Montaigne: A Biography

MONTAIGNE
Courtesy of the owner, M. le Vicomte de Gontaut-Biron

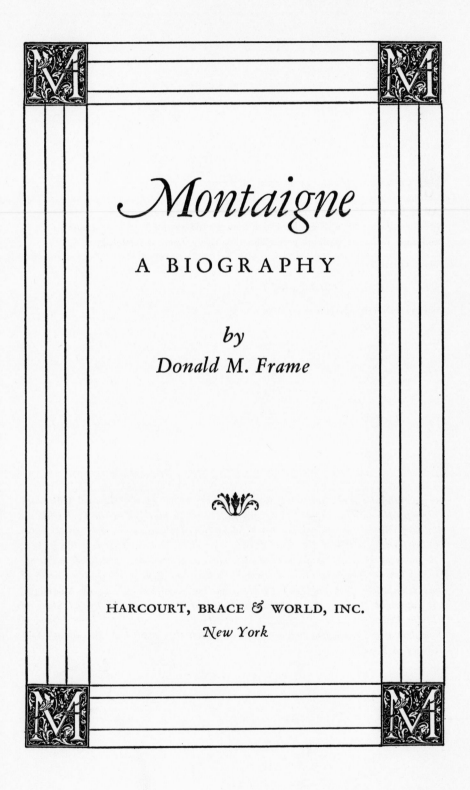

Montaigne

A BIOGRAPHY

by

Donald M. Frame

HARCOURT, BRACE & WORLD, INC.

New York

844.3
F84m
51336
Nov. '65

*I am grateful for the following permissions to reprint. To the Harvard University
Press for the translation (ch. 6) of two passages from Plutarch in the Loeb Classical
Library edition; to Alfred A. Knopf, Inc., for a passage (ch. 17) from Justin
O'Brien's translation of the* Journals of André Gide; *and to Walter J. Black, Inc.,
for some of my own translations of Montaigne that they first published in his Selected Essays. Especially great is my debt to Stanford University Press for most of
my translations first published by them in* The Complete Works of Montaigne,
© *copyright 1948, 1957, 1958 by the Board of Trustees of the Leland Stanford
Junior University, and to Columbia University Press for all that I have drawn, in
chapters 4, 9–11, 14, and 16, on my book, which they published,* Montaigne's Discovery of Man.

Preface

I HAVE TRIED to make this a scholarly and
readable biography: scholarly in presenting the evidence on which my statements
are based and in identifying conjecture
wherever I have used it in the absence of
fact; readable in making the scholarly
apparatus unobtrusive. The only footnotes
are those that have seemed necessary for
understanding the text; the bulk of the
notes—mainly references—are at the end,
where those who wish may find them.
When in doubt, I have tried to err on the
scholarly side; I hope I have not fallen between two stools, and that the nonspecial-
ist may read this book with interest, the
scholar with confidence.

D. M. F.

Contents

PREFACE   v

1: *The Eyquems of Bordeaux*   3

2: *The Lopez de Villanueva*   16

3: *The Early Years* [1533–1554]   29

4: *The Magistrate* [1554–1570]   46

5: *La Boétie* [1559–1563]   63

6: *Marriage* [1565–1592]   85

7: *Translation, Inheritance, Retirement* [1567–1571]   103

8: *At Home* [1571–1580]   116

9: *The Early* Essays [1571–1574]   142

10: *The "Apology for Raymond Sebond"*
     [1573–1576–1579]   162

11: *The Writer Finds His Theme* [1577–1580]   181

12: *Travel in Italy* [1580–1581]   201

13:　Mayor of Bordeaux [*1581–1585*]　　　　　　　　　223

14:　The Essays of 1588 [*1585–1588*]　　　　　　　　246

15:　Among the Great [*1586–1592*]　　　　　　　　　266

16:　The Final Additions [*1588–1592*]　　　　　　　289

17:　Death and Survival [*1592——*]　　　　　　　　303

　　　Appendix A: Table of Contents of Montaigne's Essays　　324

　　　Appendix B: A Sample Page Illustrating the Changes in　　327
　　　　　　　Montaigne's Text in Successive Editions

NOTES　329
INDEX　394

List of Illustrations

Montaigne　　FRONTISPIECE

　　Between pages 72 and 73
Bordeaux in 1563
Château de Montaigne
Montaigne's Library and Château
Catherine de' Medici

　　Between pages 168 and 169
Montaigne
Henry III
Marshal de Matignon
Henry IV

　　Between pages 264 and 265
A page from Montaigne's *Ephemeris:* Montaigne in the Bastille
A page of the *Essays* showing Montaigne's handwritten additions
Frontispiece of the Bordeaux Copy with Montaigne's corrections
Pierre Charron
Marie de Gournay

Montaigne: A Biography

Chapter 1: The Eyquems of Bordeaux

ICHEL DE MONTAIGNE spent most of his life in his château and in Bordeaux, thirty miles to the west. Bordeaux was the city, the place where he worked, as student, councillor, and mayor, even as his bourgeois ancestors had worked before him to amass the wealth with which his great-grandfather had bought the noble land of Montaigne. The Château de Montaigne, his birthplace, was the emblem of his status and the retreat of the country gentleman.

He loved his manor, but he often grew bored there. He had no great love for Bordeaux, as he did for Paris and Rome, but he came to find great satisfaction in the service of its inhabitants. He would have missed Bordeaux far less than Montaigne, but he needed both for his fulfillment, just as he needed public service as well as private life.

When he was born, in 1533, the château had been the family seat for three generations and fifty-six years; but the Eyquems or Ayquems—he was born Michel Eyquem de Montaigne and was the first of his family to drop the original surname—had lived in and around Bordeaux for centuries. It was the real ancestral home.

Bordeaux came into being as a port and has always remained mainly that. In the sixteenth century its walls enclosed a smaller replica of the concave crescent that the modern city forms on the left bank of the Garonne about ten miles south of the point where that already majestic river joins with the westward-flowing Dordogne to become the Gironde, a sort of elongated bay that runs northwest for about forty miles into the Atlantic Ocean. Garonne and Gironde together constitute the hypotenuse of a right triangle bounded on the west by the ocean, on the south by the Pyrenees and the Spanish border. To the north and west of Bordeaux, at the northern point of the triangle, is Médoc; to the west and south are *les Landes,* then overgrown and marshy, now sandy and studded with scrubby pine; on all sides are vineyards. In the sixteenth century, even as it has since Roman times, Bordeaux offered a sheltered harbor for ocean traffic mainly with Spain and northern Europe; it was also a key outlet for the trade of the southwest of France. With Agen and other large towns along the Garonne, especially Toulouse, far up the river to the southeast, and with the Mediterranean beyond, river boats carried on a thriving trade in the days when, as Rabelais said, roads *went,* because the best roads were water.

The principal export was the bright clear wine of the Bordeaux region, then still unrivaled by those of Burgundy and the Rhine. Claret (*clairet*), originally designating a wine between white and red but ultimately any Bordeaux red, was the reigning type, as Gaillac and then Moissac were the prized districts, England and northern France the main consumers. Another rich product was the bluish woad or pastel, the biennial plant growing in Languedoc and shipped down the Garonne in bales from Toulouse, which until the introduction of indigo was the main ingredient for black and rich blue dye. Salt fish (*la saline*), both exported and imported, was another thriving trade: salmon, sardines, shad, cod from the Newfoundland banks, above all herring; it was this that made La Rousselle the richest and most active of the twelve jurades (districts) of Bordeaux. These were the main cargoes filling the holds of the sturdy little ocean-going ships that sailed up the coast of France—still usually in fleets for fear of the ever-watchful pirates—headed for Rouen, Antwerp, or London.

Bordeaux had not yet regained much more than three quarters of the 60,000 inhabitants it once numbered under Roman rule when

its name was Burdigala; but its size and prosperity made it one of
the leading cities of France after Paris and Lyons. In the sixteenth
century it boasted many fine churches: Saint-Seurin outside the walls
to the northwest, the archbishop's church of Saint-André near
the western walls, Saint-Michel with its separate tower like Saint-
André, this one the highest building in the south of France, dominating the city and the countryside. In the main, however, these
were uncompleted, somewhat discordant, badly encumbered and almost hidden by the swarming houses and shops. The streets were
narrow, dark, and winding, overhung by eaves, studded with wells,
mills, and crosses, often dangerous, usually muddy and smelly. It was
still a medieval, feudal city, huddled and crowded within its walls.
Two fortresses, the Château Trompette to the north and the Château du Hâ to the west, stood within the city as reminders that its
allegiance now was to the king of France.

From the middle of the twelfth to the middle of the fifteenth
century, from the marriage of Eleanor of Aquitaine with Henry
Plantagenet of England to the expulsion of the English from France
at the end of the Hundred Years' War, Guienne had been an
English province and Bordeaux its capital. The city had flourished;
it had its own mayor and jurats as early as 1206; and though Charles
VII of France won over many of the common people, the bourgeois
aristocracy remained loyal to their old masters and held out against
the new. Captured by the French in 1451, Bordeaux rose to join
old Talbot ("our" Talbot, Montaigne calls him) when he landed in
1452 to renew the struggle for Guienne, and held out several months
after his defeat and death a year later. The understandable severities
of the new French masters further alienated the Bordelais; and even
the kindness of Louis XI, who restored the city's privileges and
prosperity, did not wipe away recent scars and old loyalties.

To a sixteenth-century Bordelais or other Gascon,* France meant
at least two things: the nation, and the north of France. The nation,
still short of its modern boundaries especially to the east and north,
had only lately begun to take shape out of the feudal fragmentation
with the addition since 1453 of Gascony, Burgundy, and most

* I shall use the terms "Gascon" and "Gascony" throughout this book as Montaigne
did, in their broad sense, to include the people and the large area—Bordeaux and the
Château de Montaigne as well as the deeper southwest—whose usual speech was Gascon,
a language almost as close to Spanish as to French. Montaigne did not speak Gascon, but
he thought and spoke of himself as a Gascon.

recently Brittany; outlying parts like Gascony and Languedoc still clung to their feudal independence of the central government. The idea of the nation as a natural object of allegiance was still new, and was to struggle with that of religion throughout the century before prevailing. As late as 1582 Brantôme—no profound ponderer of loyalties, to be sure, but no fool either, and a proud member of an ancient noble house—became so furious at Henry III for breaking his promise to have him succeed his brother as seneschal and governor of Périgord that he swore never to serve a king of France again and was about to go to fight for Spain when a fall from a horse crippled him for life. Even the stanchest loyalists like Montaigne, who saw in support of the monarchy the one hope for peace and order in France, were loyal less to the nation than to its unifying symbol the crown. And Montaigne considered himself less a Frenchman than a Gascon.

For the French seemed in their way foreign masters too. Whereas the English had allowed the Gascons their own tongue, the new rulers insisted on French, so that Gascon virtually disappeared as a written language during the sixteenth century. Chroniclers of the time write about Gascons fighting alongside French as they do about Germans and Swiss. A Gascon heading for Paris is said to be "going to France." One of Montaigne's letters of 1570, dedicating the French poems of his dead friend La Boétie to his fellow Gascon Paul de Foix, protests that their publication has been delayed because "up there" they were thought not polished enough to meet the public eye, although Montaigne rates them high for the "beauty and richness of the invention" and the "meaty, full, and marrowy" subject matter. "It seems," he complains, "that this judgment of theirs affects the interest of all this part of the country, from which they think nothing in the vernacular [French, as against Latin] can come that does not have a wild and barbarous flavor." This is more than ruffled regionalistic pride; it shows a sense of separateness from the preponderant north of France. This sense, increased in generally Protestant Gascony by the religious civil wars, was lessened in Catholic Bordeaux, as the century wore on, by them and by the king's high court of justice for Guienne, the Parlement of Bordeaux.

The origin of the name Eyquem is not known. The likeliest theory sees in it an archaic Gascon doublet of the old French (originally Hebrew) first name Joachim. A tenth-century document mentions a Hechelmus, and numerous records from the twelfth to the fifteenth show a host of variations—Aichelmus, Aiquelinus, Ayquelmus, and the like—leading to the Gascon forms Aiquem, Ayquem, and in the sixteenth century Eyquem. Once a first name, as shown by such forms as Aiquelmus Arnaldi and Aiquelmus Guillhelmi, it appears as a patronymic as early as the twelfth century, and with a first name (Raymund or Remundus) that was to be borne three centuries later by the first Eyquem de Montaigne. Whether the Remundus Aiquelini who witnessed a document some time between 1173 and 1178 was an ancestor of Michel we do not know; he was probably at least a relative.

From the thirteenth century to the sixteenth many Ayquems lived in and around Bordeaux, among them a number of small landholders outside the town and one important branch of merchants inside on the Rue de La Rousselle, the center of the trade in fish and woad, in the parish of Saint-Michel. A Petrus Eyquen was living in this parish in 1207. By the fourteenth century we find another Ramon Ayquem, Gaillard Ayquem, Pey (Pierre) Ayquem de la Rossella (La Rousselle)—a jurat of Bordeaux in 1358—and others, all representing this branch, from which the Montaignes sprang. Already the family was one of substance and importance.

Ramon Ayquem (or Raymond Eyquem), Montaigne's paternal great-grandfather, established the family's fortune. Born in 1402 near Blanquefort, about seven miles northwest of Bordeaux, he moved to the La Rousselle district to work in the company of a wealthy uncle, Ramon de Gaujac, became his associate and heir, married (around 1449) a rich heiress, Isabeau de Ferraignes, and became one of the richest merchants in town. His company dealt mainly in local wine, salt fish, and woad. His will reveals a man of great vigor and piety, who at seventy-one planned to make the long pilgrimage—about five hundred miles—to Santiago de Compostela. At seventy-five he bought the noble house and land of Montaigne and that of Belbeys in the barony of Montravel.

Situated in Périgord where it borders on Guienne, for over a hundred years this barony had been a subfief of the archbishops of Bordeaux. They had ceded the Montaigne house and property to the Belbeys family, which had passed it to Guillaume Duboys, who, needing money, sold it to Thomas Pons, lord of Clermont; but when

Clermont failed to pay the price agreed, Ramon Ayquem in his stead
bought the two noble houses and accompanying vineyards, woods,
fields, other lands, and mills, for 900 Bordeaux francs, on October 10, 1477. On November 30 Ramon Ayquem and Guillaume
Duboys entered the Montaigne house together; then "the said Guillaume Duboys goes out, and the said Ramon Ayquem stays and
remains inside the said house and bars the door after him, and stays
inside peacefully, as long as he pleases, taking true possession of the
said manor and house, and, this taken, the said lord Ramon Ayquem
eats and drinks to his heart's content."

Thus did Ramon Eyquem officially become the first Eyquem
de Montaigne. Less than a year later he died, leaving dowries to
his two daughters and the bulk of his estate jointly to his two sons,
Grimon and Pierre, who ran the family business together for ten
years, until Pierre died, still young and unmarried, in 1488. The
elder son, Grimon, Montaigne's grandfather, born around 1450, enjoyed, his grandson tells us, a full life of sixty-nine years without
ever tasting medicine, which he mistrusted as did his father and his
descendants. He did little with the noble manor of Montaigne beyond defending his rights to it in 1509 against a claim by the children of the previous owner. Primarily a Bordelais and a business-
man, he greatly enlarged the family's fortune and the scope of their
trade and bought many buildings and properties in Bordeaux. Active in church affairs, he was a vestryman of his parish and one of
the farmers of revenues from the archbishopric of Bordeaux and the
Ordre du Temple. The first of his family known to have entered
public service, he was one of the city's jurats, or administrative and
executive assistants to the mayor, for eighteen years (1485–1503),
and for a time provost, which meant the jurat charged with matters
of justice. Married to the daughter of another rich merchant and
jurat, Grimon du Four, Grimon Eyquem died intestate in 1519,
leaving four sons and two daughters. Parts of his estate were concealed or dissimulated by relatives, and the sons had to appeal to the
Pope to secure their own and their sisters' rights.

With the next generation the family moved steadily away from
business into careers more lustrous and more appropriate for nobles:
soldiery, the Parlement, the Church. One of Grimon's daughters
married a lawyer in the Parlement, the other a notary, secretary to
the king. His second son, Thomas de Saint-Michel, was a lawyer

in the Parlement from 1529, curate of Saint-Michel de Montaigne, and canon of the archiepiscopal church of Saint-André in Bordeaux. The third son, Pierre the younger (the eldest, Montaigne's father, was another Pierre), lord of Gaujac, took his *licence* in law at Toulouse around 1527 and became both a lawyer and a churchman. On the death of his brother Thomas he succeeded him in his curacy and canonry, becoming also curate of Caplong, Saint-Quentin, and Lahontan and canon of Saint-André and Saint-Seurin. His brother Pierre, in his will (quoted below), asked him to look out for his children and be a second father to them. Michel must have been his favorite nephew; for it was almost certainly Gaujac and not (as has always been maintained) Montaigne's father who bought a position in the Cour des Aides of Périgueux in 1554 and, some time in the next three years, transferred it to Michel; and when he died (July 24, 1573) he left him one third of his estate. He was born sickly, Michel tells us, and once fell so ill from a fever that the doctors warned him to follow their orders or die. Frightened as he was, he replied sturdily: "Then I am a dead man." "But," his nephew concludes, "God soon made this prognosis vain." Pierre de Gaujac lived to be sixty-six.

The last of the four brothers, Raymond de Bussaguet, seemed to enjoy a stronger constitution than Gaujac but lacked his salutary mistrust of medicine (still according to Michel), so that he died ten years earlier and much younger. Destined at first for the Church, he became a lawyer at the Parlement, then a councillor (1536) of great influence, a leader in both religious and political matters. He married Adrienne de La Chassaigne, daughter of councillor Geoffroy, and she bore him two sons and two daughters. He died in the same year (1563) as his good friend and his nephew's great friend Etienne de La Boétie.

The oldest son of Grimon, Pierre Eyquem de Montaigne, was the first of the family to be born at Montaigne (September 29, 1495) and the first to adopt the nobleman's true profession of arms. He too was carefully brought up. A Latin epigram of his youth shows no literary merit but sound schooling. Although he brushed up on this language when his son was learning it, he lost his command of it and found Raymond Sebond difficult except in his son's translation; but he learned to use two vernaculars more valuable for a soldier, Italian and Spanish. His son tells us that he took

part in the French invasions of Italy under Lautrec, leaving a diary
(which has not been found), and married in 1529, after his return.
It was from Italy that he brought back the scheme of early education for Michel.

By now the Eyquems de Montaigne were a leading family of
Bordeaux. Already in 1523 one of the town's streets, apparently
the Rue de Sarlat, is referred to in a document as "the street called
de Montaigne." By the end of the century the tower on the south
side of the Peugue where that stream, like its fellow the Devise, then
flowed east through the town into the Garonne, was known as the
Tower du Brisson or Tower of Eyquem-de-Montaigne. These
place names reflect not only the family's extensive properties in the
city, but also its great prestige.

Soon after Pierre Eyquem returned from the wars and married
he was elected, like his father before him, first jurat and provost of
his city (1530). In 1537 he was jurat again and deputy mayor; in
1546 first jurat again; in 1554 he was elected mayor for a two-year
term that he served under trying circumstances.

A bloody uprising in Bordeaux in 1548 over the salt tax had led
to harsh retaliation and curtailment of the city's privileges, including
that of electing their own mayor. This last had been restored, but
the full prerogatives of the office, like those of the city, had not.
To the service of his now suspect city Pierre de Montaigne gave
himself unsparingly, traveling to Paris to plead for the return of its
privileges, taking along twenty casks of local wine as the most eloquent proof of its basic soundness. "I remembered in my boyhood,"
writes his son, who admires but does not wholly approve of his
father's dedication, "having seen him old, his soul cruelly agitated
by this public turmoil, forgetting the sweet air of his home, to which
the weakness of years had attached him long since, and his household
and his health; and, truly heedless of his life, which he nearly lost
in this, engaged for them [the jurats] in long and painful journeys.
He was like that; and this disposition in him sprang from a great
goodness of nature; there was never a more kindly and public-
spirited soul."

Pierre Eyquem loved his country home and loved to build it
up. More than 250 notarized deeds dating from the years 1528–59
show how actively he bought, sold, exchanged, and exploited his
holdings, greatly enlarging the property and—with the indispensable permission of his lord, the archbishop of Bordeaux—fortifying

and embellishing the château. His son was to envy him his enjoyment of this but not to share it; he was not to ruin the house as his father had wryly predicted, but to keep it up about as he found it.

Montaigne's *Essays* abound in mentions of his father, always with high praise except in one respect: he thought him overimpressed by learning because he lacked it himself. To his regret, after giving him a remarkable education for his first six years, "that good man, being extremely afraid of failing in a thing so close to his heart, at last let himself be carried away by the common opinion, which always follows the leader like a flock of cranes, and fell in line with custom," sending the youngster to a good but regular school where he was lucky to learn anything worth while. Praising his father's idea of a public place (like a bulletin board or a want-ad column) where people could advertise such things as jobs offered or needed, goods wanted or for sale, Michel calls him "a man of very clear judgment for one who was aided only by experience and nature." He starts his long critique of human knowledge and reason, the "Apology for Raymond Sebond," with a disenchanted comment on the uncritical worship of learning characteristic of his father's generation, of the early Renaissance in France:

My house has long been open to men of learning, and is well known to them. For my father, who ruled it for fifty years and more, inflamed with that new ardor with which King Francis I embraced letters and brought them into credit, sought with great diligence and expense the acquaintance of learned men, receiving them at his house like holy persons having some particular inspiration of divine wisdom, collecting their sayings and discourses like oracles, and with all the more reverence and religion as he was less qualified to judge them; for he had no knowledge of letters, any more than his predecessors. Myself, I like them well enough, but I do not worship them.

Montaigne's disparagement shows some of the pride of the nobleman, whose profession is to fight and govern, not merely to amass learning, and some of his disconcerting Spartanism, usually stated as a preference for doing well to speaking well. Some of it is related to his mediocre opinion of the learned Sebond, whom he found himself called on to defend. Some of it is the feeling of the later Renaissance in France, already shown by the Pléiade poets, that knowledge of the ancients is sterile unless it leads beyond to emulation of their best work. Much of it is vexation that his admired father chose for his heroes men who were far less able than he and merely more learned.

At all events, if Pierre de Montaigne lacked the erudition of a Budé or a Scaliger, an Estienne, a Turnebus or a Lipsius, he was not as unlettered as his son's account suggests. His early competence in Latin, his fluency in Italian and Spanish, his care in keeping a diary, have already been noted. When as mayor, in his red-and-white satin robes, he helped welcome a new archbishop to Bordeaux, the official chronicler reports that he greeted him with "a very beautiful speech." He took great interest in the excellent new Collège de Guyenne, founded just six days before the birth of Michel, who studied there; it was he who, as deputy mayor, turned over letters of naturalization to its first principal, André de Gouvéa (Goveanus), a learned Portuguese whose Jewish descent made him anxious for the security of French citizenship; it was during his mayoralty that a great later principal, Elie Vinet, was elected to the position.

Generally Michel de Montaigne has nothing but the warmest praise for "the best father there ever was," "the good father that God gave me, who has no return from me but gratitude for his goodness." He deeply appreciated not only the painless training that made him fluent in Latin at the age of six, but also his being sent out earlier to nurse with humble people from the cradle, to bring him close to them. "If I had any male children," he writes, "I should cordially wish them my own fortune." He admires his father's ability "to keep his desires down to his means, and to be pleased with what he had," and wishes he could have bequeathed to him, instead of some part of the estate, "that passionate love that he had in his old age for his household." Nothing would have pleased Michel more than to find enjoyment in carrying on the work his father had loved. "I love to follow his example and his rules, and shall bind my successors to them as much as I can. If I could do better for him, I would. . . . God forbid that I should allow to fail in my hands any semblance of life that I could restore to so good a father."

As kindness won Michel's gratitude, other qualities won his admiration. A small man, like his son, Pierre Eyquem was "straight and well-proportioned," with "an attractive face, inclining to brown." His vigor and agility were remarkable, even in extreme old age. "He scarcely ever found a man of his condition who was his equal in any bodily exercise. . . . I have even seen some canes filled with lead, with which they say he exercised his arms to prepare for throwing the bar or the stone, and some shoes with leaded soles to train him to be lighter in running and jumping. Of his vaulting, he has left some small miracles in people's memory. I have seen him, past sixty, put our agility to shame: leap into the saddle in his furred gown, do a turn over the table on his thumb, hardly ever go up to his room without taking three or four steps at a time." Most of all, however, it was his chastity, modesty, and integrity that his son revered.

It is marvelous what stories I have heard my father tell of the chastity of his day. He was the man to tell them, being very well suited to the service of the ladies, both by nature and by art. He spoke little and well, and sprinkled his language with ornamental expressions from books in the modern vernaculars, especially Spanish. . . . His bearing was one of gentle, humble, and very modest gravity. A singular care for neatness and propriety of person and dress, whether afoot or on horseback. A prodigious fidelity in keeping his word, and a general conscientiousness and scrupulousness leaning rather toward than away from superstition. . . . On this subject of mine, he used to say that in a whole province there was scarcely one woman of quality who had a bad reputation; and he would tell of remarkable intimacies, especially of his own, with respectable women, free from any suspicion. And of himself he solemnly swore that he came to his marriage a virgin. And yet he had taken a very long part in the Italian wars. . . . Consequently he married well along in age, in the year 1528,* which was his thirty-third, on his return from Italy. Let's get back to our bottles.

Even Pierre Eyquem's vigor was not proof against illness. One of the great shocks of Michel's life, so great that the first words that nature (as he put it) wrung out of his entrails were in his nearly native Latin, came in his twenties "when I saw my father, in perfect health, fall back into my arms in a faint." A little later, at sixty-two, Pierre declared himself no longer fit for military service. For his last seven years he lived in torment from the kidney stone, which struck him at sixty-six as it was to strike his son at forty-five. "Before that," writes Michel, "he had had no threat or symptom of it, in his loins, his sides, or elsewhere. And he had lived until then in a happy state of health, and very little subject to diseases; and he lasted seven years more with this ailment, painfully dragging out the last years of his life. . . . He died extraordinarily afflicted with a large stone he had in his bladder."

Michel was not present at his deathbed. The fatal day, June 18, 1568, is that of his dedication in Paris, to his father, of the translation that Pierre Eyquem had asked him to make of the *Natural*

* 1529, new style.

Theology of Raymond Sebond. It ends with the hallowed formula favored by Montaigne and many of his contemporaries, to which the coincidence of dates gives a poignant irony but which assuredly came from Michel's heart: "Sir, I pray God to give you a very long and very happy life."

He treasured his father's memory, following his preference in dress for black and white, noting after ten years that "I have not banished from my study some long sticks that my father ordinarily carried in his hand." Eight years after that, speaking of his heroes Lucullus, Metellus, and Scipio, he writes: "They are dead. So indeed is my father, as completely as they; and he has moved as far from me and from life in eighteen years as they have in sixteen hundred. Nevertheless I do not cease to embrace and cherish his memory, his friendship, and his society, in a union that is perfect and very much alive."

Some of the flavor of Pierre de Montaigne is found in his second and final will. He wants to be buried in his parish church of Saint-Michel de Montaigne "with no ceremonies other than those for one of the poorest members of the parish," but with distribution of alms to the poor and gifts to his tenants and neighbors. His loving concern for his family's welfare and concord speaks out in his conclusion:

Since the manner of our death is as uncertain as the hour, and since I do not know whether at that passage I shall be able to give my children orally this final command, which I want to have written in their hearts, insofar as they love and esteem me: I recommend to them with all the power that God and the laws have given me over them, after the love, fear, and obedience owed to God, the king, and the country, to keep themselves united together by affection and will, to maintain among themselves the holy name of friendship, which for so long, and until death has separated us from one another, my three brothers and I have so happily kept and so inviolably maintained; and upon my eldest son [Michel] in particular, to whom I leave the most means, I enjoin to help, succor, and favor my said children, his brothers and sisters, in every way he can, and to serve them as a father in my place; and [I enjoin] upon my other sons and daughters also to bear him fraternal honor and respect as their elder, the head of the house, and that he must take my place and represent me to them. I recommend to them all to accept wholly the advice and will of my brother de Gaujac, their uncle, or to put it better their father in my place, and not to do or undertake anything without him; and also to call and join into their society and friendship the children of my brother the late lord of Bussaguet, their cousins, who all together should serve one another as brothers and sisters, as I beg them [the cousins] also for their part to do the same, in imitation of their fathers.

Among the fathers of great men there are so many caricatures, the self-righteous tyrant, the hypersensitive ineffectual, the disorderly drunkard, that it is a rare pleasure to come across one sound and able, kind and firm, one who truly deserved his son. Such a one was Pierre de Montaigne.

Though his son was the first of the family to drop his surname, with the disingenuous statement that his ancestors "were formerly surnamed Eyquem," he admired and loved his paternal ancestors: "Truly it would spring from a bad nature to be scornful of even the portraits of our friends and predecessors, the form of their clothes and their armor. I keep their handwriting, their seal, the breviary and a peculiar sword that they used. . . . What a satisfaction it would be to me to hear someone tell me, in this way, of the habits, the face, the expression, the favorite remarks, and the fortunes of my ancestors! How attentive I would be!"

We can see how Montaigne's dear friend La Boétie loved and admired the family from his dying plea to a brother of Montaigne's whose Protestant sympathies were driving him apart from the others:

But I do want to advise you, out of respect for the good reputation that the family you belong to has acquired by continual concord—a family that is as dear to me as any family in the world: Lord, what a family! from which there has never come any act other than that of a worthy man— out of respect for the will of your father, that good father to whom you owe so much, the will of your good uncle, and your brothers, to avoid these extremes.

It is in the same vein that Montaigne speaks of the Eyquems. He admires their constant concern for integrity. When he points out, apropos of his dead friend, that familial affections cannot match the perfection of those freely chosen, he hastens to add: "Not that I have not experienced all the friendship that can exist in that situation, having had the best father that ever was, and the most indulgent, even in his extreme old age, and being of a family famous and exemplary, from father to son, in this matter of brotherly concord."

It was only the name Eyquem that Montaigne dropped. The heritage lived on in him, sturdy and sound.

Chapter 2: *The Lopez de Villanueva*

ONTAIGNE, who writes so warmly of his father, tells us nothing about his mother. He mentions her just twice, noting that his brothers and sisters, who never had the kidney stone as he did, were all children of the same mother as he, and that when he was brought up on Latin alone, no one, not even his father or mother, was allowed to address him in any other language; so that both parents learned enough Latin to understand and use it. And that is all.

The main reason is probably that she was still living when he wrote. He rarely reveals much about living private persons by name; his wife and daughter, who also survived him, are not often mentioned either. His father, however, died almost three years before Michel retired and began to write in earnest; he was a notable public figure, as the mother, wife, and daughter were not; and Michel's absence from his deathbed was a further incentive for fully expressing his gratitude.

Another possibility requires exploration. The family of Antoinette de Louppes de Villeneuve, though about as eminent and prosperous as the Eyquems, were marranos, or converted Spanish

Jews. Now the stock in which Montaigne takes pride is the Eyquems; he never discusses his maternal ancestry; he might as well have been born of the Eyquems alone. He may have regretted, even deplored, the Lopez side of his heritage. However, he seems consistently sympathetic toward the Jews.

He is one of the very few writers of his time to protest against the use of torture to extract confessions from suspected criminals, heretics, or unbelievers. "As for me," he writes, "even in justice, all that goes beyond plain death seems to me pure cruelty, and especially for us who ought to have some concern about sending souls away in a good state; which cannot happen when we have agitated them and made them desperate by unbearable tortures." And more forcefully, comparing "civilized" cruelty with that of the Brazilian cannibals: "I think there is more barbarity in eating a man alive than in eating him dead; and in tearing by tortures and the rack a body still full of feeling, in roasting a man bit by bit . . . (as we have not only read but seen within fresh memory, not among ancient enemies, but among neighbors and fellow citizens, and what is worse, on the pretext of piety and religion), than in roasting and eating him after he is dead." These were subversive opinions in the age of the Inquisition; Montaigne was rebuked for them by the papal censors who examined his *Essays* in Rome in 1580–81. (The rebuke led to no change in later editions; but the same is true of the other five criticisms that he reports.) Now the Lopez de Villanueva family, his maternal ancestors, had included many martyrs of the Inquisition; they would fit his description "among neighbors and fellow citizens"; it is at least possible that the thought of them, among others, prompted his protest.

One incident suggests no prejudice on his part. During his mayoralty, on December 22, 1583, in the church of Saint-André of Bordeaux, he became the godfather of a namesake, Michel, born six days earlier to two marranos of Portuguese descent, Diogo and Guiomar (Leao) Dacosta.

His references to the Jews, though not frequent, are either neutral or mildly sympathetic. Most of the interesting ones are in the *Travel Journal*, which was not intended for publication. One tells how on Shrovetide along the Corso in Rome "they race, now four or five boys, now some Jews, now some old men stark naked." Although other accounts show these races as a nasty form of hazing, with hoots and often sticks and stones speeding the racers, Montaigne merely notes that they received prizes and that the spectator's only pleasure was in watching the runners pass. He has been blamed for his failure to protest; but it should be remembered that all we know of what he saw at these races that day is the little he tells us.

One could hardly expect the Christian Montaigne to protest at a different form of pressure exerted on the Jewish community in Rome. Among the sermons he heard in Lent was that of a converted rabbi who preached to a captive audience of sixty Jews who were obliged to hear him every Saturday. Montaigne admired the learning with which he turned their own texts and arguments against them; but it is interesting that he refers to him not as a *converted,* but as a *renegade,* rabbi.

The *Journal* reveals his curiosity about Jewish rites. In Bordeaux the "new Christians" of Jewish descent, though secure, were suspect; Montaigne could inquire more freely in Italy. Thus in Verona his secretary notes that "we also saw the Jews, and Monsieur de Montaigne was in their synagogue and had quite a talk with them about their ceremonies." In Rome too he visited a synagogue and heard a service, which he describes with the same curious and dispassionate care that he shows for Catholic and Protestant services. The same care, and even more concern for detail, mark his long account (about 750 words) of how in Rome on January 30, 1581 "he went to see the most ancient religious ceremony there is among men, and watched it very attentively and with great profit: that is, the circumcision of the Jews." (Presumably his visit to the synagogue had led to this invitation.) Many of his terms relate the ceremony to Christian ritual: it is a "mystery" performed by a "minister," resembling baptism in many details: "They give the boys a godfather and godmother, as we do. . . . The child is wrapped in our style. . . . The boy's outcry is like that of ours when they are baptized." Throughout the account Montaigne's sympathy seems clear.

In one curious passage in the *Essays,* Montaigne follows "the best Latin historian of our era," the Portuguese bishop Hieronymus Osorius, in relating how the Portuguese treated the Jews exiled from Spain in 1492 by Ferdinand and Isabella: how John II of Portugal sold them refuge for a limited time, promising ships to take them to Africa, then furnished too few for them all; how those who did get aboard were treated villainously by the sailors, who wasted so much time in transit that the Jews were forced to buy food from them at exorbitant prices that used up all their money; how on hearing of this most of those left behind accepted slavery, although "some made a show of changing religion"; how John's successor, Manuel, first set the Jews free, then resolved to convert them, set a deadline, gave them first three ports, then only one, by which to leave the country; and when they were all in that one, had all the children under fourteen taken from their parents to be brought up as Christians, with the result that many killed themselves and some their children.

Here Osorius concludes that time and habit made sincere Catholics of the converts and their descendants. Here Montaigne, entirely on his own, uses Osorius' reasons to reach the opposite conclusion: "Some turned Christians; of their faith, or of that of their descendants, even today, a hundred years later, few Portuguese are sure, though custom and length of time are far stronger counselors than any other compulsion."

Montaigne's sharp focus on the injustice done to the Jews and his low estimate of the value of their forced conversion are what the *Essays* lead us to expect. His conclusion, curiously, suggests doubt about the sincerity of "new Christians" in general, and thus by implication of the Louppes and others of Bordeaux.

There had been Jews in Bordeaux in Roman times when it was still Burdigala. Their treatment under Christian rule through the Middle Ages had been little better than elsewhere in Christendom: no right to worship, no legal status, their goods ever subject to confiscation and themselves to banishment followed by readmission at a price. They were generally given more freedom in England than in France, in Gascony under English rule than under French. In the fourteenth century they had a quarter just outside Bordeaux near Saint-Seurin, where we read of a "cemetery of the Jews" and a "plantier des Juifs"; and the nearest gate, the Porte-Dijeaux, was also known as the Porta Judaica. By the fifteenth century many must have moved quietly into town, where we read of a Street of the Jews' Well and a Judaic Street. The scant evidence of their activity for the half century after the French reconquest of Bordeaux in 1453 suggests that their numbers had already declined when in 1502 Louis XII extended edicts of banishment from the older parts of France to the entire country.

At about the same time the Spanish and Portuguese marranos, banished from Spain ten years before and then from Portugal, began to settle in Bordeaux. They numbered many eminent families: the Louppes de Villeneuve, wealthy merchants and later (dropping the name Louppes) councillors and presidents in the Parlement and jurats of the city; the distinguished Aragonese doctor Ramon de Granollers; Jean Millanges, father of Montaigne's first publisher; the lawyer Dominique Ram, whose son Thomas de Ram became lieutenant general in the seneschalsy of Bordeaux; in the 1530's André de Gouvéa, principal of the Collège de Guyenne, and his colleagues Fernandès Dacosta, Jehan Gelida, Mathieu and Jean da Costa; and many other leading citizens. Thanks in large part to Gouvéa's efforts, in 1550 Henry II granted letters patent to the "merchants and other Portuguese called New Christians," welcoming them to settle in France, wherever they wished, with their families, servants, and goods, to acquire goods and real estate, to trade, to dispose by will or gift of what they had; in short, to enjoy the privileges of their fellow townsmen, in whatever town; and promising them, on behalf of the king and his successors, a year's time, if they should be sent away again, to dispose of their property and take away their families and servants.

Their wealth and ability, however, made them formidable rivals to the natives; and since, while conforming in public to Catholic ritual, some of them continued to Judaize in private and most of them were suspected of doing so, envy, hatred, and suspicion arose against them. By 1574 their harassment by their fellow Bordelais had reached such a point that the Parlement had to forbid anyone to molest them. The Parlement, which included New Christians and their descendants and relatives by marriage, and which recognized their great contribution to the city, continued to protect them stanchly. However, their safety was imperiled by all crises, such as the approach of a Spanish army in 1590 while League passions were running high, and even more the mission of Pierre de Lancre to Guienne in 1609 to stamp out sorcery. De Lancre, an acquaintance and admirer of Montaigne, was nevertheless a fire-breathing witch burner who urged banishment and torture for the Spanish and Portuguese of Bordeaux, claiming that they were disguised Jews and, by the same token, sorcerers.

His first charge may have been valid; for more than a century later, in the more tolerant climate of the early Enlightenment, after royal letters patent in 1723 had reaffirmed those of 1550 while speaking no longer of Christians, however new, but of "the Jews of the districts of Bordeaux and of Auch, known and established in the kingdom under the title of Portuguese, otherwise called new Christians," a sober and responsible report of 1733 shows them returning openly to their ancient faith. "They have established seven synagogues or congrègues, in which they practice their cult with freedom and security, and even ostentation." Among the leading practitioners mentioned were two members of the Lopès family.

Montaigne had known that force does not make for sincere conversion; and while we cannot be sure, his remarks about the Portuguese marranos may have applied in his mind to those of Bordeaux.

Montaigne's maternal ancestry, which recent scholarship has traced far back, resembles the paternal in many ways but differs in the fact, only too often all-important, that the Lopez de Villanueva were Jews.

In the market town of Calatayúd in Aragon, about fifty miles southwest of Saragossa on the road to Madrid, there lived during the fourteenth century a Jewish family named Paçagon (or Pazagon, Patagon) whose head, Moses, a wealthy rag dealer, under the threat of persecution, became converted to Christianity, taking the name Garcia Lopez or Garcilopez, probably from an aristocratic sponsor who had consented to be his godfather. Since his home was in the less ancient part of Calatayúd called Villanueva, he came to be known as Garcilopez de Villanueva. His conversion occurred either in the late fourteenth century or more probably between 1411 and 1414; later he moved to Saragossa and was followed thither by his sons and most of his relatives from Calatayúd, including his close kinsman—probably a first cousin—Mayer Paçagon, the great-great-great-great-great-grandfather of Montaigne, who upon conversion took the name Juan Lopez de Villanueva.

(The line of descent is shown by the chart on the next page [22].)

Conversion was not final for the whole family, but was necessary for any to survive. The Inquisition was at its height in Aragon in the late fifteenth century. Its victims among the Lopez de

Montaigne's Maternal Ancestry and Some of His Relatives

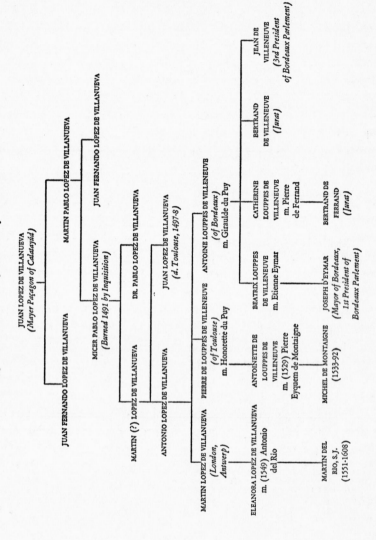

Villanueva of Saragossa include Ramon (son of Moses Paçagon), Juan Fernando (the elder, son of Mayer Paçagon) and his son Micer Fernando, Montaigne's great-great-great-grandfather Micer Pablo, all burned at the stake, as well as others burned in effigy or condemned but managing to escape. One who escaped, the merchant Garcia Lopez (condemned in 1486), was probably the first to settle in France, choosing Provence. Montaigne's great-uncle Martin Lopez, after a stay in London, moved to Antwerp by 1520 and amassed a fortune in spice. His son, another Martin, became a pillar of Dutch Protestantism; his daughter Eleanora married a Del Rio, a devout Catholic like herself, and had as a son the eminent Jesuit historian, philologist, and enemy of sorcery Martin del Rio.

Montaigne's great-uncle Antoine (de) Louppes de Villeneuve, brother of the first Martin Lopez of Antwerp, settled in Bordeaux by around 1510 and rose rapidly from agent to be "honorable homme" and one of the city's wealthiest merchants, dealing with all the leading Bordeaux businessmen and joining with his nephew by marriage, Montaigne's father, to send 800 bales of woad and eight casks of wine in a Breton ship in 1535 to brother Martin Lopez. As the table above shows, the children of Antoine Louppes de Villeneuve and his wife Giraulde du Puy moved into the magistrature, making the couple parents and grandparents of jurats, presidents of the Parlement, and a mayor of Bordeaux; and their two sons dropped the name Louppes (as Michel dropped the Eyquem) to become simply Bertrand and Jean de Villeneuve.

Montaigne's maternal grandfather Pierre de Louppes settled not in Bordeaux but in Toulouse, following his uncle Jean in 1492, who, after prospering in woad, devoted himself to good works and was a Franciscan tertiary when he died in 1497 or 1498. Pierre prospered in business—in 1540 he sent a shipment of woad to his nephew Bertrand de Villeneuve in Bordeaux—married Honorette du Puy, daughter of a merchant from Auch (and probably sister of brother Antoine's wife, Giraulde), and had several sons, one of whom was a *capitoul* (councillor) of Toulouse in 1542, and three daughters, one of whom, Antoinette, was Montaigne's mother.

Her marriage to Pierre Eyquem was probably arranged by uncle Antoine of Bordeaux, who, with another uncle, Arnaud du Puy, joined Pierre Eyquem in Bordeaux in signing the contract, by which she brought the groom a dowry of 4,000 livres tournois, of which 2,000 were to be put into lands or other revenue-bearing investments, and which he was to return to her with 2,000 more in case he died before her. A month later, on January 15, 1529, in the house of "noble Pierre Lopez" in Toulouse, the official act was drawn up and signed. The bride is styled "noble" like the groom, and of age, meaning over twelve and under twenty-five. (She was probably quite young, since her eighth and last child was born almost thirty-two years later; but we do not know her age.)

The few documents we have dealing with Antoinette de Louppes are legal and mainly unrevealing. Pierre Eyquem's first will (February 4, 1561) provides for the return to his widow of the 6,000 livres tournois stipulated in the marriage contract, plus 300 more that Pierre may have received besides, and makes Michel the general heir and official head of the family, but provides that his mother be "mistress and usufructuary, while living in widowhood, of my each and every possession, governing them like a good pater-familias and maintaining, bringing up, and providing for our sons and daughters according to the capacity of our possessions." She is made co-executrix with two of Pierre's brothers, Gaujac and Bussaguet, and the three of them, together with the two oldest sons, Michel and Thomas (de Beauregard), joint tutors of the three youngest children (Léonor, aged eight; Marie, not quite seven; and Bertrand, five months) in perfect trust, to bring them up, govern them, and see to their education and indoctrination.

Michel was not quite twenty-eight when this will was made. If we remember his father's prediction that he would ruin the estate, we may infer that Pierre Eyquem trusted his wife's managerial ability as much as he mistrusted that of his heir—at least at this age. He wanted her to keep her practiced eye and firm hand on the estate and, apparently, to run it in fact while Michel, who showed neither interest in such everyday matters nor knowledge of them, remained a figurehead.

Nine months before his death, on September 22, 1567, Pierre Eyquem made a new will that shows far more faith in Michel's responsibility and that led to an act of agreement between mother and son dated August 31, 1568 "over the doubts which have arisen between them or which might arise later over the will of the said late lord of Montaigne." It provides for payment of the money owed to Antoinette de Louppes; its most interesting parts are those that seek to settle the conflicts of authority.

The will had provided that the widow be supported from the estate of the deceased "with the same authority and in just the same way as she had been during her life, as long as she lives in chaste widowhood." The agreement specifies that this clause extends "to no superintendence and mastery other than honorary and maternal." The will enjoined upon Montaigne and the other children to "respect, honor and serve her [their mother] like good sons and daughters" and urged the mother "to love and cherish them as she has done." The agreement, in place of this, stipulates "that as long as mother and son agree to live together at Montaigne," she is to enjoy "all filial honor, respect, and service, as well as two maids and a manservant," and one hundred livres tournois a year for petty cash. The son, however, retains "the command and mastery of the said château of Montaigne in general, its accessories and its entrances and exits," while the mother and her maids and manservant have the right to go in and out and use the wells and gardens. The will had foreseen that mother and son might possibly not "live and get along congenially together in the same house," in which case Michel must provide her with another house elsewhere, suitable to her quality, comfortably furnished, plus 300 livres tournois per year. The agreement allows either party to decide to live apart, and stipulates the conditions in either case.

Since the will at one point made Michel responsible for the upbringing and maintenance of his young sisters Léonor and Marie, but elsewhere made him only co-tutor with his mother and his uncle Pierre de Gaujac, the agreement created two arbiters, Montaigne's cousin Antoine de Belcier, son of his father's sister Blanquine, and his mother's cousin Jean de Villeneuve, son of Antoine de Louppes de Villeneuve, both members of the Parlement, to settle any differences that might arise.

Although lawsuits and agreements were a favorite sport of the bourgeois aristocracy of Bordeaux, these documents, especially the agreement, suggest incompatibility between mother and son and a struggle for control in what had been her house for forty years but was now his. Whatever the faults on his side, his mother appears as a dominating woman not easily adaptable to any position except mastery. At this time her son was thirty-five and had been married for three years.

Another legal act of the following year (May 23, 1569) is interesting for other reasons, of which more later. Montaigne's third brother, Arnaud de Saint-Martin, had suddenly died of apoplexy at twenty-seven after being hit above the right ear by a court-tennis ball. Michel had discovered in his wife's coffers a gold chain left there by his dead brother. When he told his mother, she claimed it as her own; he returned it to her in the presence of his two other brothers, and a formal act was drawn up to attest this.

Her own testament, dated April 19, 1597—five years after the death of her eldest son—is that of an embittered woman. Though her daughter-in-law was still living at Montaigne, it was made in Bordeaux; the mother had probably not lived at the château for about ten years. She wills to be buried, not with her husband at Montaigne, but in the church of Saint-André in Bordeaux with two of her husband's brothers and her son Arnaud de Saint-Martin. She mentions Michel only to complain that he has enjoyed the fruits of her labors; his father mainly in the same vein; his wife, her daughter-in-law for over thirty years, not at all. Her meager affection seems to include two surviving sons, Montaigne's brothers Thomas and Bertrand, and to center on her daughter Léonor and especially Léonor's daughter Jeanne de Camain, aged fifteen, who at her marriage is to receive 1,800 livres tournois (already delivered to her father) because "the said Jehanne de Cammain, my granddaughter, in the period of twelve years or more that she has been in my company, has done me many services, both in my illnesses and my health."

This is the only nice thing that Antoinette de Louppes says about anyone in her will. Of her daughter Jeanne de Lestonnac she remarks that although her dowry explicitly canceled any inheritance claims, she is to receive one hundred crowns: "and I want her to be unable to make any further claim to my property or to dispute with my heirs named below." A similar legacy to Montaigne's daughter Léonor is couched in similar terms. The gist of Antoinette's grievance is this:

I also declare that by my marriage contract with the said late lord my husband, half of the sum brought by me as a dowry was to be placed and employed in the acquisition of real estate to take the place of my patrimony, which, to my great loss and damage, was not done. Also it is notorious that I worked for a period of forty years in the house of Montaigne with my husband in such a way that by my work, care, and management the said house has been greatly increased in value, improved and enlarged; which, with all the abovementioned, the late Michel de Montaigne, my eldest son, has enjoyed peaceably by my grant and permission, and since his death Léonor de Montaigne, daughter of the said late Michel, my son, holds and possesses almost all the property left by the said late lord of Montaigne, my husband, being very rich and opulent; thus she has no right to any claim to my property and inheritance. However, I give and leave her the sum of one hundred crowns. . . . And in case the said Léonor should not be content, I will and intend that she consider and take into account both the abovementioned hundred crowns and also the profit, advantage, and comfort that I could have received if the said acquisition in real estate had been made according to the contents of my marriage contract.

Also curious is a wary postscript which notes that this is her last will, recognizes that she is "of an age easy to circumvent" (probably nearing ninety), that she may die with no children there to help her, and that someone may try to make some other disposition of her property, and declares that she repudiates in advance any will, whether already made or yet to be made, whether signed by her or not, that does not contain the three Latin words *Deus audi me—* God, hear me.

From all this emerges the portrait of a strong-minded, capable woman, more wary than outgoing, strict, hard-working, thrifty, acquisitive, proud of her share in Pierre Eyquem's prosperity, bitter over his failure to use 2,000 crowns of her dowry in the kind of investments that the marriage contract had stipulated, and even more over being denied a share in his profits after his death and seeing the estate she had helped to build up pass to a son to whom property was a pleasant accident to enjoy and not a lifework to amass, and from him to a granddaughter who probably also took wealth for granted.

Of course she had a point. In their third generation as nobles, the time at which in those days the recently ennobled began to be regarded as genuine, the Eyquems de Montaigne, led by Pierre, started thinking about money like nobles. We do not know how much Pierre lavished on the care and upbringing of Michel, but the mother must have thought him a doting fool and the son badly spoiled, brought up with no sense of the hard realities of life. Musicians to wake him in the morning, indeed! And a tutor speaking nothing but Latin! Better that house and vineyard down the hill, or those storage sheds in Bordeaux, which would bring in a good rent and not give youngsters extravagant ideas. After all, that was what those 2,000 crowns of her dowry had been meant for.

Her son's views on the proper transmission of family authority are clearly expressed in an essay written about ten years after his father's death. Mothers, he says, should not be left dependent on their children, but "given plentiful means to maintain themselves according to the standing of their house and their age." Moreover, they should have charge of affairs, if the father is dead, until the children are of legal age. But they are prone to be so unfair, he finds, that "the father has brought the children up very badly if he cannot hope that at that age they will have more wisdom and ability than his wife, seeing the ordinary weakness of the sex." It seems likely that he wrote these words with his mother in mind.

We do not know much about Antoinette de Louppes. Unless her son's remark about the Portuguese "new Christians" is an oblique comment on her—which seems farfetched—nothing we know suggests that she was not a sincere Catholic. Nothing we know suggests that her half-Jewish descent had anything to do with her incompatibility with her son. Their contrasting attitudes toward amassing and enjoying money and property, the conflict over authority, mainly attributable to the mother's inability to accept her son as master in what for almost forty years had been *her* home, the son's grateful love for the kind father who had spared no expense for his upbringing but had left his widow to harbor, apparently with reason, a bitter grievance at his failure to provide for her as her dowry required he should—these aspects of the cold war between the sexes and the generations account for the friction between mother and son and for his reticence about her. Montaigne wrote an often-tender chapter on the affection of fathers for their children; if he wrote one on that of mothers, it has not survived.

Most attempts to explain part of Montaigne's mind and temperament by the twenty-five per cent of Jewish blood that mixed so happily with the Gascon in his veins have been responsible and therefore cautious. Probably attributable to it in some measure are his deep tolerance in an age when that was not in fashion; a rather detached attitude, typical of the marranos and natural in them, toward the religion he consistently and very conscientiously practiced; his tireless curiosity, mainly but not solely intellectual; the cosmopolitanism natural to the member of a far-flung family.

His Eyquem blood helped him send deep roots into the French soil of his native Gascony; his Lopez blood helped make him a citizen of the world.

"I WAS BORN between eleven o'clock and noon," Montaigne tells us, "on the last day of February, 1533."
He was the third child of Pierre and Antoinette
Eyquem de Montaigne; the first two must have
already died. He was followed by seven others: three
very soon, Thomas (May 17, 1534), Pierre (November 10, 1535),
and Jeanne (October 17, 1536); five years later Arnaud (September 14, 1541); then in the father's fifties and sixties Léonor (August
30, 1552), Marie (February 19, 1555), and Bertrand (August 20,
1560). The family was as varied as it was large.

Our best glimpse of Thomas Eyquem, lord of Beauregard,
is at the deathbed of Montaigne's friend La Boétie. With no
one present but Montaigne and the girls serving him, La Boétie
calls in Beauregard, thanks him for the trouble he is taking, receives permission to speak from the heart, and tells him that of all
who have sought to reform the Church, "I have never thought
there was a single one who went about it with better zeal and more
complete, sincere, and simple affection than you." He acknowledges
the imperfections in the Church that have alienated Beauregard

and led him to leave it. "I do not want to dissuade you from it now; for I do not readily ask anyone to do anything whatever against his conscience." After the already quoted plea not to shatter the family unity, La Boétie points to the analogy of civil strife: "Do not be so sharp and so violent; accommodate yourself to them. Do not form a band and body apart; unite with them. You see how many ruins these dissensions have brought into this kingdom, and I warrant you they will bring much greater ones yet. And since you are wise and good, keep from bringing these disturbances into the midst of your family. . . ."

La Boétie's words have a curious setting and sequel. The house in which he died belonged to Richard de Lestonnac and his wife, Jeanne, Montaigne's sister. The last person La Boétie had spoken to previously was his own stepdaughter Jacquette d'Arsac. Soon afterward she and Beauregard, a widower, were married. A few years later Jeanne de Lestonnac, a Protestant married to a Catholic, having failed to convert her oldest daughter (the future Catholic saint), entrusted the girl to the Beauregards, hoping that they might fare better. Montaigne brought this to the father's attention, and young Jeanne returned home a Catholic still.

At the time of La Boétie's death, to judge by Montaigne's letter, Jacquette d'Arsac did not yet seem drawn to Protestantism. Beauregard's commitment may have been very recent; for whereas in 1561 his father's first will made him co-tutor (with Michel, their mother, and two uncles) of the three youngest children, the second will, of 1567, omits an uncle (Bussaguet) who had died in 1563 and leaves all the others except Beauregard.

Fifteen years after Michel's death, in 1607, Beauregard brought an unsuccessful suit against Montaigne's widow and daughter, claiming that Pierre Eyquem had wanted him, in the event that Michel had no male heirs, to inherit the name, surname, arms, and noble house of Montaigne.

However, nothing else suggests any breach in the family unity —nothing else in the father's wills, nothing in the settlement of the second will by the four older brothers (August 22, 1568), in Montaigne's only reference to Thomas in the *Essays* (one of his estates in Médoc is being "buried under the sands that the sea spews forth"), or in the quatrain addressed to him after Montaigne's death by his *fille d'alliance,* Marie de Gournay:

> *Your race makes you a good father,*
> *Your wife calls you a good husband,*
> *Everyone says you are just and faithful,*
> *And I name you a perfect friend.*

His first marriage was to Serène Estève; his second, to Jacquette d'Arsac (who died about 1578), which made him lord of Arsac, Lilhan, Loirac, and Castera, as well as of Beauregard; his third, in 1582, to Françoise de Dampierre. This is about all we know of Thomas de Beauregard.

The third child, Pierre, lord of La Brousse near Montaigne, lived there quietly, never married, and left little trace. At twenty-five a contract for a suit of armor reveals him as a "man-at-arms" in the company of Monseigneur de Burie, the king's lieutenant general in Guienne. Marie de Gournay reports that he was charged by Michel on his deathbed with sending her his last farewell. He negotiated the arrangements for Michel's burial in the church of the Feuillants in Bordeaux, where he himself was also buried three years later. Marie de Gournay's quatrain further suggests his devotion:

> *You are the beloved brother of the very great Montaigne,*
> *La Brousse, and that point alone lends you as great luster*
> *As your nice mind, your well-formed body,*
> *And your happy wealth, or this illustrious race.*

The only reference to him in the *Essays*, made around 1574, shows him traveling with Michel during the civil wars and falling in with a gentleman of good appearance who pretended to be a Catholic but whose uneasy conscience gave him away—at least to Montaigne—each time they passed through a town loyal to the king. The account suggests that the brothers often traveled together and clearly shows that Pierre, like Michel, was a Catholic loyalist. Devoted, modest, and helpful, Pierre de La Brousse died on November 27, 1595, at the age of sixty.

We have already noted that the fourth child, Jeanne, became the Protestant mother of a Catholic saint. At the age of eighteen (May 5, 1555) she married Richard de Lestonnac, lord of Espaigne or of Le Parc, a councillor at the Bordeaux Parlement. He was then, and remained, a Catholic; she turned to Protestantism, toward which she may have leaned for some time, probably not before 1558, when her namesake was two years old. A learned person like her husband, her superb command of Greek (as well as Latin) gave rise to stories. Once, it is said, a colleague of her husband came to the house to invite him to an amorous escapade, and, seeing his wife there, couched his invitation in Greek; whereupon she berated him in the same language and promptly sent him on his way alone.

With the help of her brother Beauregard and his second wife, she tried to bring up her six children as Calvinists. However, her daughter Jeanne (1556–1640) clung to her father's faith and was thinking of entering a convent when her parents in 1573 prevailed on her to marry instead. Her uncle Michel was a signer of her marriage contract. Her husband, Gaston de Montferrant, baron of Landiras, a devoted Catholic like herself, left her a widow around 1595; and in spite of her children, whom she had brought up most piously, she entered orders soon after, leaving them only to found (1605) the "Nuns of Our Lady" (Les Religieuses de Notre-Dame). This order, affiliated with the Benedictines and dedicated to the teaching of girls, so closely resembled the Society of Jesus in its rules that the members were popularly called the Jesuitines. It spread widely, mainly in France but also in Spain. The founder, who served for many years as superior, died in 1640 and was declared venerable in 1834, beatified in 1900, and canonized on May 15, 1949.

The biographers of Saint Jeanne de Lestonnac agree that as a girl she was the apple of her uncle Michel's eye; that he saw nothing girlish in her lively mind and sound judgment, and so admired her beauty of body and soul as to call her a masterpiece of nature; and that he played a decisive role in keeping her in (or possibly restoring her to) the Catholic fold, warning her father of the danger she was running at the Beauregards', so that Richard de Lestonnac brought her back under his own wing. On the occasion of her canonization, the late Pope Pius XII acknowledged Montaigne's role and expressed his wish and belief that some day soon the *Essays* might be removed from the Index of Prohibited Books. "Why yes," he is quoted as saying, "it is thanks to him that the little girl became a Catholic."

To return to Michel's brothers and sisters, the fifth child and fourth son, Arnaud, lord of Saint-Martin, is known to have been a student at the Collège de Guyenne and for only two other things: the manner of his sudden death and the puzzling episode, already noted, that followed when Michel found a gold chain of Arnaud's in his own wife's coffers, heard it claimed by his mother as hers, and formalized his return of it to her in a legal document. Arnaud had died suddenly at the age of twenty-seven (Montaigne says twenty-three, but he often miscounts) of a freakish accident: "A brother of mine, Captain Saint-Martin, twenty-three years old, who had already given pretty good proof of his valor, while playing tennis was struck by a ball a little above the right ear, with no sign of contusion or wound. He did not sit down or rest, but five or six hours later he died of an apoplexy that this blow gave him."

The sixth child and second sister, Léonor, was almost twenty years younger than Michel, who served as her godfather at the baptism. On September 2, 1581, she married Thibaud de Camain, lord of La Tour de Camet and of Courtezelles, a future councillor at the Bordeaux Parlement. As we have seen, she was probably her mother's favorite child; her daughter Jeanne spent twelve of her first fifteen years in her grandmother's company; and mother and daughter are kindly remembered in the will of Antoinette de Louppes. Marie de Gournay's wish for her is that her daughter may become like her. Montaigne's friend and imitator Pierre Charron left her 500 crowns in his will (January 31, 1602); and on her husband's death in 1628 it fell to her to succeed him in administering a fund of 7,200 crowns left by Charron to provide dowries for needy unmarried girls and scholarship aid for poor students.

Even less known to us is the next child, Marie. In 1577, she and Mattecoulon helped baptize Montaigne's fifth daughter, without ceremony, before the child died. Two years later, at the age of twenty-four, she married Bernard (or Bertrand) de Cazalis, lord of Freyche, and died childless soon after. He may be the same Cazalis who went to Italy a year later with Michel, leaving the party in Padua to stay on there, apparently as a student.

The eighth and last child, Bertrand-Charles, was born when his oldest brother was twenty-seven. At eight, on his father's death, he became lord of Mattecoulon, a few miles north of Montaigne. Michel, obeying his father's wishes, sought to fill his place for the boy. When Bertrand was twenty, he took him along on his trip to Rome. We read of his sending him to visit a wounded count and learn that his wounds were not mortal; taking him and others

on side trips to Lake Garda and Montalcino; bringing him to
be presented to the Pope and kiss his feet; and finally, when summoned back to serve his term as mayor of Bordeaux, leaving him
in Rome in a nice little rented room "with forty-three gold crowns,
with which, he had decided, he could stay there and learn fencing
for five months."

Apparently he was an apt pupil; but as Montaigne was to remark, "We go and learn fencing in Italy, and practice it at the
expense of our lives before we learn it." This nearly happened to
the warlike Bertrand, who, still—or again—in Rome on June 6,
1583, was called on to second one Esparezat, "a gentleman he hardly
knew," in a duel with La Villate, whose second was the baron de
Salligny. As Montaigne comments, he was trapped in the code of
honor, which so often clashes with that of reason, first because his
immediate adversary, Salligny, was "much closer and better known
to him" than Esparezat, and then by his obligation after he had
killed Salligny, which led him to join his principal in killing the protesting La Villate. Brantôme, who feels that Mattecoulon had to
do what he did, reports that he answered: "And how do I know?
If you had killed Esparezat you would come and kill me if you
could." Montaigne deplores his brother's dilemma but shows his sympathy over it:

After having disposed of his man, seeing the two principals still on their
feet and intact, he went to the relief of his teammate. What less could he do?
Should he have kept still and, if chance had so willed it, watched the man
for whose defense he had come there being defeated? . . .

He could be neither just nor courteous at the risk of the man to whom
he had lent himself. Accordingly he was delivered from the prisons of Italy
by a very prompt and solemn recommendation of our king.

On his return to France he took service under Henry of
Navarre and became gentleman in ordinary of his chamber, captain,
and governor of Casteljaloux. Despite his choice of sides, he was
an intransigent Catholic. His château was ruined by the Protestants; once in the court of Navarre he struck a man for speaking
irreverently of the Virgin and the saints. When his nephew
Charles de Gamaches says that Mattecoulon rose as he grew
older from the love of beautiful human forms to that of angelic and
saintly souls, he is probably suggesting not so much a platonic matu-

rity as a lusty youth. At the age of thirty-one (September 10, 1591), he married Charlotte d'Eymar, daughter of a president of the Bordeaux Parlement (and a relative on his mother's side), who bore him two children. After Michel's death he made frequent use of his calendar of important events, the copy of Beuther's *Ephemeris historica,* and added about ten notes, one of them (August 14, 1622) a touching epitaph to his dead son: "He was a gentle knight. . . . God give him peace." Marie de Gournay addresses this quatrain to him:

> You whose armed strength is my security,
> Brave Mattecoulon, O son of victory,
> If Hercules had seen the glory of your mighty sword,
> He would have dropped his club and been a soldier.

Since she praises all Montaignes in every way she can, we may infer that Mattecoulon's main qualities were military courage and prowess.

Such were Montaigne's four brothers and three sisters, differing widely in age, interests, temperament, and convictions. Here are no more merchants but two soldiers, the first in the family after their father, and two lords of their manors like Michel. Only two did not marry, one of these dying too early; only three were childless. The marriages were all to nobles, mostly of the aristocratic families of the Bordeaux Parlement. Their most striking characteristic in an age of religious civil warfare which began when the oldest was twenty-nine, the youngest not yet two, is the deep family unity beneath the diversity of religious convictions. It is clear that Jeanne was an ardent Protestant for life, and Thomas at least for some time in the 1560's. The religious issue was alive in the family when Michel was not beyond his early teens. Men were executed for Lutheranism in Bordeaux in 1544. It must have been between 1538 and 1546 that Pierre Bunel, a learned humanist from Toulouse who had been drawn toward the Reform but not won over to it, spent a few days at Montaigne and on his departure left his host Pierre a copy of Raymond Sebond's *Theologia naturalis,* recommending it to him as a good antidote to the menacing spread of Lutheranism.

At a time when religion set brother in arms against brother, son against father, it was rare to find such concord in a religiously divided family. Firm as he was in his own convictions, Pierre de Montaigne, like Etienne de La Boétie, set freedom of conscience above all. It was a tolerant atmosphere in which Michel grew up.

He was born at a moment when the moderate, peaceful religious reform sought by Erasmus, Lefèvre d'Etaples, and their admirers was widely popular in France and seemed not unlikely to prevail. This type of reform and humanism went hand in hand, aiming to use the new philology to gain a better understanding of the Bible, and, by scholarly translation, to make it better known and understood by all. The innovators found violent opponents in the powerful conservative theologians of the Sorbonne but two strong protectors in Queen Margaret of Navarre, sister of the king of France, who had embraced the doctrines of Lefèvre, and King Francis himself, whose feud with the Sorbonne dated from his Concordat of 1516 with the Pope, which gave him great power over the French Church through the right to nominate, for the Pope's approval, the candidates for most high ecclesiastical positions. Just three years before Montaigne was born Francis I, after long urging by the great Hellenist Guillaume Budé, had delighted the evangelical humanists by founding the first French nontheological institution of higher learning, the future Collège de France, and he continued to support it against the fury of Noël Béda and his Sorbonne colleagues. Marot in verse and Rabelais in prose were only the most eminent of the writers who ridiculed the conservative theologians as obscurantists and rejoiced in the golden age of learning inaugurated by the new academy.

Before Montaigne was two years old, however, the day of the moderates was over. Pope Clement VII had excommunicated Henry VIII because of Anne Boleyn and had persuaded Francis I to put pressure on his heretical subjects. Convinced that these had become seditious by the "Affair of the Placards," the posting, in Paris and even on the door of the king's chamber in Amboise, of violent attacks on the papacy and the Mass (October 17–18, 1534), Francis began persecution in earnest. Calvin fled to prepare his *Institutes* and soon to make Geneva a citadel of militant reform.

During Montaigne's boyhood and young manhood, until the outbreak of the religious civil wars in 1562, Calvinism, though mainly underground, spread widely and steadily throughout France despite repression that was stern under Francis I and violent under

his son Henry II (1547-59). Henry's death and that of his son
Francis II soon after left the crown very weak, with the other sons
minors and the regent, Catherine de' Medici, a woman and a foreigner. Catholics and Protestants, princes of the blood and other
great nobles, subjected her to great pressure. An attempt to reconcile doctrinal differences, the Colloquy of Poissy, failed. The massacre of over twenty Protestants, worshiping illegally at Vassy on
March 1, 1562, by the Catholic leader François de Guise, led to
open war that was to continue intermittently for the rest of Montaigne's life and even after.

The Château de Montaigne, where he grew up and spent
most of his life, stands on a sort of plateau a few miles north of the
Dordogne. Bordeaux lies about thirty miles to the west. To the east,
a dozen miles upstream, is Sainte-Foy-la-Grande, with Bergerac as
far again beyond; about as far to the west is Libourne, where the
Isle joins the Dordogne from the north and flows with it to meet
the Garonne fifteen miles downstream; on the way to Libourne
lies Castillon on the river and Saint-Emilion on its heights above.
From prehistoric times nature here has been hospitable to man, and
man has been responsive; here he and his dwellings and his animals
fit into the landscape in unusually civilized fashion. Through woods,
grasslands, and above all the ever-present grapevines, the road rises
steadily up one of the chain of gentle hills that overlooks the serene
Dordogne, then levels off on top of the plateau to pass through the
village of Saint-Michel de Montaigne on its way to the manor.

The main part of the château, rebuilt after a fire in 1885,
is not as it was in Montaigne's time; but his and another tower and
the wall between still stand, and old accounts and sketches give us a
good picture of how it used to be. You entered, then as now,
from the southeast, by a gate under the tower at that corner, from
which on your left walls stretched some fifty yards toward a main
building to the west, and on your right the same distance to another
tower. The tower by the entrance was to be Montaigne's, the other
his wife's. The entrance brings the visitor into a large square courtyard bounded on the west by the main building and on the other
three sides by walls, with a gallery along the opposite wall connecting
the two towers. Buildings, walls, and towers were of yellowish
stone and masonry, the roofs dark red. The old parts are all still

sturdy; as Montaigne says, though he made no attempt to fortify it himself, it was strong for the time when it was built. To the east of the court lay a large garden of about the same size; to the north a poultry yard as long as the court and about half as wide; both were fully walled. Beyond the main building to the west lay (and still lies) a lovely balustraded terrace, overlooking the valley of the Lidoire, with a splendid view of the hills and castles to the west and north. Here you know how the estate got its name and why Montaigne says it is "perched on a little hill" and "exposed to the winds."

Of Montaigne's tower and library more later; he is not yet ready to make them his own. Enough to imagine him now roaming and playing—absent-mindedly and lazily, he tells us—in the sturdy red-roofed manor, the spacious court and garden, the animated poultry yard, and among the hilly meadows, woods, and vineyards of his father's ever-growing estate. Child, youth, and grown man, this was his home.

His birth was anxiously awaited, since two children had already died, and Antoinette de Louppes had been carrying him for eleven months. It must have been his father who chose him a name new to the family, Michel, as a bond between them; for though the son was not born on Michaelmas Day (September 29), the father was. The name the youngster probably heard most was the nickname Micheau, which his father loved and used in both his wills, even when his son was a married man in his thirties and a councillor in the Bordeaux Parlement.

Pierre Eyquem spared neither pains nor money to mold the boy wisely from the cradle. His grateful son writes later that he "had me held over the baptismal font by people of the lowliest class, to bind and attach me to them." Noblemen usually hired nurses for their children; Montaigne's father, seeing a further use for this custom,

sent me from the cradle to be brought up in a poor village of his, and kept me there as long as I was nursing, and even longer, training me to the humblest and commonest way of life. . . . His notion aimed . . . to ally me with the people and that class of men that needs our help; and he considered that I was duty bound to look rather to the man who extends his arms to me than to the one who turns his back on me. . . .

His plan has succeeeded not at all badly. I am prone to devote myself to the little people, whether because there is more vainglory in it, or through natural compassion, which has infinite power over me.

Tradition has it that Montaigne's nurse lived in the nearby hamlet of Papessus.

Back home he was brought up "by reason, and by wisdom and tact. . . . They say that in all my childhood I felt the rod only twice, and that very softly." Since his father had been impressed by the theory "that it troubles the tender brains of children to wake them in the morning with a start, and to snatch them suddenly and violently from their sleep, in which they are plunged much more deeply than we are, he had me awakened by the sound of some instrument; and I was never without a man to do this for me." In every way Pierre de Montaigne sought "to teach me to enjoy knowledge and duty by my own free will and desire, and to educate my mind in all gentleness and freedom, without rigor and constraint."

Latin, though losing ground in France to the vernacular, was still the great international language of educated men; but it was as hard to learn well then as now. Certain patriotic theorists (with whom Montaigne does not agree), among them the poet Du Bellay, claimed that the main reason why the French did not match the learning of the Greeks and Romans was the time it took them to learn their languages. So while young Micheau was still nursing and before the first loosening of his tongue, his father put him in the care of a German doctor, Horstanus, later to be a teacher at the Collège de Guyenne, who spoke very good Latin but no French.

This man [Montaigne writes], whom he had sent for expressly, and who was very highly paid, had me constantly in his hands. There were also two others with him, less learned, to attend me and relieve him. These spoke to me in no other language than Latin. As for the rest of my father's household, it was an inviolable rule that neither my father himself, nor my mother, nor any valet or housemaid, should speak anything in my presence but such Latin words as each had learned in order to jabber with me.

It is wonderful how everyone profited from this. My father and mother learned enough Latin in this way to understand it, and acquired sufficient skill to use it when necessary, as did also the servants who were most attached to my service. Altogether, we Latinized ourselves so much that it overflowed all the way to our villages on every side, where there still remain several Latin names for artisans and tools that have taken root by usage. As for me, I was over six before I understood any more French or Perigordian than Arabic. And without artificial means, without a book, without grammar or precept, without the whip and without tears, I had learned a Latin quite as pure as what my schoolmaster knew, for I could not have contaminated or altered it.

Less practical but more lustrous than Latin was the language of Plato, Aristotle, and the New Testament. Pierre de Montaigne wanted this too for his heir, but also without tears. "As for Greek," Michel wrote later, "of which I have practically no knowledge at all, my father planned to have me taught it artificially, but in a new way, in the form of amusement and exercise. We volleyed our conjugations back and forth, like those who learn arithmetic and geometry by such games as checkers and chess."

Young Michel, however, by his own account at least, was sluggish, slow, and unretentive. His father, dismayed at the scant yield of his elaborate plan and deprived of the advice of its proponents, sent the boy to the new school in Bordeaux, the Collège de Guyenne, one of the finest in France. Many of the distinguished humanists on its faculty—the Gouvéas, Buchanan, Muret, and others—leaned toward Erasmian religious reform and later inculcated or at least insinuated heretical views. If young Michel noticed any of this, he does not mention it; nor does it seem to have lessened his father's pride and trust in the school. The former first jurat, provost, and deputy mayor arranged for tutors (regular teachers wishing to supplement their meager income) for his son and even held out for certain practices (which the son does not specify) not normally allowed. Michel's brilliant Latin led him to skip immediately to an upper grade, probably sixth (he finished the twelve-year course in seven years), forced his teachers to give him special exercises turning, not French into Latin, but bad Latin into good, and made some of the finest Latinists of his day, his private tutors Nicholas Grouchy, Guillaume Guerente, and George Buchanan, afraid to accost him, so great was his fluency. It helped also, in his last year or two of school, to win him lead roles in the Latin tragedies of Buchanan, Guerente, and Muret (probably the *Baptistes* and *Jephthes* of Buchanan and the excellent *Julius Caesar* of Muret), "which," he says, "were performed with dignity in our Collège de Guyenne," adding that "in this matter, as in all other parts of his job, Andreas Goveanus, our principal, was incomparably the greatest principal of France; and I was considered a master craftsman."

"But for all that," Montaigne sums up, "it was still school. My Latin promptly degenerated, and since then, for lack of practice, I have lost all use of it. . . . When I left the school at thirteen, I had finished my course (as they call it), and in truth without any benefit that I can place in evidence now."

The main reason is not far to seek. For all its excellent faculty, the school's curriculum aimed mainly to teach Latin to students who knew none when they entered. Since they were obliged to speak it before they knew it, their jargon might well corrupt Montaigne's pure Latin.

Though most of the teachers followed Erasmus in seeking to make learning palatable, Montaigne considers himself fortunate to have avoided getting "nothing out of school but a hatred of books, as do nearly all our noblemen." In his first or second year of school he learned to love books—not the usual light reading of the time, the *Amadis de Gaule, Huon de Bordeaux,* or other such romances, but Ovid's *Metamorphoses*—so much that he would steal away from any other pleasure to read them. As he grew more careless about his regular lessons, he was lucky to come in contact with a very understanding tutor (quite possibly his fifth-grade teacher, the learned young Jean Talpin, future author of many sound pages on education), who, probably impressed by the youngster's enjoyment of a work that his classmates would only sample a few years later, "knew enough to connive cleverly at this frivolity of mine and others like it." He was indeed astute. "Pretending to see nothing, he whetted my appetite, letting me gorge myself with these books only in secret, and gently keeping me at my work on the regular studies." Thus Montaigne, always lured on by his enjoyment, went through Virgil's *Aeneid,* Terence, Plautus, and finally, undeterred by an unfamiliar vernacular, some Italian comedies. Thanks to this man, his school years were by no means wholly wasted.

Disappointed in an education that did little but fill the memory, the gently reared youngster was indignant at school discipline:

They are a real jail of captive youth. They make them slack, by punishing them for slackness before they show it. Go in at lesson time: you hear nothing but cries, both from tortured boys and from masters drunk with rage. What a way to arouse zest for their lesson in these tender and timid souls, to guide

them to it with a horrible scowl and hands armed with rods! . . . Where
their profit is, let their frolic be also.

The system is dangerous, since nothing "so depraves and stupefies a
well-born nature" as violence and compulsion: "If you would like
him to fear shame and chastisement, don't harden him to them."
Moreover, it does not work:

There is nothing like arousing appetite and affection; otherwise all you make
out of them is asses loaded with books. By dint of whipping, they are given
their pocketful of learning for safekeeping; but if learning is to do us good,
we must not merely lodge it within us, we must espouse it.

As Michel de Montaigne looked back in his forties and fifties
on the schoolboy Micheau, he saw in him health, tractability, maturity in judgment, but also laziness and inertia. No wonder, he
says, his father's excellent cultivation brought no fruit from such
sterile soil:

Though my health was sound and complete and my nature gentle and
tractable, I was withal so sluggish, lax, and drowsy that they could not
tear me from my sloth, not even to make me play. What I saw, I saw well,
and beneath this inert appearance nourished bold ideas and opinions beyond
my years. I had a slow mind, which would go only as far as it was led; a
tardy understanding, a weak imagination, and on top of all an incredible
lack of memory. It is no wonder if he could get nothing worth while from
all this.

His character was of a piece with his mind: "No one predicted that
I should become wicked, but only useless. . . . The danger was
not that I should do ill, but that I should do nothing."

For the next eight to eleven years, from thirteen to twenty-
one or twenty-four, from schoolboy to magistrate, we lose almost all
trace of Montaigne. At fifteen he witnessed the terrible revolt over
the salt tax in Bordeaux in the late summer of 1548 and the
pathetic death of Tristan de Moneins, the king's hapless lieutenant
in Guienne, at the hands of a frenzied mob in the streets; he blames
him not for going out to confront the mob but for losing his nerve
when he did. And this is all we really know.

About these years conjectures naturally abound. Montaigne
may have had a year off at home to ride, hunt, visit, and read all
he wanted. He may have spent a few years at one of the academies
where young nobles were taught polite manners, genealogy, the rudi-

ments of political knowledge, and above all the arts of fighting, whether in tourneys, duels, or war. He may have been given a few years free to spend in Paris at court and studying with members of the future Collège de France. (He must have been north early, for he says that Paris had his heart since his childhood.) He may have studied with Muret and others at the Faculty of Arts of the University of Bordeaux.

But his likeliest occupation for at least part of this period is still the study of law. By now his father clearly intended him for a career as magistrate, not for arms or the Church. Members of a sovereign court were supposed to have the *licence* in law (though exceptions were frequent), and a royal edict of 1546 required of councillors seeking admission to a Parlement an open-book examination on legal texts and practice. Though these tests were rarely severe, Pierre de Montaigne probably wanted his eldest son suitably prepared for his career.

The University of Bordeaux law school was weak, losing students, low in morale. Much better was that of Toulouse, where Montaigne's uncle Pierre de Gaujac had studied. Its brilliant faculty included the Latin poet Jean de Boyssoné; the renowned teacher Jean Corras; the great young renovator of the study of Roman law Jacques Cujas (1520–90); and his colleague and former teacher Arnaud du Ferrier, a future friend of Montaigne. Michel would have found there aunts, cousins, and uncles (one of them a *capitoul*) to welcome him to his mother's native city.

Unquestionably Montaigne spent some time in Toulouse as a youth. It may have been then or later that he heard there the story of the woman who, after passing through the hands of soldiers, exclaimed: "God be praised that at least once in my life I have had my fill without sin!" Some time in his "childhood" he either witnessed or read about the famous Martin Guerre case of impersonation, tried in the Parlement of Toulouse and later reported in print by Jean Corras; but he was in his late twenties when it happened. His encounter with Dr. Simon Thomas took place in Toulouse in his youth. Meeting Michel at the house of a rich old consumptive and discussing possible cures, Thomas told his patient "that one of these would be to give me occasion to enjoy his company; and that by fixing his eyes on the freshness of my face and his thoughts on the blitheness and overflowing vigor of my youth, and filling all his

senses with my flourishing condition, he might improve his constitution. But he forgot to say that mine might get worse at the same
time."

Montaigne was to have many friends or acquaintances who were
at Toulouse, mostly as law students, at the time when he would
have been: Estienne Pasquier, Henri de Mesmes, the men
Mesmes mentions as his own teachers (Corras and Du Ferrier)
and friends (Pierre Bunel, Simon Thomas, Adrianus Turnebus),
and the two Gascons Guy du Faur de Pibrac and Paul de
Foix. Pasquier tells us of his friendship; Montaigne himself mentions every one of the others: Corras and Thomas as we have just
seen, Bunel as the friend of his father who left him Sebond's
Natural Theology, Turnebus four times with the highest praise.
On his trip to Italy in 1581 he visited Du Ferrier, then the French
ambassador, in Venice, and his letters show the two in close contact
four years later. Mesmes and Foix are two of the important persons
to whom Montaigne dedicated works of La Boétie in 1570.
While Foix was ambassador to Rome, Montaigne visited with him
at least twice. The deaths of Foix and Pibrac in 1584 drew from
him this eloquent eulogy:

Good Monsieur de Pibrac, whom we have just lost, such a noble mind, such
sound opinions, such a gentle character! This loss, and that of Monsieur de
Foix, which we suffered at the same time, are important losses to our crown.
I do not know if France has another pair left, comparable in sincerity and
ability, to substitute for these two Gascons in the councils of our kings.
They were souls beautiful in different ways, and certainly rare and beautiful
by the standards of our time, each in his own way. But who placed them
in this age, they who were so out of tune and proportion with our corruption
and tempests?

The law school of the University of Toulouse had seen violence in the years of Reform. The faculty was humanistic and
generally sympathetic to the new ideas; the students, sharply divided; the townspeople, mainly conservative. The fiery Etienne
Dolet had shone there, done battle, and finally been banished.
Rabelais had noted not long before that the students not only
learned to dance and use the two-handled sword, but also "burned
their *régens* [professors] alive like kippered herring."

The law student's life was not easy. "We were up at four
o'clock," writes Henri de Mesmes (a normal hour then was seven in

winter, six in summer), "and, having prayed to God, at five o'clock went to our studies, our big books under our arm, our inkstands and our candlesticks in our hands." For five straight hours they had classes, or "readings," in which the teacher commented on the chosen texts. A hasty review of notes was followed by the midday meal; and then, to relax, they read in Sophocles, Aristophanes, Euripides, or sometimes Demosthenes, Cicero, Virgil, or Horace. Classes again from one to five; another hour to put notes in order and check the teacher's citations; "then we had supper, then read in Greek or Latin." Only Sunday provided such frivolities as music and walks, and then only after Mass and vespers. To be sure, many students got through by hook or by crook; but for most, as for Montaigne's friend Pierre de Brach later, the course was memorable for its rigor and discomforts.

All this, of course, is in no sense proof. Indeed, if Montaigne did study law there, it is amazing that he never mentions any of these many friends, or is mentioned by them, in this relation. But since he was to be attached to the Cour des Aides of Périgueux as a councillor at—or soon after—twenty-one, before the legal age, it is likely that he studied law somewhere. If he did, it was probably at Toulouse.

FFICIAL RECORDS outline Montaigne's years as a magistrate; his comments on justice and its administration show his feelings; an occasional glimpse reveals him in action. The picture is incomplete but coherent.

It has long been assumed that he replaced his father and served three years in the Cour des Aides of Périgueux before that body was incorporated (December 3, 1557) into the Bordeaux Parlement; but in all probability he was given the post not by his father but by his uncle, Pierre Eyquem, lord of Gaujac, and some scholars doubt that he served long—if at all—at Périgueux. He probably did serve there, however. In the abundant records of the Bordeaux Parlement for these years we find no sign that, although under age, he needed a special dispensation to become a member; which probably means that he had one for the Cour des Aides and did not need another. Furthermore, his name appears—to be sure, after the suppression of the Aides—in the king's letters patent of October, 1557, on the list of the Périgueux officers to be received into the Bordeaux Parlement.

The Cour des Aides, or Cour des Généraux, of Périgueux

had sovereign jurisdiction, civil and criminal, in Guienne, Auvergne, and Poitou, over all cases concerning taxes and duties: taille (a national, personal tax), gabelle (a heavy tax on salt, the purchase of which was compulsory), aides (levies for state expenses), customs, and the like. It was empowered to register titles of nobility, judge its own candidates and those of courts under its jurisdiction, and serve as court of appeal for decisions of minor tax bureaus and magistrates. Like the Parlements but in a narrower domain, it was an arm of the king's judicial power. It was mainly to raise money, however, that Henry II created it. The offices were farmed out for a lump sum of 50,000 crowns for resale by the mayor and consuls of Périgueux.

Venality of public offices had become royal policy under Francis I. It abetted the rise of the rich bourgeois and their alliance with the king, helping to create a new nobility, of the robe against the sword, or the long robe against the short. Surprisingly, it seems not to have damaged the quality of the judiciary. However, low salaries led the magistrates to make the *épices*—originally presents of spice or candy to a judge by a grateful litigant—a tax paid to the court by all parties. Combined with the proliferation of minor venal offices and thus of fees, this made justice a luxury all too often unavailable to the poor. Montaigne lived with this system and followed its rules, but protested strongly against the venality and high cost of justice.

The new court in Périgueux encountered bitter opposition. Though the jurisdictions reduced were those of the Cours des Aides of Paris and Montpellier, the main early protest came from the Bordeaux Parlement, hopeful of enlarging its domain and smarting from its temporary suppression after the salt-tax revolt of 1548 and from recent royal encroachments that inflated its numbers and created within it new divisions such as the Chambre des Requêtes, a sort of Chamber of Petitions, with primary but not final jurisdiction in cases involving nobles whose "letters of committimus" let them appear before special courts. Established in 1543 but not yet constituted, it was soon to be filled by the members of the Cour des Aides of Périgueux.

The royal edict creating the Périgueux court (March, 1554) led to a protest by the Bordeaux Parlement, seconded by the Cour des Aides of Paris in the hope that the new court might be

simply abolished. And so for a time it was, by another edict in
May; but a counterprotest by the Perigordians brought about a third
edict (July, 1554) re-establishing the Aides in their city in return
for the 50,000 crowns already mentioned. The First President was a
former advocate general at the Bordeaux Parlement, Fronton de
Béraud; the Second President, Antoine Poynet, lieutenant general
at the court in Bergerac. There were eleven councillors: Bertrand
Macanan, Pierre (and later, presumably, Michel) Eyquem de
Montaigne, Bertrand Lambert, Jean Saint-Angel, Etienne Daringes, François Fayard, Jacques Brusac, Jean Barbarin, Pierre
Blanchier, François Merle, and Jean Faure; an advocate general, a
procurator general, and six lesser functionaries. In salary the presidents each received 1,000 crowns, the advocate and the procurator
600, the councillors 500.

In December, 1554, the town of Périgueux spent 4,000 crowns
to prepare a magnificent ceremony in which President Pierre de
Carle of the Bordeaux Parlement (brother-in-law of Montaigne's
future friend La Boétie) invested with their functions the black-
robed presidents and the scarlet-robed councillors of the Cour des
Aides.

The new court lasted less than two and one half years. Located
some eighty miles from Bordeaux, the main seat of justice in the
area, it was inconvenient for many of those it served. A bitter complaint by the Cour des Aides of Montpellier led to another edict
(May, 1557) restoring its earlier domain, suppressing the Cour des
Aides of Périgueux, and transferring that court's reduced jurisdiction to the Bordeaux Parlement, which, however, had to incorporate the Périgueux magistrates into its existing chambers without
examination, as full-fledged members. Two presidents of the Parlement, sent to complain to the king, obtained one concession: that the
Périgueux group, as regular members, should form the still-unconsti-
tuted Chambre des Requêtes (without final jurisdiction in their
domain) and continue to serve as a Cour des Aides for Guienne
with final jurisdiction in tax cases, still at a higher salary than their
new Bordeaux colleagues. The Parlement had to submit, but did
so grudgingly.

The Bordeaux Parlement was one of eight groups composing
the Parlement, the highest court of justice in France, and, in the
latter half of the sixteenth century, a moving force in the administra-

tion. Its right to register edicts allowed it to delay the promulgation necessary for their execution and even to add conditions. When it delayed, the king would send jussive letters ordering promulgation, and if these failed, hold a *lit de justice* ("bed of justice") in which he simply told the Parlement what it must do. The Parlement could present remonstrances to the king; it was usually asked to ratify treaties. As the king's right arm in the administration of justice, it often supplanted the nobility and local officials. During the religious civil wars, when a weak monarchy left a power vacuum, it played a role in determining policy. It was a unique and potent institution.

Its eight members were the Parlements of Paris, Toulouse, Bordeaux, Grenoble, Dijon, Rouen, Aix, and Rennes. Officials of one Parlement could sit with the others, as Montaigne once did in Paris. The oldest and strongest was the Paris Parlement, close to the court of France and having vast jurisdiction to the north (except in Normandy) and as far as Lyons to the south. Toulouse was second in age and dignity, while Grenoble, founded in 1454, disputed the third place with Bordeaux.

The Bordeaux Parlement, established in 1451, functioned briefly until the revolt of Guienne under Talbot led Charles VII to withdraw its privilege, which Louis XI restored in 1462. From one chamber in 1500 with two presidents and eighteen councillors (nine clerical, nine lay), it had grown by mid-century to five chambers, five presidents, forty lay and fifteen clerical councillors. Suspended in 1548 in punishment for the salt-tax revolt, it was reinstated in 1550. Its chambers were the short-lived Requêtes, whose function we have noted; two Chambres des Enquêtes, reporting, with only primary jurisdiction, on civil cases up for appeal; the Grand' Chambre, or Chamber of Pleas, which judged these cases; and the Tournelle, filled in rotation by members of the other chambers, which sat on criminal cases.* It was a learned and hardworking body, whose sessions in the massive Palais de l'Ombrière started between six and seven in the morning and lasted into the late afternoon.

Montaigne found many relatives here: a brother of his father,

* By 1569 the Tournelle had its own membership (*Archives Historiques de la Gironde*, XXIX, 475). A different sort of chamber was the Chambre des Vacations, a skeleton court set up annually during the long vacation (September 7–November 11) to handle urgent cases.

the influential councillor Raymond de Bussaguet; a first cousin of
his mother, Jean de Villeneuve, councillor and future Third President, and the son of another, the future First President Joseph d'Eymar. Councillor Richard de Lestonnac was married to Montaigne's sister Jeanne. Within eight years Montaigne himself was to
marry a daughter and granddaughter of presidents in the Parlement,
Françoise de La Chassaigne. Besides relatives, he soon found there his
beloved friend Etienne de La Boétie.

If the newcomers from Périgueux were wary of the welcome
awaiting them, they can hardly have expected quite what they got.
Their reception was delayed, not only beyond the long vacation and
the reopening, but for more than three weeks after. On December 3,
1557, they were brought in and seated together behind the second
bar of the main courtroom, near the clock, before the assembled
Bordeaux Parlement. The acting First President, Roffignac, refused from the outset to recognize their claim, as Aides, to final
jurisdiction in tax cases, and received them only as a Chambre des
Requêtes, with limited primary jurisdiction. When they protested
that the king had granted them both functions and the right to vote
in all assemblies of the whole Parlement, Roffignac replied dryly that
the court would rule on that. They saw no recourse but to take the
oath in this reduced capacity, and, with one knee on the floor, swore
that they had paid no money (for their offices) to anyone but the
king. For his address of welcome Roffignac exhorted them to emulate the moderation of their new colleagues in the exaction of *épices*.
Fronton de Béraud, First President of the Aides, was refused his
promised position as Fifth President of the Parlement until he gave
up, as he did three months later, his original presidency. In short,
despite explicit advance assurances, the king's orders were not carried
out.

Nor was this all. For their deliberations the newcomers were
assigned inadequate space in the court clerk's chamber and forced
to struggle even for that with the seneschalsy and other groups.
Petty harassment was the rule. They were refused the standard privilege of being preceded within the Palais de l'Ombrière by ushers
carrying their rods of office. When, claiming their rights as a Cour
des Aides, they fined the Présidial, a lesser civil court, for its effron-
tery in disputing them a room, the Grand' Chambre, on appeal,

charged them with encroaching on the king's authority and reversed their decision as insolent sedition. Their first four years were a series of frustrating denials of their rights. Once their Second President, Antoine Poynet, losing all patience, led them into the assembly of the chambers and, despite orders and threats, for some time flatly refused to leave.

Finally Charles IX issued an edict (August, 1561) suppressing both the Cour des Aides and the Chambre des Requêtes and ordering that the councillors in these courts, with their salaries reduced to 375 livres to match those of their colleagues, be incorporated into the "regular" chambers of the Bordeaux Parlement. The resulting remonstrances led to royal jussive letters (September 20) forcing the Parlement finally (November 13) to register the edict and execute it. This too was done grudgingly. The Aides were obliged each to declare who their relatives were in the other chambers; which Montaigne, who had many, is said to have done with some irony. Worse, they were treated as newcomers and denied precedence over councillors admitted later whom they had preceded already.

To this we owe our first glimpse of Montaigne as a magistrate; for although still under age at twenty-eight, he was chosen to speak for the injured group. The official report reads as follows:

Maître Antoine Poynet, President in the said Requêtes, both on his own behalf and on that of his fellow councillors here present . . . asked for a delay to deliberate with them on this, which was granted; and soon after, the said councillors of the said Requêtes returned, who said, with one of them, Maître Michel Eyquem de Montaigne, as spokesman, that it was not reasonable for the said Lalanne * to precede them, because they were received into the said Court earlier than the said Lalanne, and because the king, by his jussive edict, wanted them to have the same rank as they had acquired at the time of their reception into the said Requêtes; also because they had been present and deliberated at the reception and examination of the said Lalanne, and being councillors of the Requêtes they were members of the body of the Court, and moreover this disagreement had been adjudicated by the decision given on their reception into the said Requêtes; and for the said incorporation the Court was having them take no other oath than the one they had taken at first when they were invested with the said offices of president and councillors in these [Requêtes]; and furthermore they had

* Sarran de Lalanne, a councillor admitted two years after the Aides were incorporated into the Parlement but given precedence over them in 1561.

preceded the said Lalanne in the processions and public acts in which the Court had been present as a court, without any complaint from the said Lalanne.

Despite Montaigne's plea, the Parlement ruled in favor of Lalanne; and if Poynet appealed to the king, as he said he would, it was in vain.

More important problems confronted the Bordeaux Parlement. Though the city was Catholic, Protestantism had been gaining strength for twenty years. As early as 1538 eleven Reformists were condemned by the Parlement to "make honorable amends." In the 1540's several were executed. The troubles of 1548 aided the new sect, and the 1550's saw a swift increase in their worship and their acts of iconoclasm, which led to stern countermeasures. By 1561, in a city of about 50,000, the Protestants numbered about 7,000—one person in seven. Even before strife became nationwide in 1562, there was real civil war around Bordeaux.

The First President of the Bordeaux Parlement since 1555, in whose absence Roffignac had been serving in 1557, was a stalwart moderate, Jacques Benoist de Lagebaston, trusted agent of Henry II as he had been of Francis I—whom he so resembled that some said he was an illegitimate son—and friend and protégé of Chancellor Michel de L'Hôpital. In carrying out the tolerant policy of L'Hôpital and the queen mother, he had help from the king's lieutenant general in Guienne, Charles de Coucy, lord of Burie. But Protestantism was spreading on all sides and, especially in divided communities, meeting repression with counteraggression—image-breaking, church-burning, and terrorism. Even the terrible Blaise de Monluc, leader of the king's army in the southwest, could not keep it down. Many Catholics, thinking Burie and Lagebaston too lenient, formed leagues to combat the rebels. One league had Roffignac among its leaders; another, many friends of Montaigne: Antoine Prévost de Sansac, archbishop of Bordeaux; Christophe de Foix de Candale, bishop of Aire; his brother Fédéric de Foix de Candale; and their cousin, Montaigne's choleric neighbor and sponsor, the former ambassador to England, Germain-Gaston de Foix, marquis de Trans, an inveterate enemy of Lagebaston.

These men exerted constant political pressure and led vigilante actions against the Reformists, with some success; but the Parlement and the Jurade opposed them for encroaching on their own authority, and the crown supported the law-abiding moderates.

The Edict of January, 1562, which gave French Protestants great freedom of worship (allowing those around Bordeaux to worship in the suburbs), inflamed Catholic resistance. In the name of the Catholic nobility of Guienne, Fédéric de Foix de Candale, both in person and through Roffignac and Charles de Malvin de Cessac in the Parlement, repeatedly challenged Lagebaston as a judge in cases involving Protestants. Lagebaston defended himself stoutly in the Parlement and in letters to the king and queen mother, accusing Candale's league of usurping royal authority. On July 25, 1562, the Bordeaux Parlement struck at the tolerationists by voting to put into effect a rule enacted in 1543 requiring of all its members a formal profession of Catholic faith.

Montaigne, at court on just what business we do not know, was one of thirteen members absent at the time. However, six weeks earlier (June 12) he had asked to be admitted to sit with the Paris Parlement, which had already voted (June 6) to require the same profession of faith. It is not surprising that he then took the oath, but it is noteworthy that the king's advocate, Baptiste du Mesnil, then rose to remark "that it was easy to tell that the decision and ordinance of this court, which it had itself begun to carry out, had been found good and holy and had been well received by each and every one, as all could see. . . ." It has been said that Montaigne took the oath only because he had to; but the official report suggests that he did so gladly.

Again and again in 1562–63 Bordeaux was in serious danger from Protestant troops. After the assassination of François de Guise early in 1563, the Peace of Amboise (March 19) restored some order for a time and again gave Protestant nobles much freedom of worship. Later in the year the struggle in the Bordeaux Parlement was renewed by another enemy of Lagebaston, François de Péruse d'Escars (or des Cars), grand seneschal of Guienne for Antoine de Bourbon, king of Navarre. Navarre had no love for Lagebaston, who had worked to reduce his independence in favor of the crown by trying to persuade him to exchange the remains of his kingdom for equivalent domains in the interior.

When the Bordeaux Parlement reopened on November 12,

1563, d'Escars appeared in high state and brought his halberdiers into the hearing room, but yielded when the court withdrew in protest. Four weeks later, however, he returned to object to Lagebaston on the grounds that Navarre had once ordered him to request his removal. In reply Lagebaston protested all the members of the court who, he said, advised d'Escars on his affairs and "often went to eat and drink with the sieur d'Escars, which made them contemptible, to the point where the sieur d'Escars sent for them at any time and used them on such negotiations as he pleased." Summoned to name them, he cited Presidents Roffignac and La Chassaigne, the archbishop of Bordeaux, and councillors Fauguerolles, Malvin de Cessac, Gautier, Belot, La Guyonie, d'Eymar, Lecomte, and Montaigne.

Now d'Escars was a supporter of Candale and Trans, in effect a member of their league. It was at his home that Montaigne's dearest friend, La Boétie, had been exercising, only a few months earlier, when he contracted his fatal illness. One protested councillor, Jean de Belot, was a close friend of La Boétie and Montaigne, who wrote him four years later from his château to warn the Parlement of nearby Protestant troop movements. D'Eymar was a relative, Malvin de Cessac a friend, as were probably La Guyonie and Gautier; President La Chassaigne was soon to become his grandfather-in-law.

When the challenged magistrates were heard, Montaigne's counterprotest was officially recorded as follows:

When it came to be Michel de Montaigne's turn to speak, he expressed himself with all the vivacity of his character, and said there was no reason for them to leave, and that the First President was not qualified to offer to challenge anyone, by way of remonstrance or otherwise, when he himself was challenged; then he left saying *that he named the whole Court.* He is called back. The Court orders him to say what he means by these words, *that he named the whole Court;* whereupon the said Eyquem said that he had no feelings in the present matter nor any enmity against the First President, but that they are friends and the said First President has been a friend of all those of the house of the said Eyquem; but seeing the bad prospects offered for justice, *jacta erat alea,** and that accused persons were being allowed, contrary to the rules of the Court, to challenge other judges who were not interested parties any more than himself, he had said that if it were permitted, he could also challenge the whole Court; but he did not

* The die was cast.

intend for all that to name anyone, and he withdrew his remark about naming the whole Court.

Montaigne at thirty, we see, was a man of vehement reactions. Lagebaston, he felt, was breaking the rules, accusing him of partiality, and worst of all impugning the memory of the fairest man he had ever known, La Boétie, not three months dead, who had indeed been a friend of d'Escars but the creature of no man.

La Boétie had advocated firmness against the Protestants, but without malice. Nor is there malice in Montaigne's indignant outburst. He still looks on Lagebaston as a friend and claims he can judge fairly between him and d'Escars. (Indeed, it appears he opposed d'Escars's later attempts to oust Lagebaston.) Though apparently not yet the trusted friend of Protestant leaders, neither is he a Catholic extremist like his friends Candale, Trans, d'Escars, and Monluc, but a stanch loyalist, stoutly independent in his personal allegiances.

He showed no fear of speaking out in an unpopular cause. Just over a year after this outburst the Bordeaux Parlement was preparing to receive young Charles IX, then on a tour of his country seeking to strengthen allegiance and ease tensions. On January 12, 1565, all the councillors were invited to consider what the king might say and what they might reply. The air was tense; the Parlement had put off registering many royal edicts, and was to yield later only to the sharp commands of the king in person; the councillors wanted their pay raised. On January 24 Montaigne's suggestions were reported as follows:

The said d'Eyquem said that, in speaking to the King, we must imprint on his mind by strong reasons how good it is for a good king to visit the lands of his subjects often and how many advantages this brings to the affairs of his state; that the disesteem and the whole disorder of justice comes from the infinite number of officers that are put in it;

from the bad order of their election and the fact that everything is venal;

that we must request that all these faults be corrected and especially all removed that concern justice;

that we must make no request that tends to increase or augment what we gain from our positions.

Nothing suggests that Montaigne's colleagues welcomed his recommendations or brought them to the ear of the king, whose April visit was a grand occasion. All the city must have turned out; much of it was in the procession: mayor, jurats, archbishop, Parlement, University, sergeants, boys, even the "King of the Basoche" and his men leading twelve "captive nations," which included "Utopians, Taprobanians [Ceylonese], Amerisks, Indians, Canadians, Savages, and Brazilians." (Montaigne was not alone in his fascination with the New World.) While the councillors listened, resplendent in red robes and furred hoods, First President Lagebaston, in scarlet robe and scarlet ermine-trimmed cloak, kneeling before the fourteen-year-old king, addressed him at such length that the monarch cut him short, praising his royal justice and promising short shrift for any who took up arms. At his "bed of justice" later he strictly commanded mild treatment of the Protestants. Chancellor L'Hôpital twice rebuked the Parlement for stubbornness, avarice, irregularity, and other vices; and a request to have Lagebaston ousted was peremptorily dismissed.

It is hard to gain much insight into Montaigne's day-to-day work as a magistrate. We have his reports on five cases, terse, impersonal, all but one very short, none revealing. Here is a sample:

Between François de Verneuil, appellant from the presidial judges of Périgueux, on the one hand;

And Master Guillaume, priest, and Martial de Verneuil, appellees, on the other.

Seen the case, the act of appeal, responses to this, extracts from the clerk's registers, of the Presidial of the said Périgueux, of the sixth, twentieth, twenty-sixth, twenty-seventh, and twenty-eighth of September, 1560, and other pieces and documents produced by the parties:

It shall be said, without regard to the objections claimed by the said appellees, that a bad and null judgment was made by the said presidial judges; and, amending their judgment, we order that the sentence of the ordinary judge shall take its full and entire effect; condemn the said appellees to pay to the said appellant the expenses incurred both before the said presidials and in the Court, except for the tax on these to the said Court.

(signed)   *De Guionie*
Michel de Montaigne, relator *
Monsieur le président La Guionie
Messrs. *La Boétie, Beringuiet, Macei, Lataste, Rignac,*
Makanan, Fayard, St.-Angel, Montaigne, relator

* The document is in Montaigne's own hand. At the lower left another hand has added: "Habeat relator six ecus" ("The reporter is to receive six crowns").

It may be partly accident that as against Montaigne's five reports we have twenty-two of La Boétie's; but it seems quite clear that La Boétie took to the work of the Parlement more than did his friend.

Much of Montaigne's time during these years was spent at the court of France. He was there at least once before the death of Henry II in July, 1559; again—or possibly still—in September, 1559, when Francis II in Bar-le-Duc received a self-portrait from King René of Sicily; and again in the following summer, when he writes that silk had gone out of fashion after "we had hardly been a year wearing broadcloth at court in mourning for King Henry II." On November 26, 1561, the Bordeaux Parlement sent a message to the king by Montaigne, going to court for other matters. He took the oath in the Paris Parlement (June 12, 1562) on yet another trip, followed the court in October to the siege of Protestant-held Rouen, where he met three Brazilian cannibals, and probably remained at court until February, 1563. In November, 1564, and again just a year later, the registers of the Bordeaux Parlement show him absent and at court. He was in Paris on June 18, 1568, dedicating his translation of Raymond Sebond, and two years later (August and—perhaps again—September, 1570), having La Boétie's works published. Altogether nine or ten trips during these years seem clear, and more are not unlikely.

We do not know what Montaigne wanted at court. Magistrates of the Parlement were persons of some importance. Montaigne's colleagues may have welcomed all his trips as giving them an intelligent observer—and perhaps an effective spokesman—at court. Certain events of the 1570's, which we shall examine later, suggest that Montaigne was already well thought of there.

When the Chambre des Requêtes was abolished Montaigne was assigned to the Chambre des Enquêtes. During his nine years there he became the friend, then the mourner, of La Boétie, the husband of Françoise de La Chassaigne, head of his own family, and lord of Montaigne. In 1569, one year after his father died, his turn came up to be considered for a higher chamber, and he was pronounced incompatible for either one because his brother-in-law Richard de Lestonnac was in the Grand' Chambre and his father-in-law, Joseph de La Chassaigne, President of the Tournelle. The refusal was a matter of course; but Montaigne was apparently expected to seek his one remaining recourse by an appeal to the king for a dispensation. Instead he resigned his position, presumably for the usual price of that office, to his chosen successor, Florimond de Raemond, a stalwart Catholic and later a very militant one. The transfer was made official on July 23, 1570, by letters patent from the king.

Montaigne probably had many reasons for retiring from the Parlement at thirty-seven. A husband and father, lord of a fine estate, he was probably drawn to the life of a country squire. He wanted to commemorate his friend and try to live up to him. His tower was an excellent place to read, meditate, and write; though what to write he did not yet know. He was doubtless saddened by his country's plight and the policy of compromise that he and La Boétie had opposed, and certainly tired of his routine duties in the Parlement. The Grand' Chambre may have seemed worth a try; the Chambre des Enquêtes would no longer do.

Two distinguished friends of Montaigne speak of his work in the Parlement. The magistrate and historian Jacques-Auguste de Thou brackets Montaigne as a councillor with his friend La Boétie as "*assessor dignissimus*—a most worthy magistrate." The lawyer Estienne Pasquier states that "No man cared less for chicanery and legal technicality than he; for his profession was entirely different."

To be sure, Montaigne sprinkles through his book such terms as "mortgaging" his will, his work, or the freedom of his soul, "gains ceasing and . . . damages ensuing," and begins several paragraphs of one chapter with the legal term "Item." But considering his long exposure to such terms, they leave few traces in his style, which he sought to make "not lawyer-like, but rather soldierly." Most of them, as Pasquier wryly noted, are used for comic effect, like Montaigne's defense of the male member, accused of rebellion against our will:

> To conclude, I would say this in defense of the honorable member whom I represent: May it please the court to take into consideration that in this matter, although my client's case is inseparably and indistinguishably linked with that of an accessory, nevertheless he alone has been brought to trial; and that the arguments and charges against him are such as cannot— in view of the status of the parties—be in any manner pertinent or relevant

to the aforesaid accessory.* Whereby is revealed his accusers' manifest animosity and disrespect for law. However that may be, Nature will meanwhile go her way, protesting that the lawyers and judges quarrel and pass sentence in vain.

When Montaigne writes of the Parlement and his colleagues, his usual stress is on ceremony, pedantry, and hypocrisy. Although he commends those Parlements which, like that of Bordeaux, examine new candidates on their judgment as well as their learning, he has known a magistrate who prided himself on piling up two hundred quotations in one single decision, which to Montaigne was hardly a thing to boast of. A memorable figure is "a councillor of my acquaintance who, after disgorging a boatload of paragraphs with extreme effort and equal ineptitude, retired from the council chamber to the Palace urinal, where he was heard muttering very conscientiously between his teeth: '*Non nobis, Domine, non nobis, sed nomini tuo da gloriam.*' " † An uglier glimpse is this: "From this same sheet of paper on which he has just written the sentence against an adulterer, the judge steals a scrap for a billet-doux to his colleague's wife."

Montaigne was less dismayed, however, by the magistrates than by the inadequacy of justice. Well aware of the limitations of the law, he was annoyed that legislators were not. Laws should be few and simple, but were many and complex; should be just and humane, but were often unjust and cruel. The whole system showed the frailty of the human mind and the vanity of trying to legislate goodness.

We have in France more laws than all the rest of the world together. . . . And yet we have left so much room for opinion and decision to our judges, that there never was such a powerful and licentious freedom. . . . The most desirable laws are those that are rarest, simplest, and most general; and I even think that it would be better to have none at all than to have them in such numbers as we have.

The "princes of this art," seeking absolute accuracy, "have so weighed every syllable, so minutely examined every sort of combination," as to make the language unintelligible. Interpretations only multiply the difficulty, for they too must be interpreted:

* Here the 1595 edition of the *Essays* adds: "for it is indeed in the nature of my client to solicit inopportunely at times, but never to refuse; and to solicit wordlessly and silently at that."

† "Not unto us, O Lord, not unto us, but unto thy name give glory . . ." (Psalms 115: 1).

Aristotle wrote to be understood; if he did not succeed, still less will another man, less able, and not treating his own ideas.

·   ·   ·   ·   ·   ·   ·

This is best seen in law practice. We give legal authority to numberless doctors, numberless decisions, and as many interpretations. Do we therefore find any end to the need of interpreting? Do we see any progress . . . ? Do we need fewer lawyers and judges . . . ? On the contrary, we obscure and bury the meaning. . . .

Human variability makes justice inconsistent. Quoting a saying of the Parlement lawyers about the criminal who finds a judge in a lenient mood: *"gaudeat de bona fortuna*—let him rejoice in this good fortune," Montaigne comments:

For it is certain that judgments come sometimes more intent on condemnation, thornier and harsher, and sometimes more easygoing, indulgent, and inclined to pardon.

·   ·   ·   ·   ·   ·   ·

However good a judge's intentions are, unless he listens closely to himself, which few people amuse themselves in doing, his inclination to friendship, kinship, beauty, and vengeance, and not only things so weighty, but that fortuitous instinct that makes us favor one thing more than another and that assigns us, without leave of our reason, our choice between two like objects, or some shadow of equal emptiness, can insinuate insensibly into his judgment the favor or disfavor of a cause, and tip the scales.

A truly honest judge, Montaigne believes, would imitate one he knew of who, where authorities were at odds, "used to put in the margin of his book 'Question for my friend'; that is to say, that the truth was so embroiled and disputed that in a similar case he could favor whichever of the parties he saw fit." After all, Montaigne adds, "it was only for lack of wit and competence that he could not write everywhere: 'Question for my friend.' "

For Montaigne, the horrible thing about justice was its injustice. It frightened innocent people like the peasants who reported finding a badly wounded man but not daring to help him lest they be accused of being his assailants. "What could I say to them?" Montaigne asks. "It is certain that this act of humanity would have got them into trouble."

There is the injustice of magistrates who have closed their minds. Montaigne tells how certain men recently had been condemned to death for a murder when news came that some prisoners of a nearby court had confessed to it and been found clearly guilty.

For fear of a bad precedent, the first court ruled "that the sentence has been passed according to law, and that the judges have no right to change their minds." "In short," Montaigne concludes, "these poor devils are sacrificed to the forms of justice."

He has often been outraged at seeing judges use fraud and deceit to lure a criminal into confession. "That is a malicious justice," he comments; "and I consider it no less harmed by itself than by others."

The cruelty of penalties in his time appalls him:

As for me, even in justice, all that goes beyond plain death seems to me pure cruelty, and especially for us who ought to have some concern about sending souls away in a good state; which cannot happen when we have agitated them and made them desperate by unbearable tortures.

          .   .   .   .

I would advise that these examples of severity, by means of which they want to keep the people at their duty, be exercised against the corpses of criminals.

Even as a judge (presumably when on duty in the Tournelle) he could not always bring himself to apply the full rigor of the law:

I am so squeamish about hurting that for the service of reason itself I cannot do it. And when occasions have summoned me to sentencing criminals, I have tended to fall short of justice.

The problem is more than one of temperamental squeamishness or compassion. As Montaigne points out, "Justice in itself, natural and universal" is a different, nobler thing than "that other, special, national justice, constrained to the need of our governments."

Consider the form of this justice that governs us: it is a true testimony of human imbecility, so full it is of contradiction and error.

          .   .   .   .

How many condemnations I have seen more criminal than the crime!

          .   .   .   .

Now laws remain in credit not because they are just, but because they are laws. That is the mystic foundation of their authority; they have no other. . . . They are often made by fools, more often by people * who, in their hatred of equality, are wanting in equity; but always by men, vain and irresolute authors.

There is nothing so grossly and widely and ordinarily faulty as the laws. Whoever obeys them because they are just, does not obey them for just the reason he should.

_____

* Montaigne had written at first: "more often by wicked men. . . ."

The product of long experience and serious thought, Montaigne's criticism of the law was neither casual nor solely destructive.* In 1584 Henry of Navarre consulted him about a plan for judiciary reform. On the question of different treatment for different classes, Montaigne wrote: "Have only one justice"; on that of the plurality of judges on one case: "Better five than one." He opposed limiting the number of lawyers as "not very good for the state." He again urged that justice be rendered at no cost. Two articles financially favoring, one judges against litigants, the other rich against poor, elicit the comment: "Cannot be." A central conviction, that the main hope lies in good judges, dictates his final note: "See to it that men of virtue, learning, and integrity administer justice."

For all his disillusionment, Montaigne had learned much during his thirteen years in the Bordeaux Parlement. He had enriched his experience of human behavior, especially of human sham and cussedness. He had developed his "capacity to sift the truth," using it to weigh evidence and probe motivation. He had probably confirmed his moralist's conviction that, however complex the problem, actions are at bottom either right or wrong, and that thoughtful investigation must lead to right judgment between good and evil.

His distaste for routine, probably inborn, must have been sharpened, and with it his mistrust of ceremony, the outward display that masks the inner truth. Most important, his critique of the law shows a quality all his own, not evident in his family or in La Boétie: a tough-minded awareness of the frailty of human institutions, the subjectivity and relativity of truth, and the variability of human judgment. It did not take Sextus Empiricus or Cornelius Agrippa to teach him his skeptical temper; it had ripened for thirteen long years in the halls of the Bordeaux Parlement.

---

* In the closing session (August 22, 1582) of the Special Court of Justice of Guienne set up in Bordeaux to handle all cases concerning the latest edict of pacification, Montaigne was highly complimented for his work as magistrate and mayor by the eminent Parisian jurist Antoine Loisel.

NE EVENT made the years in the Bordeaux Parlement worthwhile: Montaigne's closest bond, his friendship with Etienne de La Boétie.* It lasted four or five years before his friend died and made his later life seem hollow. He devoted himself to his friend's memory, never quite replaced him, never ceased to mourn him. La Boétie satisfied his deepest need, for complete communication. The lack of this later was one of Montaigne's reasons for writing the *Essays*.

Montaigne was in his mid-twenties when they met and just thirty when his friend died. The cliché of the sage in his tower amid his books is inadequate for his maturity, inaccurate for his youth. He may have exaggerated his early giddiness in the contrast with his older self, failing in body and struggling to avoid going sour; but the young man he looks back on so wistfully is a sprightly one.

He is short and thickset, with a sturdy build well suited for horseback and "a face not fat but full." He credits himself with certain attractive features—broad round forehead, clear soft eyes,

* Now pronounced approximately La Bo-ay-seé, but in his lifetime La Bwettie. The name Montaigne was then pronounced Montagne.

nose of moderate form, suitably small ears and mouth, teeth white and regular, smooth thick chestnut beard, well-rounded head, fresh color, pleasant facial expression, odorless body, well-proportioned limbs—but only to add that even these cannot make a small man handsome. Something in his carriage and in certain gestures reveals a vain and stupid pride. His taste in dress leans to black and white, after his father; but he likes adornment, which becomes him, and an aristocratic carelessness: "a cloak worn like a scarf, the hood over one shoulder, a neglected stocking. . . . If I have one shoe on wrong, I also leave my shirt and my cloak on wrong; I scorn to reform halfway." He smiles at a sort of dandyism that leads to his carrying a rod or a stick and even "trying to be elegant and resting on it in an affected manner." He is affable, every ready to tip his hat, never failing—except to his servants—to return this salute.

His health is perfect: "vigorous, full, lazy . . . not merely entire, but even blithe and ebullient . . . full of verdure and cheer," of the kind that "kindles in the mind vivid, bright flashes beyond our natural capacity, and some of the lustiest, if not the most extravagant, enthusiasms." His energy is almost beyond control. He eats greedily, in his haste often biting his tongue and—being little addicted to the newfangled forks and spoons—his fingers. He is a loud talker, quick to anger, incurably restless:

> My walk is quick and firm; and I know not which of the two, my mind or my body, I have had more difficulty in keeping in one place. That preacher is indeed a friend of mine who holds my attention through a whole sermon. In solemn places, where everyone has such a strained expression, where I have seen the ladies keep even their eyes so steady, I have never succeeded in keeping some part of me from always wandering; even though I may be seated there, I am hardly settled there. . . . People might have said of me from my childhood that I was crazy in the feet, or had quicksilver in them, so fidgety and restless are they, wherever I place them.

He cannot think well sitting down; he has to be walking or—for his best ideas—in bed, at table, preferably on horseback.

He has no adroitness or agility whatever. Whereas his father was unmatched in all bodily exercises, the converse is true of him:

> I have scarcely found any [man] who did not surpass me, except in running, in which I was just fair. Of music, either vocal, for which my voice is very inept, or instrumental, they never succeeded in teaching me anything. At dancing, tennis, wrestling, I have never been able to acquire any but very slight and ordinary ability; at swimming, fencing, vaulting, and jump-

ing, none at all. My hands are so clumsy that I cannot even write so I can read it; so that I would rather do over what I have scribbled than give myself the trouble of unscrambling it. And I read hardly any better. I feel that I weigh upon my listeners. Otherwise, a good scholar. I cannot close a letter the right way, nor could I ever cut a pen, or carve at table worth a rap, or saddle a horse, or properly carry a bird and release it, or talk to dogs, birds, or horses.

All his life Montaigne loved freedom and independence. "I have a distaste for mastery," he wrote, "both active and passive." As a child his thoughts, though slow, were all his own. Brought up freely, he "likes to give his freedom elbowroom in all directions." He hates involvement and worry, and has cultivated this inborn trait: he would lend his blood as readily as his care. He is happier now with no money of his own than he will be soon with the wealth and the worries of the estate. However, he loathes obligation and takes pleasure in paying debts. Even to ask a favor is painful, because of "a little natural pride, inability to endure refusal, limitation of my desires and designs, incapacity for any kind of business, and my very favorite qualities, idleness and freedom." Not often has he given advice; never that he can remember has he taken it. Impatient of all constraint, he strenuously combats that of habit. He learns better from good fortune than bad, from contrast than example.

One of his favorite freedoms is frankness. He loves it on moral ground, since truth is "the first and fundamental part of virtue" and "we are men, and hold together, only by our word." It is also a temperamental need; for he cannot bear to be misunderstood. In addressing people of different parties he will change his tone but not his meaning. In his amorous approaches he is candid, even blunt. He would rather be importunate and indiscreet than a dissimulating flatterer.

Vexed as a youngster when men would not compete with him in earnest, he has always wanted to be treated as a man. Too much, he finds, is made of mere age; we are used too late in public office. If we have any stuff in us, we show signs of it at twenty.

For all his love of freedom, Montaigne is no rebel but a stanch conservative. His main convictions he has held from childhood. It is easier, he finds, to maintain an opinion than choose one; and the burden of proof rests on the innovator. In politics he has never wavered at all; in religion, only a little. He was once overready to make light of what he took for superstition in certain Catholic observances; if anything were to have tempted his youth, it would have been the hazards of Reform. He has thought through his objection to Protestantism: that besides unwisely subordinating works to faith, by rejecting the Church's authority as the one sure interpreter of Scripture, it opens the gates to the presumption of individual human reason and leads inevitably to atheism. But his conservatism is temperamental too. He is gratefully free from anxiety because the laws have given him a master and God has given him a belief based "on the eternal foundation of his holy word." Awareness of his changeability has given his opinions a certain constancy:

For whatever appearance of truth there may be in novelty, I do not change easily, for fear of losing in the change. And since I am not capable of choosing, I accept other people's choice and stay in the position where God put me. Otherwise I could not keep myself from rolling about incessantly. Thus I have, by the grace of God, kept myself intact, without agitation or disturbance of conscience, in the ancient beliefs of our religion, in the midst of so many sects and divisions that our century has produced.

Love of glory shows in Montaigne's desire for the Order of Saint Michael, ostentation in his youthful studies and certain purchases of books. He is neither markedly ambitious nor without ambition. The court attracts him again and again. Neither gregarious nor withdrawn, he dislikes small talk and thrives on candid communication. He is keen to enjoy life: except for avoiding finicality— he had to be trained to like sweets, but relishes all wines and sauces —he follows his natural love of pleasure. One of his favorite pleasures is the pursuit of women.

Like many ancients and contemporaries, he regards them with more delight than admiration as decorative lightweights, incapable of wisdom, spirituality, or true friendship. They are wrong to vie with men in theology and other serious studies and should stick to poetry (which Montaigne also loves) as "an amusement suited to their needs; . . . a wanton and subtle art, in fancy dress, wordy, all pleasure, all show, like themselves." Yet their company is one of his favorites; the essays that he dedicates he dedicates to women; and his most licentious chapter, "On Some Verses of Virgil" (III: 5), aims to have them bring his book from the salon into the boudoir.

His first amorous experience, he tells us, came by chance and before the age of choice: "I do not remember about myself so far back. And my lot may be coupled with that of Quartilla, who had no memory of her maidenhood." Finding sexual desire natural, he has rarely fought it:

And in my youth . . . I lent myself as licentiously and thoughtlessly as any other man to the desire that held me in its grip,
    And fought my battles not without distinction;

Horace

more, however, in continuation and endurance than in violence:
    I scarce remember lasting up to six.

Ovid

He once let passion carry him away, burned himself at it, and suffered all the pangs that the poets assign to uncontrolled love; since then he has learned his lesson: "It is madness to fasten all our thoughts upon it and to become involved in a furious and reckless passion."

When really smitten, he has written his share of love letters, some of which he thinks were not bad and might interest the idle youngsters now afflicted with this mania. He well remembers how "the close kisses of youth, savory, greedy, and sticky" left their scent for hours on his thick mustache.

Timing is the key to successful courting, and his has not always been good: respect and fear of offending have sometimes made him lack enterprise. Yet for all this "stupid bashfulness," he is "impertinently genital" in his approaches and absurdly fair to his lady loves.

I swore to them only what I felt. . . . I think I have carried out more than I promised or owed. They have found me faithful even to the point of serving . . . an avowed and sometimes multiplied inconstancy. . . . I have never broken with them to the point of scorn or hatred. . . . I have kept my word in things in which I might easily have been excused. . . . I have more than once, in the interest of their honor, made pleasure yield in its greatest stress; and when reason urged me, I have armed them against myself. . . .

As much as I could, I have taken upon myself alone the risk of our assignations, to free them of it. . . .

Caring as he did about the lady's mind and will as well (though not as much) as about her body, and wanting "to make the pleasure keener by difficulty, by desire, and by a certain glory," he has had little traffic with prostitutes and got off with two slight and incipient touches of venereal disease. All in all, as he looks back on it, he recommends sexual involvement to anyone who can use it in moderation.

It is a vain occupation, it is true, unbecoming, shameful, and illegitimate; but carried on in this fashion, I consider it healthy, proper to enliven a heavy body and soul; and as a physician, I would prescribe it to a man of my temperament and condition. . . .

.   .   .   .

I have no other passion to keep me in breath. . . . It would restore to me vigilance, sobriety, grace, care for my person . . . take me back to sane and wise studies . . . divert me from a thousand troublesome thoughts . . . warm up again, at least in dreams, this blood that nature is abandoning; . . . hold up the chin and stretch out a little the muscles and the soul's vigor and blitheness for this poor man who is going full speed toward his ruin.

Montaigne was no slave to pleasure, however. Even his youthful hedonism was judicious. Once fond of games of chance, with cards or dice, "I gave them up long ago for this reason only, that however good a face I put upon my losses, I did not fail to feel stung by them within." Since his youth he has occasionally skipped a meal, to sharpen his appetite, conserve his vigor for some action, cure a sick stomach, or for want of proper company. Once he used to have his sleep interrupted to "gain a glimpse of it."

Seeking to control his own sexual desire, he has watched it "come to life, grow, and increase in spite of my resistance, and finally seize me, alive and watching, and possess me," but has found it governable at its onset, and Venus less imperious than many chaster men claim. Generally he has been able to keep sexuality in its place: "In this business I did not let myself go entirely; I took pleasure in it, but I did not forget myself; I preserved entire the little sense and discretion that nature has given me, for their service and mine: a little excitement, but no folly." Looking back later, he credits himself with doing rather well: "When I consider the behavior of my youth in comparison with that of my old age, I find that I have generally conducted myself in orderly fashion, according to my lights; that is all my resistance can accomplish."

Judgment, conscientiousness, and self-control are among the serious traits of this lively young magistrate. Another is his constant concern with death—not so much anxiety as a keen awareness of its imminence.

Since my earliest days, there is nothing with which I have occupied my mind more than with images of death. Even in the most licentious season of my life . . . amid ladies and games, someone would think me involved in digesting some jealousy by myself, or the uncertainty of some hope, while I was thinking about I don't remember whom, who had been overtaken a few days before by a hot fever and by death, on leaving a similar feast, his head full of idleness, love, and a good time, like myself; and thinking that the same chance was hanging from my ear. . . .

   I did not wrinkle my forehead any more over that thought than any other. . . . Otherwise for my part I should be in continual fright and frenzy; for never did a man so distrust his life, never did a man set less faith in his duration.

   Montaigne's friend Etienne de La Boétie was in many ways very different. Two and a third years older, he was married, settled, an accomplished writer, a trusted negotiator for the Parlement, disciplined, idealistic, sure of his standards and aims.

   Though both men were keen students of human nature, neither can tell just what drew them together. There may be a significant clue in their mutual use of the term "brother." Montaigne, brought up in complete freedom as an eldest child, may have craved the steadying influence of a wise older brother; and La Boétie, brotherless and orphaned early, may have welcomed such a link with the brilliant but still somewhat rudderless Montaigne. Real brotherhood is accidental and involves rivalry; an elective one has no such drawbacks. Their compact was soon sealed for each man's life.

   They probably met in 1559, more than a year after Montaigne entered the Bordeaux Parlement, and by chance, though each knew of the other already:

We sought each other before we met because of the reports we heard of each other, which had more effect on our affection than such reports would reasonably have; I think it was by some ordinance from heaven. We embraced each other by our names. And at our first meeting, which by chance came at a great feast and gathering in the city, we found ourselves so taken with each other, so well acquainted, so bound together, that from that time on nothing was so close to us as each other.

   Montaigne's first glimpse of his future friend may have been a mild shock, for he esteemed beauty highly, and his friend—as Montaigne writes after some hesitation—though well formed, was ugly:

We also call ugliness an unattractiveness at first glance, which resides chiefly in the face, and often arouses our distaste for very slight causes: the complexion, a spot, a rugged expression, or some inexplicable cause, when the limbs are symmetrical and perfect.

The ugliness which clothed a very beautiful soul in La Boétie was in this category. This superficial ugliness, which is very imperious for all that, is less prejudicial to the state of the spirit and not very certain in its effect on men's opinion.

Disconcerting or not, it was no obstacle to the friendship.

Etienne de La Boétie was born in Sarlat, just north of the Dordogne about seventy-five miles east of Montaigne, on November 1, 1530, to a distinguished civil servant and the sister of a president of the Bordeaux Parlement. Soon after he was ten his father died, and probably his mother too; for Etienne was brought up by his namesake, uncle, and godfather, Etienne de La Boétie, curate of Bouilhonnas, to whom he paid this dying tribute:

Everything a very wise, very good, and very liberal father could have done for his son, you have done all that for me, both in the care that was needed to instruct me in humane letters, and when you were pleased to push me into public employment; so that the whole course of my life has been full of great and commendable friendly services from you. In short, whatever I have, I hold from you, I so acknowledge it, I am indebted to you for it; you are my true father.

La Boétie received his *licence* in law at the University of Orléans in 1553 after studying under the renowned teacher and future martyr Anne du Bourg. Letters patent from the king authorized Guillaume de Lur, known as de Longa, appointed to the Paris Parlement, to resign his office in that of Bordeaux in favor of young La Boétie, and ordered the court to receive him, though under age, in view of his high ability; which it did on May 17, 1554. It must have been soon after that La Boétie married Marguerite de Carle, sister of a president in the Parlement (Pierre) and of the famous bishop of Riez (Lancelot), and since 1552 widow of Jean, lord of Arsac. Mother of two children, one of whom married Montaigne's brother and was only fifteen years younger than La Boétie, she was probably older than her husband. Theirs seems to have been a very happy marriage.

He played a distinguished role in the Parlement, serving as censor of Latin plays put on by the Collège de Guyenne, on a mission to Charles IX, and, with lieutenant general de Burie, in bringing justice and order to Agen, a hotbed of religious controversy, with the firmness and fairness that won the respect of his older colleagues for all his work.

He was an able humanist and man of letters. A gifted poet in French and especially in Latin, on good terms with the rising Pléiade group, he was a friend of Jean Dorat and Jean-Antoine de Baïf and seems to have known Ronsard personally. The noted critic Julius Caesar Scaliger praised his verse. An eminent Hellenist, he translated Xenophon's "Oeconomicus" and Plutarch's "Rules of Marriage" and "Letter of Consolation to His Wife" and annotated his treatise "On Love."

He is best known as a writer for his *Discourse on Voluntary Servitude,* often nicknamed *Contr'Un* (*Anti-One*), composed probably at law school in Orléans and later revised. Montaigne's curious presentation of it is best explained as follows. He planned to give it a central place in his first book of *Essays,* announced it in his chapter "Of Friendship," learned that it had been published already by Protestants, decided it might be used against the crown if republished in "so unpleasant a season," withheld it, and offered in its place twenty-nine of La Boétie's sonnets, meanwhile leaving his original introduction to the work unchanged. After 1588, however, he altered his statement of La Boétie's age when he wrote the work. "He wrote it," Montaigne reported, "by way of essay in his early youth"; and added, but after 1588 deleted: "not having reached his eighteenth year." The end of his introduction first read: "But let us listen a while to this boy of eighteen"; after 1588 he changed "eighteen" to "sixteen." Incidentally, the way La Boétie speaks of the Pléiade poets suggests that they have already published substantial work, in which case the *Voluntary Servitude* was revised, if not composed, when La Boétie was in his twenties.

All this in no way invalidates Montaigne's claim that "if I had not supported with all my strength a friend that I lost, they would have torn him into a thousand contrasting appearances," and his explanation for withdrawing the *Voluntary Servitude:*

Because I have found that this work has since been brought to light, and with evil intent, by those who seek to disturb and change the state of our government without worrying whether they will improve it, and because they have mixed his work up with some of their own concoctions,

I have changed my mind about putting it in here. . . . This subject was treated by him in his boyhood, only by way of an exercise, as a common theme hashed over in a thousand places in books. I have no doubt that he believed what he wrote, for he was so conscientious as not to lie even in jest. . . . But he had another maxim sovereignly imprinted in his soul, to obey and submit most religiously to the laws under which he was born. There never was a better citizen, or one more devoted to the tranquillity of his country, or more hostile to the commotions and innovations of his time. He would much rather have used his ability to suppress them than to give them material that would excite them further. His mind was molded in the pattern of other ages than this.

The *Discourse* opens with the argument that any absolute master is a great misfortune, goes on to express amazement that hundreds of thousands, nay, a million millions, will serve a tyrant, and marvels at their blind cowardice. Such servility is unnatural but understandable; for since the habit of slavery undermines valor, "the primary reason for voluntary servitude is habit." La Boétie studies this and other causes in some detail, shows how a tyrant's henchmen help preserve him in power, and concludes in wonder at their pusillanimous folly.

The most striking feature of the work is La Boétie's formidable erudition and the masterly control that never lets it mute his eloquence. Its timelessness is shown by its second English translation and first American publication in 1942, with the title *Anti-Dictator* and headings relating it to Mussolini and Hitler.

Of almost equal interest is La Boétie's *Memoir Concerning the Edict of January 1562,* which Montaigne also knew but also decided not to publish in the 1570's, and which remained lost for three and a half centuries. This edict was an early attempt by Catherine de' Medici and L'Hôpital to propitiate the Protestants by giving them great freedom of worship. Writing later in the same year, after the outbreak of civil war but before Catholic doctrine had been crystallized by the Council of Trent, La Boétie warns of the danger of the split. Two religions and two hostile parties, he argues, can only breed strife, disrespect for law, and anarchy. The Church has much to answer for; the indulgences of 1517 should have been condemned when Luther pointed them out; but concessions have led only to increased demands. There are three choices: to maintain the old religion, support the new, or uphold both under law.

Bordeaux in 1563

Château de Montaigne

*Montaigne's Library
and Château*

LES EDITIONS "TITO,"
MAURICE BERJAUD, BORDEAUX

Catherine de' Medici

The second alternative would go against the faith of the king and nearly all his subjects. The third would invite foreign intervention, and the king could not in conscience allow it either. The only solution is a Catholic France reformed not by the Church but by the king, acting mainly through his Parlements. Protestant leaders should be punished as rebels; the worst abuses of the Church should be rigorously corrected (for example, priests should be grown men who serve as priests); all superficial differences should be reconciled. This done, Protestants must return to the religion of their fathers or leave the country. Only then will France regain law, order, and unity.

If the modern reader finds this intolerant, he should remember that the Protestants also opposed the coexistence of cults unless they gained by it. History seemed to prove that this simply would not work. Accepting this as a lesson, La Boétie shows a constructive fairness rare in his time. Montaigne, as we have noted, stood squarely on the Catholic side, apparently with less regard than later for the Protestant rebels. He probably agreed with his friend's recommendations.

Montaigne, who survived La Boétie by nearly thirty years, is our chief authority on their relationship. His main account is in his chapter "Of Friendship" (I: 28), unique in its warmth and eloquence. It was by the *Voluntary Servitude,* he writes, that he first heard of La Boétie, "long before I had seen him . . . thus starting on its way this friendship which together we fostered, as long as God willed, so entire and so perfect that certainly you will hardly hear of the like, and among men of today you see no trace of it in practice. So many coincidences are needed to build up such a friendship that it is a lot if fortune can do it once in three centuries." Most human relationships—natural, social, hospitable, erotic, and casual—fall short of the ideal.

What we ordinarily call friends and friendships are nothing but acquaintanceships and familiarities formed by some chance or convenience, by means of which our souls are bound to each other. In the friendship I speak of, our souls mingle and blend with each other so completely that they efface the seam that joined them, and cannot find it again. If you press me to tell why I loved him, I feel that this cannot be expressed, except by answering: Because it was he, because it was I.

Beyond all my understanding, beyond what I can say about this in particular, there was I know not what inexplicable and fateful force that was the mediator of this union.

After telling of their first meeting, Montaigne goes on:

He wrote an excellent Latin satire, which is published, in which he excuses and explains the precipitancy of our mutual understanding, so promptly grown to its perfection. Having so little time to last, and having begun so late, for we were both grown men, and he a few years older than I, it could not lose time and conform to the pattern of mild and regular friendships, which need so many precautions in the form of long preliminary association. Our friendship has no other model than itself, and can be compared only with itself. It is not one special consideration, nor two, nor three, nor four, nor a thousand: it is I know not what quintessence of all this mixture, which, having seized my whole will, led it to plunge and lose itself in his; which, having seized his whole will, led it to plunge and lose itself in mine, with equal hunger, equal rivalry. I say lose, in truth, for neither of us reserved anything for himself, nor was anything either his or mine.

In a perfect friendship, says Montaigne, the greatest possible favor is for one friend to let the other do him a service. No man can have two such friendships; each is all-embracing. Menander was right to call that man happy who has known even the shadow of a friend.

For in truth, if I compare all the rest of my life—though by the grace of God I have spent it pleasantly, comfortably, and, except for the loss of such a friend, free from any grievous affliction, and full of tranquillity of mind . . .—if I compare it all, I say, with the four years which were granted me to enjoy the sweet company and society of that man, it is nothing but smoke, nothing but dark and dreary night. Since the day I lost him . . . I only drag on a weary life. And the very pleasures that come my way, instead of consoling me, redouble my grief for his loss. We went halves in everything; it seems to me that I am robbing him of his share. . . . I was already so formed and accustomed to being a second self everywhere that only half of me seems to be alive now. . . . There is no action or thought in which I do not miss him, as indeed he would have missed me. For just as he surpassed me infinitely in every other ability and virtue, so he did in the duty of friendship.

La Boétie, in his only account, places the friendship on the same exalted level. Many wise men, he says, mistrust any bond not tested by time:

But a love little more than a year old has joined us, and yet it has left nothing undone to attain the highest point of love. Perhaps this is by chance; but it is sacrilegious to speak so, and there is no sage, however morose, who, when he knows us both, and our interests and ways, would inquire into the years our bond has lasted and would not gladly applaud so great a love. There is no reason to fear that our descendants, if only the fates permit, will begrudge placing our names among those of famous friends.

.   .   .   .

You have been bound to me, Montaigne, both by the power of nature and by virtue, which is the sweet allurement of love. . . . No power is more effective in bringing men together and kindling in them a beautiful love.

The pictures that the friends give of each other are of unequal value. Montaigne's remarks about La Boétie, all written after his death, are a little too pious to be truly revealing. His friend, he writes, was an excellent citizen, "the greatest man of our time, in my opinion," "one of the men most fit and needed for the highest offices in France"; eminent in virtue, piety, justice, liveliness of mind, soundness of judgment, imagination, learning, love of country, hatred of vice; so nearly miraculous that Montaigne cannot do him justice; full of "a million graces, perfections, and virtues which molded idle in the midst of so fair a soul"; a poet of pith and marrow. His magistrate's robe concealed "a soldierly vigor." To be sure, even he does not quite equal the great ancients; but then, no one does.

And the greatest man I have known in person, I mean for natural qualities of the soul, and the best endowed, was Etienne de La Boétie. He was truly a full soul, handsome from every point of view; a soul of the old stamp, who would have achieved great results if fortune had willed it, for he had added much to this rich nature by learning and study.

La Boétie, writing to his living friend, tells us more. Three of his Latin poems are addressed to Montaigne. One of these, directed to him and Jean de Belot jointly, expresses La Boétie's anguish at his country's self-destruction and his resolve to begin life afresh in the New World. Of the two poems to Montaigne alone, the first (in order of presentation; we do not know the order or time of composition) shows Michel seeking virtue in his father's footsteps but needing support; for La Boétie asks whether his own youth will make him ridiculous if he gives advice. Virtue, he says, selects those born to conquer and shows them her full austerity. Thus (pursuing the ancient fable) Virtue and Pleasure appeared to the young Hercules, and Virtue convinced him of her rival's ugliness and the glorious difficulty of following herself.

The third poem, the "Latin satire," is much longer: 322 lines
as against seventy-two. After paying tribute to the friendship, it
represents Montaigne as born for neither mediocre virtues nor vices,
as an Alcibiades, who Socrates predicted would be the ruin or the
glory of Athens. Such natures require the discipline of virtue but
may reject it. Before young Montaigne, gently reared, noble, rich,
vigorous, passionate, lies a world of pleasure. "Shall I bend," he
protests, "with sleepless care, to harass all these volumes? Shall I
alone, now that I am older, be ignorant of Venus? My house sup-
plies ample riches, my age ample powers. Here, surely, here is the
proper use of wealth and verdant youth. And indeed a sweet girl
is smiling at me, but secretly, a lovely occasion for guilt even for
a gray head." All La Boétie can do is try to restrain him by a
detailed account of the miseries of fornication and an exhortation to
virtue.

Though exaggerated praise is endemic in humanistic poetry,
Montaigne's promise is as clear as his susceptibility. La Boétie likens
him to a Cyclops, to Alcibiades, twice to Hercules, calls him eager,
able, and free, "with winged foot already near the goal, alert to
pluck the crowns." Where he himself is mediocre in ability, virtue,
and promise, Montaigne's capacities are infinite. He seems already
to be what he will be at his retirement about ten years later: a man
of great ability in search of his function. He is no mere rake—he
sounds inexperienced, and La Boétie's verses are monitory, not de-
scriptive—but he is strongly tempted to be, and La Boétie is
worried.

La Boétie is clearly the moral mentor; yet his high moral
strenuousness seems to leave little room for love of life. He badly
wants a greater place than he feels is given him. The good life seems
to him an unending struggle for perfection. Montaigne's freedom
from any such compulsion was probably part of his charm for La
Boétie, who, loving and admiring him, could see in him his own right
to demand less of himself.

We have one glimpse of their discussions in an early essay when
Montaigne says he has always maintained, "against the opinion of
many, and even of Etienne de La Boétie," that dying people in a
coma are probably not suffering keenly. Our main view is in Montaigne's account of his friend's last days, published in 1570 as "Extract from a Letter that Monsieur de Montaigne the Councillor

Wrote to Monsieur de Montaigne His Father concerning Certain Details that He Noted in the Illness and Death of the Late Monsieur de La Boétie." He probably wrote it soon after the event, but may have retouched—or indeed written—it at any time between 1563 and 1570.

On Monday, August 9, 1563, La Boétie came down with an intestinal ailment as he was about to leave for Médoc. Montaigne, returning from the Parlement, sent to invite him to dinner at his house, and learned that La Boétie was feeling ill and wanted Montaigne to come to see him instead. He found him unwell, with diarrhea and stomach pains following overexposure after exercise. Both men feared the plague raging in Périgord and Agenais, where La Boétie had recently been on missions for the Parlement; and there was enough of it near La Boétie's house in Bordeaux for Montaigne to encourage him to go two leagues to Germignan and stay with the Lestonnacs, Montaigne's sister and brother-in-law.

The next morning (Tuesday) Madame de La Boétie sent for Montaigne with the news that her husband seemed very ill. He came and at their request spent the night, did the same on Thursday, and returned on Saturday to find a worn La Boétie who "told me then that his illness was a bit contagious and moreover unpleasant and melancholic; that he knew my nature very well and asked me to be with him only for short periods but as often as I could. I did not leave him again."

On Sunday La Boétie felt very weak and had chaotic visions, not painful, but in his view no better than death. Beginning to lose hope, at Montaigne's suggestion he put his domestic affairs in order, urging Montaigne to watch over his wife and uncle, lest grief drive them frantic, telling all three of his will and of his gratitude for their love and help, and saying to Montaigne:

"My brother, whom I love so dearly and whom I chose out of so many men in order to renew with you that virtuous and sincere friendship, the practice of which has for so long been driven from among us by our vices that there remain of it only a few old traces in the memory of antiquity, I entreat you to accept as a legacy my library and my books, which I give you as a sign of my affection toward you: a very small present, but one which comes from a willing heart and which is appropriate for you because of your fondness for letters. It will be μνημόσυνον *tui sodalis*." *

* "A remembrance of your friend" (adapted from Catullus).

This done, he could consider his conscience. "I am a Christian," he said, "I am a Catholic; as such have I lived, as such do I intend to end my life. Let a priest be sent for, for I will not fail in this last duty of a Christian."

At this point he looked much better, and Montaigne had a glimmer of hope. It was not to last; soon the friends began preparing for La Boétie's death. Here is part of their conversation:

But two or three hours later, both to keep up his great courage, and because I wished, in the zeal I have had all my life for his glory and honor, that there should be more people in the room to witness so many fine proofs of greatness of soul, I told him that I had blushed for shame that my courage had failed on hearing what he, who was suffering this illness, had had the courage to tell me. That up to then I had thought that God gave us no such great power against human calamities, and I had had difficulty believing what I had come across on this subject in the histories; but that having felt such a proof of it, I praised God that this had been in a person by whom I was so loved and whom I loved so dearly; and that this would serve me as an example, to play this same part in my turn.

He interrupted me to beg me to use it in this way, and to show in action that the talks we had had together during our health had been not merely borne in our mouths but deeply engraved on heart and in soul, in such a way as to be put into execution on the first occasions that offered; adding that this was the true object of our studies, and of philosophy. And, taking me by the hand, he said: "My brother, my friend, I assure you that I have done many things in my life, it seems to me, with as much pain and difficulty as I do this. And when all is said, I had been prepared for it for a very long time and had known my lesson all by heart."

La Boétie added that he had lived healthy and happy, simply and without malice, long enough; old age might well have brought ambition and avarice. As it was, he was sure he would find God and the abode of the blessed. At this Montaigne flinched, and La Boétie reminded him that he must be strong.

In the evening the notary took down La Boétie's will, which he dictated rapidly and surely. He bade farewell to his niece and stepdaughter, encouraging them to virtue, and in private to Montaigne's Protestant brother Thomas, urging him not to disrupt the family.

The next morning, Monday, La Boétie had lost all hope and reproached Montaigne for keeping him alive and in pain. He was icy cold, with a mortal sweat and almost no pulse. He made his confession, but had to wait a full day for Mass and the sacrament; stated his profession of faith; asked the priest, his uncle, and Montaigne to pray for him; and cordially greeted a visitor, his friend Jean de Belot. Two or three times he called out: "All right! All right! Let it come when it will, I'm waiting for it, strong and firm of foot." In the evening he had visions which he could describe only as "Great, great . . . but, my brother, I cannot express them: they are marvelous, infinite, and ineffable." After trying to comfort his wife's anguish, he sent her away, saying that he was going off, only to add quickly: "to sleep."

Having taken what proved to be his last leave of her, he urged Montaigne to stay close to him. He began to toss violently, his voice grew loud, his remarks poignant:

Then, among other things, he began to entreat me again and again with extreme affection to give him a place; so that I was afraid that his judgment was shaken. Even when I had remonstrated with him very gently that he was letting the illness carry him away and that these were not the words of a man in his sound mind, he did not give in at first and repeated even more strongly: "My brother, my brother, do *you* refuse me a place?" This until he forced me to convince him by reason and tell him that since he was breathing and speaking and had a body, consequently he had his place. "True, true," he answered me then, "I have one, but it is not the one I need; and then when all is said, I have no being left." "God will give you a better one very soon," said I. "Would that I were there already," he replied. "For three days now I have been straining to leave."
      In this distress he often called me simply to know whether I was near him.

By two in the morning he began to rest; Montaigne left the room and rejoiced with La Boétie's wife at this good sign.

But an hour later, or thereabouts, speaking my name once or twice and then heaving a great sigh to himself, he gave up the ghost, at about three o'clock on the Wednesday morning, August 18th, 1563, after living 32 years, 9 months, and 17 days. . . .

There may be some embellishment, in Montaigne's letter and chapter, of his friend and their friendship. The Socratic touches are evident: equable discussions on death, comfort to the weeping wife and friends. But there are reasons for trusting Montaigne's account pretty far. La Boétie might well seek—successfully—to emulate Socrates, who after all is not the only model of a peaceful and courageous death. Many details have no savor of hagiography: the dying man's poignant reproaches and complaints, Montaigne's comment

that his speeches to his niece and stepdaugher were "a little long."
Except for its date, on which Montaigne errs by one unimportant
day, La Boétie's will tallies fully, as far as it goes, with Montaigne's account. Most important, La Boétie's version of the
friendship and Montaigne's other remarks outside the chapter and
the letter fully confirm his main accounts. It has been said that
when Montaigne writes of the friendship, "absence, imagination and
literature all contribute their part"; but we need not exaggerate that
part.

When Montaigne retired he had the following memorial to La
Boétie and his books inscribed in his study:

[To the shades of Etienne de La Boétie], the tenderest, sweetest, and closest
companion, than whom our age has seen no one better, more learned, more
charming, or indeed more perfect, Michel de Montaigne, miserably bereft
of so dear a support of his life, remembering the mutual love and dear
feeling that bound them together, wanting to set up some unique monument,
and unable to do so more meaningfully, has dedicated this excellent apparatus for the mind.

Montaigne's references to his friend and the friendship elsewhere
in the *Essays* are so frequent that a sampling must suffice. He knows
by experience, he says, that separation may allow each friend to live
more fully, since the arms of friendship can reach around the world:

In other days I made use and advantage of our separation. We filled and
extended our possession of life better by separating: he lived, he enjoyed,
he saw for me, and I for him, as fully as if he had been there. One part of
us remained idle when we were together; we were fused into one. Separation
in space made the conjunction of our wills richer.

Once, after a wistful wish to pass on his domestic responsibilities
to a younger man, Montaigne added: "Three and four times happy
the man who can entrust his pitiful old age into a friendly hand."
This passage was later crossed out, though probably not by him;
but what follows was not:

And will it ever be said enough how precious is a friend, and how different
a thing from these civil bonds [marriage]? Even the image of friendship
that I see in the animals, so pure, how religiously I respect it!

To this passage he added another which was also crossed out later but,
in the 1595 edition of the *Essays*, restored further on:

As I know by too certain experience, there is no consolation so sweet in
the loss of our friends as that which comes to us from the knowledge of
not having forgotten to tell them anything and of having had perfect and
entire communication with them. O my friend! Am I better off for having
had the taste of it, or am I worse off? Certainly I am better off. My regret
for him consoles and honors me. Is it not a pious and pleasant duty of my
life to be forever performing his obsequies? Is there an enjoyment that is
worth this privation?

Another remark, more matter-of-fact but equally telling, is
strong proof of Montaigne's feeling, since it was not intended for
publication. On May 11, 1581, nearly eighteen years after La Boétie's death, Montaigne, at the baths of La Villa near Lucca,
wrote in his *Travel Journal*:

This same morning, writing to Monsieur d'Ossat, I was overcome by such
painful thoughts about Monsieur de La Boétie, and I was in this mood so
long, without recovering, that it did me much harm.

There is much to show that the *Essays* themselves are—
among other things—a compensation for the loss of La Boétie.
Montaigne's need for communication is deep; he is "sociable to excess," "hungry to make myself known," "all in the open and in
full view, born for company and friendship." He is hard to please
and "somewhat barren and cool" in ordinary relationships because
"by nature I find it hard to communicate myself by halves and
moderately." In true friendship, however, he is expert and at ease:
"I am very capable of forming and maintaining rare and exquisite
friendships, inasmuch as I grasp so hungrily at any acquaintances that
suit my taste, I make advances and I throw myself at them so avidly,
that I hardly fail to attach myself and to make an impression wherever
I land. I have often made happy proof of this."

He has missed a congenial friend on his travels to share his
experiences with:

It is rare good fortune, but inestimably comforting, to have a worthy man,
of sound understanding and ways that conform with yours, who likes to
go with you. I have missed such a man extremely on all my travels. . . .

No pleasure has any savor for me without communication. Not even
a merry thought comes to my mind without my being vexed at having
produced it alone without anyone to offer it to. . . . I like the idea of
Archytas, that it would be unpleasant to be even in heaven and to wander
among those great and divine celestial bodies, without the presence of a
companion.

Again and again in his late years Montaigne reaches out for a friend. Marie de Gournay, who in 1588 became his *fille d'alliance*,* was a welcome friend but no La Boétie. He craved a more equal, frank, and vigorous bond; to find it he would go far.

If there are any persons, any good company, in country or city, in France or elsewhere, residing or traveling, who like my humors and whose humors I like, they have only to whistle in their palm and I will go furnish them with essays in flesh and bone.

The sense of the *Essays* as a kind of bottle, or multitude of bottles, in the sea, is clear in the following call from the depths of loneliness:

Besides this profit that I derive from writing about myself, I hope for this other advantage, that if my humors happen to please and suit some worthy man before I die, he will try to meet me. I give him a big advantage in ground covered; for all that long acquaintance and familiarity could have gained for him in several years, he can see in three days in this record, and more surely and exactly.

Amusing notion: many things that I would not want to tell anyone, I tell the public; and for my most secret knowledge and thoughts I send my most faithful friends to a bookseller's shop. . . .

If by such good signs I knew of a man who was suited to me, truly I would go very far to find him; for the sweetness of harmonious and agreeable company cannot be bought too dearly, in my opinion. Oh, a friend! How true is that old saying, that the enjoyment of one is sweeter and more necessary than that of the elements of water and fire!

It was a mood brought on by the loss of La Boétie that led Montaigne to write in the first place: "It was a melancholy humor, and consequently a humor very hostile to my natural disposition, produced by the gloom of the solitude into which I had cast myself some years ago, that first put into my head this daydream of meddling with writing."

La Boétie was the only man Montaigne fully trusted as witness to his life. With him dead, the *Essays* must serve instead. After all, if Montaigne had wanted merely to know himself better, he need not have written, let alone published, his book. One of its main purposes was to testify faithfully to what he was.

I know well that I will leave behind no sponsor anywhere near as affectionate and understanding about me as I was about him [La Boétie]. There

---

* Usually rendered "adoptive daughter" or "covenant daughter," this title was one of many by which often, in Montaigne's time, persons unrelated by blood laid mutual claim to spiritual kinship.

is no one to whom I would be willing to entrust myself fully for a portrait; he alone enjoyed my true image, and carried it away. That is why I myself decipher myself so painstakingly.

If La Boétie had lived, Montaigne would probably have written in the form of letters:

Letter writing . . . is a kind of work in which my friends think I have some ability. And I would have preferred to adopt this form to publish my sallies, if I had had someone to talk to. I needed what I once had, a certain relationship to lead me on, sustain me, and raise me up. . . . I would have been more attentive and confident, with a strong friend to address, than I am now, when I consider the various tastes of a whole public. And if I am not mistaken, I would have been more successful.

Though we may disagree with the last sentence, the passage is another proof of La Boétie's close connection with the *Essays*. Montaigne's loneliness led him to write; the lack of his friend, leaving him no one to address in letters, made him seek a form of his own that would be both a testimony to his life and a means of communication which might bring him another good friend and thus fill the void in his heart.

The influence of La Boétie and his death is strongest for the next ten years (1563–73) of Montaigne's life. After two years of seeking to divert his grief in various amours, he let himself be married, but with the inauspicious conviction that marriage ranked far below friendship. When he resigned from the Parlement, where La Boétie no longer sat, he promptly published his friend's works severally, with dedications to important persons. He took pride in protecting La Boétie's memory against misinterpretation. In all these acts and in his chapter on friendship, centrally placed in Book One of the *Essays* and worked over with loving care, he seems to consider himself as mainly the guardian of La Boétie's shrine.

Nor is this all. For the same ten years Montaigne tried hard to follow in La Boétie's footsteps. As long as his friend lived—to judge by our few glimpses of the two—Montaigne preached and practiced a code and ideal more natural for himself and less rigorous than La Boétie's. After 1573 he was to renew his quest for a way of his own. For the ten years in between he was under the sway—almost the shadow—of his friend's ideals.

It was mainly La Boétie's death that gave him such influence. We may argue with a living friend and still idolize his values when he dies. After all, as Montaigne told him, it was only then that he learned how bravely a man could meet pain and death. Only then did he resolve to play the same part in his turn.

The stoical humanism of the early essays echoes the spirit of La Boétie, as his dying words echo in "To Philosophize Is to Learn to Die" (I: 20). There are literary influences too—direct, for Montaigne is more bookish than he likes to admit, and through La Boétie, who was unashamedly bookish. Seneca, Cicero, Lucretius, and countless other authors played a part in changing Montaigne in his thirties from a reflective but gay young hedonist into an apprehensive stoical humanist. But the major part, in life and even more so in death, was played by Etienne de La Boétie.

Chapter 6: Marriage [1565–1592]

ONTAIGNE'S MARRIAGE is a controversial topic. There is far more evidence than agreement over what is pertinent and what it shows. One document has sensational meaning for some, little for others; many of his acerb remarks about wives and marriage may or may not apply to his own. We had best approach the question from firm ground.

Françoise de La Chassaigne, Montaigne's wife, was born on December 13, 1544, into a distinguished Catholic family of Bordeaux. Her grandfather Geoffroy, Second President of the Parlement, was the chief hostage of the salt-tax rebels in 1548 and a leading adversary of Protestantism until he died around 1568; he and Montaigne were among those challenged by Lagebaston in 1563. Her aunt Adrienne had married Montaigne's uncle, councillor Raymond de Bussaguet. Her father, Joseph, lord of Pressac, was a councillor in the Parlement for twenty-five years, then Fifth President from 1569 until his death in 1572. Late in 1569, heading a mission to court, he was seized by Protestant rebels from Blaye and held about a year as a hostage. Françoise had an older sister and two younger brothers, one of whom, Geoffroy, lord of Pressac, student and translator of Seneca, wrote a treatise on honor and valor, *Cléandre* (1582), which shows some apparent borrowings from his brother-in-law's *Essays*.

Françoise de La Chassaigne was twenty and Montaigne thirty-two when they were married on September 23, 1565. She brought him a dowry of 7,000 livres tournois, payable 4,000 in six months, the other 3,000 in four years; each spouse presented the other with 2,000 livres, to go to the survivor; and Pierre de Montaigne gave Michel one quarter of the revenue coming from all the estate except the château and other buildings.

She bore him six children (1570–83), all girls, of whom five died within a few months. The other, Léonor (1571–1616), lived to marry at eighteen, lost her husband four years later, remarried at thirty-seven, and had one daughter by each marriage. Madame de Montaigne survived her daughter by eleven years and her husband by nearly thirty-five, dying on March 7, 1627, at the age of eighty-two. We have nineteen letters of her old age to her spiritual director.

Witnesses other than her husband tell us relatively little. Apparently she was a good hostess. Jacques-Auguste de Thou stopped at the château in 1589 only to learn that his friend Montaigne was in Bordeaux, and wrote of being "most elegantly entertained" by his wife. Marie de Gournay, who after Montaigne's death spent over a year with his widow and daughter, wrote eloquently of her piety toward Montaigne's remains, his book, and his memory, had the highest praise for their hospitality, and hailed Françoise in typically lavish terms:

> In married love Alcestis you recall,
> In grace and beauty, that celestial Greek,
> Daughter of Tyndareus. Now and of old,
> Your husband's greatness makes your lot unique.

Montaigne's old friend and colleague Charles de Malvin de Cessac, in a letter of condolence on his death, recognizes the magnitude of the widow's grief and the vanity of any consolation, offers services and friendship, and states his trust in her "virtue and prudence, aided by the grace of God," to give her strength in her bereavement.

Montaigne's son-in-law, Charles de Gamaches, in *The Sensible Man Reasoning about Passages from the Holy Writ, against the Pretended Reformists* (1623), traces his daughter's piety to her fondness for her grandmother, who is so devout that at seventy-seven she observes fasts not only each Friday but for half of Lent "with a face as well composed as in the first days of the second year of your widowhood." He says that she was a full partner of her great husband in every way, attracting him physically by her "surpassing beauty" and fully wedded to him in mind as well.

This tribute from a son-in-law who lived many years at Montaigne, whose aunt had married Françoise's brother Geoffroy, and whose debt to Montaigne on education is clear, seems conclusive; yet except in regard to Françoise's piety we may question his competence. Montaigne had been dead thirty years when he wrote, sixteen when he married Léonor. Gamaches probably never knew him personally, or he would presumably have mentioned it; his allusion to Françoise's second year of widowhood suggests that he first came to know the family then. His praise of the marriage probably parrots the wife and daughter, and lacks authority.

We learn something of Françoise de La Chassaigne in her seventies from her correspondence. All the letters we have are addressed to her spiritual director, Dom Marc-Antoine de Saint-Bernard, between August 14, 1617, and probably 1625. She has many material concerns: sending him quince marmalade, thanking him for lemons and especially some oranges that help her appetite; having a jeweled feeding cup like her own made for the Countess of Gurson; arranging about a set of coral spoons, two of which she had from her late father and wants to keep all her life; asking apologetically to have someone send her some muslin and taffeta for a dress for her granddaughter; arranging for Dom Marc-Antoine to get some hay from her; asking him to buy her a thirty- or forty-pound tub of good English butter. There are legal and financial problems: endowments for burial, prayers, and masses for her husband, her daughter, and herself; a donation requested by her correspondent, of which she is wary; plans concerning her chapel in the church of the Feuillants in Bordeaux. For all these she is glad to lean on Joseph de Bussaguet (grandson of her aunt Adrienne and Montaigne's uncle Raymond), who understands legal matters better than she. She is charitable, but wants her giving to be voluntary (else "I should have no merit in it of my own") and not to encroach on her other obligations.

Money is a frequent concern. She would like to end her days in Bordeaux with Dom Marc-Antoine and her other friends, but lacks the necessary funds. Repeatedly and reluctantly she asks him to repay half of the 200 crowns that he owes her; to avoid doing so she has borrowed 700 livres. Her chapel is provided at her own expense, not from her husband's estate; if others want burial there they must pay the remaining costs. Her last letter shows great relief over a business deal: "By this God has given me a means of supporting this house of my late husband and my children." Her obligations make it hard to give freely: "So many kinds of charity come before our eyes that in truth one does not know which one to run to; and my two grandchildren, one of whom by his father's bad management is cast into poverty and misery. My husband, from whom came all the property I possess, recommended them to me so!" *

She is devoted to her spiritual director. Her first letter describes her as "crushed" at having no news of him. She has been sick for nine months, and "hardly a day has passed when I have not thought of you and wished to receive your consolations. Good Lord, how I have wanted to see you! . . . Truly I do not know whether I would not rather choose to die than to know that you are going away." Again and again she urges him to come to see her; yet her eagerness does not make her inconsiderate. She understands why he cannot come, and twice urges him not to try when it would be dangerous. "I would rather die than have you take the road in this miserable weather."

She is naturally much concerned with infirmities and approaching death. "My health," she writes simply in 1624, "is amazingly enfeebled; yesterday evening I thought I would die; but God is always very gracious to me." Her last letter urges Dom Marc-Antoine to remember her, for she is helpless: "Truly it is time for you

---

* "My two grandchildren" (or "little children," *"petits enfants"*) are probably her great-grandson Charles de Lur-Saluces and her unmarried granddaughter Marie de Gamaches, both born after the death of Montaigne, whose recommendation was obviously a general one.

to help me to offer my soul to God and resolve to do His holy will. . . ."

The traits revealed in her letters—piety, devotion to her spiritual director, emphatic statement, concern with material matters, anxiety over conflicting demands on her property, determination to preserve her husband's estate for their descendants and to prepare for death—are natural for a widow in her seventies. They may not tell us much about her as a wife and mother from her twenties to her forties. Let us return to her as a younger woman.

Much sensational conjecture springs from the following document:

> Today, the 23rd day of the month of May, 1569, in the château of Montaigne in Périgord, there appeared the noble Michel de Montaigne, lord of the said place, speaking to the lady Antoinette de Louppes, his mother, declared to her that he had found in his wife's coffers a gold chain that the late Arnaud de Montaigne, lord of Saint-Martin, his brother, had left there; which [chain] the said lady de Louppes said belonged to her, and demands that it be returned to her. And this gold chain the said lord of Montaigne, in the presence and with the consent of the nobles Thomas de Montaigne, lord of Beauregard, and Pierre de Montaigne, lord of La Brousse, brothers of the said late de Saint-Martin, presently left and delivered to the said de Louppes, and she received it. . . .
>
> . . . Done in the presence of the said noble men Thomas de Montaigne, lord of Beauregard, and Pierre de Montaigne, lord of La Brousse, sons and brothers of the said lady de Louppes and lord of Montaigne, and the said lady and the lord of Montaigne have signed below.
>
> Signed: A. de Louppes, Montaigne, Thomas de Montaigne, Pierre de Montaigne.
>   Signed: Dumas, royal notary.

In publishing this curious document, Théophile Malvezin wondered whether the chain was a flirtatious gift from young Arnaud —the brother who was killed by a court-tennis ball—to his sister-in-law. Most scholars have ignored his conjecture, presumably as inconclusive. However, Alexandre Nicolaï and M. Maurice Rat have interpreted the episode as evidence of adultery between the two. M. Rat summarizes their case as follows.

Montaigne's austere notion of marriage predisposed him for a pair of horns. Françoise was "what the peasants of Gascony call a beautiful woman, that is to say a fresh and robust and lusty woman."

So she "found consolation for her vexation by abandoning herself, a few months after the wedding, to Captain Saint-Martin, Montaigne's younger brother, who was young and handsome and did not hesitate, finding the opportunity convenient and his sister-in-law pleasing, to show her that she was attractive and to teach her immodesty." Came the death of the "handsome captain," who "loved to adorn himself and, among other jewels, rather frequently wore a handsome gold chain which looked well on his doublet." Montaigne, presiding over the partition of his brother's property and not finding the chain, "became very worried over this disappearance, and perhaps not without connecting it with certain suspicions, for he searched everywhere and even in his wife's coffer, where indeed he found it." Françoise, taken aback at first, sought the help of her mother-in-law, who got along badly with her but was always ready to join her against that bad housekeeper Montaigne. Antoinette de Louppes now appears and "claims ownership of the gold chain, which, so she says, she had loaned to Saint-Martin and ultimately entrusted to her daughter-in-law."

This account rests on few facts. We know little of young Françoise's beauty,* nothing of her lustiness; nothing of Saint-Martin's appearance or dress, or whether he ever wore the chain. Montaigne's worry, suspicions, and frenzied search are pure supposition. There probably was bad feeling between wife and mother, but nothing shows the mother saying she loaned the chain to Arnaud and later entrusted it to Françoise.

A major assumption of Nicolaï's is that Françoise expected the full fruits of love in marriage and was appalled by Montaigne's prudery. To the modern reader this seems reasonable; yet authorities agree that in the Renaissance marriage was no place to look for passionate love. Ruth Kelso's summary of typical views is almost a paraphrase of Montaigne:

The great danger, men were warned, was that the girl who came to the marriage bed a virgin in body and mind might become debauched by the excesses and lack of modesty of her own husband. A husband who inflames his wife is to blame if afterwards she admits a lover. . . . He must treat her as a husband and not as a lover. . . . For that, good judgment and

---

* Our only contemporary testimony is that of Montaigne as reported by Florimond de Raemond (see below, p. 93); but the context makes such a tribute too nearly inevitable to be conclusive.

not mere passion is necessary. Many writers would have eliminated all pleasure from the marital act if they could, and went so far even as to recommend methods that insure the least possible satisfaction to the wife.

Altogether, the enigmatic affair of the gold chain is probably best explained—insofar as our present knowledge can explain it—as a product of the struggle between mother and son, after the father's death, over property and authority in the household. Less than nine months earlier, Montaigne and Antoinette de Louppes signed the agreement spelling out in detail the rights remaining to his mother. Nothing suggests that the chain did not indeed belong to her. A grasping woman, she may have made such a fuss over it as to provoke Montaigne—and possibly his brothers—into formalizing its return. If it was hers, Saint-Martin's act in leaving it in his sister-in-law's coffers seems hardly sinister. Moreover, if Montaigne, who deplored scandal and hostility in marriage, suspected that its presence there implied his wife's guilt, he would hardly have given this fact even the limited publicity of a formal act. We cannot of course be sure that Madame de Montaigne did not betray her husband; but nothing clearly suggests that she did.

It is time to consult our main authority, Michel de Montaigne. As we have noted, La Boétie's death was a heavy blow. "Needing some violent diversion to distract me from it, by art and study I made myself fall in love, in which my youth helped me. Love solaced me and withdrew me from the affliction caused by friendship." Just over two years later, without enthusiasm, he married.

Of my own choice, I would have avoided marrying Wisdom herself, if she had wanted me. But say what we will, the custom and practice of ordinary life bears us along. . . . I did not really bid myself to it, I was led to it, and borne by extraneous circumstances. . . . And I was borne to it certainly more ill-prepared and contrary than I am now after having tried it. And, licentious as I am thought to be, I have in truth observed the laws of marriage more strictly than I had either promised or expected.

He thinks he married at a good age, close to Aristotle's ideal of thirty-five, and is glad his marriage was planned by others:

Connections and means have, with reason, as much weight in it as graces and beauty, or more. We do not marry for ourselves, whatever we say; we marry just as much or more for our posterity, for our family. . . . Therefore I like this fashion of arranging it rather by a third hand than by our own, and by the sense of others rather than by our own. How opposite is all this to the conventions of love!

In a good marriage ("if such there be," Montaigne adds), love is dangerous; friendship should be the model. To be sure, in theory both feelings may combine to involve the body as well as the soul and make the resulting union more complete; but this has never happened, and women's incapacity even for friendship makes it virtually impossible. Whereas friendship is a steady warmth, love (which for Montaigne means sexual desire) is a fitful flame. Least successful is the marriage based on beauty and desire. It needs a more solid and stable base; ardor is no good for it. The ultimate absurdity is for a man to marry a woman he has enjoyed as his mistress; Montaigne's comment on this is pungent.

Nor is this all. In Montaigne's eyes, the wantonness of ordinary sexual love is an offense against the dignity of marriage, "a kind of incest" when employed "in this venerable and sacred alliance," this "religious and holy bond." Our pleasure should be restrained, serious, and austere; since the aim of marriage is generation, perhaps we should not make love to our wives except for that purpose. If any excessively eager husbands still exist, they should know that philosophy and theology alike command restraint. "Those shameless excesses that our first heat suggests to us in this sport are not only indecently but detrimentally practiced on our wives. Let them at least learn shamelessness from another hand. They are always aroused enough for our need."

Feeling as he does, Montaigne naturally reveals little about his sexual relations with his wife. "I have never," he says, "followed in that any but the simple instruction of nature." He advises married people to make love infrequently and take their time when they do. He says he likes to sleep alone and without a woman (or without his wife: *sans femme* could mean either), and that advancing years have so enslaved him to habit that "I cannot, without an effort . . . make a child except before going to sleep, or"—curious limitation in this austere relationship—"make one standing up." One remark which seems to stress a wife's sexual appetite sounds as though it applied to his own:

We have not made a bargain, in getting married, to keep continually tied to each other by the tail, like some little animals or other that we see, or like the bewitched people of Karenty, in doglike fashion. And a wife should not have her eyes so greedily fixed on the front of her husband that she cannot see the back of him, if need be.

For all his outspokenness, Montaigne was extremely bashful about exposing to anyone at all "the members and acts that our custom orders us to cover up." This modesty extended to his wife. His friend and successor in the Parlement, Florimond de Raemond, in a marginal note on his copy of the *Essays*, marvels at the austerity that he reports:

I have often heard the author [Montaigne] say that although he, full of love, ardor, and youth, had married his very beautiful and very lovable wife, yet the fact is that he had never played with her except with respect for the honor that the marriage bed requires, without ever having seen anything but her hands and face uncovered, and not even her breast, although among other women he was extremely playful and debauched. I refer the truth of what I say about this to his conscience.

The only letter we have from Montaigne to Françoise is his dedication (1570) of La Boétie's translation of Plutarch's "Letter of Consolation to His Wife." As they neared their fifth anniversary, their long-awaited first child, Thoinette, had just died at the age of two months. Montaigne's greeting suggests a cordial understanding:

My wife, you understand very well that it is not the act of a gallant man, according to the rules of the present day, still to pay court and show affection to you. For they say that an intelligent man may well take a wife, but that to espouse her is for a fool to do.
Let us let them talk. For my part I hold to the simple ways of the old days—as indeed my hair is beginning to show. And in truth innovation has been costing this poor state so dear up to now (and yet I do not know if the bidding will not go still higher), that in every way and every place I give it up. You and me, my wife, let us live in the old French way.

He goes on to tell how he received from the dying La Boétie, "that dear brother and inviolable companion of mine," his papers and books, now the most treasured adornment of his library, and wants to communicate them to his friends, among whom "I have, so I believe, none more intimate than you." He regrets the appropriateness of his present, praises Plutarch for saying all that he could have said but better, commends himself very strongly to her good graces, and signs himself "Your good husband."

Any good effect of this cordial letter must have been annulled by the clumsiest of blunders. The baby had lived about two months; the printed text regrets that "you had to lose her in the second year of her life." It is hard to say how much Montaigne is to blame for the slip. He was unconcerned about having children and cared little about them until they began to be persons. Once he wrote of losing "two or three" as though not even sure of his count. Though he seems wistful over having no son, he would probably rather have produced a perfectly formed child "by intercourse with the muses than by intercourse with my wife." Moreover, it is hard to imagine the printer of his letter mistaking *an* (year) for *mois* (month).

On the other hand, our only authority for the error is Montaigne himself. Less careless about his children's births and deaths than we might suppose, he recorded them all in his copy of Beuther's *Ephemeris*. His laconic style, natural for such a register, suggests controlled feeling, not a lack of it.

June 28.   1570. There was born to Françoise de La Chassaigne and to me a daughter, whom my mother and President de La Chassaigne, my wife's father, surnamed Thoinette. She is the first child of my marriage and died two months later.

September 9.   In the year 1571, around two o'clock in the afternoon, Françoise de La Chassaigne, my wife, was delivered at Montaigne of my daughter Léonor, second child of our marriage, whom Pierre Eyquem de Montaigne lord of Gaujac and my sister Léonor baptized.

July 5.   In the year 1573 around five o'clock in the morning there was born to Françoise de La Chassaigne, my wife, and to me, at Montaigne, a daughter who was the third child of our marriage. Monsieur l'abbé de Verteuil, my wife's uncle, and Mademoiselle de Mons held her on the fonts in the chapel here and named her Anne. She lived only seven weeks.

December 27.   1574. There was born to Françoise de la Chassaigne, my wife, and me a daughter, fourth child of our marriage. Died about three months later and was baptized in a flurry under pressure of necessity.*

May 16.   1577. There was born to Françoise de La Chassaigne, my wife, the fifth child of our marriage. It was a girl, who died one month later. My brother, lord of Mattecoulon, and my sister Marie baptized her without ceremony.

* The names of this and the next daughter are not known.

February 21. 1583. We had one more daughter, who was named Marie, baptized by the lord of Javerlhac, councillor in the court of the Parlement, her uncle, and my daughter Léonor. She died a few days later.

It seems likely that Montaigne and his wife reacted quite differently to all these losses; his expressions of relative unconcern may well be responses to what he considered her excessive distress. If so, they had a share in pushing the two spiritually apart.

The occasional glimpses that Montaigne gives us of his family life reveal little but suggest an amiable household. "We have just now at my house," he once writes, "been playing a game to see who could find the most things that meet at their two extremes: as Sire is a title that is given to . . . the king, and is also given to the vulgar, as to tradesmen, and applies to no one in between." Card games with his wife and daughter are no rarity: "I handle the cards and keep score for a couple of pennies just as for double doubloons; when winning or losing, against my wife and daughter, is indifferent to me, just as when playing for keeps." When he was being carried home from a dangerous collision on horseback with no memory and little consciousness, one of his first thoughts—though he discounts it as a reflex action—was to order a horse for his wife, who was having trouble on the steep, rugged road.

Montaigne and his wife agreed fully on bringing up their only surviving child gently. Convinced that force can do nothing that reason, wisdom, and tact cannot, and having himself as a child felt the rod "only twice, and that very softly," Montaigne favors mildness: "I have owed the same to the children I have had; they all die on me at nurse; but Léonor, one single daughter who escaped that misfortune, is over six years old now,* and has never been guided or punished for her childish faults—her mother's indulgence easily concurring—by anything but words, and very gentle ones." He believes that girls must be brought up by women, and keeps his hands off, though not without an occasional ironic smile:

My daughter (she is the only child I have) is at the age at which the laws allow the most ardent of them [women] to marry. She is of a backward constitution, slight and soft, and has been brought up by her mother ac-

* Another of Montaigne's erratic dates. Since this passage first appeared in 1588 (not 1580 or 1582), Léonor was presumably at least eleven when this was written.

cordingly, in a retired and private manner; so that she is now only just beginning to grow out of the naïveté of childhood.

She was reading a French book in my presence. The word *fouteau* * occurred, the name of a familiar tree. The woman she has to train her stopped her short somewhat roughly and made her skip over that perilous passage. I let her go ahead in order not to disturb their rules, for I do not involve myself at all in directing her: the government of women has a mysterious way of proceeding; we must leave it to them. But if I am not mistaken, the company of twenty lackeys could not have imprinted in her imagination in six months the understanding and use and all the consequences of the sound of those wicked syllables as did this good old woman by her reprimand and interdict. . . .

Montaigne considers women poor educators and heads of families, whose preference among children shows a "disordered appetite and sick taste" and goes always "to the weakest and most ill-favored, or to those, if they have any, who are still hanging about their necks." He deplores the passion which makes some people, presumably women, hug infants when they are barely born and have nothing to make them lovable. "I have not," he adds, "willingly suffered them to be brought up near me." Infants are best reared naturally, as he was: not by their parents, certainly not by their mothers. A widow should govern her family only until her sons are grown; for unless they have been badly brought up, they will then be wiser than she, "seeing the ordinary weakness of the sex."

In marriage as everywhere, Montaigne wants self-sufficiency and privacy. Early in his retirement it is the former that he stresses more: "We must reserve a back shop all our own, entirely free, in which to establish our real liberty and our principal retreat and solitude. . . . Here we must talk and laugh as if without wife, without children, without possessions, without retinue and servants, so that, when the time comes to lose them, it will be nothing new to us to do without them." Later his love of privacy makes him rejoice that his tower gives him such a "back shop" and makes it a little hard to reach and out of the way.

There is my throne. I try to make my authority over it absolute, and to withdraw this one corner from all society, conjugal, filial, and civil. Everywhere else I have only a verbal authority, essentially divided. Sorry the man, to my mind, who has not in his own home a place to be all by himself,

---

* *Fouteau* means *beech* but suggests forms of the verb *foutre*, whose primary meaning is "to have sexual intercourse."

to pay his court privately to himself, to hide. . . . I find it measurably more endurable to be always alone than never to be able to be alone.

There have been few more reluctant householders than Montaigne. Although the task is less difficult than annoying, it is not for him; he came to it too late to learn to like it.

At home I am responsible for all that goes wrong. Few masters—I am speaking of those of medium condition like me, and if there are any, they are more fortunate—can rely so much on another that a good part of the load does not remain on their shoulders. That tends to make me less gracious in entertaining visitors—and I may perhaps have kept one or another of them here more by my kitchen than by my graciousness, as bores do—and takes away much of the pleasure I should derive at home from the visits and gatherings of my friends.

Running the household is the wife's job; skill at it (which few have, though Madame de Montaigne appears to be one) is her greatest asset.

Don't tell me! From what experience has taught me, I require of a married woman, above all other virtues, the virtues of a good housewife. I place my wife in a position to show these, leaving the entire government of my affairs in her hands by my absence. . . . If the husband provides the matter, Nature herself wills that the wife provide the form.

Since his wife seems to lack the virtue of economy, Montaigne is more involved in household matters than he likes: "My presence, ignorant and uninterested as I am, is very helpful in my domestic affairs. I take part in them, but grudgingly. Besides, there is this about my household, that while I burn the candle privately at my end, the other end is not spared in the least."

One of the joys of travel is freedom from domesticity; but this is an expensive luxury; since Montaigne likes to make his trips with a "decent" retinue, he must postpone them until "skimmings and reserves" come to hand. Though he trusts his wife to manage in his absence, he would not turn to her for permanent relief. He would like to find a son-in-law "in whose hands I could deposit full sovereignty over the management and use of my possessions, that he might do with them as I do, and enjoy my present profits in my place."

The main trouble with running a household is the countless petty knaveries and other such vexations:

Trivial pinpricks: sometimes trivial, but always pinpricks. . . . The throng of petty troubles pains us more than the violence of a single one, however great it may be. The more crowded and sharp these domestic thorns are, the

more sharply and without warning they prick us, easily catching us unawares. . . .

Life is a tender thing and easy to disturb. . . . These regular drippings
wear me down.

A constant problem in the household is anger. Montaigne holds
that while it grips us we should never punish a servant; but, recognizing the danger of suppressed resentment, he is as candid with his
family as he can be: "We incorporate anger by hiding it. . . . I advise that we rather give our valet a slap on the cheek a little out of
season than strain our inclination to represent this wise bearing. . . .
My passions . . . grow languid when they have vent and expression." Thus when he gets angry, he does so "as keenly, but also as
briefly and privately, as I can." He loses his temper in haste and violence, but normally only with his tongue, and always pertinently; less
on great occasions than on small. What disturbs him about "those
in my family who have the right to get angry" (which seems to mean
mainly his wife; his mother was probably living elsewhere) is lack of
gradation and direction:

The scolding you give a servant for stealing is not felt, because it is the
very same that he has heard you use against him a hundred times for a
glass badly rinsed or a stool badly placed. I admonish . . . my family not to
get angry in the air, and to see to it that their reprimand reaches the person
they are complaining about: for ordinarily they are yelling before he is in
their presence and continue yelling for ages after he has left. . . . No one is
punished or affected by it, except someone who has to put up with the racket
of their voice.

The strongest suggestion that countless "pinpricks" have made
Montaigne weary of his wife is the final item in a list of domestic
annoyances: the poverty and oppression of your tenants, a quarrel
between neighbors, their encroachments on you, the rigors of the
weather and the resultant gloom of your steward: "Add to that the
new and well-shaped shoe of the man of days gone by, which hurts
your foot; and the fact that a stranger does not understand how much
it costs you and how much you sacrifice to keep up that appearance
of order which people see in your family, and that perhaps you buy
it too dear." The story of the well-shaped shoe appears twice in Plutarch: once in the "Rules of Marriage," of which Montaigne had
published La Boétie's translation, and more fully in the "Life of
Aemilius Paulus," where the account is this:

A Roman once divorced his wife, and when his friends admonished him, saying: "Is she not discreet? is she not beautiful? is she not fruitful?" he held out his shoe . . . saying: "Is this not handsome? is it not new? but no one of you can tell me where it pinches my foot." For, as a matter of fact, it is great and notorious faults that separate many wives from their husbands; but the slight and frequent frictions arising from some unpleasantness or incongruity of characters, unnoticed as they may be by everybody else, also produce incurable alienations in those whose lives are linked together.

Here is the lesson Plutarch draws in the "Rules of Marriage":

A wife, then, ought not to rely on her dowry or birth or beauty, but on things in which she gains the greatest hold on her husband, namely conversation, character, and comradeship, which she must render not perverse or vexatious day by day, but accommodating, inoffensive and agreeable. For . . . it is the petty, continual, daily clashes between man and wife, unnoticed by the great majority, that disrupt and mar married life.

Finally, one of the most vexing things about marital irritations is the difficulty of getting them off our chest:

The bitternesses of marriage, like the sweets, are kept secret by the wise. And among the other annoying conditions that are found in it, this, for a talkative man like myself, is one of the main ones: that custom makes it improper and prejudicial to communicate to anyone all that we know and feel about it.

Although Montaigne clearly found many "domestic thorns" in marriage, he has many good things to say about it. "A good marriage . . . is a sweet association of life, full of constancy, trust, and an infinite number of useful and solid services and mutual obligations. . . . If you form it well and take it rightly, there is no finer relationship in our society. We cannot do without it, and yet we go about debasing it." He has no wish for conjugal enmity: "I am too soft for such thorny plans." He is less opposed to matrimony than when he went into it; he has followed its laws better than he had promised or expected. "It is treachery," he writes, "to get married without getting wedded." He knows that he should be thankful for his household and estate and should enjoy them more:

"What do you lack? Is not your house open to fine healthy air, sufficiently furnished, and more than sufficiently capacious? Royal majesty with all its pomp has put up there more than once. Are there not more families below yours in orderliness than there are above it in eminence? Is some extraordinary and indigestible domestic worry festering in you? . . . If a man has no contentment with such just occasion for it, where does he expect to find it?"

All his talk about wanting to get away now and then clearly reflects the pressure on him to stay and is partly caused by it. He rightly argues that he loves his home and family the better for an occasional vacation: "Marital love . . . is readily cooled by too continual association, and harmed by assiduity. . . . These interruptions fill me with a fresh love for my family and give me back a sweeter enjoyment of my home."

Probably the best summary is a remark of Montaigne's, made after about twenty years of marriage, whose banality has concealed the significance of the balance it suggests.

> Whoever supposes, to see me look sometimes coldly, sometimes lovingly, on my wife, that either look is feigned, is a fool.

In short, the clear and central evidence shows Montaigne's marriage to have been neither miserable nor delightful, basically satisfactory, though—whenever it encroached on his freedom—often irritating.

His more general remarks about wives and marriage are normally sardonic. He begins his chapter "Of Three Good Wives" (II: 35): "They don't come by the dozen, as everyone knows, and especially in the duties of marriage." Wedlock, to him, is a battleground in the war between the sexes:

> Wives always have a proclivity for disagreeing with their husbands. They seize with both hands every pretext to go contrary to them; the first excuse serves them as plenary justification. . . . No responsibility seems to them to have sufficient dignity if it comes by the husband's concession. They have to usurp it either by cunning or by insolence, and always unjustly, to give it grace and authority.

Since he wishes he could keep up a good talk with a carpenter or a gardener, it is probably in his own family that he finds the "mean and sickly minds" which weaken and erode our own: "There is no contagion that spreads like that one. I know by enough experience how much it is worth per yard." Reason has no power against unreasonable women: "They love themselves best wherever they are most in the wrong. Unfairness allures them." The way to treat headstrong women is to infuriate them, as we do "when we oppose silence and coldness to their agitation, and disdain to feed their rage." A shrewish wife is a stiff trial of patience. Whereas Epaminondas took pride in his duel with poverty, Socrates, in Montaigne's opinion, "tested himself still more roughly, keeping for his exercise the malignity of his wife, which is a test with the naked blade."

Jealousy in a wife, which Montaigne claims to know, "at least by sight," is the worst vice of all:

I do not know if a man can suffer anything worse from them than jealousy. It is the most dangerous of their conditions, as the head is of their members. Pittacus used to say that everyone had his weakness, and that his was his wife's bad temper: except for that, he would consider himself happy in every respect. It is a very grievous misfortune where a man so just, so wise, so valiant, feels the whole state of his life altered by it; what are we small fry to do?

A pet aversion of Montaigne's is insincere mourning, which he sees all about him:

In our age wives more commonly reserve the display of their good offices and the vehemence of their affection toward their husbands until they have lost them. . . . They prove by that rather that they love them only dead.
. . . They may tear their hair and scratch themselves in vain; I go straight to the ear of a chambermaid or a secretary: "How did they get on? How did they live together?"
. . . Is it not enough to make me come back to life out of spite, to have someone who spat in my face while I existed come and rub my feet when I am beginning to exist no longer?

Montaigne talks much about cuckoldry, always to affirm that there is no real dishonor in it for the victim: "I know a hundred honorable men who are cuckolded, honorably and not very discreditably." It is possible, as some suspect, that he is covertly alluding to himself. However, his scruples about personal references do not keep him from making harsh allusions (like the "well-shaped shoe") by indirection in other areas; and he is fully capable of concern over problems not confronting himself. Not one of his remarks about cuckoldry sounds like a reference to a plight of his own.

Considering all the evidence about Montaigne's marriage—clear and dubious, central and peripheral—and allowing for the influence of an old literary and masculine tradition, we must conclude that he found it a fairly even mixture of satisfaction and frustration,

better than he had expected, but one in which the roses were out-
numbered by the thorns.

Did Madame de Montaigne ever read the *Essays* during her husband's life? She came from a learned family, and her brother Geoffroy
borrowed from them; she honored them and served them well after
her husband died; but his increasingly free allusions to the trials of
marriage suggest to me that she did not read them. Were the two
intellectually close enough for him to have been tempted to encourage her to? It seems unlikely. If he ever was, his diffidence about his
plan before the *Essays* were first published in 1580 may have checked
him until too late. Her concern about the book after his death is no
proof of acquaintance with it. Probably she took his word that he
was pottering about, up in his tower with all those books, on a bi-
zarre project that might well make him ridiculous. ("But what is it
you're writing about?" "Why, about me." "Oh . . .") Apparently
a dutiful and pious wife, she may never have read her husband's book.
If not, in many important ways she may have understood him less
well than have thousands of readers in his own time and since. And
this sums up the limits of the marriage.

Chapter 7: Translation, Inheritance, Retirement
[*1567–1571*]

ONTAIGNE's first published work was a translation, made at his father's behest, of the Latin *Book of Creatures, or Natural Theology* by the fifteenth-century Spaniard Raymond Sebond,* who taught medicine, theology, and philosophy at Toulouse in the 1430's and died there on April 29, 1436, after writing his book in the last two years of his life. We know little else about him.

Though not published for about fifty years (in 1484), the *Natural Theology* was a great success in Holland and Germany at first, and from 1509 on in France. It seeks to demonstrate all the truths of Christianity by the evidence of the creation, the book of nature, which Sebond claims is surer, more convincing, and more demonstrative than theology or even Scripture—though, as he later acknowledges, less lofty and authoritative than the latter. His main purpose was apparently to refute the fideism of the Nominalists, who opposed reason to faith.

* The name appears in many spellings including Sabaude, Sabonde, Sabunde, Sabiende, Sabieude, Sebon, Sebonde, Sebeyde, Sibiude. The one used here is the one Montaigne used.

Sebond opens with a Prologue * full of the highest claims for his doctrine, which he says can teach man in a few months, and infallibly, all he needs to know about the nature of God and man and the relation between them. The first of his 330 chapters, "Of the Ladder of Nature," sets forth his central observation and some of its consequences. Each member of God's creation has one or more of four faculties: being, life, feeling, and understanding. At the lowest level are inanimate objects, which have being alone; next vegetation, which also has life; then the animal kingdom, which has feeling as well; and at the top man, who alone has understanding, and with it free will. Since man did not make himself, he must have been created by a higher power, God, whose nature and infinite faculties Sebond deduces (ch. 3–45). God created the world out of no necessity and for himself alone; man is the only creature that can know him. From God's creation of the world there follows naturally his creation of his Son and of the Holy Spirit (46–55). Sebond then compares and contrasts man with the creatures of the lower levels (56–63). This comparison reveals the law that all creatures act, and should act, to their own advantage; and this law applies to belief in Christ and to the main articles of Christian faith (64–81).

From a consideration of free will, which separates man from the animals (82–83), Sebond moves to man's obligations toward God (84–96), not only for himself but for all creation, since it is all made for him (97–101). Man's nature reveals this debt (102–108), which he can repay in just one way, by love (109–112). The behavior of the creatures toward us can show us our duty toward God (113–119); our love of God should lead us to love men, our brothers and fellow images of God (120–128). Since love ennobles or debases the will, according as the thing loved is good or bad (129–136), and since our first love must be either for God or for ourselves (137–140), all our goodness and happiness, or evil and misery, in this world and the next, follow from our choice of our first love (141–165). From our duty to love God follow other duties: to hate our own self-love even as we fear, honor, and glorify God (165–205). In these lie our highest advantage and happiness.

God's care for his own honor is one of the proofs that Jesus Christ is truly his Son (206). Christianity is founded in truth (207–210). The tone of the Bible bespeaks God's authorship; for, as

* He calls it "Prologue"; Montaigne calls it "Préface."

befits him, he does not argue but asserts, does not prove but commands (211–217). The nature of angels (218–222) bears a resemblance to that of man, whose perpetual disobedience to his Creator is a proof of his fall from original innocence, perfection, bliss, and dominion over creation (223–235). Woman was more to blame for this than man, but both were seduced by that fallen angel, the devil, into his power and that of sin (236–252). Man's slavery could be ended only by the Redemption (253–269), which sets the Christian free (270–280). To give man this continuing grace, Jesus instituted the seven sacraments. Sebond examines these individually at great length (281–321) before showing in conclusion the necessity and desirability of the Last Judgment (322–330).

A good summary of the ground covered up to the final argument is provided by Sebond himself:

> Since, as I was saying at the beginning, this book, or this knowledge, is about man, I am obliged to omit nothing that concerns his state and his progress in any way. Now up to the present I have taught him to know himself, I have taught him how God had made him, how God had made all things for him, how he was extremely obligated for this, and with what coin he should acquit his debt; I have shown that, in that he is a man, he is subject to punishment or recompense for his works; I have treated his duty, his fall and his reparation, the sacraments which bring and lead him back to his first state and make him apt to do works that are good and worthy of him.

How did Montaigne come to translate the book? The earliest evidence is his dedication of the translation to his father, dated June 18, 1568. Here he says he has worked for about a year, at his father's behest, to clothe Sebond's lofty conceptions in a civilized garb:

> Sir, in carrying out the task you set me last year at your home at Montaigne, I have cut out and trimmed with my own hand for Raymond Sebond, that great Spanish theologian and philosopher, a costume in the French style, and have stripped him, as well as I could, of that wild bearing and barbaric demeanor that you saw in him at first; so that in my opinion he has enough style and *savoir-faire* to present himself in any good company. . . .
> . . . To you he owes all the improvement and correction he has here. However . . . if you are pleased to have a reckoning with him, it will be you that will owe him much in the end. For in exchange for his excellent and very religious arguments, his lofty and as it were divine conceptions . . . you for your part have brought to him only words and language: a merchandise so vulgar and so vile that the more of it a man has, the less, peradventure, he is worth.

About ten years later, however, Montaigne offers a fuller account in his longest essay (II: 12), entitled "Apology for Raymond Sebond." His father, he now tells us, worshiped learned men and loved to entertain them "with all the more reverence and religion as he was less qualified to judge them; for he had no knowledge of letters." One such man, Pierre Bunel, a guest at Montaigne for a few days with some others, gave him Sebond's book as a parting present.

And because the Italian and Spanish languages were familiar to my father, and this book was composed in a Spanish scrambled up with Latin endings, Bunel hoped that with a very little help he could make his profit of it, and recommended it to him as a very useful book and suited to the time in which he gave it to him; this was when the innovations of Luther were beginning to gain favor and to shake our old belief in many places.

In this he was very well advised. . . .

Now some days before his death, my father, having by chance come across this book under a pile of other abandoned papers, commanded me to put it into French for him. It is nice to translate authors like this one, where there is hardly anything but the matter to reproduce. . . . It was a very strange and a new occupation for me; but being by chance at leisure at the time, and being unable to disobey any command of the best father there ever was, I got through it as best I could; at which he was singularly pleased, and ordered it to be printed; and this was done after his death.

Montaigne goes on to praise Sebond for fulfilling his "bold and courageous" purpose—of proving all the articles of Christianity by human and natural reason—as well as can be done, and to tell of asking Adrianus Turnebus about this unknown author and his work.

There are curious things about all this. Montaigne now suggests that his translation was a labor of merely "some days" (or "a few days": *quelques jours*) and almost pure accident: the book was under a pile of other abandoned papers, his father came across it by chance and commanded him to translate it, he happened to be at leisure at the time and could not refuse. Yet a thousand-page book would take more than a few days to translate, especially for a novice; and Montaigne's interest in it, on his own showing, must go back at least to before June 12, 1565, the day Turnebus died. When Montaigne wrote this part of the "Apology" (probably around 1579) he was clearly ill at ease as the champion of Sebond and anxious to ascribe his association with him to chance.

His opinion of the book and its author when he translated it is less clear: apparently better, but in some ways similar. His praise of

Sebond in his dedication is high indeed, unlike his manner in the "Apology." His translation, free in detail, is in general very faithful. However, in translating the Prologue he sharply reduces Sebond's extravagant claims, as the following passage will show. The parts radically altered by Montaigne in translation are here italicized and followed by the sense of Sebond's original text in square brackets.

There follows the doctrine of the book of creation, or book of Nature: . . . a doctrine *suitable, natural, and useful to every man* [which is necessary to every man, and natural and suitable to him], by which he is enlightened to know himself, his Creator, and *almost everything* [everything] for which he is responsible as a man. . . .
    Besides, this doctrine teaches every man to see with his own eyes, without difficulty or pains, *the truth, as far as this is possible to natural reason* [every truth necessary to man], for the knowledge of God and of himself . . . *gives him great access to the understanding of what the Holy Scriptures prescribe for him and command him* [And by this knowledge man knows, without difficulty and in reality, whatever is contained in the Holy Scripture; and whatever is said and prescribed in the Holy Scripture, by this knowledge is known infallibly, with great certainty . . .], and brings it about that human understanding is *delivered from several doubts* [all doubt removed], and *boldly consents to what the Scriptures contain concerning the knowledge of God or of oneself* [assents to all the Holy Scripture, and is made certain, so that it cannot doubt about any question in this knowledge. And by this knowledge can be resolved every question that should be known both about God and about oneself, and this without difficulty].
    In this book are revealed *the* [all the] ancient errors of the pagans and infidel philosophers, and by its teaching *the Catholic faith* [all the Catholic faith, infallibly] is maintained and known. The creatures, joined together and coupled to one another . . . contain the knowledge that is *necessary for us before any other* [necessary].

    Other similar changes in the six-page Prologue are these: "The foundation of all the knowledge that is necessary to man" is translated "the little foundations of the doctrine that pertains to man"; "the foundation and root of all truth" is changed to "a fountain of salutary truth"; "this [knowledge] is the first and necessary to man" becomes simply "it is the first"; "this knowledge argues with infallible arguments, which no one can contradict" is rendered "It does not use obscure arguments, which need deep and long reflection"; and "he [the reader] will know more in less than a month from this knowledge than by studying the learned doctors for a hundred years" becomes "by this doctrine he will in a few months become learned and versed in many things, for the knowledge of which he would need to spend a long time in reading many books."

These changes clearly prove that Montaigne, even while translating Sebond, had serious misgivings about his claims to necessity, infallibility, and absolute truth. They may, however, spring from more than one motive. The *Natural Theology* had been placed on the 1558–59 Index of Prohibited Books; when this list was revised in 1564, the text was removed from the Index but the Prologue retained. In all probability Montaigne knew this. Concern to affirm his own orthodoxy by making the Prologue innocent (as far as we know it was never censured in his translation) was probably one of his motives; but it is virtually certain that the changes he made represented his own estimate of the book, for they all tally perfectly with his reservations about Sebond later in the "Apology."

To be sure, Montaigne found some congenial ideas in the *Natural Theology*. Among the major themes are man's natural inclination to seek truth; the importance of experience in the quest; the value of self-study as our proper starting point, principal domain, and point to which we must return. There are minor affinities on such subjects as glory, names and their relation to the objects they represent, and the rebellious nature of the male member. In these areas Sebond may well have had a modest influence on Montaigne's thinking. And despite his stress on man's glory as the kingpin of God's creation, he is firm in pointing out the other side: man's nullity compared to God (ch. 11), his vileness and misery if he sets his love on himself (200–201), the infinity and perfection of God (21–23), and the justice of our having to accept the Bible on Divine authority (209–212).

But the differences in thinking between the two men makes these affinities—which are mostly either minute or very general—unimpressive. Though Montaigne apparently esteemed Sebond more highly when he translated him than when he later undertook to defend him, he clearly saw the weakness of his optimistic dogmatism.

Then why did Montaigne undertake the considerable labor of translating this work of nearly a thousand pages?

The main reason is probably the obvious one: that his father set him this task (as he says in his dedication), perhaps (as he says twice in the "Apology") as an outright command.

Pierre Bunel must have left the book at Montaigne between
1538 and 1546. Young Michel, still a child, was probably not present.
Pierre de Montaigne had had a good grounding in Latin and an in-
direct refresher course when Michel was learning to prattle, but he
apparently read it only with difficulty. He may well have dipped
into the book and, already prejudiced in its favor by Bunel, been
much impressed with it. Active in public life when the book was
given to him, he may have returned to it after his term as mayor of
Bordeaux ended in 1556. His son had presumably read at least some
of it and discussed it with him before he consulted Turnebus about
it no later than 1565.

Pierre de Montaigne must have worried a good bit about his
brilliant but unproductive eldest son, who, even as a grown man, had
not found in the Bordeaux Parlement the function he needed. He
had arranged his marriage and settled him down; but his heir was a
reluctant householder and still childless. Translation was an important and honored occupation; witness the high repute of Jacques
Amyot, translator of Plutarch. Michel was at home with books as his
father never was; his Latin was as good as any man's. Pierre de Montaigne presumably set his son this task quite firmly, for his own
good, to give him something useful to do that might open up to him
new fields of activity. Their relationship was such, however, that he
would hardly have done so if his son had been strongly opposed to it.
Michel was presumably willing (though not eager), but needed the
spur of a command or a challenge to set him in motion. He probably
started work on the translation some time in 1567 and took a year or
a year and a half to complete it; for although the dedication is dated
June 18, 1568, the privilege is of October 27, and the date of completed printing is December 30. In the original text of the "Apology,"
after stating that his father liked the translation and ordered it to be
published, which was done after his death, Montaigne added "with
the nonchalance that may be seen by the infinite number of mistakes
left in it by the printer, who alone had charge of this." He suppressed this passage from 1582 on, having meanwhile (1581) published a second edition of his translation, carefully corrected, presumably by himself. In short, if he did not choose the role of translator, he took interest and pride in his version, even after the publication of his own "Apology for Raymond Sebond" and other *Essays*.

Montaigne had at least two good reasons of his own for doing his father's bidding. A lover and connoisseur of books, the friend of an erudite author and translator, he must have had some desire to try his hand at writing. Soon after publishing his translation, he multiplied dedicatory letters introducing La Boétie's works, then less than a year later retired and started to write a book of his own. Probably more important is the value he saw in Sebond's work, for all its weaknesses, as a peaceful but effective antidote to Protestantism and atheism. His concern about this problem appears clearly in 1570 in his dedicatory letter to Henri de Mesmes.

At least one earlier translator had held this view. Although Montaigne probably did not know an anonymous French translation of Sebond (1519), he apparently did know Jean Martin's French version (called *Natural Theology;* 1551) of the fifteenth-century Latin abridgment by Pierre Dorland, entitled first *Viola Animae* and later *Dialogi de Natura Hominis.*** Both these works had been well received; Martin's was reprinted in 1555 and 1566, Dorland's four times between 1544 and 1568. Martin had presented his as an aid to the faithful that would bring atheists back to the light.

The clearest sign that Montaigne shared Martin's view is in one of the few passages where he amplifies his author in translating him. Sebond's conclusion to chapter 208 had rather dryly noted the security arising from belief and the weakness of the arguments against it:

From all these things it follows that it is sure indeed to believe in Jesus Christ and follow him; and that it is indeed detestable and reproachable and in no way excusable not to believe in him; because those who do not believe can allege nothing in their favor, and have no argument against those who believe, and nothing can be alleged against the believers. Nor can God in heaven rebuke them for anything nor blame them nor confute them. For they have followed his Son and believed in him as sent by God, and if they have been or should have been deceived, they would have been deceived in the name of the Son of God, which the Supreme Deity could not allow.

In translating this Montaigne takes the bit in his teeth and launches into an eloquent contrast between the anxiety of unbelief and the joyful security of Christian belief:

All this teaches us clearly how much advantage and security there is in our religion, seeing that, even if we should err out of ignorance (which we

---

* *Violet of the Soul; Dialogues on the Nature of Man.*

cannot do, for it is incredible that God should have permitted an abuse so evident and so general to be born under the name of his Son), we would still be more excusable toward him, erring as a result of so many so pressing appearances, full of piety and reverence toward his divine authority, than those who disdain it [our religion] on the authority of their mere bare fancy, having nothing on their side but vain imaginings, nothing with any power to turn us aside or shake us. Now compare the condition of Christians, full of so many great fair hopes and so much trust, with that of infidels. Compare the repose and assurance that is in our soul with the turbulent, inconstant, and doubtful error that continually torments and martyrizes the understandings that have strayed from this holy belief, ignorant, doubting, and uncertain in what principally concerns them as men; for indubitably they cannot solve their problems except by imaginary opinion based on frail foundations subject to debate and controversy in a thousand ways: so that all that incessantly presents itself to their soul in this irresolution is a horror and frightful terror of the threats of God, a continual fear of having made a mistake in a matter in which the sovereign good and the ultimate evil of man are concerned; they incessantly ruminate and reconsider the great disparity between their condition and ours, and see, with great vexation and desperate remorse in their conscience, how from our mistake (if it were possible that there could be one) we can incur no danger and no loss, and the worst we can do is fall back merely into that same state which they hope and propose for themselves; whereas their state pushes and plunges them headlong into an abyss of unhappiness and eternal anguish.

The large part of this that is Montaigne's own proves clearly that in translating Sebond he hoped to coax the strayed sheep back into the fold.

Another thing the translation shows is Montaigne's literary skill before he started the *Essays*. Sebond is prolix and pedestrian, meager in resources and heavy-handed. He piles up synonyms and redundant phrases, repeats terms and formulas in awkwardly close proximity, moves from point to point with a relentlessly tedious string of *quoniam, quia,* and *quare*.* Montaigne assumes intelligence in his reader. As Coppin well says, he "lets in light and air," and with them clarity and movement. He gives the book life by bringing the reader and his own opponents into the discussion, as he will do so often in the *Essays*. Freshness and color come from his apt and abundant metaphors, for which Sebond is often merely a point of departure. Let one short sample of his style do for many. Sebond had written (ch. 108) that our debt to God is most manifest, "written

* Since, because, wherefore.

by the finger of God on every creature, on man himself, both body and soul; and it is patent to all, and anyone can read it in the book of nature." Montaigne translates thus: "God has written it in us, in our soul, in our body, in each creature; and then has stitched it eternally into the pages of the book of nature." If he had not gone on to write the *Essays*, we might pay more attention to his admirable translation.

The quality of his version allows us to check some of his later statements about his style. He likes to deprecate the irregularity of the *Essays*: "I would have done it better elsewhere, but the work would have been less my own. . . . My language has no ease or polish; it is harsh and disdainful, with a free and unruly disposition." At times he suggests, and once clearly states, that he cannot do otherwise: "If I should attempt to follow that other style that is even, smooth, and orderly, I could not attain it." Now if all he means by this is that he cannot write like Raymond Sebond, we may well agree and be thankful. But if he means what he seems to—that he cannot write orderly, controlled French prose—then his own translation convicts him of sacrificing candor to modesty. He could and did write this sort of prose, with every appearance of ease, as part of his apprenticeship. The freedom with which he treats the language in his maturity comes not from ineptitude but from mastery.

Pierre Eyquem lay dying at Montaigne while his son was in Paris attending to the publication of his translation. Michel had marveled at the agility with which that best of fathers, even in his sixties, leapt into the saddle in his furred gown, did a turn over a table on his thumb, and climbed the stairs to his room three or four at a time; but had also sorrowed at seeing him risk his health and indeed nearly lose his life on long and painful journeys as mayor of Bordeaux. At sixty-two Pierre had declared himself no longer fit for military duty. His son twice connects his death with the torment he suffered in his last seven years, "painfully dragging out the last years of his life." The timing of Pierre's second will, drawn up two full years after his son's marriage but only nine months before his own death, suggests that his health may then have just taken a turn for the worse; and its phrasing is that of a man gazing steadily at death from no great distance.

The fact that Montaigne dated from Paris the dedication of his translation to his father on the very day of the latter's death (presumably at Montaigne) is a natural source of speculation. His closing greeting ("Sir, I pray God to give you a very long and very happy life") suggests sheer coincidence, and the letter gives no hint of concern. It seems clear that Montaigne was in Paris at the time, hence unable to be at his father's deathbed. It seems likely that he had composed his dedication before his father died or at least before he knew of it, and decided, on hearing the news—as he did with his introduction to La Boétie's *Voluntary Servitude*—to let it stand as testimony of his feeling while he worked on the translation. The dating, if not coincidence, was probably Montaigne's way of explaining his absence and marking the dedication as his farewell to his father.

He must have returned home quite promptly; for barely two months later (August 22, 1568) he and his three adult brothers signed an agreement about their respective shares of the estate. Michel was the residuary legatee; Thomas, the next in age, inherited the noble house of Beauregard near Bordeaux, but on condition of paying 2,600 livres to the third brother, Pierre, who also received the "fief and territory" of La Brousse near Montaigne. The fourth brother, Arnaud, already lord of Saint-Martin, inherited all his father's possessions on the island of Macau, and got 1,700 livres tournois from Michel. The only other adult child, Jeanne de Lestonnac, had received a dowry when she married and had thus been excluded from any inheritance; the other three children, Léonor, Marie, and Bertrand, were still minors. The document suggests a thoroughly friendly agreement.

Nine days later there was a less pleasant settlement, the one between Montaigne and his mother, which spelled out so specifically her rights in the household—and their limitations.

Arrangements such as these concerning his estate explain why Montaigne, busy at home, left it to the printer in Paris to handle alone the publication of the Sebond translation, which appeared— probably quite early—in 1569.

Some time late in 1568 or early in 1569—probably in April or May, 1569—came the shocking accident to Montaigne's twenty-seven-year-old brother, captain Arnaud, struck over the ear by a ball while playing court tennis and dead five or six hours later of apoplexy brought on by the blow. There followed on May 23 the curious incident, discussed in our last chapter, of the gold chain.

Around this time (probably late 1569, possibly early 1570) Montaigne himself had a close brush with death when he was knocked hard off his horse in an accidental collision on a narrow lane with a bigger man on a bigger horse. It was on this occasion that the semi-conscious Michel thought to order a horse for his wife. We shall return to this accident later.

Montaigne's solicitude need not, but may well, have been caused by his wife's pregnancy; for it must have been around the end of September, 1569, during the long vacation from the Bordeaux Parlement, that their first child was conceived, the ill-fated Thoinette, born June 28, 1570, dead two months later.

It was on his return to the Parlement from this long vacation, on November 14, 1569, that Montaigne sought to be promoted from the Chambre des Enquêtes, and was declared ineligible for either higher chamber because of a brother-in-law in the Grand' Chambre and a father-in-law in the Tournelle. Rather than seek a dispensation from the king, he chose to resign, and sold his position on April 10, 1570 to Florimond de Raemond. The king legalized the transaction by letters patent dated July 23, and Raemond was sworn in to the Parlement on October 2.

For all the importance of these events of 1570—birth of a first child, retirement from the Bordeaux Parlement after thirteen long years—the activity that involved Montaigne most was the publication of La Boétie's works. Just twenty days after signing his contract with Raemond, Michel dated from Montaigne (April 30, 1570) his dedications respectively to Michel de L'Hôpital, Chancellor of France, and Henri de Mesmes of the king's Privy Council, of La Boétie's Latin poems and his translation of Plutarch's "Rules of Marriage." Montaigne resigned his councillorship into the hands of the king by means of an agent; this was not occasion enough to bring him to Paris; but the publication of La Boétie's works took him there either twice or for one long stay in the late summer of 1570. His task included locating everything of La Boétie's that he could— as he had been doing for seven years since his friend's death—as well as composing the dedications and editing the works.

Less than six months later Montaigne celebrated his thirty-eighth birthday by having painted, on the wall of the little room next to his library-study, a Latin inscription commemorating his retirement and representing his life up to then as a slavery to the cares of court and Parlement, from which at last he was escaping to invite his soul in peace and freedom.

In the year of Christ 1571, at the age of thirty-eight, on the last day of February, anniversary of his birth, Michel de Montaigne, long weary of the servitude of the court and of public employments, while still entire, retired to the bosom of the learned Virgins,* where in calm and freedom from all cares he will spend what little remains of his life now more than half run out. If the fates permit he will complete this abode,† this sweet ancestral retreat; and he has consecrated it to his freedom, tranquillity, and leisure.

Montaigne's new leisure was to be neither uninterrupted nor an unmixed blessing; but out of it were to come the *Essays*.

* The Muses.
† His château.

HE FRENCH COUNTRY GENTLEMAN of the sixteenth century was no longer a puissant feudal lord and not yet a comic clod or foppish courtier. Generally he mistrusted city and court and chose to live on the land, which repaid his love, its absolute value rising throughout the century while money sank to one third its worth. His life centered in his home. His class, alone entitled to bear arms, administered much local justice and made up most of the army, in which, as at court, they still served only three months a year. Living close to the soil, personally concerned with their cattle and poultry, vines and other crops, they were on friendly man-to-man terms with their peasants, with whom they shared the benefits and blows of the weather. Little affected by the new learning, their energy sought mainly physical outlets and enjoyed food and wine, women, strenuous sports, dances, and practical jokes, with coarse gaiety. Lawsuits and even armed fights, often over minor prerogatives, testify to their combativity.

The religious civil wars did much to uproot them. They were often called to arms; heavy expenses and poor pay—if any—drove them into debt; the devastation of the country hit them hard. Catherine de' Medici worked to weaken them to the advantage of the crown, drawing them to court and army, multiplying the administrators responsible only to the king. Thus from the 1560's on many country nobles, trained for arms alone, turned to battling and often mere banditry, even in times of official peace. After 1576, with three parties claiming allegiance, there was always a pretext for trouble. By the end of the century the nobility had almost lost its identity as enforcer of peace and justice.

Montaigne was not a typical noble, but he had much in common with his many friends who were. Fond as he was of travel and—despite his Latin inscription—of the court, he spent most of his time at home. Most of his transactions were in land and its products. Without augmenting his estate, he did not deplete it. He cares for his peasants without condescension and respects their courage. His gaiety is often simple and coarse. Though he claims to be "virgin of lawsuits," the records suggest otherwise. Though he took no part in lawlessness, he had harsh experience of it, and a brother was imprisoned for his role in a duel.

His fellow nobles differed widely in their attitude toward learning. Verse and song had been treasured long before in the courts of Provence and Champagne, and more recently Charles d'Orléans had been his country's finest poet after Villon. But the ideal of the learned noble, like other Renaissance phenomena, came to France mainly from Italy in such works as Castiglione's *Courtier* (1528). Erudition came in fashion under Francis I, fostered by his sister, Margaret of Navarre, who wrote poetry, plays, and tales. When Montaigne retired, the noble Ronsard was the greatest French poet; Du Bellay had been the second until his death. Charles IX addressed verses to Ronsard and sponsored the Academy of the Palace; Henry III revived this as the Academy of Poetry and Music. Chancellor Michel de L'Hôpital, Henri de Mesmes, and Paul de Foix were among the lettered nobles to whom Montaigne dedicated La Boétie's works. On the Protestant side were such men as Bèze and Du Plessis-Mornay. Friends nearer home included François de Candale and Montaigne's brother-in-law Geoffroy de La Chassaigne. Even warrior nobles like La Noue, Monluc, Brantôme were memoir writers.

On the other hand many nobles, especially of the oldest families, despised learning as fit only for the bourgeois. The great Constable

Anne de Montmorency was illiterate. Brantôme, whose château was fifty miles northeast of Montaigne, approves of Mattecoulon's conduct in his duel but likes to twit Michel as an ink-stained lover of peace. Telling of a man who practiced on the duke of Milan's portrait until one day he stabbed the duke seven times and killed him, he comments: "What an essay! I think the sieur de Montaigne never made or wrote the like among his." His preface to the story that the marquis de Trans gave the Order of Saint-Michel to Montaigne out of contempt, as he did to his own *maître d'hôtel,* is this: "We have seen councillors leave the Parlement, give up the gown and square bonnet, and start dragging a sword, and immediately load themselves with this collar, without any other manner of making war, as did the sieur de Montaigne, whose vocation was rather to continue with his pen, writing his *Essays,* than to change it for a sword that did not become him so well." Brantôme's position is extreme; when the noble Protestant leader La Noue urged soldiers to return to work once war is over, Brantôme called it evil "that the hands which have handled [arms] so nobly and so cleanly should sully and debase themselves by a mechanical plowing or a vile and dirty trade"; better that they leave the country—as he did—and serve abroad. Yet he is a more typical noble than Montaigne.

Pierre de Montaigne, first a soldier then a public official, revered the learning he lacked and obviously wanted it for his son Michel. How far his desire went we do not know; Michel, his third-born, may for a time have had an older brother destined for a specifically noble career.

Michel adored learning much less. The Pléiade poets had declared it a necessary apprenticeship that must be justified in use. The poet must devour the Greek and Latin masterpieces, incorporate them, convert them into blood and food. Montaigne has similar views on all education. What we learn we must digest and make our own, lest we become asses loaded with books. If learning is not moral, we are better off without it.

He may well have felt pushed toward two opposite extremes: military prowess and erudition. His desire to be a proper nobleman leads to much of his apparent anti-intellectualism. The fourth noble head of his house, he was only the second born Eyquem de Montaigne; and normally acceptance as a true noble came only in the third generation. He loves to contrast speaking well with doing well, calls culture the enemy of valor, lauds Sparta at the expense of Athens, and extols the aristocratic ability to command and to fight. Learning, he finds, is better applied "to conducting a war, governing a people, or gaining the friendship of a prince or a foreign nation, than to constructing a dialectical argument, pleading an appeal, or prescribing a mass of pills." The test of quality is courage against pain: "If we need not sleep on hard ground, sustain fully armed the heat of noon, feed on a horse or an ass, watch ourselves being sliced open and a bullet torn out from between our bones, let ourselves be sewn up again, cauterized, and probed, how shall we acquire the advantage that we wish to have over the common herd?" It is largely as brave commanders that Montaigne admires Alexander, Caesar, Cyrus, Epaminondas, François de Guise, Leonidas, Philopoemen, Pompey, and the Scipios. He would rather, he says, be a good horseman than a good logician.

The same desire explains some of his coyness about being a writer —he is "less a maker of books than of anything else," and would "rather be a fool in all respects" than employ his ability so badly— and some of his nobiliary vanity. He writes that his château "is my birthplace and that of most of my ancestors; they set on it their affection and their name"; but the name Montaigne came from the château, and his only ancestor born there was his father. He says that his family was "formerly surnamed Eyquem"; but he was the first to drop the surname. He likes to refer to himself as a soldier, and lauds the joys of military life, just as though this avocation had really been his career. Such talk, which gave Brantôme reason to sneer at his modest military record, reflects Montaigne's split feelings about what a nobleman should be.

For although he calls the military profession "the proper, the only, the essential, form of nobility in France," he condemns the French overemphasis on valor in a man as he does that on chastity alone in a woman. He regrets that his main contacts are with men "who have little care for the culture of the soul, and to whom one can suggest no other blessing than honor, and no other perfection than valor." He is shocked by the conflict between justice and honor: "What could be more barbarous than that by the code of arms the man who endures an insult should be degraded from honor and nobility, and by the civil code he who avenges an insult should incur capital punishment? . . . And that of these two bodies . . . one should have charge of peace, the other of war; one should have gain as its share, the other honor; one knowledge, the other virtue; one words, the other action; one justice, the other valor; one reason, the other force; one the long robe, the other the short?"

These two pressures are suggested in an early essay when Montaigne chooses precisely these vocations of soldier and scholar to satirize:

The man you see climbing atop the ruins of that wall, frenzied and beside himself, a mark for so many harquebus shots; and that other, all scarred, pale and faint with hunger, determined to die rather than open the gates to him—do you think they are there for their own sake? They are there for the sake of a man whom perhaps they never saw, who is not in the least concerned about their doings, and who at that very moment is plunged in idleness and pleasures.

This fellow, all dirty, with running nose and eyes, whom you see coming out of his study after midnight, do you think he is seeking among his books how to make himself a better, happier, and wiser man? No such news. He is going to teach posterity the meter of Plautus' verses and the true spelling of a Latin word, or die in the attempt.

Montaigne at home means Montaigne in the book-lined study in his tower, where at dawn and sunset a great bell rings the *Ave Maria*. The room is well lighted; the windows look out in all directions. On the beams of the ceiling are fifty-odd quotations in Greek and Latin, probably inscribed early in his retirement, stressing man's frailty and ignorance but including, where Montaigne's eye fell on it often, Terence's statement of human solidarity:

Homo sum, humani a me nil alienum puto.*

He calls it handsome for a village library and claims to have a thousand volumes:

When at home, I turn aside a little more often to my library, from which at one sweep I command a view of my household. I am over the entrance, and see below me my garden, my farmyard, my courtyard, and into most of the parts of my house. There I leaf through now one book, now another, without order and without plan, by disconnected fragments. One moment I muse, another moment I set down or dictate, walking back and forth, these fancies of mine that you see here.

It is on the third floor of a tower; the first is my chapel, the second a bedroom and dressing room, where I often sleep in order to be alone. Above

* I am a man; I consider nothing human foreign to me.

it is a great wardrobe. In the past it was the most useless place in my house. In my library I spend most of the days of my life, and most of the hours of the day. I am never there at night. Adjoining it is a rather elegant little room, in which a fire may be laid in winter, very pleasantly lighted by a window. . . . Every place of retirement requires a place to walk. . . . My mind will not budge unless my legs move it. Those who study without a book are all in the same boat.

The shape of my library is round, the only flat side being the part needed for my table and chair; and curving round me it presents at a glance all my books, arranged in five rows of shelves on all sides. It offers free and rich views in three directions, and sixteen paces of free space in diameter.

In winter I am not there so continually; for my house is perched on a little hill, as its name indicates, and contains no room more exposed to the winds than this one, which I like for being a little hard to reach and out of the way, for the benefit of the exercise as much as to keep the crowd away. There is my throne.

If we place Montaigne mainly in his tower, we must not hold him to it. His best ideas never come to him there, but at table, in bed, and "mostly on horseback, where my thoughts range most widely." Books are a diversion from his proper work; he uses them little more than those who do not know them, and will always leave them for better company; but they do have the great advantage of being always there.

To see him truly we must see him in his favorite spot, on horseback; as Emerson said, "we can't afford to take the horse out of Montaigne's essays." He prefers it to coach or litter, even to walking; he was once good at riding post. He corrects his seat in the saddle by watching not a good rider but a bad one—a lawyer or a Venetian. Even in agony from the kidney stone he can hold out for ten hours on horseback; and when he bleeds from the kidneys at the slightest movements, he does not give up "moving about as before and pricking after my hounds with youthful and insolent ardor." If he could live his life as he wishes, "I should choose to spend it with my rear in the saddle."

A collision on horseback gives us a glimpse of Montaigne at home.

During our third civil war, or the second . . . I went riding one day about a league from my house, which is situated at the very hub of all the turmoil of the civil wars of France. Thinking myself perfectly safe . . . I took a very easy but not very strong horse. On my return . . . one of my men, big and strong, riding a powerful work horse . . . in order to show his daring and get ahead of his companions, spurred his horse at full speed up the path behind me, came down like a colossus on the little man and little horse, and hit us like a thunderbolt with all his strength and weight, sending us both head over heels. So that there lay the horse bowled over and stunned, and I ten or twelve paces beyond, dead, stretched on my back, my face all bruised and skinned, my sword, which I had had in my hand, more than ten paces away, my belt in pieces, having no more motion or feeling than a log. It is the only swoon that I have experienced to this day.

Those who were with me, after having tried all the means they could to bring me round, thinking me dead, took me in their arms and were carrying me with great difficulty to my house, which was about half a French league from there. On the way . . . I began to move and breathe. . . . They set me up on my feet, where I threw up a whole bucketful of clots of pure blood, and several times on the way I had to do the same thing. In so doing I began to recover a little life, but . . . my first feelings were much closer to death. . . .

When I began to see . . . I could still distinguish nothing but the light. . . . My doublet was stained all over with the blood I had thrown up. The first thought that came to me was that I had gotten a harquebus shot in the head; indeed several were being fired around us at the time of the accident. It seemed to me that my life was hanging only by the tip of my lips; I closed my eyes . . . to help push it out, and took pleasure in growing languid and letting myself go. It was an idea . . . not only free from distress but mingled with that sweet feeling that people have who let themselves slide into sleep. . . .

. . . From the first, while wholly unconscious, I was laboring to rip open my doublet with my nails (for I was not in armor); and yet I know that I felt nothing in my imagination that hurt me. . . . My stomach was oppressed with the clotted blood; my hands flew to it of their own accord. . . .

As I approached my house, where the alarm of my fall had already come, and the members of my family had met me with the outcries customary in such cases, not only did I make some sort of answer to what was asked me, but also (they say) I thought of ordering them to give a horse to my wife, whom I saw stumbling and having trouble on the road, which is steep and rugged. . . .

Meanwhile . . . I felt . . . a languor and an extreme weakness, without any pain. I saw my house without recognizing it. When they had put me to bed, I felt infinite sweetness in this repose, for I had been villainously yanked about by those poor fellows, who had taken the pains to carry me in their arms over a long and very bad road. . . . They offered me many remedies, of which I accepted none, holding it for certain that I was mortally wounded in the head. It would, in truth, have been a very happy death. . . .

When I came back to life and regained my powers . . . two or three hours later, I felt myself all of a sudden caught up again in the pains . . .

and I felt so bad two or three nights after that I thought I was going to die all over again, but by a more painful death; and I still feel the effect of the shock of that collision.

. . . The last thing I was able to recover was the memory of this accident; I had people repeat to me several times where I was going, where I was coming from, at what time it had happened to me, before I could take it in. As for the manner of my fall, they concealed it from me and made up other versions for the sake of the man who had been the cause of it. But . . . the next day, when my memory came to open up and picture to me the state I had been in at the instant I had perceived that horse bearing down on me (for I had seen him at my heels and thought I was a dead man, but . . . I had no time to be afraid), it seemed to me that a flash of lightning was striking my soul with a violent shock, and that I was coming back from the other world.

All around Montaigne's château are birds and animals. He has a strong sense of kinship with them, placing us neither above them nor below, and recognizing some difference, but "under the aspect of one and the same nature." His distaste for cruelty to them is rare in an age of hunting: "I have not even been able without distress to see pursued and killed an innocent animal which is defenseless and which does us no harm. . . . I hardly take any animal alive that I do not give it back the freedom of the fields." We owe them kindness as fellow creatures, virtual equals with feelings like our own; Montaigne cannot refuse to play with his dog if he asks for it even outside the proper time, and his cat makes him wonder who is playing with whom: "When I play with my cat, who knows if I am not a pastime to her more than she is to me? We entertain each other with reciprocal monkey tricks. If I have my time to begin or to refuse, so has she hers."

Montaigne tells how his father once saw a cat lock gazes with a bird on a treetop until "the bird let itself fall as if dead between the cat's paws, either intoxicated by its own imagination or drawn by some attracting power of the cat." He notes how neighborhood children are suckled by nanny goats, who come when called, but only to their own human nurslings; how hens and chickens fear certain animals and birds but not other larger ones: sparrow hawks but not geese, cats but not dogs. He tells of putting out to stud an old horse sated with his own mares but uncontrollable at the scent of others. He considers animals more beautiful than humans, and draws on observation for many examples of their intelligence in the "Apology."

In his many servants he considers mainly fitness for their functions, not whether his lackey is unchaste, his mule driver a gambler, or his cook profane. He regards it as unjust and inhuman to make much of rank, that "accidental privilege of fortune," knows we may learn from "a cowherd, a mason . . . a page's prank, a servant's blunder," and envies those "who know how to be familiar with the humblest of their retinue and carry on a conversation with their own servants." Unable to remember their names, he has to call them by their job or their region. When he scolds his valet, he does so wholeheartedly; but once finished, he will do him a favor if he needs one. Long in his service was a simple crude fellow who had spent many years among the cannibals in Brazil and who told him all about them, brought sailors and merchants who had been there to see him, and probably gave him some of their bread, which tasted sweet and a little flat. He has taken beggar boys into his service who soon went back to their former life; he found one gathering mussels in the dump and urged him, in vain, to return. He knows that they have "their splendors and their sensual pleasures" as well as the rich, and he wonders how they look at the world: "Thinking about the poor beggar at my door, often merrier and healthier than myself, I put myself in his place, I try to fit my mind to his bias."

He approves the French custom of placing noble children in other houses as pages, and laments the death of one of his when they fell among enemies: "They killed miserably, among others, an Italian page of mine, a gentleman, whom I was bringing up carefully; and in him was extinguished a very fine young life full of great promise."

In handling money he went through three stages. For almost twenty years since "childhood" he depended on others, often had to borrow, worried little, and was "never better off." Then—presumably after either his marriage (1565) or his father's death (1568)—he came into money, tried to provide for all emergencies, and worried constantly. After four or five years, the pleasure of a very costly trip pulled him out of this "vile and stupid" study of money, and since then he lives contentedly from day to day. In his eighteen years of managing an estate—and this not out of philosophical scorn but childish laziness—he has not been able to force himself really to study a title deed or his main affairs. "What would I not do rather than read a contract, rather than go and disturb those dusty masses of papers, a slave to my affairs?" He has none of the knowledge that a householder needs: "I cannot reckon. . . . Most of our coins I do not know; nor do I know the difference between one grain and another . . . the names of the chief household implements, or the roughest principles of agriculture. . . . I know still less of the mechanical arts, of trade and merchandise, of the diversity and nature of fruits, wines, and foods, and of how to train a bird, or doctor a horse or dog. . . . Not a month ago I was caught ignorant that leaven was used to make bread, and what was meant by fermenting wine. . . . If you give me all the equipment of a kitchen, I shall starve."

His house is always open; its only protection is an old-fashioned porter who does not so much defend the door as offer it with more decorum and grace. He marvels that it is still "virgin of blood and pillage, under so long a storm," and hopes it may not tempt marauders. When he flees before the plague in 1586, he leaves it unguarded and abandoned. Often threatened in it, even with death, he resents owing his escape to either the benignity of the great or his own and his ancestors' affability. "For what if I were different? If my conduct and the frankness of my dealings obligate my neighbors or my kinsmen, it is cruel that they can acquit themselves by letting me live, and say: 'We grant him leave to continue to hold the divine service freely in the chapel of his house, all the churches around having been emptied and ruined by us; and we grant him the use of his property, and his life, since he shelters our wives and our cattle in time of need.' "

Carefully trained in etiquette, whose forms, he notes, vary even from town to town, he could run a school of it and generally likes to follow it; but not at home, where everyone does as he pleases. If someone takes offense, he cannot help it; better to offend him once than himself every day; there is no use fleeing the servitude of courts if we then bring some of it "right home to our lair."

Indolence of taste . . . attaches me forcibly to solitude, even at home, in the midst of a numerous household and as many visitors as anywhere. I see enough people there, but rarely those with whom I like to converse; and there I reserve, both for myself and for others, an unusual freedom. There we have a truce on ceremony, on waiting on people and escorting them here and away, and other such troublesome prescriptions of our code of manners (oh, what a servile and bothersome practice!); everyone there behaves as he pleases; anyone who wants to, communes with his own thoughts; I remain mute, dreamy, and locked up in my thoughts, without my guests' taking offense.

Good talk is one of Montaigne's favorite occupations, and he deplores its rarity. Like the long concluding harangues, offers, and prayers in letters, in speech he hates "those verbose compliments imposed by the ceremonial laws of our etiquette." Unable to talk except in earnest, he lacks the knack of amusing the first comer, holding the attention of a group, or keeping a prince entertained: "Princes are not very fond of serious talk, nor I of telling stories." Conversations must have vigor and effort, and either weight and depth or pleasantness and beauty; in their absence, in abject and feeble small talk, "I make silly and stupid remarks and replies, ridiculous and unworthy of a child, or, still more awkwardly and impolitely, maintain an obstinate silence. I have a dreamy way of withdrawing into myself, and . . . a dull and childish ignorance of many common things. . . . Five or six stories can be truthfully told about me, as silly as can be told about any man whatever."

He devotes one whole chapter, a favorite of Pascal's, to "The Art of Discussion," which he considers so enjoyable and fruitful that he would rather even lose his sight than his hearing or speech. The study of books is tame, but discussion offers both instruction and exercise. Montaigne is bored by agreement but stimulated by "a stiff jouster": "No propositions astonish me, no belief offends me." Opposition arouses his attention, not his anger; wherever he finds truth, he welcomes it and surrenders to it cheerfully. However, he finds much discussion spoiled by pedantry, irrelevance, and desire to win at any cost:

One goes east, the other west; they lose the main point and mislay it in the throng of incidentals. After an hour of stormy argument, they do not know what they are looking for; one is low, another high, another wide of the mark. One man catches at a word or a simile. One is no longer aware of his opponent's points, so involved is he in the course of his argument; and he is thinking about following himself, not you. One man, finding his back too weak, fears everything, denies everything, mixes up and confuses the point from the outset, or, at the height of the debate, rebels and is flatly silent, through spiteful ignorance affecting a haughty contempt or a stupidly modest avoidance of contention. One man, provided he can strike, does not care how much he lays himself open. Another counts his words, and weighs them as reasons. This one uses only the advantage of his voice and lungs. Here is one who concludes against himself. And this one, who deafens you with useless preambles and digressions. This other arms himself with sheer insults and seeks a German quarrel * to get rid of the

* A quarrel without any reason.

company and conversation of a mind that presses his own hard. This last fellow sees nothing in reason, but holds you besieged with the dialectical enclosure of his clauses and with the formulas of his art.

Arrogance is another disastrous vice. Montaigne once heard a man of rank and fortune drop this pronouncement into a light discussion: " 'It can only be a liar or an ignoramus who will say otherwise than,' and so on." "Pursue that philosophical point," Montaigne comments, "dagger in hand." Stubbornness is almost as bad: "This man must have fallen on his nose a hundred times in one day; there he stands . . . as positive and unshaken as before. . . . Obstinacy and heat of opinion is the surest proof of stupidity. Is there anything so certain, resolute, disdainful, contemplative, grave, and serious as an ass?"

Montaigne seeks men free from these vices, urbane, pertinent, direct: "the rarest type among us," the *honnestes et habiles hommes* that he did much to foster: "The object of this association is simply intimacy, fellowship, and conversation: exercise of minds, without any other fruit. In our talks all subjects are alike to me. I do not care if there is neither weight nor depth in them; charm and pertinency are always there; everything is imbued with mature and constant good sense, and mingled with kindliness, frankness, gaiety, and friendliness."

He thinks he talks better than he writes, since talk readily grows animated in "men who move about briskly, as I do, and become heated." He is always frank even to his cost; his freedom toward the great is often indiscreet; often they have had to ask him to moderate his tone. When wounded or sick, he finds it costly and tiring to use his voice, for it is loud and strained. At home he likes to have meals short and listen to stories after; "for it tires me and disagrees with me to talk on a full stomach, whereas I find it a very healthy and pleasant exercise to shout and argue before a meal." Despite his scruples, his lively, noisy way of speaking often leads him into hyperbole: "I magnify and inflate my subject by voice, movements, vigor and power of words, and further by extension and amplification, not without prejudice to the simple truth. But . . . for the first man who catches me up and asks me for the naked and unvarnished truth, I promptly abandon my straining and give it to him without exaggeration, without overemphasis or padding." Florimond de Raemond describes his conversation as "the sweetest and most enriched with graces and shining with diverse perfections that one could have wished for."

Montaigne's century was subject to boredom but not yet aware of it as a problem. He had noted, after Seneca, that men "seek business only for busyness"; but Pascal's searching analysis was yet to come. He was little subject to it but not immune; it explains his love of travel and many of his pastimes. Inept at checkers and chess (which he loved), he once liked cards and dice, still enjoys cards with his wife and daughter, and tells of playing a game in his house "to see who could find the most things that meet at their two extremes." He has watched trick dancers who seek attention by perilous leaps, as apprentice clowns overact. He enjoys how a blind acquaintance (Louis VI de Rohan, prince de Guémené) spurs his horse after a hare and rejoices at his comrades' catch, strokes a tennis ball and fires a harquebus at random, takes his godson in his arms and says: "My, what a handsome boy! How good it is to see him! What a gay face he has!" He marvels at the little man from Nantes who stopped at Montaigne to earn a little money, born without arms and calling his feet his hands: "he carves, he loads a pistol and fires it, he threads his needle, he sews, he writes, he doffs his hat, he combs his hair, he plays cards and dice, and moves them with as much dexterity as any other could do." As a child Montaigne had seen another like him handle a sword and halberd in the crook of his neck, throw them in the air and catch them, hurl a dagger, and crack a whip as well as the best wagoner in France. He is tired of performing dogs, but greatly impressed with the "reasoning and intelligence" of those of blind men, which leads them to "stop at certain doors where they have been accustomed to receive alms" and "avoid being hit by coaches and carts, even when for their part they have enough room to pass"; he has seen one "leave a smooth flat path and take a worse one, to keep his master away from the ditch."

Entertainment may lead to perspective, as did Montaigne's talk with a Brazilian cannibal at Rouen in 1562: "When I asked him what profit he gained from his superior position among his people (for he was a captain, and our sailors called him king), he told me that it was to march foremost in war. How many men followed him? He pointed to a piece of ground, to signify as many as such a space could hold; it might have been four or five thousand men. Did all his authority expire with the war? He said that this much remained, that when he visited the villages dependent on him, they made paths for him through the underbrush by which he might pass quite comfortably." There is the "monstrous child" that he describes (II: 30) with clinical sympathy, fourteen months old, shown about for a penny or so by his father, an uncle, and an aunt who served as nurse; fastened below the breast to another child, without a head, "as if a smaller child were trying to embrace a bigger one around the neck." A few inches of flesh connected them between the nipples and the navel. "All of the imperfect child that was not attached, as the arms, buttocks, thighs, and legs, remained hanging and dangling on the other and might reach halfway down his legs. The nurse also told us that he urinated from both places." At first Montaigne adds only that he will leave this case for the doctors and that some people would call it a good prognostic for France. In 1588 he notes another freak he has seen in Médoc. His comment after 1588 shows that to him nothing natural is foreign:

What we call monsters are not so to God, who sees in the immensity of his work the infinity of forms that he has comprised in it; and it is for us to believe that this figure that astonishes us is related and linked to some other figure of the same kind unknown to man. From his infinite wisdom there proceeds nothing but that is good and ordinary and regular; but we do not see its arrangement and relationship. . . .

We call contrary to nature what happens contrary to custom; nothing is anything but according to nature, whatever it may be. Let this universal and natural reason drive out of us the error and astonishment that novelty brings us.

Other sights and stories are reminders of man's cruelty, courage, anger, and folly. Montaigne has seen a peasant "left for dead stark naked in a ditch, his neck all bruised and swollen from a halter that was still hanging from it, by which he had been dragged along all night at a horse's tail, his body pierced in a hundred places with stabs from daggers . . . who had endured all that . . . rather than promise anything." He tells how several years ago a nearby villager came home one day after long being exasperated by his wife's jealousy: "and when she welcomed him with her customary yelling, he went into such a fury that then and there, with the billhook that he was still holding in his hands, he reaped clean off the parts that put her in such a fever, and threw them in her face." Just a few days back a woman of nearby Bergerac, beaten by her surly husband, matured a plan all night, got up, chatted with her neighbors as usual, recommended her affairs to them, led her sister by the hand onto the bridge, took leave of her as if in jest, and then, without a sign of change or alteration, "threw herself down headlong into the river, where she perished."

In the comic vein is a gentleman suspected of impotence who, a few days after his wedding, "went around boldly swearing that he had ridden twenty stages the night before; which was afterward used to convict him of pure ignorance and to annul his marriage." Montaigne has seen many supposed miracles, one in a village two leagues away, which drew great crowds from far and near. A young man pretended to be a spirit, and, when his joke succeeded, took in two associates: "And from preaching at home they went on to preaching in public, hiding under the altar of the church, speaking only at night, and forbidding anyone to bring any light. From words tending to the conversion of the world and the threat of judgment day (. . . subjects under whose authority and reverence imposture most easily hides), they proceeded to some visions and actions so silly and ridiculous that there is hardly anything so crude in children's play. Yet if fortune had seen fit to favor them a little, who knows to what point this buffoonery would have grown?"

Incredible tales are of course a commonplace:

My ears are battered by a thousand stories like this: "Three people saw him on such-and-such a day in the east; three saw him the next day in the west, at such-and-such a time, in such-and-such a place, dressed thus." Truly, I would not believe my own self about this. How much more natural and likely it seems to me that two men are lying than that one man should pass with the winds in twelve hours from the east to the west! How much more natural that our understanding should be carried away from its base by the volatility of our untracked mind than that one of us, in flesh and bone, should be wafted up a chimney on a broomstick by a strange spirit!

Stories of all sorts made up the news and helped pass the time in the red-roofed château. It is no wonder that they abound in the *Essays*.

So do incidents. We imagine Montaigne listening to his curate as we read: "When the vines freeze in my village, my priest infers that the wrath of God is upon the human race, and judges that the cannibals already have the pip." Watching a hired painter suggests his setting La Boétie's *Voluntary Servitude* in the middle of his own Book I: "He chooses the best spot, the middle of each wall, to put a picture labored over with all his skill, and the empty space all around

it he fills with grotesques . . . paintings whose only charm lies in
their variety and strangeness." Montaigne once persuaded a bishop
friend to be cut open for a stone in the bladder. Alas! "When he
was dead and was opened up, they found that his only trouble was in
the kidneys." Once, before his first attack of the kidney stone, hearing that the blood of a specially fed billy goat was a cure, Montaigne
had one put aside in the summer heat, fed on laxative herbs and
white wine, and finally killed. In the paunch his cook felt "two or
three big balls that rattled against one another." Montaigne had the
entrails cut open. "Out came three big lumps, light as sponges, so
that they appeared to be hollow, moreover hard and firm on the outside, and spotted with several dull colors." Montaigne concluded
wryly that a cure seemed unlikely "from the blood of an animal on
its way to dying of a similar disease."

Many events are grim. There are deaths—Montaigne's young
brother, five of his children, and others—whose trappings oppress
him with "the cries of mothers, wives, and children; the visits of
people dazed and benumbed by grief; the presence of a number of
pale and weeping servants; a darkened room; lighted candles; our
bedside besieged by doctors and preachers; in short, everything
horror and fright around us."

There are brutal crimes, whose victims people are afraid to help:

Some peasants have just informed me hastily that a moment ago they
left in a wood that belongs to me a man stabbed in a hundred places, who
is still breathing, and who begged them for pity's sake to bring him some
water and help him to get up. They say that they did not dare go near him,
and ran away, for fear that the officers of the law would catch them there
and hold them accountable for the accident—as is done with those who are
found near a murdered man—to their total ruin, since they had neither
ability nor money to defend their innocence. What could I say to them? It
is certain that this act of humanity would have got them into trouble.

Once Montaigne was held up on the road during a truce by
fifteen or twenty masked gentlemen and a troop of mounted archers
—made prisoner, taken deep into a nearby forest, unhorsed, valises
and money box seized, coffers searched, horses and equipment divided among his captors. "We were a long time in that thicket disputing over the matter of my ransom, which they set so high that it
was quite apparent that I was scarcely known to them. They started
a big dispute over my life. . . . Many threatening circumstances

. . . showed the danger I was in." He stood on his rights, under the truce, to give them no ransom beyond the large sum they had already taken. After two or three hours they were having him led away by fifteen or twenty musketeers, on a slow horse, by a different route from his scattered men, for a distance of two or three harquebus shots, when suddenly they changed their minds. "I saw the leader return to me with gentler words, taking pains to search for my belongings scattered among the troop, and having them returned to me as far as they could be recovered, even including my money box. The best present they made me was finally my freedom; the rest did not concern me much at that time." The leader, who took off his mask and revealed his name, told Montaigne it was his frank manner that made them change their plans.

To the same openness he owes his escape from the plot of a neighbor, "to some extent a relative," who came to his door one day completely terrified, his horse panting and worn, and pressed to be let in. When Montaigne opened to him, as he did to everyone, "He entertained me with this bit of fiction: that he had just been set upon half a league away by an enemy of his . . . having been surprised in disarray and weaker in number, he had sought safety at my door." Naïvely, Montaigne tried to reassure him. "Soon after, up came four or five of his soldiers, with the same bearing and the same fright, wanting to come in; and then others and still others after them, well equipped and well armed, until there were twenty-five or thirty, pretending to have the enemy at their heels." Montaigne grew suspicious, but, seeing no point in showing it, followed the simple natural course and had them come in: the men on horseback in the courtyard, the leader inside with him. "He saw himself master of his undertaking, and nothing now remained but its execution. He has often said since, for he was not afraid to tell this story, that my face and my frankness had disarmed him of his treachery. He remounted his horse, his men constantly keeping their eyes on him to see what signal he would give them, very astonished to see him go away and abandon his advantage."

Though he lives in a "backward region" and rarely has contact with anyone "who understands the Latin of his Paternoster" or even French, he sees many congenial people. He travels with his brother Pierre de La Brousse, visits a kinsman at Armagnac and learns about the man known as The Thief, and tries to divert a widow from her grief. He has a visit from Madame de Duras (probably with her husband and the count and countess of Gramont) as he is working on the last chapter of Book II, and from an unnamed friend who reads "Of Pedantry" and asks for more. He dedicates his chapter on paternal affection (II: 8) to Madame d'Estissac, a widow devoted to her children, one of whom Montaigne later took on his Italian trip. A touching scene shows the terrible marshal Blaise de Monluc, after the death of his young son, lamenting to Montaigne that he had never shown him his esteem and love.

Montaigne was proxy for Louis de Foix, count de Gurson, when he contracted to marry his cousin Diane de Foix, to whom Montaigne was to dedicate his chapter on education. At the wedding feast was a disappointed suitor. Many friends, and notably one old lady, feared he might cast a spell to make Gurson impotent on his wedding night. Montaigne reassured the old lady, dug out of his coffers a flat gold piece given him by Jacques Peletier as a protection against headache and sunstroke, and promised the groom, in return for secrecy, to perform a miracle for him if necessary. When they brought the newlyweds the midnight meal, Gurson gave the signal.

I told him then that he should get up on the pretext of chasing us out, and playfully take the bathrobe that I had on (we were very close in height) and put it on him until he had carried out my prescription, which was this: when we had left, he should withdraw to pass water, say certain prayers three times and go through certain motions; each of these three times he should tie the ribbon I was putting in his hand around him and very carefully lay the medal that was attached to it on his kidneys, with the figure in such and such a position; this done, having tied this ribbon firmly so that it could neither come untied nor slip from its place, he should return to his business with complete assurance and not forget to spread my robe over his bed so that it should cover them both. . . . The characters on my medal proved themselves more venereal than solar, more useful for action than for prevention.

The *Essays* are full of sketches of noble acquaintances. Some illustrate the treatment of children by their fathers. One youth, caught stealing a lady's rings, confessed to Montaigne that he could no longer keep off "this filthy path," on which his father's rigor and avarice had set him. One "lord of good understanding," when asked why he hoarded his riches, told him it was in order to retain his authority. He once boldly urged a good friend, a lively old widower, who was bothered by all the entertaining done by his grown son and

marriageable daughters, to give his son his main house and retire to
another near by; which he did "and was well off for it."

Florimond de Raemond identifies many others whom Montaigne
sketches without naming them. A Huguenot captain, René de Valzargues, is the friend who, despite Montaigne's arguments, rushed
eagerly and for no apparent reason "to the first death that came his
way crowned with a gleam of honor." François IV de La Rochefoucauld, asked why he always blew his nose in his hand, replied with
the question "what privilege this dirty excrement had that we should
prepare a fine delicate piece of linen to receive it, and then, what is
more, wrap it up and carry it carefully on us." The old prelate who
entrusted all his affairs to others is Antoine Prévost de Sansac, archbishop of Bordeaux. François de Candale, bishop of Aire, is the churchman who, to justify his obsessive quest of the philosopher's stone,
cited five or six passages from Scripture which Montaigne found very
appropriate to the defense of "that fine science." It was the wife of
his second cousin Joseph d'Eymar who told him of the "widow of
chaste reputation" who found herself mysteriously pregnant, promised to marry the man who had made her so, and learned that one
holiday, after too much wine, she had been found asleep in an inde-
cent posture and thus enjoyed by one of her young farmhands, to
whom she is still married. The great officer and prospective heir who
died poor and deep in debt at over fifty while his mother enjoyed
all his late father's estate is Marshal François de Montmorency, eldest
son of Constable Anne. There is the lord who mocked the princely
pretensions of his friends (Bertrand de Baylens de Poyanne); the
prince who as a youth tried his father's hair shirt, to his regret (Louis,
duc de Montpensier); the worthy gentleman who "nearly drove
himself out of his mind" by his passionate concern for his master
Henry of Navarre (Jacques de Ségur, baron de Pardaillan); the lady,
"one of the greatest," who cannot bear to be seen chewing and tries
not to appear in public with an appetite (Margaret of Valois); the
gouty prince (Nemours) who "by the power of his imagination persuaded his legs and put them to sleep for a few hours, so that he
derived from them a service that they had long since forgotten"; the
gentleman who claimed to have gone from Madrid to Lisbon in midsummer without drinking (Jean de Vivonne, marquis de Pisani).
Marshal Jacques de Matignon is the friendly lord who almost per-

suaded Montaigne that the evening dew was more dangerous earlier than at nightfall. A sorry figure is Gilbert, duc de Ventadour, whose "organ" for venting wind Montaigne calls "so turbulent and unruly, that for forty years it has kept its master farting with a constant and unremitting wind and compulsion, and is thus taking him to his death."

Other unnamed characters in Montaigne's pages include the three Henrys (Henry III, Guise, and Navarre), of whom more later, and the marquis de Trans, former ambassador to England, a lifelong friend and sponsor to whom Montaigne was devoted, who conferred the Order of Saint Michael on him and later played a part in his selection to be mayor of Bordeaux. Florimond de Raemond identifies Trans twice in the *Essays*. When three sons of that stanch loyalist died in the same battle fighting for Henry of Navarre, Montaigne comments that Trans "cheated divine justice; for the violent death of three grown-up children having been sent him in one day as a bitter scourge . . . he all but took it as a favor." Elsewhere Montaigne presents him as the most tempestuous master in France.

He strikes, he bites, he swears. . . . He is eaten up by care and vigilance. . . . All that is just a farce. . . . Everybody is living it up in various corners of his house, gaming, spending, and exchanging stories about his vain anger and foresight. . . . How many times has he boasted to me of the check he kept on his household . . . and how clearly he saw into his own affairs! . . . I know no man who can bring to bear more qualities . . . fit to preserve mastery . . . and yet he has fallen from authority like a child. . . .

. . . Does he dismiss a servant? He packs his bundle, there he is gone— but only out of his presence. . . . He will live and do his job in the same house for a year without being perceived. . . . Does Monsieur take some step or send some dispatch that displeases? They suppress it. . . . No letters from outside are brought to him first. . . . If by accident he gets hold of one, the person on whom he relies to read his letters to him promptly finds in it whatever he chooses. . . . In fine, he sees his affairs only in an image arranged . . . so as not to rouse his bad humor and anger.

It is time to turn to Michel de Montaigne himself. We have seen him as son, magistrate, friend, husband, and householder; we have sketched his portrait at thirty. Subject to the power of imagination, he likes foreign things better than his own; would weep, if he could, to keep others company; is moved by military and church music and pained by the very names of dear ones lost. Strenuously independent, he avoids commitments as too binding; he has given advice freely when asked, which was not often, and never taken any. Centering his attention inward, as men should, he has affection, though not esteem, for himself. He considers his opinions worse than his conduct, and can better defend a position than choose one. A man of good will, he hates no one, and wishes that fewer people made up for his deficiency.

He takes pride in being fair and scrupulous, for it is rare in his day to see a man "moderate in his revenge, slow to resent offenses, religious in keeping his word, neither double-dealing nor shifty, nor accommodating his faith to the will of others or to the occasion." "If anyone," he says, "should see right into my soul, still he would not find me guilty either of anyone's affliction or ruin, or of vengeance or envy, or of public offense against the laws, or of innovation and disturbance, or of failing in my word; and in spite of what the license of the times allows and teaches each man, still I have not put my hand either upon the property or into the purse of any Frenchman, and have lived only on my own, both in war and in peace; nor have I used any man's work without paying his wages." He is conscience-stricken if he chances to see other people's letters; he can be cheated, because he prefers to trust others; when falsely accused, he makes things worse by silence or "an ironic and mocking confession," as though it were "compromising my conscience to plead for it"; he lets his friends lecture him, but often finds their reproach or praise so inappropriate "that I would hardly have erred to err rather than to do good in their fashion." He is thankful that he has never been brought before a judge or seen the inside of a prison— as he was to do in 1588. He strongly condemns judging by party labels: "Should we not dare say of a thief that he has a fine leg? And if she is a whore, must she also necessarily have bad breath?"

He stresses his variability the better to convince us of our own:

I who spy on myself more closely, who have my eyes unceasingly intent on myself . . . I would hardly dare tell of the vanity and weakness that I find in myself. . . . If my health smiles upon me, and the brightness of a beautiful day, I am a fine fellow; if I have a corn bothering my toe, I am surly, unpleasant, and unapproachable. . . . Now I am ready to do anything, now to do nothing. . . . Either the melancholic humor grips me, or the choleric; and at this moment sadness predominates in me by its own private authority, at that moment good cheer.

He has learned from this same variability, however. Fearing to change lest he lose by it, he has kept his Catholic faith serenely intact amid all the new sects and divisions. He holds services in his chapel when the Protestants have ruined all the churches around. Some of his habits related to religion are swearing only with the mild "Par Dieu!"; crossing himself—"a sign that I revere and continually use, even when I yawn"; using the Lord's Prayer often and recommending it when-ever appropriate: "on sitting down to table and rising from it, on getting up and going to bed, and on all particular actions with which we are accustomed to associate prayers."

Though the kidney stone lies not far ahead, Montaigne at re-tirement has enjoyed excellent health, thanks largely, he believes, to his freedom from medicine, even when threatened by doctors. His quarrel is not with them, for he has known "many decent and lovable men among them," but with their art, which feeds upon the public folly. "I call them into my company when I am sick if they happen to be at hand, and I expect to be entertained by them, and I pay them as others do. I give them authority to order me to cover up warmly, if I like it better that way than another way; between leeks and lettuce they can choose what they want my broth to be made of, and prescribe for me either white wine or claret; and so with all other things that are indifferent to my appetite and habit." He is not merely flippant; he senses what medicine needs; but as long as it is anything but a science, he follows nature and experience: what he likes and is used to, what agrees with him. His faith in experience leads him to record the regimen—the same in sickness as in health—that has brought him into his late fifties; much of this holds for his forties as well.

He avoids enslavement to habit and keeps his ways and tastes flexible:

I cannot, without an effort, sleep by day, or eat between meals, or breakfast, or go to bed without a long interval, of about three full hours, after supper, or make a child except before going to sleep, or make one standing up, or endure my sweat, or quench my thirst with pure water or pure wine, or remain bareheaded for long, or have my hair cut after dinner; and I would feel as uncomfortable without my gloves as without my shirt, or without washing when I leave the table or get up in the morning, or without canopy and curtains for my bed, as I would be without really necessary things. . . . I . . . indulge my preference for a glass of a certain shape and do not willingly drink from a common glass, any more than I like to be served by a common hand. . . .

I owe many such weaknesses to habit. Nature too . . . has brought me her share: such as no longer being able to stand two full meals a day without overloading my stomach, or complete abstinence from one of those meals without filling myself with wind, drying up my mouth, and numbing my appetite; and suffering from too long exposure to the night air. . . . In the military service, when whole nights are spent on duty . . . after five or six hours I begin to be troubled by my stomach, as well as by a violent headache, and I do not last until daytime without vomiting. As the others are going off to breakfast I go off to sleep, and after that I am as gay as before.

He rises at seven or after (late for his time) and does not dine before eleven or sup before six. To go back to sleep in the morning is to regret it later. He sleeps "hard and alone, even without a woman, in the royal style, rather well covered up"; never has his bed heated, but in his late years sometimes uses cloths to warm his feet and stomach; can get along with very little sleep, but enjoys eight or nine hours at a stretch. He likes leisure for defecation, which he hates to have interrupted; as for his bowels, "mine and I never fail the moment of our assignation, which is when I jump out of bed, unless some violent occupation or illness disturbs us."

At table he is not choosy; he dislikes a crowd of dishes and courses, attacks the nearest thing, and is loth to change. Though he likes salt meats, he eats bread without salt, against the custom of his region. He wants his meat rare and well-hung, even gamy, never tough. Even fish, which he prefers to meat and will not mix with it, may be too fresh and firm for him. Oysters he loves; also all sauces; among salads and fruits, only melons. His appetite and digestion vary: he first liked white wine, then claret, then white again; radishes once agreed with him, then disagreed, then agreed again. From his youth he has often skipped a meal, sometimes to whet his appetite; but if he wants to fast, he must avoid the supper table. He eats greedily, sometimes biting tongue and even fingers; not using newfangled forks and spoons, he likes plenty of napkins, both at table and to rub his teeth before and after meals and in the morning.

Healthy or sick, he rarely gets thirsty, and drinks only when eating. His capacity is fair for a smallish man, but still modest; when once, to be sociable, he undertook to drink heavily, he could not swallow a drop. He hates smoke and stuffy, smelly air; among the hardships of war he reckons the dust that buries a moving army all day in summer. "The first repairs I hurried to make in my house," he writes, "were in the chimneys and the privies, which as a rule are unbearably defective in old buildings." He loves Venice and Paris the less for the stench of their marshes and mud. Any heat from fire— French fireplaces or German stoves—makes him feel weak and heavy; he prefers the Roman steam-heated walls. He marvels at a man he saw studying amid the din of his servants; his own mind is "sensitive and ready to take flight; . . . the slightest buzz of a fly is the death of it."

He has a quick firm walk, tends to scratch his ears, and suffers more from summer heat than winter cold. Strong light dazzles him: "I could not eat dinner seated opposite a blazing, bright fire." Though he has good distant vision and no need for spectacles, his eyes tire easily, especially from reading toward sundown and at night. When he reads a lot he lays a piece of glass on his book to relieve the brightness of the paper. He dresses in black and white, like his father, and often carelessly. Even in winter he wears only silk hose; but illness and age make him keep head and stomach progressively warmer, leading him from a cap to a kerchief, and from a bonnet to a lined hat. "The padding of my doublet serves now only for orna- ment; it is no good unless I add a rabbit's skin or a vulture's, and a skullcap for my head. Follow these steps and you will go at a fine pace." All his powers decline with age: "Here is a step backward, just barely perceptible. I shall draw back another step, from the second to the third, from the third to the fourth, so quietly that I shall have to be a confirmed blind man before I feel the decadence and old age of my sight." Though he retires in his late thirties and wants as many years more of life, mostly he feels old, on the shelf, with an empty road ahead to death.

As a councillor in the Bordeaux Parlement Montaigne had often been away—sometimes on business—at Paris and the court. In his early retirement especially (1571–80) he was often absent from home. He writes, he says, "only when pressed by too unnerving an idleness, and nowhere but at home . . . with diverse interruptions and inter- vals, as occasions sometimes detain me elsewhere for several months." Of these occasions we know little. Montaigne may have gone to Paris (and the court) in 1571 to see to the publication of part of La

Boétie's *Posthumous Works*. The fact that he received the Order of Saint Michael in 1571 and became a gentleman in ordinary of the king's chamber by 1573 suggests that he was esteemed at court; but eminent persons like Trans usually sponsored many minor nobles and helped them obtain honors.

In May 1574 Charles de Montferrand, governor of Bordeaux, worried about the dispute over command in Périgord, in the absence of Losse, between Limeuil and Bourdeille, a brother of Brantôme (whose ill will toward Montaigne may have sprung from this incident), sent Montaigne to confer with Louis de Bourbon, duc de Montpensier, commander of the royal army in the southwest. On his return to Bordeaux with letters from Montpensier, Montaigne asked to address the Parlement and received a cordial greeting:

The said Montaigne having entered, he presented letters from the said de Montpensier addressed to the said Court, a reading of which was made; and, this done, Montaigne made a long speech about his trip. . . . And, the said speech made, Montaigne was thanked by the said de Villeneuve, President, for the fine duty he had done in his said trip, being assured that the company, in general and individually, would gratify and honor him all it could for the good and laudable virtues it saw in him and for having been one of their colleagues. For which the said Montaigne very humbly thanked the said Court, assuring it that in all that depended on his power, it would find him always ready to do it very humble service, both in general and in particular; and went out.

The historian and magistrate Jacques-Auguste de Thou reports that Montaigne, at the Estates of Blois in 1588, told him of trying to mediate between Guise and Navarre. As the context shows, these were the two Henrys; the attempt could only have been made between 1572 (when Navarre came to court to be married and was greeted by the Saint Bartholomew's Day Massacre and a forced abjuration) and 1576, when he escaped to lead the Protestants in the southwest. This mediation may have caused the expensive trip that freed Montaigne from concern over money. De Thou shows him attempting a delicate task at a time when nothing else suggests any important activity of his.

Michel de Montaigne . . . had been at court, and was then at Blois. . . . When he discussed the causes of these tumults, he had this to say (for he had once sought to mediate between Navarre and Guise, when they were together at court): that Guise had striven to gain Navarre's friendship by every possible service and assiduity, but when he felt that Navarre, whom he had tried to placate and have as a friend, was deluding him, shutting him out with dissimulation, and, completely insensible, treating him as an enemy, he had considered that he had to resort to the extreme remedy of arms to protect himself and the honor of his family; that the alienation of these two spirits from each other was the beginning of what had lately burst into the flames of war, from which he saw no other way out than the destruction of one or the other: for on the one hand Guise, as long as Navarre is alive, despairs of his own life and the safety of his people, and on the other hand Navarre is not confident that with Guise living he can defend his right to the succession to the crown. That religion, which is alleged by both, is used speciously as a pretext by those who follow them; for the rest, neither one regards it. For Navarre, if he did not fear to be deserted by his followers, would be ready to return of his own accord to the religion of his forefathers; and Guise, if there were no danger, would not be averse to the Augsburg Confession,* of which he had once had a certain taste under his paternal uncle Charles, the cardinal.† These were the feelings that he had observed in them both when he was conferring between them.

This is all we know of Montaigne's doings away from home in the years when he composed the first *Essays;* but it suggests much activity, some of it important. Even as he was formulating the boldly original plan of his book, he was not content to be merely a "maker of books."

* The main early Protestant statement of belief, prepared by Melanchthon and published in 1530.

† Charles, cardinal of Lorraine.

Chapter 9: *The Early* Essays [1571-1574]

THE AIM of Montaigne's retirement, as announced in his inscription, was to rest from the fatigues of court and Parlement in the bosom of the muses and enjoy the remainder of his life at leisure. He could then be no clearer than that; he knew better what he fled than what he sought. His fine early education, the promise his friend had seen in him, had borne little apparent fruit; fourteen undistinguished years in the Bordeaux Parlement, a vain attempt at an important mediation, a successful translation, were modest achievements for him at thirty-eight. His greatest experience had been his friendship. Now he misses La Boétie sorely and makes a cult of his memory. With all his advantages, he is a lonely man in search of his function.

Though wary of bookishness and often disdainful of letters as a profession, he loves books far more than he usually admits. Their company is a great resource. "It is at my side throughout my course, and accompanies me everywhere. It consoles me in old age and in solitude. It relieves me of the weight of a tedious idleness, and releases me at any time from disagreeable company. It dulls the pangs of sorrow, unless they are extreme and overpowering. To be diverted from a troublesome idea, I need only have recourse to books: they easily turn my thoughts to themselves and steal away the others. . . . It is the best provision I have found for this human journey."

He learned to love them early, at seven or eight, when Ovid's *Metamorphoses* delighted him so that "I would steal away from any other pleasure to read them." From these, disdaining the popular romances, he went on through the *Aeneid,* Terence and Plautus, and some Italian comedies. He had bought a complete Virgil before he was sixteen. His early thirties reveal a fondness for history and memoirs. Around 1564 or 1565 he covered the margins of his copy of Nicole Gilles's *Annals and Chronicles of France* with comments criticizing them on the authority of Aemilius Paulus, Commines, Du Tillet, Ferron, Froissart, Gaguin, Sleidan, noting that Gilles's commentator Denis Sauvage had not "studied his lesson well," and showing his own familiarity with Saint Augustine, Plutarch, Sallust, and others. Montaigne's corrections extend even to small factual details; his judgments are often severe, as here: "In truth this is sewn throughout with so many mistakes that one unlearns more than one learns." A few years later he wrote general judgments on three other books, by Martin Du Bellay, whom he finds too partial to France, Guicciardini, whom he blames for seeing evil motives everywhere, and Philippe de Commines (the *Memoirs*):

Here you will find the language pleasant and agreeable, of a natural simplicity; the narrative pure, and the author's good faith showing through it clearly, free from vanity in speaking of himself, and of partiality or envy in speaking of others; his ideas and exhortations accompanied more by good zeal and truth than by any exquisite capacity; and, throughout, authority and gravity, representing the man of good background and brought up in great affairs.

The annotations reveal a more scholarly, less casual reader than Montaigne is wont to suggest—careful, attentive, ready with criticisms of fact or judgment and with comparisons drawn from other readings, interested in the man behind the book. His commitment to the literary enterprise is clear.

When he retires he is no novice; he has worked with care and skill over a translation of nearly a thousand pages. An active reader, he cannot long be satisfied merely to read. Retirement is not an unmixed delight; he needs action. He says later that a "melancholy humor . . . produced by the gloom of the solitude into which I had cast myself some years ago" first made him think of writing. His mind would not settle down; he must harness it:

> Lately when I retired to my home, determined so far as possible to bother about nothing except spending the little life I have left in rest and seclusion, it seemed to me I could do my mind no greater favor than to let it entertain itself in full idleness and stay and settle in itself, which I hoped it might do more easily now, having become weightier and riper with time. But I find . . . that, on the contrary, like a runaway horse, it gives itself a hundred times more trouble than it took for others, and gives birth to so many chimeras and fantastic monsters, one after another, without order or purpose, that in order to contemplate their ineptitude and strangeness at my pleasure, I have begun to put them in writing, hoping in time to make my mind ashamed of itself.

In short, for many reasons, he must write. But what? Montaigne was of the many for whom this is one of the hardest questions. Essays? The concept and the term were still (so far as we can tell) as foreign to their inventor as to his contemporaries. The plan of self-portrayal also lay several years ahead. Montaigne was interested in war, in history and biography, in philosophy, especially as it concerned man's nature and duties.

In this he was of his time. The French Renaissance had eagerly welcomed the moral insights of the ancients; Stoicism and Platonism, more or less successfully reconciled with Christianity, captivated many good minds, and others too; Cato and Socrates, Seneca and Plutarch, were heroes and guides to many besides Montaigne. In his *Colloquies* and *Adages* especially, Erasmus was one of the great, and original, popularizers; mediocre works abounded and flourished: the *Moral Distichs* attributed to Cato, the *Sententiae* of Stobaeus, the *Memorable Deeds and Words* of Valerius Maximus, the *Officina* of Ravisius Textor. A more attractive type was even more popular: that of the "varied lessons" that grouped together illustrations of a single theme: the *Attic Nights* of Aulus Gellius, Coelius Rhodiginus' *Ancient Lessons*, Crinito's *Honorable Teaching*, Pedro de Mexia's *Forest of Varied Lessons*, and the *Golden Epistles* of Antonio de Guevara.

These are the works that Montaigne's earliest chapters most resemble. Although they had far greater antecedents—Plutarch's *Moralia* or *Moral Essays*, Machiavelli's *Discourses*—many of them were little more than short groups of related anecdotes with a brief moral, in the tradition of Rhodiginus and Mexia. Here is a fairly typical example, short enough to be quoted in full.

BOOK I, CHAPTER 7. THAT INTENTION IS JUDGE OF OUR ACTIONS

Death, they say, acquits us of all our obligations. I know those who have taken this in a strange sense. Henry VII, king of England, made an agreement with Don Philip, son of Emperor Maximilian—or, to place him more honorably, father of Emperor Charles V—that the said Philip would deliver into his hands the duke of Suffolk of the White Rose, his enemy, who had escaped and withdrawn to the Low Countries, in exchange for which Henry promised to make no attempt on the life of the said duke. However, nearing death, Henry ordered in his will that his son should have the duke killed as soon as he, Henry, was dead.

Recently, in the tragedy that the duke of Alva showed us in Brussels involving the counts of Horn and of Egmont, whose heads he had cut off, there were plenty of noteworthy events, among them that the said count of Egmont, on whose faith and assurance the count of Horn had come and given himself up to the duke of Alva, demanded most insistently that he should himself be killed the first, so that his death should free him from his obligation to the said count of Horn.

It seems to me that death did not discharge King Henry from his promise, and that the count of Egmont was quit of his even without dying. We cannot be bound beyond our powers and means. For this reason— that we have no power to effect and accomplish, that there is nothing really in our power but will—all man's rules of duty are necessarily founded and established in our will. Thus the count of Egmont, considering his soul and will in debt to his promise, though the power to carry it out was not in his hands, was certainly absolved of his duty even had he survived the count of Horn. But the king of England, in intentionally breaking his word, cannot be excused merely on the ground that he delayed the execution of his dishonest plan until after his death; any more than Herodotus' mason, who, having loyally kept during his life the secret of the treasures of his master the king of Egypt, revealed it to his children as he died.

At the end of the present volume (pp. 324–326) the reader will find a table of contents of the three books of *Essays*, with the approximate dates of their composition and their length in their final form. Books I and II were published in 1580 by Simon Millanges in Bordeaux. A second edition soon followed (1582), again by Millanges, with very slight additions and revisions; between 1582 and 1587 there apparently was a third, now lost, reproducing the second; for the 1587 Paris edition by Jean Richer is still the same as that of 1582. The second important edition, labeled "fifth" and published by Abel L'Angelier in Paris (1588), adds the entire third book and many passages of considerable length, though no new chapters, to Books I and II. The third important text is the so-called "Bordeaux

Copy" of the 1588 edition, on the margins of which Montaigne, while adding no new books or chapters, made many additions to the existing ones. This document, now available in phototypic and other reproductions, is the basic text for the *Essays* in their final form; but because a heedless binder, in trimming the pages, cut off some of Montaigne's additions, it often needs to be completed by the posthumous 1595 edition (by Marie de Gournay), which, though not always wholly reliable, was prepared from a rough copy of the "Bordeaux Copy."

Thus there are three books of comparable length, which appeared (in their original form, without the later additions) in 1580 (I–II) and 1588 (III); and three main strata of comparable length: pre-1580, 1580–1588, and post-1588. The chapters vary greatly in size, ranging from about a dozen of a page or so to three of nearly a hundred pages and one of two hundred-odd; they are longer in Book III, which has only thirteen, than in I and II, which have fifty-seven and thirty-seven respectively. Though we think of them as "essays" and may properly call them so today, Montaigne labeled them "chapters" and normally used the term "essays" to refer not to these chapters but to the whole enterprise of self-assessment.

Our concern now is with the ninety-four chapters of Books I and II in their original form, which Montaigne composed between 1571 and 1580. These are not arranged in any order that can be simply stated; though much of Book II was composed later than much of Book I, the places Montaigne assigned to many chapters for special reasons make any brief account useless.

About half of the ninety-four chapters were composed at least in the main in the first four years of Montaigne's retirement, between 1571 and 1574. A number of these (Book I, chapters 5–7, 13, 15–17, 24, 34, 45), like the one just quoted, are little more than strings of anecdotes with a brief conclusion: "Whether the Governor of a Besieged Place Should Go Out to Parley"; "Parley Time Is Dangerous"; "Ceremony of Interviews between Kings"; "A Trait of Certain Ambassadors," and the like. These illustrate Montaigne's first manner, in which there is little of himself. More interesting but still relatively impersonal are the many chapters (I: 2–4, 9–11, 18, 21–23, 33, 36–38, 43–44, 46–48) that treat one aspect of behavior or custom, usually stressing some paradox of our frailty and inconsistency: "Our Feelings Reach Out beyond Us"; "How the Soul Discharges

Its Passions on False Objects When the True Are Wanting"; "Of Liars"; "Of Fear"; "Of the Power of the Imagination," and the like.

The most interesting of these earliest chapters are those which show Montaigne wrestling with his greatest problem of the moment, that of pain and death. These include "That the Taste of Good and Evil Depends in Large Part on the Opinion We Have of Them" (I: 14); "That to Philosophize Is to Learn to Die" (I: 20); "Of Solitude" (I: 39); "Of the Inequality That Is between Us" (I: 42); and "Of the Inconsistency of Our Actions" (II: 1). Of all the early essays it is in these that Montaigne's conclusions are most elaborated and most his own; but it is these same conclusions that are to change most during the twenty years in which he composed his *Essays*.

The question of change has been much debated. Shortly after the turn of the century Fortunat Strowski (1906) and, more thoroughly, Pierre Villey (1908), showed that much of Montaigne's apparent inconsistency results from preoccupations and statements that are different at different moments in the composition of his book. Villey took pains, in the second edition (1933) of his *Sources and Evolution of Montaigne's Essays,* to point out that what he had demonstrated was the evolution of the book, not the man. Yet Montaigne himself proclaimed the book consubstantial with its author, and Villey often spoke of the evolution as that of the man. Since the death of Arthur Armaingaud, most serious students of Montaigne have accepted the notion of some measure of development in the *Essays;* but many discount any theory of important change in a thoughtful man who first began to write at the age of thirty-eight.

Of course many sides of Montaigne change little if at all. His temper is always skeptical; he looks before any mental leap. His perspective shows him that the convictions of his time, his region, and himself may be anything but absolute truths. He is more aware of diversity than of uniformity, and mistrusts the oversimplification that lurks in any statement. The change he finds everywhere, without and within, makes him wonder whether men ever harbor perfect truth, or know it if they do.

His skepticism never precludes action. If perfect knowledge is denied us, he finds us capable of a practical kind of knowledge adequate for living well. Nor does skepticism undermine his Catholic faith; indeed, it supports it by undermining its enemy, the Protestant trust in individual reason as judge of the meaning of Scripture. For Montaigne, God alone *is;* man and nature are only becoming and not being. Perfect truth resides with God alone; he alone can raise us up, and by his grace, not our merit. It is for us to obey, for God to know and to command. But God leaves us free to work out our lives on human terms with a clear conscience.

Montaigne's central concern was always man and his life, why we behave as we do, how we should. Few men have been less metaphysical. His interest is in the here and now, not in the unknowable hereafter. A psychologist of curiosity and acumen, he is ultimately a moralist seeking to assess, as well as understand, his actions and those of others. He ridicules the more innocuous vices, such as presumption and her daughter ambition, and hates those that harm others: falsity, hypocrisy, treachery, cruelty. He reveres nature, and urges that we follow her as our best guide, gentle and wise.

Over his last twenty years, however, Montaigne's writings show a number of striking modifications at least in statement. He first calls death the goal of life and philosophy a learning to die; later it is philosophy that teaches us to live, and death is the end but not the goal of life. Early he calls our well-being only the privation of being ill; later he proclaims that God has made all things good, and we should accept them gratefully. After urging a tense defense against the ills of life, he later says we do better to relax and rely on nature. After seeing little but diversity in man and in life, he comes to see unity as well. These are only a few of the important alterations in his statements about some of his main concerns.

He himself observes both permanence and change within him. Part of the change is simply aging, but not all; most of the permanence is in his major commitments. Awareness of his mutability has, as we have seen, bred in him a certain constancy of opinions: "I am nearly always in place, like heavy and inert bodies. . . . The firmest and most general ideas I have are those which, in a manner of speaking, were born with me." Yet he recognizes changes in himself when he says of his book: "I do not correct my first imaginings by my second. . . . I want to represent the course of my humors, and I want people to see each part at its birth. It would give me pleasure to have begun earlier, and to be able to trace the course of my mutations." New ideas can alter his very self: "I aim here only at revealing myself, who will perhaps be different tomorrow, if I learn something new which changes me." His portrait must record the mutability that is our essence: "I do not portray being: I portray passing . . . from day to day, from minute to minute. My history needs to be adapted to the moment. I may presently change, not only by chance, but also by intention. This is a record . . . of irresolute and, when it so befalls, contradictory ideas: whether I am different myself, or whether I take hold of my subjects in different circumstances and aspects."

In short, Montaigne, though alert to change in himself and ready to acknowledge it, recognizes that his may be a matter of circumstance and aspect. This is close to the heart of the question. When he states that death is the goal of life, he is berating the vulgar for not getting used to the idea of it; when he says it is not, he is criticizing the learned for excessive anxiety about it; the two criticisms are reconcilable. But in between, Montaigne has learned that simple peasants, without premeditation, meet death bravely. He is always ready to let new experiences alter his opinions and attitudes.

There is one kind of change, however, that hardly deserves the name. At first Montaigne had preached premeditation of death as our only freedom; later he tells us to forget about it and leave it to nature. Part of this is a real change of attitude, of which more later; but part of it is that his preparation for death has succeeded and hence is no longer necessary. His accident on horseback makes him realize that imagination magnifies his fear of illness: "I hope that the same thing will happen to me with death, and that it is not worth the trouble I take, the many preparations that I make, and all the many aids that I invoke. . . . But at all events, we can never be well enough prepared." In between his bouts with the kidney stone he returns to his normal ways, talks, laughs, and studies without concern, "since my soul," he says, "takes no other alarm than that which comes from the senses and the body; which I certainly owe to the care I have taken to prepare myself, by study and reason, for such accidents."

The great problem is this: how much of Montaigne's apparent change is merely a matter of tactics, of order of presentation? Generally the early essays, the "Apology for Raymond Sebond" (mainly 1576) and those composed before it, are critical, pessimistic, rather negative; they stress man's impotence, ignorance, and misery. The later ones, generally optimistic and positive, stress the great resources of man and life, for all their limitations. Having presented one side of a complex truth, Montaigne then presents the other; but sometimes he actually contradicts his own earlier statements. Is he at first merely cutting man down to size to prepare for building him up later in the proper ways? To quite an extent, I feel sure, but not completely. Montaigne's Pyrrhonistic arguments are in large part paradox; they are too often shown as such to be taken as entire conviction. But when he returns later to some of his pessimistic statements, he will not let them stand unchallenged. Where at first he wrote that "if simplicity leads us on the way to having no pain, it leads us to a very happy state for our condition," he later adds: "Yet we must not imagine it so leaden as to be totally without feeling. . . . I am glad not to be sick; but if I am, I want to know I am. . . . He who would eradicate the knowledge of evil would at the same time extirpate the knowledge of pleasure, and in fine would annihilate man."

In short, there is change in Montaigne, some of which is more than a tactic and involves not just the book but the man. Looking back on his first essays later, he writes: "Since then I have grown older by a long stretch of time, but certainly I have not grown an inch wiser. Myself now and myself a while ago are indeed two; but when better, I simply cannot say."

Montaigne's early remarks about life show a rather bleak pessimism: "The wretchedness of our condition makes us have less to desire than to fear. . . . We do not feel perfect health as we do the slightest of illnesses. . . . Our well-being is but the privation of being ill. . . . To have no ill is to have the happiest state of well-being that man can hope for."

The earliest essays are not gay; their author seems quite different from the hedonistic young friend of La Boétie and the smiling sage of the third book. This is not wholly surprising; for when he retired, his last ten years had been full of the pain and death of those dearest to him. In 1561 his father, without warning, had fallen grievously ill of the kidney stone, which killed him after seven painful years. Two years later his beloved La Boétie, not yet thirty-three, had been stricken with dysentery and soon died. A tennis ball had killed his brother Arnaud in his twenties. His long-awaited first child had lived only two months; though the second, Léonor, survived, he lost a third in 1573, and later the fourth, the fifth, and the sixth, all as infants. August, 1572 brought the terrible Massacre of Saint Bartholomew's Day, which was almost as bad in Bordeaux as in Paris. Montaigne himself, from a mere peaceful collision on horseback, had for a while been taken for dead by himself and others. "With such frequent and ordinary examples passing before our eyes," he writes of his brother's death, "how can we possibly rid ourselves of the thought of death and of the idea that at every moment it is gripping us by the throat?"

The heaviest loss is that of his friend. "Since the day I lost him . . . I only drag on a weary life." His other bereavements leave less obvious scars. Fifteen years later the very names of the deceased can still give pain: " 'My poor master!' or 'My great friend!' 'Alas, my dear father!' or 'My sweet daughter!' " His desire for aloofness is that of a man who has been hurt:

We must reserve a back shop all our own . . . ; here we must talk and laugh as if without wife, without children, without possessions, without retinue and servants, so that, when the time comes to lose them, it will be nothing new to us to do without them. . . .
. . . We must untie these bonds that are so powerful, and henceforth love this and that, but be wedded only to ourselves. That is to say, let the other things be ours, but not joined and glued to us so strongly that they cannot be detached without tearing off our skin and some part of our flesh as well.

When Montaigne lists the main threats to human happiness, he once mentions contempt, twice poverty, and always pain and death. Contempt did not bother him for long; he learned to rely on his own laws to judge himself. He knew that what we fear most in poverty is pain. Pain and death were the great enemies: death, which is inevitable; pain, which is what we fear even in death. Pain, magnified by imagination, had long worried him, even leading him to toy with the idea of suicide; death had always been on his mind.

He told La Boétie he had never believed God gave us such power over human accidents as he saw in him; and he continued to marvel at his example. His musings echo the talk of his dying friend. Death is the test of our lives and our studies, the aim of philosophy, our chance to prove we have learned its lesson; our death should be an example to others. Our task is of course not just to die, but to die well.

The early essays are full of the problem. In one, "That Our Happiness Must Not Be Judged until after Our Death" (I: 19), Montaigne approves Solon's view, since only then can we truly judge a man's philosophy and courage: "In everything else there may be sham. . . . But in the last scene, between death and ourselves, there is no more pretending; we must talk plain French, we must show what there is that is good and clean at the bottom of the pot. . . . That is why all the other actions of our life must be tried and tested by this last act. It is the master day, the day that is judge of all the others." And, remembering La Boétie, Montaigne concludes: "I leave it to death to test the fruit of my studies. We shall see then whether my reasonings come from my mouth or from my heart."

In "Judging of the Death of Others" (II: 13), Montaigne calls death "without doubt the most noteworthy action of human life." To assess it we must know whether it was met in full awareness. In those who die unawares or rush to get it over with, heroism may be more apparent than real. The truly glorious deaths are "studied and digested" like those of Socrates and Cato. Montaigne approves of the Stoic who told Tullius Marcellinus that "it is no great thing to live—your valets and the animals live—but it is a great thing to die honorably, wisely, and with constancy."

Montaigne relates his closest approach to death, which occurred between 1567 and 1570, a few years later in "Practice" (II: 6), which in some ways is typical of his "death cycle" and in other ways brings it to a close. Still greatly concerned with preparing to meet his end, he now proposes to do so by becoming familiar with similar phenomena, sleep and unconsciousness. The collision that knocked him from his horse brought his first swoon and made him think he was dying. He had hoped that death, like unconsciousness, might well be painless, perhaps even desirable; he had argued in this vein against La Boétie. Still apprehensive, he notes that we cannot give ourselves too much advantage; but now he has reason to hope that death does not require all his worried preparation and that, as with his illnesses, "the power of my apprehension made its object appear almost half again as fearful as it was in its truth and essence."

Apprendre (to learn) comes very close to *apprehend* in Montaigne's main chapter on death, "That to Philosophize Is to Learn to Die" (I: 20), a mosaic, generally Stoical in tone, by an eclectic humanist full of Pliny, Plutarch, and Lucretius, as well as Cicero and

Seneca. All sects and opinions, he argues, agree that reason must seek our contentment by helping us get over the fear of death, our only inevitable threat. The "brutish stupidity" of thoughtlessness is no use; it costs too much when the time comes. Then, among the unprepared common herd, "what torments, what cries, what frenzy, what despair overwhelms them!" We must grow used to death, have nothing else so much on our minds, recognize the possibility "at the stumbling of a horse, the fall of a tile, the slightest pinprick," and thereupon "tense ourselves and make an effort." Premeditation of death is premeditation of liberty.

As we noted earlier, Montaigne himself has had death in his imagination always, even in his most licentious years. Only recently someone found among his papers a note about something he wanted done after he died; he had written it in the best of health one league from his house, but not confident of reaching home alive. We must go right on and act, he insists; he hopes death will find him planting his cabbages, careless of death and still more of his unfinished garden. But first we must prepare. Nature can help in this: by making us ill, insensible, or simply familiar with the idea, by giving us wise advice that we should heed. Leave life, she tells us, as simply and unafraid as you entered it; your death is part of your life and part of that great order of things that you should not even wish to change.

In an uneasy afterthought, possibly written later, Montaigne wonders why simple villagers of low estate, a valet or a chambermaid, often meet death without fear. His only answer now is that the rest of us let its trappings intimidate us; what we fear is its mask. He will put his trust later in nature; now he relies on tension and premeditation.

The problem of pain is similar. Montaigne examines the truth of his chapter title, "That the Taste of Good and Evil Depends in Large Part on the Opinion We Have of Them" (I: 14), and finds it valid for death, less so for pain. "Here all does not consist in imagination. We have opinions about the rest; here it is certain knowledge that plays its part. Even our senses are judges of it." Pain is what we fear in poverty and death. Courage against it is the mark of the wise nobleman; even common people have met it blithely; if it is violent it cannot be long; and there is always the resource of suicide. Mainly, however, our hope is in the power of the soul: "we must resist it and tense ourselves against it."

Thus for Montaigne in the earliest essays life seems to be mainly bad, and its main facts pain and death. For pain the only sure solution is death, the next-best tension and resistance; for death, premeditation, apprehension, and—again—tension. In his tower Montaigne is like a man besieged—by his preparations as well as by what he fears—or like a hunted man. In what is probably an early essay he tells a curious and revealing story of a Roman noble who, fleeing the Triumvirate, had had countless narrow escapes from capture. When a troop of horsemen just missed finding him hiding in his thicket, he finally called them back to end the long agony of his anxiety. "To call out for the hand of the enemy," Montaigne comments, "is a rather extreme measure, yet a better one, I think, than to remain in continual fever over an accident that has no remedy." Montaigne's near-obsession in his late thirties with death never reached such a fever pitch; but even without his comment, the story would remind us of him.

Montaigne clearly feels that man's bleak condition obliges the noble humanist to seek help from his studies of the ancients and gird up his soul to meet the ills of life head on. But, one may ask, precisely why?

He seems not very pleased with his earliest explanation that the cost of unpreparedness is too great; for he never repeats it. He knows that common people, cowards, and whole nations have shown great unpremeditated courage. He will call on the body to help the soul; he welcomes as permissible, even laudable, any honorable assistance against the ills of life; if death were avoidable, he says, he would hide under a calf's skin to escape it.

But he feels that the humanist noble has a duty to meet pain and death not only adequately but well; and this requires preparation. This is how the superior man can and must distinguish himself. Montaigne still has the typical humanist's contempt for the fearful, unthinking vulgar and admiration for the sage, the "man of understanding," who knows how to combat fear, has lost nothing if he still has himself, and would not stoop to the "brutish nonchalance" of not thinking about death. "I cannot believe," he writes, "that meanness of understanding can do more than vigor, or that the effects of reason cannot match the effects of habit." If reason fails, it must be through misuse. When he first tells how Pyrrho, in a storm at sea, reassured his fellow passengers by pointing to a tranquil pig in their boat, Montaigne asks: "The intelligence that has been given us for our greatest good, shall we use it for our ruin, combating the plan of nature . . . ?"

In fact we should be grateful for pain, since it gives us our greatest chance to show our mettle. Without it, how could we exercise valor and magnanimity? How else than by bearing it with triumphant calm "shall we acquire the advantage that we wish to have over the common herd"?

Actually, bravery is not the only distinction between the noble sage and the vulgar; there is also consistency, which always preoccupied Montaigne. In "The Inconsistency of Our Actions" (II: 1), he scans all antiquity and finds hardly a dozen men who have fashioned a uniform will. The greatest of these is Cato the Younger, "a harmony of perfectly concordant sounds, which cannot conflict." Most men are mere playthings of whim and chance: "Our ordinary practice is to follow the inclinations of our appetite, to the left, to the right, uphill and down, as the wind of circumstance carries us. . . . We change like that animal which takes the color of the place you set it on. What we have just now planned, we presently change, and presently again we retrace our steps: nothing but oscillation and inconsistency. . . . We do not go; we are carried away, like floating objects. . . . Every day a new fancy, and our humors shift with the shifts in the weather." Indeed, such a patchwork of conflicting impulses are we that "there is as much difference between us and ourselves as between us and others."

Greater even than this difference, however, is that between the herd and the sage. Montaigne begins "Of the Inequality That Is Between Us" (I: 42) with another paradox: "there is more distance from a given man to a given man than from a given man to a given animal." We are prone to judge men by their trappings, not themselves, to see a vast distinction between a peasant and a king, who, subject alike to mortal ills, "are different, so to speak, only in their breeches." The emperor whose pomp dazzles us in public, seen behind the curtain, is an ordinary man, perhaps viler than the least of his subjects. The true distinction is between the enlightened humanist and the common herd:

The pedestal is not part of the statue. Measure him without his stilts; let him put aside his riches and honors, let him present himself in his shirt. Has he a body fit for its functions, healthy and blithe? What sort of soul has he? Is it beautiful, capable, and happily furnished with all its parts? Is it rich of its own riches, or of others'? Has fortune nothing to do with it? If open-eyed he awaits the drawn swords; if he cares not whether his life expires by the mouth or the neck; if his soul is composed, equable, and content: this is what we must see, and by this judge the extreme differences that are between us. Is he

> wise, and master of himself . . . ?

Such a man is five hundred fathoms above kingdoms and duchies; he is himself his own empire and riches; he lives satisfied, happy, and blithe. And to the man who has that, what is there left to want? . . . Compare with him the common run of men today, ignorant, stupid, and asleep, base, servile, full of fever and fright, unstable, and continually floating in the tempest of the diverse passions that drive and toss them about; depending entirely on others. There is more distance between them than between heaven and earth.

Thus Montaigne's problem in the early *Essays* is not merely the general human one of seeking freedom from fear, but that of the humanist, whose ability to meet pain and death bravely raises him above the common herd. Nor is his solution specifically Stoic, much as he admires Cato; it is that of an eclectic humanist who seeks arms in books, in the sages, in self-mastery by reason and the power of the soul, against a sea of troubles. The way he tries to raise the siege of apprehension is the humanist's way.

Most of the very earliest essays, which we have been considering up to now, were probably composed in 1572 or early 1573. In those that soon followed (1573–74) the problem remains the same, but the initial solution comes under critical scrutiny. Montaigne's frequent lip service later to the ideal of Stoical humanism has led some critics to treat his abandonment of it as an act of "impotence and flabbiness," that of "a weak man who falls in love with the strong." Though the relative merits of this and his later ideal are of course debatable, I find these critics too ready to believe that he gave up what he considered best. It is probably more important that he came to see serious weaknesses in the attitude he had so much admired. He had argued against it with La Boétie but sought to adopt it when death made his friend the object of his cult. If anything was an aberration in his development, it was not his flight from Stoical humanism but his attraction to it. Plutarch, working against his other favorite, Seneca, helped him come out of it and become himself again.

Part of his change comes with experience. Though his serious illness of the kidney stone was yet to come, from 1573 on he knew kidney trouble well. Here, as with his first approximation of death, familiarity showed him the exaggeration of his imaginings and gave him confidence.

Even the earliest essays show that Montaigne is not the perfect humanist sage—or apprentice sage. "Crawling in the slime of the earth," he writes, "I do not fail to observe, even in the clouds, the loftiness of certain heroic souls." The statement shows unconcern as well as admiration, a sense not so much of inferiority as of incompatibility. (Later he will add the adjective "inimitable" to modify "loftiness.") To feel different, for Montaigne, is not to feel (like a Romantic) therefore superior; nor is it to feel inferior. Already he considers us responsible only for intentions, not for results; these are beyond our control.

For all his variability, Montaigne is basically conservative, not radical, an accepter, not a reformer, seeking harmony, not conflict, within. By around 1573 he begins to note that men do not even wish to change much. Calling it a malady to disdain ourselves, he goes on: "It is by a similar vanity that we wish to be something other than we are. The object of such a desire does not really affect us, inasmuch as the desire contradicts and hinders itself within. A man who wishes to be made into an angel does nothing for himself. For when he is no more, he will no longer have the wherewithal to rejoice in this improvement and feel it." Our very inconsistency is tempered by a certain immutability. Neither ideas nor ideals can be of use to us unless they are our very own: "Even if we could be learned with other men's learning, at least wise we cannot be except with our own wisdom."

It is drastic change, now as later, that Montaigne feels we cannot make. Some improvement is possible; but it should concentrate on essentials, whereas Stoicism considers all vices equal. And it should be in our own terms, appropriate to our nature. If we try too hard, we can do nothing. The male member, which may lie down on the job if we urge it too strongly not to, is Montaigne's favorite proof that our will is not omnipotent; but he finds this true of the soul in general: "I know by very personal and ordinary experience that natural condition that cannot endure vehement premeditation. . . . The anxiety to do well, and that tension of the soul that is too strained and intent on its enterprise, racks it and confuses it."

Since Stoical humanism vainly ignores, or seeks to suppress, man's basic contrariness, Montaigne soon grows wary of it. He notes that ignorance and habit have done more for ordinary people than study and effort for the philosophers. True sages are rare. Gradually he comes to consider his earlier ideal impractical as well as unsound.

He had hoped to find consistency in it, but soon came to feel that this could not be—at least in precisely the heroic actions and attitudes he had most admired. Since man cannot live consistently on such a high level, the greatest deeds of the greatest heroes are aberrations:

> When we hear our martyrs cry out to the tyrant in the midst of the flames: "It's roasted enough on that side . . . start in again on the other side!" . . . surely we must confess that in those souls there is some alteration and some frenzy, however holy it be. When we come to these Stoic sallies: "I would rather be insane than voluptuous" . . . when Epicurus . . . cheerfully defies ills and, scorning the less severe pains . . . invokes and wishes for pains strong and biting . . . who does not judge that those are sallies of a courage flung out of its abode? Our soul from its seat could not reach so high; it must leave it and rise, and, taking the bit in its teeth, ravish and carry away its man so far that afterward he is himself astonished at his deed. . . . Aristotle . . . is right to call madness any transport, however laudable, that transcends our own judgment and reason; inasmuch as wisdom is an orderly management of our soul, which she conducts with measure and proportion.

Incompatible with consistency and wisdom in its highest flights, the philosophy of tension is often comically histrionic. Even in one of his earliest essays Montaigne recognized this when he first told the story of Posidonius, who was painfully ill when a visitor apologized for coming at a bad time. Though Posidonius replied that pain could not keep him from expressing his contempt for it, it forced him to exclaim: "You may do your worst, pain, yet I will not say that you are an evil." Montaigne's comment is derisive: "This tale that they make so much of, what has it to do with contempt of pain? He is only arguing about the word; and meanwhile if these pangs do not move him, why does he interrupt his talk for their sake? Why does he think he is doing a lot by not calling pain an evil?"

He is beginning to view Stoical humanism as a philosophy of death, and to rally to the defense of life. Seneca's advice to Lucilius to quit his life of pomp or quit life itself sounds to him like "Stoical harshness" but is actually borrowed from Epicurus; he contrasts it sharply with "Christian moderation."

Immodest as well as immoderate, humanistic philosophy errs morally as well as intellectually in refusing to recognize man's inherent frailty. Even its sage cannot live up to what it claims man can do; nature is too strong. In "Drunkenness" (II: 2), the inane question whether wine can overcome the soul of the sage draws this broadside from Montaigne:

Out of a thousand souls, there is not one that is straight and composed for a single moment in a lifetime; and it may be questioned, given the soul's natural condition, whether it can ever be so. But as for combining this with constancy, that is the soul's ultimate perfection; I mean even if nothing should jar it. . . .

For all his wisdom, the sage is still a man; what is there more vulnerable, more wretched, and more null? Wisdom does not overcome our natural conditions. He must blink his eyes at the blow that threatens him; he must shudder if you plant him on the edge of a precipice. . . . Enough for him to curb and moderate his inclinations; for to do away with them is not in him.

Stoical humanism authorizes suicide as man's unalienable right, which anyone but a coward will avail himself of in misery. In his earliest essays Montaigne often echoes this view and seems to approve of it. Now, in "A Custom of the Island of Cea" (II: 3), he examines both sides of the question. He does not commit himself clearly; but the movement of the chapter as a whole in its original form— arguments for suicide; arguments against; occasions and motives that may sometimes sanction it—clearly limits its justifiability and seems rather to condemn than to approve it in general. It contains many serious criticisms of suicide which conform with Montaigne's basic convictions and which he nowhere later contradicts.

In the first place, Christianity condemns it. Both the Church itself and "other philosophers" (presumably Christian) maintain that God has put us here as in a garrison, "not for ourselves alone but for his glory and the service of others," and that it is for him alone to release us; if we take this liberty ourselves, we are punished in the afterlife as deserters from our post.

Moreover, Christianity apart, suicide is the easy way out. It takes more constancy to wear out our chains than to break them. "It is an act of cowardice, not of virtue, to go and hide in a hole, under a massive tomb, in order to avoid the blows of fortune." And insofar as it shows contempt for life, it is the act of a mind diseased: "The opinion that disdains our life is ridiculous in us. For after all it is our being, it is our all. Things that have a nobler and richer being may accuse ours; but it is against nature that we despise ourselves and care nothing about ourselves. It is a malady peculiar to man, and not seen in any other creature, to hate and combat himself."

Thus suicide and the doctrine that approves it are both un-Christian and unnatural. For Montaigne these two things are much the same. His Christianity virtually identifies the order of nature with the order of God. He seeks God less in the Bible through revelation than—like Sebond, of all people—in the creation through reason. For him what is Christian may be natural or supernatural; what is natural is nearly always Christian.

He considers Christian virtue moderate, in contrast with Stoical —and Epicurean—harshness. Any virtue that is not moderate and natural is for him no true virtue, either by purely human or by Christian standards. "A man may both love virtue too much," he writes, "and behave immoderately in a just and virtuous action. The Holy Writ may be adapted to this angle: 'Be not wiser than you should, but be soberly wise.'" Extreme austerity of the Stoical type is one of man's sorriest attempts to improve on nature. Our misery is of our own making: "Isn't man a miserable animal? Hardly is it in his power, by his natural condition, to taste a single pleasure pure and entire, and still he is at pains to cut it down by reason. He is not wretched enough unless by art and study he augments his misery."

Thus Montaigne attacks Stoical humanism for ignoring not only the limitations imposed on us by nature but also her generous gifts. He is beginning to dwell on her benignity, which he will stress more later, often apropos of Socrates, who becomes his greatest hero after 1576. He notes her kindness to all creatures close to her—animals, savages, beggars, common folk. Simple, unopinionated, and relaxed, they follow their natural inclinations. Compared with these trusting children of nature, the humanist sages are foolish prodigals. Their dogmatic philosophy is unsound, impractical, inconsistent, immoderate, comically presumptuous, un-Christian, and unnatural. In the years before the "Apology for Raymond Sebond," all these points are clearly made. In that chapter, Montaigne will blithely develop them into a devastating critique of all dogmatic philosophy.

Chapter 10: The "Apology for Raymond Sebond"
[*1573–1576–1579*]

HIS CHAPTER (II:12), by far Montaigne's longest, has been his most influential and remains his most puzzling. In its final form it is three times as long as the next-longest and comprises nearly one sixth of the entire work; its original version was nearly five times as long as any other chapter of Books I and II and filled nearly one fourth of the 1580 edition.

Here we find the fullest expression of Montaigne's doubt, summed up in the famous formula "What do I know?" which he used for a time as his motto. For Bacon, Descartes, and Pascal this was a starting point, a demonstrated position that must be faced and overcome: by the experimental method, by reason, by faith. For about a century many religious believers and doubters alike, and for another century mainly doubters, drew freely on Montaigne's arguments: in England Glanvill, Browne, Blount, Sheffield, Pope, in France Raemond, Charron, Pierre Camus, La Mothe Le Vayer, Diderot, Rousseau. His French adversaries include Garasse, Silhon, Bossuet, Malebranche, Pascal and his Jansenist colleagues. For Sainte-

Beuve in his *Port-Royal* (though apparently not later) this is the perfidious, tortuous, calculating center of the apparently innocent *Essays,* in which Montaigne, "an accursed enchanter, a malignant demon," leads his reader imperceptibly ever deeper into the caves of doubt, only then to blow out the light. André Gide in our own time held a somewhat similar view; yet most modern scholars reject this theory.

Montaigne opens with the brief keynote statement that knowledge is not the sovereign good and that he likes learned men but (unlike his father) does not worship them. He then spends three pages * introducing his author in the curious way noted earlier (chapter 7). Pierre Bunel left Sebond's book, as an antidote to Lutheranism and atheism, with Montaigne's father, who, a few days before his death, happened to come across it in a pile of abandoned papers and ordered Michel to put it into French for him. His son, by chance at leisure and unable to refuse, did his best; the father, pleased, arranged to have it printed.

The first objection raised against the book is "that Christians do themselves harm in trying to support their belief by human reasons, since it is conceived only by faith and by a particular inspiration of divine grace." Montaigne finds in this "a certain pious zeal" and deals with it mildly, for the very good reason that he clearly shares it. After two pages showing that rational demonstration may be of some help, he spends five more on the oblique defense that what passes for Christianity in France is so bad that it must have been received by human means; thus Sebond may yet be useful.

The second objection, that Sebond's arguments are "weak and unfit to prove what he proposes," makes some critics think they can shatter them with ease. These men, more dangerous and malicious than the others, must be shaken up roughly. Montaigne's method will be "to crush and trample underfoot human arrogance and pride; to make them feel the inanity, the vanity and nothingness, of man; to wrest from their hands the puny weapons of their reason; to make them bow their heads and bite the ground beneath the authority and reverence of divine majesty."

His introduction ended, Montaigne sets out to demolish man's

---

* All the following references to page lengths are based on the Dezeimeris and Barckhausen re-edition (Bordeaux: Gounouilhou, 1870–73, 2 vols.) of the original 1580 edition of the *Essays.*

presumption. "Let us see then if man has within his power other reasons more powerful than those of Sebond, or indeed if it is in him to arrive at any certainty by argument and reason." Since the second type of critic rejects the authority of religion, the object of the counterattack will be man without God: "Let us then consider for the moment man alone, without outside assistance, armed solely with his own weapons, and deprived of divine grace and knowledge, which is his whole honor, his strength, and the foundation of his being. Let us see how much presence he has in this fine array." In the very next sentence, completely abandoning Sebond, Montaigne announces the first part of his counterattack, against man's delusions of superiority over the animals. "Let him help me to understand, by the force of his reason, on what foundations he has built these great advantages that he thinks he has over other creatures." A few pages on man's nothingness in regard to infinity, and Montaigne is off for a forty-three-page romp—longer than any other whole chapter in the 1580 edition—with the animals.

As he extols their intelligence, courage, charity, magnanimity, and other virtues at the expense of ours, Montaigne gives his critical judgment the day off and revels in the joy of argument. He presents as true examples which Pliny and Herodotus had reported as incredible and false. His main source is Plutarch, whose dialogues "That Brute Beasts Make Use of Reason" (between Ulysses and Circe's captive swine, once a man, Gryllus) and "Whether Land or Water Animals Are Cleverer" are clearly presented as paradoxes by Plutarch but used in apparent earnest by Montaigne. (Two facts about these dialogues are worth noting: they flatly oppose Stoic doctrine, as Plutarch often does elsewhere, in crediting animals with intelligence; and the French translator, Montaigne's friend Jacques Amyot, Grand Almoner of France and bishop of Auxerre, praises the "Gryllus" as well suited to Christianity by its rejection of man's arrogant rationalism and atheism.)

We are not worse treated than the beasts, Montaigne argues; but to our cost we have abandoned nature's way. We belong right among them: not below, but certainly not among the gods and angels.

Suppose, however, man does have some kind of reason and imagination that the animals lack. Does it make him happier, or better? To both questions—in about twelve pages for the first, three for the second—Montaigne answers an emphatic No. Reason is the source of ambition, lust, greed, anxiety, arrogance, and most of our other vices. Did intelligence exempt Varro and Aristotle from human pains? "Did they derive from logic some consolation for the gout?" Here we meet Posidonius again, refusing to call pain pain: "Nothing but wind and words." Here are Pyrrho and the pig again; but where Montaigne had concluded earlier that we must use our reason better, now he finds no use in knowledge or philosophy: "But even if knowledge would actually do what they say, blunt and lessen something of the stings of the pain and the keenness of the misfortunes that pursue us, what does it do but what ignorance does much more purely and evidently? . . . Philosophy, at the end of her precepts, sends us back to the examples of an athlete or a muleteer."

Reason, knowledge, and imagination may be not merely useless but detrimental to happiness. Anticipation and apprehension, Montaigne's earlier aids against the fear of death, now seem to do more harm than good: "When real evils fail us, knowledge lends us hers. . . . Compare the life of a man enslaved to such imaginings with that of a plowman letting himself follow his natural appetites, measuring things only by the present taste of them, without knowledge and without prognostication, who has pain only when he has it; whereas the other often has the stone in his soul before he has it in his loins. As if he were not in time to suffer the pain when he is in it, he anticipates it in imagination and runs to meet it."

Knowledge itself seeks help in affliction from ignorance by telling us to forget the painful present for the happy past. This trick is unworthy and not even good; it would not comfort us against pain even if it worked, and it will not work because it is psychologically unsound. We cannot forget at will. "For memory sets before us, not what we choose, but what it pleases. Indeed there is nothing that imprints a thing so vividly on our memory as the desire to forget it." Suicide, philosophy's last resort, is a confession of her impotence, an appeal to ignorance, insensibility, and nonexistence.

Rational philosophy has no more power to make us good than happy. "As by simplicity life becomes pleasanter," Montaigne goes on, "so also does it become better and more innocent. . . . The simple and ignorant, says Saint Paul, raise themselves to heaven, and take possession of it; and we, with all our learning, plunge ourselves into the infernal abyss." The nations of the New World live better without magistrates and laws than ours that are overrun with them.

Humility, fear, obedience, amenability, the main Christian and social
virtues, usually go hand in hand with ignorance. Christians, knowing
the cause of man's fall, should need no reminder of the dangers of
the lust for knowledge. This and our absurd pride lead us even to try
to define and limit God, to whom our concepts do not apply at all.
"It is for God alone to interpret his works and to know himself.
. . . Our faith is not of our own acquiring, it is a pure present of
another's liberality. It is not by reasoning or by our understanding
that we have received our religion; it is by external authority and
command. . . . It is by the mediation of our ignorance more than
of our knowledge that we are learned with that divine learning. . . .
Let us bring to it nothing of our own but obedience and submission."

For the remaining three-fifths of the chapter, Montaigne turns
to the question whether we have, or can have, true knowledge. "Yet
must I see at last whether it is in the power of man to find what he
seeks, and whether that quest that he has been making for so many
centuries has enriched him with any new power and any solid truth."
It is the second of these questions that he tackles first. Scorning to
use the unthinking herd to make a fool of man, he proposes instead
the philosopher and sage: "I wish to take man in his highest estate.
Let us consider him in that small number of excellent and select men
who, having been endowed with fine and particular natural ability,
have further strengthened and sharpened it by care, by study, and
by art, and have raised it to the highest pitch that it can attain. . . .
It is in them that the utmost height of human nature is found. . . .
I shall take into account only these people. . . . The infirmities and
defects that we shall find in this assembly the world may well boldly
acknowledge as its own."

He divides philosophers into three classes according to their respective claims: that they have found the truth; that it cannot be
found; that they are still looking for it. The brashest of these are
the first class, the dogmatists—Aristotle, Epicurus, the Stoics, and
others. Clitomachus, Carneades, and the Academics, who deny that
man can find the truth, have had the largest and noblest following;
but even their denial is dogmatic. Only those are really sound who
confess their ignorance and go on searching, like Socrates, whom
Montaigne for the first time describes as "the wisest man that ever
was," and like the skeptics who follow Pyrrho. These use their reason
to question and debate, but abstain from final judgment. They be-

have simply and sociably, not presuming to think they know better. The most responsible and humane of human philosophies, theirs is also the ideal preparation for Christianity, presenting man "naked and empty, acknowledging his natural weakness, fit to receive from above some outside power; stripped of human knowledge, and all the more apt to lodge divine instruction and belief."

Most of the dogmatists, Montaigne goes on, were really skeptics who hated to admit it and wanted to show how far their search for truth had led them. They loved the quest for its own sake, like Democritus, who, intrigued to find a flavor of honey in some figs, was happily theorizing about the soil they came from, when his maid told him they had been in a jar that had held honey; whereat he scolded her angrily and went on theorizing anyway.

Montaigne now examines, as a test of their knowledge, the philosophers' beliefs about God or the gods (thirteen pages), man in general (eight pages), his soul or reason (fourteen pages), and his body (one page). Some of their notions about the Deity are hard to explain. "For what is there, for example, more vain than to try to regulate God and the world by our capacity and our laws?" The most excusable religion that Saint Paul found in Athens was the worship of an unknown God. Of all merely human ancient opinions about God, the most plausible considered him "an incomprehensible power, origin and preserver of all things, all goodness, all perfection, accepting and taking in good part the honor and reverence that human beings rendered him, under whatever aspect and in whatever manner it might be." Our arrogance in this domain is our ultimate presumption and folly. As soon as human reason leaves the beaten path of the Church, it is lost in the troubled sea of human opinions, since man can be only what he is, and imagine only within his reach.

Turning to our knowledge of ourselves, Montaigne finds it as scant and irresponsible as any other. The omniscient critics of Sebond do not even know how spirit works on body. Men never test ideas, but accept them on credit. We are not even allowed to challenge Aristotle; yet that "god of scholastic knowledge" is no better than the rest. Allow another man's first principles, and you are at his mercy; challenge them, and he will not even argue with such a skeptic. Now men cannot know first principles unless by divine revelation. Nothing else is certain, not even common sense, which the philosophers have so ingeniously ruined for themselves. They fall back on reason as their touchstone, but it is false and impotent, and knows nothing even of itself or of the soul. Here too the philosophers— Plato and Aristotle, Stoics and Epicureans—offer the wildest non-sense, refusing to recognize the vulnerability of the soul to hydro-phobia, fever, or even wine. As for the body, a sampling of our theories of reproduction is quick, decisive proof that we know noth-ing about it either. In short, man knows no more of himself—his nearest object of perception—than he does of God.

This concludes Montaigne's demonstration of our ignorance and sets the stage for two pages warning an unnamed princess (Margaret of Valois) to content herself with the ordinary ways of defending Sebond, to avoid the fencer's trick of losing your weapons to make your adversary lose his, in short to use what follows only as a last resort. For what follows is the long climactic part (forty-eight pages), Montaigne's proof that man is incapable of having true knowledge— or, if by any chance he ever should have it, of knowing it for what it is.

The Academic philosophers maintained that while we could not know what is true, we could recognize what is probable. Montaigne denies this on the ground, especially cogent in French, that if we do not know the true (*le vray*) we cannot know what resembles it (*le vraysemblable*). "Either we can judge absolutely, or we absolutely cannot."

Even our judgment is insecure, as we see by its constant varia-tion. "What I hold today and what I believe, I hold and believe it with all my belief. . . . But has it not happened to me, not once, but a hundred times, a thousand times, and every day, to have em-braced with these same instruments, in this same condition, something else that I have since judged false?" Our condition is flux; we must learn its lesson. We are subject to so many passions, vicissitudes, and alterations, that "we can hardly find a single hour in our life when our judgment is in its proper seat." We should know, if nothing else, that without outside help we cannot attain absolute truth; we should learn from the spectacle of our own weakness.

Our soul is affected not only by our body's passions but even more by its own, which make us see things otherwise than does tranquillity. Which way is true, or even truer, Pyrrho does not know.

In the race, as in the individual, change is the one constant. It

LE SEIGNEVR DE MONTAIGNE

Montaigne, by Thomas de Leu

Henry III

Marshal de Matignon

Henry IV

would have been Pyrrhonizing, a thousand years earlier, to doubt the accepted cosmography and suspect the existence of whole continents that have since been discovered. The best products of our judgment and understanding—laws, customs, beliefs, moral codes—are subject to the laws of nature and thus of flux; they are born, grow, dwindle, and die, like us and like all other creatures. But "truth must have one face, the same and universal." It is not to be found among even the best of our ideas.

Our senses are the surest proof of our ignorance. "Knowledge begins through them and is resolved into them." Yet we cannot be sure of their testimony. Often the five that we have conflict; perhaps we need eight or ten. The Epicureans, desperately and absurdly, say we must believe them anyway, or we know nothing. Combine this, Montaigne will add later, with the Stoics' denial that the senses can be trusted at all, and "we shall conclude, at the expense of these two great dogmatic sects, that there is no knowledge." The senses have great power and make fools of us if we challenge them. Touch overthrows "all those beautiful Stoical resolutions, and compels the man to cry out at his stomach who has established with all resolute-ness this doctrine in his soul, that the colic, like every other malady and pain, is an indifferent thing, not having the power to reduce at all the sovereign happiness and felicity in which the sage is lodged by his virtue." Suspend a philosopher in a net between the towers of Notre-Dame and for all his philosophy he is terrified. Our natural condition is too strong.

When we and the animals disagree, whose senses shall we trust? We need to agree with them and with ourselves, but we cannot. To know when we are right, when wrong, we would need a judge whom no conditions could influence, such a judge as never was; or some judicatory machine, which in turn must be verified, and the verifier verified, and so ad infinitum.

Moreover, the soul has no direct contact with the outside world. The mediating senses present to it not the object but only the impact this makes on them. We simply cannot be sure that this corresponds to the object, "just as a man who does not know Socrates, seeing his portrait, cannot say that it resembles him."

Finally, we can have no true knowledge of the created world because both we and it are perpetually changing. Flux cannot truly know flux. Nor can flux have communication with being. Montaigne follows Plutarch (in Amyot's translation) almost word for word for three pages in showing that God alone *is*, has being, does not change, and thus can know perfect truth, which like him is eternal and immutable. To this "most religious conclusion of a pagan" he adds the remark of another, Seneca: "O what a vile and abject thing is man, if he does not raise himself above humanity!" Thus in conclusion he returns to the lofty aspiration of Stoical humanism, and dismisses it as presumptuous and pointless: "There is no truer saying in all his Stoic school than that one. But to make the handful bigger than the hand, the armful bigger than the arm, and to hope to straddle more than the reach of our legs, is impossible and unnatural. Nor can man raise himself above himself and humanity; for he can see only with his own eyes, and seize only with his own grasp. He will rise, if God lends him his hand; he will rise by abandoning and renouncing his own means, and letting himself be raised and uplifted by divine grace; but not otherwise."

The chapter is puzzling because it is a defense of Sebond in little but name, which, as one critic has put it, "supports Sebond . . . as the rope supports the hanged man." Though the two have common adversaries in the Protestants, Montaigne's critique draws blood not only from them but from his author as well. Hence the common charge of betrayal. Montaigne, it is alleged, is far too intelligent not to know what he is doing. His skepticism is often a mockery of Sebond and apparently of Christianity itself; this must be conscious and intentional.

However, this view is hard to accept. Montaigne protests his truthfulness earnestly and often; he constantly speaks and acts like a Catholic; if he is perfidious, he must be a thoroughgoing fraud. His fideism (religious faith based on skepticism about human reason) was acceptable to the Church of his time and was not even criticized by the papal censors when they examined his book in Rome in 1580–81; he could hardly know that its unorthodoxy a hundred years later would contribute to placing it on the Index of Forbidden Books. Nor is it his fault that later admirers applied his critique of philosophy and of other religions to Catholicism, which he had set above the reach of reason.

There is at least one explanation of Montaigne's treatment of Sebond besides forgetfulness and betrayal, and that is unconcern.

Even when translating him, he had made clear his disagreement with
the Spaniard's extravagant claims. In the "Apology" he labors to say
something good about his man, but mainly seeks to dissociate himself
from him. He seems to regard him as a rather weak thinker whom
many readers admire, who is on the right side, means well, and may
be useful. The proportions of the chapter suggest how little Montaigne is concerned with Sebond. He undertakes to defend him against
two groups of objectors, thus leading us to expect an introduction,
two main parts, and a conclusion. But there is almost no defense;
the beginning and the conclusion relate to the counterattack against
the second group of critics, which fills over nine tenths of the
whole chapter and is obviously Montaigne's main concern.

It is about two thirds of the way through that Montaigne stops
to address the noble lady for whom he says he has extended this
work beyond his wont, and urges her to defend "your Sebond" with
the customary arguments, using those that follow only with great
caution, "if one of these new doctors tries to show off his ingenuity
in your presence, at the risk of his salvation and yours." The "new
doctors" are the Protestants; the lady is Margaret of Valois, sister of
Henry III and wife of the Protestant Navarre. Montaigne knew her
already. A passage in her *Memoirs* shows her reading with much comfort in 1576 a book that can only be Sebond's, presumably in Montaigne's translation. One comment of Montaigne's is enlightening:
"Because many people are busy reading it, and especially the ladies,
to whom we owe additional help, I have often found myself in a
position to help them by clearing their book of two principal objections that are made against it." It seems virtually certain that Margaret asked Montaigne to write in defense of his author, and highly
probable that she did so in 1578–79, when she joined her husband in
Gascony and found herself surrounded by Protestants eager to convert her.

However, there is good reason to believe, with Villey and Zeitlin, that large parts of the chapter were composed a good deal earlier,
one around 1573, another around 1576. The frequent inconsistencies
and lapses in order—fruitless circularity and the like—support the
theory of strata in the original 1580 version, as do its disproportionate
length and Montaigne's remark about having labored "to extend so
long a work contrary to my custom." On this theory, most of the
enigma of Montaigne's tactics is explained by his piecing together,

as a command performance, mainly out of materials already composed, a defense of an author whom he did not greatly admire. He had probably written a chapter on human presumption—perhaps incomplete; perhaps more than one; perhaps with that title, later given to another—to humiliate it for the sake of Christian obedience, without Sebond in mind, when Margaret asked him to defend him. Perhaps remembering the recent and popular *Apology for Herodotus* by the Protestant Henri Estienne, which was anything but a defense of that historian, and having aimed his earlier chapter precisely against those who were Sebond's main critics, Montaigne probably decided he could set it so as to make it a satisfactory "Apology for Raymond Sebond."

The following tables show my version of this theory and of the theoretical and actual parts of the chapter that may usefully be distinguished, with the page numbers in my translation (S) and in the Dezeimeris and Barckhausen edition (DB), which reproduces the original text of 1580. Montaigne, of course, made no formal divisions of the chapter whatever.

APOLOGY FOR RAYMOND SEBOND

1. Simplified Plan Showing Strata of Composition

  I. Introduction—c. 1579 (S 319–28; DB 17–29)
 II. Presumption of Man without God: Man No Better than the Animals—
      c. 1573 (S 328–70; DB 29–90)
III. Man's Ignorance without God—c. 1573 (parts of S 370–87; DB 90–
      106)
 IV. Skepticism—c. 1576 (parts of S 371–80; DB 92–100)
IIIA. Man's Ignorance (continued)—c. 1576 (S 387–418; DB 106–36)
                    of God (S 387–400; DB 106–13)
                    of Man: Soul and Body (S 400–18; DB 113–36)
  V. Warning to the Princess—c. 1579 (S 418–20; DB 136–38)
 VI. Man's Incapacity for Knowledge without God—c. 1579 (S 420–57;
      DB 138–86)

2. Detailed Plan of Contents

KEYNOTE: Knowledge Is Useful but Overrated	S 319;	DB 17
INTRODUCTION: Sebond and His Book	S 319;	DB 17
FIRST OBJECTION AND DEFENSE	S 321;	DB 20
Conclusion	S 326;	DB 26
SECOND OBJECTION: The Objectors	S 327;	DB 27
Defense	S 328;	DB 28

COUNTERATTACK: The Vanity of Man and of
                    Man's Knowledge without God   S 328–457; DB 29–186
  1. General   S 328; DB 29
  2. Man Is No Better than the Animals   S 330; DB 32
  3. Man's Knowledge Cannot Make
                    Him Happy—   S 358; DB 75
  4.   or Good   S 367; DB 87
  5. Man Has No Knowledge   S 370; DB 90
     a. Skepticism the Only Wisdom   S 371; DB 92
     b. Man's Ignorance of God (or gods)   S 380; DB 100
     c. Man's Ignorance of Man in General— S 400; DB 113
     d.   of His Soul and Reason S 405; DB 121
     e.   of His Body   S 417; DB 135
  6. Warning to the Princess   S 418; DB 136
  7. Man Can Have No Knowledge   S 420; DB 138
     a. The Lesson of Flux   S 420; DB 138
     b. The Senses Are Inadequate   S 443; DB 166
     c. Flux Cannot Know Flux   S 455; DB 182
     d. Flux Cannot Know Being   S 455; DB 183
  8. Conclusion: Man Is Nothing without God   S 457; DB 186

If indeed there was an earlier chapter which Montaigne made into an "Apology for Raymond Sebond," it may well have ended in one of two places:

1. Just before the "Warning to the Princess" (S 418, OC 539, DB 136) with Montaigne's statement that he has "sufficiently demonstrated" how little human reason "understands about itself." This would be a natural place, since Montaigne then issues his warning and goes on to show that we not only do not but cannot know.

2. With the following passage on man's ignorance of the divine (S 386–87, OC 500–01, DB 105–06):

Reason does nothing but go astray in everything, but especially when it meddles with divine things. Who feels this more evidently than we? For even though we have given it certain and infallible principles, even though we light its steps with the holy lamp of the truth which it has pleased God to communicate to us, nevertheless we see daily how, when it strays however little from the beaten path and deviates or wanders from the way traced and trodden by the Church, immediately it is lost, it grows embarrassed and entangled, whirling round and floating in that vast, troubled, and undulating sea of human opinions, unbridled and aimless. As soon as it loses that great common highroad it breaks up and disperses onto a thousand different roads.

Man can be only what he is, and imagine only within his reach.

This seems a likely ending to an earlier shorter chapter because of its conclusiveness—it wraps up earlier themes and leads to a summarizing punch line; its close similarity in moral to the 1580 conclusion, quoted above (p. 170), which Montaigne may have modeled on it; his declaration sixteen pages earlier (S 370, OC 480, DB 90) that he must see "at last" whether man can learn or has learned anything—which seems to announce an ending that otherwise is very long in coming; and his statement to the princess thirty pages later that he has "taken the pains to extend so long a work contrary to my custom," which may well mean that he has much enlarged, at her request, something already written before he penned the warning.

There are other possibilities, of course; an earlier chapter might have ended with the statement (S 405, OC 523, DB 120) that "reason . . . is a touchstone full of falsity, error, weakness, and impotence." If there was such a chapter, it received, on any theory, additions before being published: borrowings from books by La Primaudaye (1577), Laurent Joubert (1578), and the like. If it was composed around 1573, the parts on Pyrrhonism were probably added around 1576—or possibly later, after Queen Margaret's request. Montaigne's statement (S 362, OC 470, DB 80) about the man who "has the stone in his soul before he has it in his loins" may have been added, as Villey believed, after he himself got it in his loins in 1578; but such was his earlier fear of it that this may be part of his original text.

The dating of the possible original chapter on man and the animals at 1573 is supported by references to themes of other chapters. Montaigne here writes of the inequality of men as of a subject already treated (I: 42; c. 1572–73), and twice of the Brazilian cannibals as though his chapter on them (I: 31; c. 1578–80) were not yet written. Much of his material here resembles other early discussions of strange manners and conventions, such as "Of Custom" (I: 23; c. 1573). He relies heavily for his animal stories on Plutarch's *Moral Essays*, from which he borrowed especially freely around 1573. He acknowledges this debt when he tells Margaret that she should have given the task of defending Sebond to a professional writer, who would have enriched and supported this theme better "and would have used others than our Plutarch to make his compilation."

The dating of the part on Pyrrhonian skepticism at around 1576 rests largely on two medals which Montaigne had struck, both bearing that date, his name and coat of arms, a pair of scales in balance, and the Pyrrhonian motto Ἐπέχω (I abstain); one with the additional number 42, the other with 43, which were his ages in 1576 before and after February 28. Ἐπέχω was among the seventeen Pyrrhonian maxims inscribed on the beams of Montaigne's library; but we do not know when this was done; we assume around 1576. The chief source of Pyrrho's doctrines, Sextus Empiricus' *Outlines of Pyrrhonism*, had been available since 1562 in Henri Estienne's Latin translation from the Greek.

The date 1579 is assigned to the Introduction and the Warning (plus a few references to Margaret and to Sebond) on the theory that at about that date Montaigne, at Margaret's request, arranged some material already composed so as to make it an "Apology for Raymond Sebond." As for the final part after the Warning, on man's incapacity for knowledge without God's help, Villey attributed it to 1576 because it includes much material from Pyrrho, especially the critique of the senses (S 443–55, OC 571–84, DB 166–82). Zeitlin assigns that critique to 1576, for the same reason, and regards what immediately precedes (S 420–43, OC 542–71, DB 138–66) as partly composed in 1576, partly composed and retouched in 1579, when Montaigne often criticizes Pyrrhonism. I lean to 1579 for this whole section, partly because of Montaigne's critique of Pyrrhonism, partly because all that follows the Warning seems to do so in time as well as in order of presentation.

All this division and dating of parts of the chapter is of course entirely hypothetical. Its justification is that no simpler, surer explanation of the chapter's enigmas seems tenable, and that it fits what we otherwise know about the development of Montaigne's thought.

It is striking, but not surprising in view of Montaigne's personal concerns in the "Apology," that his conclusion is not an affirmation of Pyrrhonism but a repudiation of Stoicism. For all its importance in the chapter, Montaigne's Pyrrhonism is neither brand-new, absolute, all-embracing, nor a complete commitment. His doubting temper is manifest before and after; Villey's theory of a "skeptical crisis" seems excessive. The "Apology" is Montaigne's most thorough exploration and statement of the case for doubt, whose composition centered in a time when Sextus Empiricus had just made him recognize the dialectical power of Pyrrho's position. His sweeping skepticism here is less an end in itself than a means of confounding dogmatism. Montaigne is playing Pyrrhonist. Where the Pyrrhonists use uncritical arguments because they do not presume to judge, he uses them but still judges. His account of their method in argument describes his own in this chapter: "They do not fear contradiction in their discussion. When they say that heavy things go down, they would be very sorry to have anyone take their word for it; and they seek to be contradicted, so as to create doubt and suspension of judgment, which is their goal. They advance their propositions only to combat those they think we believe in."

Montaigne's delight in the game of paradox often leads him into inconsistencies. He tells of his talk with an innovation-monger who maintained that the ancients were mistaken about the winds. " 'What?' I said to him. 'Then did those who navigated under the laws of Theophrastus go west when they headed east? Did they go sideways, or backward?' 'That was luck,' he replied; 'at all events they miscalculated.' I then replied to him that I would rather follow facts than reason. Now these are things that often clash." One sentence later he makes his point completely clear: "And the Pyrrhonists use their arguments and their reason only to combat and ruin the apparent facts of experience; and it is marvelous how far the suppleness of our reason has followed them in this plan of combating the evidence of the facts." Much earlier, shortly after his first presentation of the Pyrrhonist case, Montaigne urged that we meet initial assumptions in argument by assuming the very opposite: "For every human presupposition and every enunciation has as much authority as another, unless reason shows the difference between them." From these examples we see that Montaigne prefers facts to even the most ingenious rational undermining of them, such as Pyrrhonism, and considers reason helpless—except where it helps.*

As we have noted, some of this may be less inconsistency than change of attitude. If around 1576 Montaigne became infatuated with systematic Pyrrhonism, he soon got over it. Several chapters composed in 1578–80 reveal viewpoints contrasting with the skeptical

---

* Much of the inconsistency or change in Montaigne's treatment of reason is mainly verbal, since he uses it to mean at least two very different faculties: theoretical reason, which is always dangerous, and practical reason, which is always good. However, he never makes this distinction explicit; and after using the term in the "Apology" almost always in its bad sense, he turns to its good sense in the chapters (I: 26; II: 8; etc.) written just afterward, in 1578–80.

themes of the "Apology." In a passage placed immediately before that chapter he speaks with marked detachment about the uncritical praise of animals that he displays in it. Elsewhere he shows equal detachment from its misanthropy. Once he introduces Pyrrho as "the one who built such an amusing science out of ignorance." And he states that though we must make concessions to nature, "reason alone must guide our inclinations."

As his statements of purpose show, his skepticism is limited in extent as well as in degree. Man's false opinion of knowledge and its value, the vanity and presumption that results—these are his targets; when he hits others it is often because his relish for the sport makes him inattentive. It is in their lunatic fringes—our claims to know what we cannot know—that he attacks human reason and knowledge. He never suggests that we can know too much or reason too much about our conduct.

He is beginning to put his faith in experience, which—since it deals rather with what happens than with why—he finds more dependable than reason. Many arguments for our intellectual impotence in the final part of his chapter—our changes and illusions—are drawn not from books but from his own life.

Although the "Apology" denies our capacity for perfect knowledge, especially of the unfathomable, it often recognizes much value in the imperfect kind that we can have. Apparently without any special divine dispensation, Montaigne has learned many useful things even from his variations. Like him, we must learn the lesson of flux. "At least we must become wise at our own expense." Presumably if we must, we can. If it cannot be perfect, our knowledge can be useful. And this is what matters to Montaigne.

All these limitations apply to Montaigne's intellectual commitment to Pyrrhonism as a critique of knowledge. Much of its appeal is as a way of life. Critical as he now is of Stoical humanism as a guide to conduct, he has not yet—or has barely—discovered his later model Socrates. Meanwhile Pyrrho will do nicely. In the presumably later chapter where Montaigne speaks of Pyrrho as building an amusing science out of ignorance, he accepts as true all the comic stories of his eccentricities; but here he wants him as a model and rejects them firmly:

As for the actions of life, they [the Pyrrhonists] are of the common fashion in that. They lend and accommodate themselves to natural in-

clinations, to the impulsion and constraint of passions, to the constitutions
of laws and customs, and to the tradition of the arts . . . without any
taking sides or judgment. Which is why I cannot very well reconcile with
this principle what Laertius says about the life of Pyrrho, and in which
Lucian, Aulus Gellius, and others seem to agree: for they portray him stupid
and immobile, adopting a wild and unsociable way of life, waiting for carts
to hit him, risking himself on precipices, refusing to conform to the laws.
That is outdoing his doctrine. He did not want to make himself a stump
or a stone; he wanted to make himself a living, thinking, reasoning man,
enjoying all natural pleasures and comforts, employing and using all his
bodily and spiritual faculties. The fantastic, imaginary, false privileges that
man has arrogated to himself, of judging, knowing, ordering, and establish-
ing, he honestly renounced and gave up.

If Montaigne's intellectual skepticism, limited and not wholly
consistent, is mainly a means to other ends, what are these ends?
Under the general aim of humbling the pride of the intellect, he
seeks to discredit three specific groups: the Protestants, the ancient
dogmatic philosophers, and the followers of Stoical humanism.

The Protestants are the only ones identified as Sebond's second
group of critics. Their presumption in setting their individual reason
above that of the Church, with its centuries of established knowledge, makes them natural objects of Montaigne's attack. In his opinion, the initial rejection of authority involved in the change from
Catholicism to Protestantism leads easily and naturally to "an execrable atheism":

For the common herd (and almost everyone is of this sort), not having
the faculty of judging things in themselves and by reason, let themselves
be carried away by chance and by appearances, when once they have been
given the temerity to despise and judge the opinions that they have held
in extreme reverence, such as those in which salvation is concerned. . . .
They will soon after cast easily into like uncertainty all the other parts of
their belief . . . and they shake off as a tyrannical yoke all the impressions
they had once received from the authority of the laws or the reverence of
ancient usage; determined from then on to accept nothing to which they
have not applied their judgment and granted their consent.

Although Montaigne condemns the evil of the wars impartially
in both sides, his doctrinal allegiance is clear and undeviating. He
considers these "new doctors" great enemies of peace and order and
the greatest threats to the salvation of the faithful. His Christian
skepticism, though never official Church doctrine, came to be an
important instrument of the Counter Reformation.

The Protestants may be even more important here than they seem. Montaigne's action in holding back from publication La Boétie's *Voluntary Servitude* and *Memoir Concerning the Edict of January 1562* shows that he avoided inflammatory polemic and sought rather to convince and reconcile. Thus he treats the Protestants here as erring brothers, reserving his ridicule for the ancients. The latter may be serving as object lessons for the former, who have fallen heir to their presumption; but if so, only to a limited extent. Despite its title, the whole essay is not about the critics of Sebond, who appear rarely and vaguely, but about the ancient dogmatic philosophers and their follies. Montaigne is not even attacking the many modern humanists whose worship of these ancients may endanger their faith. His man without divine grace or knowledge, who might seem a remote abstraction theologically, seems to be rather the philosophers' man—man as the pagan ancients saw him or had reason to see him. For it is mere man—man as he would be if God had not made him in his own image and redeemed him with the blood of his Son—who struts comically through the pages of the ancients and of the "Apology for Raymond Sebond."

Protestantism is not a live issue for Montaigne himself. What is, is the development of a moral code suited to, and attainable by, himself and others. The ideal of Stoical humanism, that man should raise himself by his bootstraps above humanity, is intrinsically unattainable and therefore futile. Ethically as well as intellectually, Pyrrhonism is sounder—ethically for setting up an attainable ideal, intellectually for making us a blank page on which God may write clearly if he will; and thus ethically again for fostering humility and combating presumption.

As Montaigne began work on the essay that was to become the "Apology," he was critically examining the moral ideal that had long attracted him and that La Boétie had revered. By the end of his work on the essay for the 1580 edition, he had finished with that ideal; he was convinced that Stoical humanism was not for him, nor for mankind either.

The steps in his repudiation are apparent. Man and his reason are presumptuous. He is neither wiser, happier, nor better than the animals. His self-conscious premeditation of troubles is less valuable than simple and trusting acceptance of life as it comes. Even the philosophers admit this without meaning to. Their dogmatic pride is absurd, since they have not found truth, and cannot. Their presumption is a barrier to Christian faith and becomes blasphemous impudence when they seek to define and limit God by human analogies and reasonings. The best human philosophy, in itself and as a basis for Christianity, is Pyrrhonism, or at least a Pyrrhonistic view of our capacities. Stoical humanism errs by ignoring the nature and condition of man. Without God's grace we are incapable of true knowledge. The mechanism of our cognition precludes any perfect grasp of externals; our instability, of stable and eternal truth. What can we do as creatures of flux? Learn its lesson, know ourselves for what we truly are.

The "Apology" is Montaigne's declaration of complete intellectual independence. Even Pyrrho is in no sense a master, but an ally. The Stoical humanists, once his heroes and in some measure his teachers, have proven inadequate and become his targets. Free of their tutelage at last, he is ready to look within himself for instruction.

HE LAST two or three years of Montaigne's work on the first *Essays,* until at last he noted the date—March 1, 1580—on his foreword to the reader, were very productive. He composed much of the "Apology for Raymond Sebond" and about thirty entire chapters (a few in Book I: 26, 31, 53; most of them in Book II: 7–11, 16–37), which include some of his finest—"Of the Education of Children," "Of Cannibals," "Of the Affection of Fathers for Their Children," "Of Books," "Of Cruelty," "Of Glory," "Of Presumption," "Of Giving the Lie," "Of the Resemblance of Children to Fathers"—and make up about one third of the first two books in their original form. He came to recognize his subject, and explored it with the joy of a man who has found his function at last.

In the vanity of man and his knowledge he confronted much the same dilemma as did Bacon, Descartes, and Pascal later; but they had his conclusions to start from, and they were harder to satisfy. They demanded perfect truth; he was content with self-knowledge and happiness. Convinced that Stoical humanism did not lead to these, he abandoned it for a new method and a new resource—self-study.

If he had placed any hope in Christian ethics, he seems to have given it up by now. Though his faith is sincere, his God is far above man's moral or intellectual reach, and apparently raises few men up by his extraordinary grace. The appalling practices of the time seem to prove that Christianity has little effect on conduct. What passes for it is a pretext for treachery and cruelty. Without any overt—perhaps even any conscious—break, Montaigne seems to ignore Christianity as he seeks a man-centered moral code that man has no excuse to infringe.

Self-study was of course no invention of Montaigne's. The maxim "Know thyself" was on the temple of Apollo at Delphi and the lips of Socrates. Even Calvin endorsed it in his *Institutes*. Sebond preached it to the translator of his *Natural Theology:* "Since nothing created is closer to man than himself, he will remain very assured and very enlightened about everything that is proved concerning him. . . . That is why man and his nature must serve as means, argument, and testimony to prove everything about man, to prove all that concerns his salvation, his happiness, his unhappiness, his evil, and his good. . . . So, if he wants to know his former value, his nature, his pristine beauty, let him return to himself and come back home." However, where most of Montaigne's predecessors sought in the self evidence for already formed theories about human nature and conduct, Montaigne is more inquiring. Morality, he believes, depends largely on psychology; what we should expect to be, on what we are; and about this we have much to learn.

He was always fascinated by human motivation and behavior. His judgments of authors read before he began to write show the same curiosity as he feels about his ancestors. From the first the essays reveal his interest in the "lofty and hazardous undertaking" and his awareness of what it requires: "We must probe the inside and discover what springs set men in motion."

The value of self-study is suggested in the earliest essays. In treating "The Inconsistency of Our Actions" (II: 1) Montaigne may have himself in mind as an example. He finds our education barren of knowledge for and of ourselves. The outline of his plan appears in the original conclusion of "Practice" (II: 6) when he draws this lesson from his nearly fatal fall from a horse: "This account of so trivial an event would be rather pointless, were it not for the instruction that I have derived from it for myself. . . . Now as Pliny says, each man is a very good education to himself, provided he has the capacity to spy on himself from close up. This is not my teaching, this is my study; and it is not a lesson for others, it is for me."

Though not a principal theme in the "Apology," self-study is recognized as man's most proper concern. The know-it-alls who criticize Sebond seem unaware even of the difficulty of knowing themselves. If man can know anything, it must be himself; he is nearest and most accessible. Self-study has taught Montaigne the lesson of flux: "I who spy on myself more closely, who have my eyes incessantly intent on myself, as one who has not much business elsewhere . . . I would hardly dare tell of the vanity and weakness that I find in myself." Others too can learn our frailties in themselves better than in Pyrrho: "each man can furnish himself with as many examples as he pleases."

The theme becomes clear in the essays of 1578–80. Montaigne is impatient with the cocky theorists who "perch astride the epicycle of Mercury" and are experts on the eighth sphere and the ebb and flow of the Nile, when they cannot explain what makes themselves tick. Not yet sure that self-knowledge is knowledge of man, he is sure that it is genuine knowledge of one man. For this, reasoning and theory, the Renaissance view of man as the microcosm, are as useless as scholastic logic; we are far too "vain, diverse, and undulating." Montaigne has seen from the first that we must probe for motive and follow a man's traces long and carefully. What truly reveals us is rarely our public behavior, often the trivial, always the everyday. Obviously there is no one whom we can observe as carefully, know as inwardly, as ourselves: "there is no sure witness except each man to himself."

For self-study the material is experience, the instrument judgment. Though at times Montaigne almost equates this with common sense, he normally makes the sharp distinction that judgment, by recognizing its limitations and our own, can truly raise man above himself. It is almost identical with understanding and with reason in the sense of *right reason,* but, unlike reason as *wrong reasoning,* it is close to the facts, responsible, teachable, scrupulous in reaching conclusions. Far more important than knowledge, it has no necessary connection with it. Its training is the heart of education. Its jurisdiction is infinite, including morals as well as intellect, determining not only what is true but what is good. It is the faculty that teaches man how to live.

At the same time, self-study is a school of judgment. Montaigne's sense of this appears clearly from the sequence of ideas that follows: "I find my opinions infinitely bold and constant in condemning my inadequacy. In truth, this too is a subject on which I exercise my judgment as much as on any other. . . . Others always go elsewhere, if they stop to think about it; they always go forward; as for me, I roll about in myself. This capacity for sifting truth . . . I owe principally to myself."

The greatest importance of self-study is that it teaches us to live. Montaigne approves Socrates' view that all other knowledge is a waste of time. "I make no account," he writes, "of the goods that I have been unable to employ in the service of my life. . . . I have put all my efforts into forming my life. That is my trade and my work."

Though Montaigne's claims are still very discreet, already he finds his new method the surest way to the most important knowledge man can attain. He is ready to make himself the subject of his book.

It seems to have been only around 1578 that Montaigne first found the title of his work. Although the best account of his plan cannot be dated, all the others are of 1578 or later. The term "essay" (*essai*) was his own invention, tentative in every way, not yet crystallized or hackneyed. In the discursive personal treatise his chief antecedents are Plutarch's *Moralia* or *Moral Essays* (as they are often called today), Machiavelli's *Discourses on the First Ten Books of Livy*, Erasmus' *Colloquies*, and the various books of "selected lessons" noted earlier. None of these works are as personal as Montaigne's; none of the authors have the brashness to take themselves as subject—nor, for that matter, will Francis Bacon, the next writer to use the title. The name may have come to Montaigne from a practice in the Floral Games in his mother's home town, Toulouse, established in 1540 with the title *examen* (changed the next year to *essay*), of breaking a tie among the leading versifiers by setting them a last line on which to construct an impromptu poem.

Before Montaigne began to write of his project as a series of trials, tests, attempts, or occasionally samplings (*essais*), he had often used the verb *essayer* (in modern French, normally *to try*) in ways close to his project, related to experience, with the sense of trying out or testing. Here are a few samples, in which the italicized verbs translate the French *essayer:* "Having *found* by experience . . . that the sciences and arts . . . are formed and shaped little by little . . . I do not leave off sounding and *testing* what my powers cannot discover." "I have *experienced* . . . that things often appear greater to us from a distance than near." "The reason why we doubt hardly anything is that we never *test* common opinions." At least once he uses it reflexively: "And whoever wants to *essay himself* in the same way, and get rid of this violent prejudice of custom . . . when the mask is torn off . . . he will feel his judgment as it were all upset, and nevertheless restored to a much surer status." The greatest concentration of these is in the ten pages of "Practice" (II: 6), where the verb is used four times (of a total of six) in a richer sense than simply "to try." "As for death, we can *try* it out only once." "It seems to me, however, that there is a certain way of familiarizing ourselves with death and *trying* it out to some extent. We can have an experience of it." Montaigne's excellent early health made illnesses seem so horrible "that when I came to *experience* them I found their pains mild and easy compared with my fears." And finally, apropos of his theory that the groans and writhings of unconscious people do not prove real suffering: "Now I have no doubt, now that I have *tried* this out by experience, that I judged this matter rightly all along." The whole chapter treats Montaigne's attempt to *essayer* death, to have some experience of it, which he now considers better than premeditation.

The term *essais* he uses five times in the 1580 edition, once in about the modern sense of his book: "If these essays were worthy of being judged . . ." Twice he says that this is the *essai* of "my natural faculties," once adding for emphasis "and not at all of the acquired ones"; twice he says these are the *essais* of his judgment. And although judgment can be trained, he still considers it (especially in contrast with learning) a natural faculty, as the following passage shows: "As for the natural faculties that are in me, of which this is the essay, I feel them bending under the load: my conceptions and my judgment move only by groping, staggering, stumbling, and blundering." He comes to recognize that whatever he writes about, he is always judging; that this is the center of his portrait, which shows not only the conclusions but also the tests of his judgment:

Judgment is a tool to use on all subjects, and comes in everywhere. Therefore in the tests [*essais*] that I make of it here, I use every sort of occasion. If it is a subject I do not understand at all, even on that I essay [*essaie*] my judgment, sounding the ford from a good distance; and then, finding it too deep for my height, I stick to the bank. And this acknowledgment that I cannot cross over is a token of its action, indeed one of those it is most proud of. Sometimes in a vain and nonexistent subject I try [*essaye*] to see if it will find the wherewithal to give it body, prop it up, and support it. Sometimes I lead it to a noble and well-worn subject in which it has nothing original to discover, the road being so opened up and beaten that it can walk only in others' footsteps. There it plays its part by choosing the way that seems best to it, and of a thousand paths it says that this one or that was the most wisely chosen.

For the rest, I let chance itself furnish me with subjects, since they are all equally good to me; and moreover I do not undertake to develop them completely and to the bottom of the vat. Of a thousand aspects that they each have, I take the one I please. I am prone to grasp them by some unusual and fanciful angle. I would certainly pick out richer and fuller subjects, if I had any other purpose set than the one I have.

Every action is fit to make us known.

Montaigne does not yet claim universality for his self-portrait; but he recognizes that there is such a thing as moral science, and in "Presumption" (II: 17), after stating that the subject of his study is man, he stresses two traits in the self-portrait that follows: his general ordinariness and his one ability, judgment. Later he will show how the first of these traits makes a man a representative human to be studied, while the second allows him to assess himself with impartiality. Thus his final insight, that self-study leads to knowledge of mankind as well as of self, though still implicit, is already foreshadowed here.

Montaigne's only account of the genesis of his plan, though too disparaging to be taken at face value, is useful for his timing and his reasons. "If strangeness and novelty . . . do not save me," he writes, "I shall never come out of this stupid enterprise with honor. . . . It was a melancholy humor, and consequently a humor very hostile to my natural disposition, produced by the gloom of the solitude into which I had cast myself some years ago, that first put into my head this daydream of meddling with writing. And then, finding myself entirely destitute and void of any other matter, I presented myself to myself as theme and subject. It is a wild and monstrous plan."

His task is to see and describe himself as accurately as he can. His ideas may not be true; his account of them must be. What he aims to make known, he says, is not things but himself; not the measure of things but the measure of his sight. The only certainty he guarantees is "to make known what I think, and to what point, at this moment, extends the knowledge I have of what I am treating." Hence he speaks out freely even outside his competence. "For likewise these are my humors and opinions; I offer them as what I believe, not what is to be believed."

He likes his language just as it is, "dry and thorny, with free and unruly movements." His order need not be logical; it must be that of his mind: "I have no other marshal but fortune to arrange my bits. . . . I want people to see my natural and ordinary pace, however off the track it is. I let myself go as I am." For the style must be part of the man and of his portrait.

A true portrait must change as the subject changes. Montaigne wants to show the course of his humors and the birth of each part; he wishes he had begun earlier. If something new he learns alters him tomorrow, this too must be shown. Handsome or ugly, he must paint a faithful likeness: "Whatever these absurdities may be, I have had no intention of concealing them, any more than I would a bald and graying portrait of myself, in which the painter had drawn not a perfect face, but mine. . . . Even if I had been able to adopt some other style than my own ordinary one and some other better and more honorable form, I would not have done it. . . . I want to be seen here in my simple, natural, ordinary fashion, without straining or artifice; for it is myself that I portray."

When he speaks of his plan in the late 1570's, just before the first publication of his book, Montaigne is always disparaging. There is something much like stage fright in his fear that his readers may consider any trivial talk of self a proof of presumption. He knows that such a view is throwing out the baby with the bath, and that his judgment is trustworthy; he defends his plan sturdily in "Presumption." But most of the time he apparently feels that in order to be accepted as truthful he must be less truthful than modest. We have seen some of his remarks about "this stupid enterprise," "a wild and monstrous plan," "these absurdities," and the like. Elsewhere it is "the meanness of my subject," "such inept and trivial remarks," or "these stupidities"; and here is a fairly typical summary: "I see well enough how little value and weight all this has, and the boldness and temerity of my plan. . . . I have not obliged myself not to say stupid things, provided I do not fool myself and that I recognize them as such."

Even such self-disparagement applies only to self-portrayal, never to self-study. By knowing his own nature Montaigne seeks to learn his privileges and duties. Our attitudes, principles, and rules of conduct must be our own, based on what we are, rooted in our being; if not, they are useless. Independence and naturalness are indispensable to consistency, wisdom, and happiness. Moreover, self-study reveals our natural resources; and on these, not those of Stoical humanism, Montaigne now proposes to rely.

In the mid-1570's and later Montaigne becomes aware of two benign paradoxes rich in consequences for happiness. The first he expresses around 1575–76. Much of his earlier apprehension had been based on our insecurity. Now, however, apparently for the first time, he questions Seneca's argument for despising life, that we can enjoy nothing which we fear to lose, and finds that on the contrary security begets boredom. "Difficulty gives value to things. . . . To forbid us something is to make us want it . . . to give it up to us completely is to breed in us contempt for it." Thus our very ephemerality may be no kill-joy but a condition of the only happiness we can enjoy.

The other paradox is that the arbitrariness of the soul, which makes what it will of sense impressions, is not only, as Montaigne often insists in the "Apology," a proof of our ignorance, but also a guarantee that we can be happy. He devotes one of his earliest essays to the question of the soul's ability to take things as it chooses. Though he finds this considerable toward poverty and death, against pain all we can do is tense ourselves and resist. In the "Apology" he plays many variations on the new theme. It arises from his view of the mechanics of cognition: "Our conception is not itself applied to foreign objects, but is conceived through the mediation of the senses; and the senses do not comprehend the foreign object, but only their own impressions." Once he attributes this arbitrariness to the animals as well as to us: "The privilege in which our soul glories, of reducing to her condition all that she conceives . . . of constraining all the things that she considers worthy of her acquaintance to . . . leave aside . . . all accidents of sense, in order to accommodate them to her immortal and spiritual condition . . . —this same privilege, I say, seems very evidently to belong to the beasts."

His main proof of it is the diversity of human opinion: "That things do not lodge in us in their own form and essence, or make their entry into us by their own power and authority, we see clearly enough. Because, if that were so, we should receive them in the same way: the taste of wine would be the same in the mouth of a sick man as in the mouth of a healthy man. . . . Thus external objects surrender to our mercy; they dwell in us as we please." For cognition is active, not passive; we know things by our faculty of knowing, not "through the power and according to the law of their own essence."

However, already in the "Apology" Montaigne senses the possibilities of this phenomenon for our happiness, as he raises again the question how much we can choose how to take external events: "Moreover, since the accidents of illnesses, madness, or sleep make things appear to us otherwise than they appear to healthy people, wise men, and waking people; since this condition has the power to give things another essence than the one they have . . . is it not likely that our normal state and our natural disposition can also assign to things an essence corresponding to their own condition, and accommodate them to themselves . . . ? And that our health is as capable of giving them some appearance as our sickness?"

After 1588, in the final additions to the essays, Montaigne shows the full flowering of this idea. "The soul," he then says, ". . . molds to itself and to its every condition the feelings of the body and all other accidents. . . . Out of the many thousands of attitudes at its disposal, let us give it one conducive to our repose and preservation, and we shall be not only sheltered from all harm, but even gratified and flattered, if it please, by ills and pains." Here is his strongest statement of this theme: "Things in themselves may have their own weights and measures and qualities; but once inside, within us, she [the soul] allots them their qualities as she sees fit. . . . Health, conscience, authority, knowledge, riches, beauty, and their opposites— all are stripped on entry and receive from the soul new clothing, and the coloring that she chooses—brown, green, bright, dark, bitter, sweet, deep, superficial—and which each individual soul chooses; for . . . each one is queen in her realm. Wherefore let us no longer make the external qualities of things our excuse; it is up to us to reckon them as we will. Our good and our ill depend on ourselves alone."

In the essays of 1576–80 Montaigne's sense of the power of the soul appears to be growing. Earlier he had stressed the help the body can give the soul: "I, who have a soft and commonplace soul, must help support myself by bodily comforts." Now it is the reverse: "We must order the soul . . . to rally to the body, embrace it, cherish it, assist it, control it, advise it, set it right and bring it back when it goes astray; in short, to marry it and be a real husband to it." But the important concept is the one now emerging: that not the strength of the soul but its very arbitrariness gives it virtually complete control over our happiness. If not fully developed in the "Apology," this concept is foreshadowed there and thoroughly prepared by the play of his mind upon the positive as well as the negative aspects of the idea.

For all Montaigne's independence in the "Apology," for all its affirmative implications and consequences, when most of it was written his new method and resources had not been tested. His liberation from apprehensive tutelage was still somewhat theoretical. The test came in 1578 with the acute pain of renal calculus, or the kidney stone.

In a curious judgment, the Romantic historian Jules Michelet attributed to Montaigne's sickness a certain morbidity that he could not stand. "I find in him at each moment," he wrote, "a certain nauseating taste, as of a sickroom where the stale air is impregnated with the sad perfumes of the pharmacy. All this is *natural*, no doubt; this sick man is *Nature's man*, yes, but in his infirmities. When I find myself shut up in this padded library, I need air."

Montaigne's sickness was quite as important as Michelet suggests, but with precisely the opposite effect. He never had a healthier outlook, or loved health more, than after it first struck. His first experience of it was about as pivotal a point as the work of the "Apology." His brush with death had reduced his fear of it; but until his illness he still feared pain.

Until he was around forty his health had been "blithe and ebullient." From around 1573 to 1578 he had some illness in the kidneys, but mild. In his last fourteen years he suffered from headaches, dyspepsia, tooth trouble, failing eyesight, the quinsy that actually killed him, and worst of all the kidney stone, one of the most dreaded

diseases of his and earlier times. He knew and quoted Pliny's statement: "There are only three kinds of diseases that people have been
accustomed to escape from by killing themselves: the fiercest of all
is the stone in the kidney when the urine is held back by it." His
Travel Journal shows the nature and frequency of his attacks. Often
every few days, once three times in two days, a stone would form in
his kidney, block his urine, and cause intense pain until finally
voided. Often the pain was acute even without a stone. At least once
it made him seriously consider suicide.

The stone had been precisely the ailment he feared most, knowing it only by the cries of those who could not bear it. His father had
got it at sixty-six, when Michel was twenty-eight, and died seven
years later in great pain; Michel knew he might fall heir to it. Fear
of it had led him, in perfect health, to toy with the idea of suicide.
"I felt and protested enough that it was time to leave, that I should
cut off life in the quick and in the breast, following the rule of the
surgeons when they have to cut off some limb. But those were vain
propositions."

In the spring or summer of 1578 came the first fierce attack.
Montaigne got some help from the baths of Aigues-Caudes—no immediate effect, no purgation, but a year without affliction—and, when
the next attack came, from those of Bagnères—gravel voided, bowels
loosened, but only two months' respite, followed by a very bad bout.
After a year and a half, in the winter of 1579–80, convinced that
the illness was there to stay, and "tested . . . pretty roughly for a
beginner," he assesses the result in "The Resemblance of Children to
Fathers." Now he makes light of his earlier notions of suicide: "I
was so far from being ready to do that then, that in the eighteen
months or thereabouts that I have been in this charming state, I
have already learned to adapt myself to it. I am already growing reconciled to this colicky life; I find food in it for consolation and
hope. So bewitched are men by their wretched existence, that there
is no condition so harsh that they will not accept it to keep alive."

It is a sign of Montaigne's good cheer that he is now ready to
make fun of himself. He does so again when he brands his freedom
from purely psychic pain "a stupid and insensible disposition"—and
then calls it "one of the best parts of my natural condition." Physical
pains he feels keenly, but his fear of them had been far worse: "I had
conceived them in my imagination so unendurable that in truth I had

more fear of them than I have found harm in them. Wherefore I continue to confirm this belief, that most of the faculties of our soul trouble the repose of life more than they help us in it." For now he is at grips with the most sudden, painful, mortal, and hopeless of diseases; and he is doing very nicely indeed.

I have already experienced five or six very long and painful bouts of it. However, either I flatter myself or else there is even in this condition enough to bear up a man whose soul is unburdened of the fear of death and unburdened of the threats, sentences, and consequences with which medicine gives us a headache. But the very impact of the pain has not such sharp and piercing bitterness that a well-poised man should therefore go mad or give up hope. . . .

Now that he can endure, even enjoy, a life of pain, he can attack the histrionics of Stoical humanism with authority. The insistence on rigid composure has always seemed to him foolish. "Why does philosophy, which has regard only for real substance and actions, go playing around with these vain and external appearances, as if it were training men for acting in a comedy?" Its business is to keep the soul firm in a pain-racked body, aware of itself, not prostrated but excited by the struggle. It is cruelty to ask for more. If it helps the body to twist and cry out, let it do so: "We have enough labor with the pain without adding a new labor by our reason."

But Montaigne is not making excuses for himself. He has found to his delight that he can endure the pain like a sage—or like a man:

I say this to excuse those whom we see ordinarily crying out and storming in the shocks of the pain of this sickness. For as for me, I have passed through it until now with a little better countenance. Not that I give myself trouble, however, to maintain this external decorum; for I take little account of such an advantage. In this respect I lend the pain as much as it likes. But either my pains are not so excessive, or I bring to them more firmness than most people. I complain, I fret when the sharp pains afflict me, but I do not come to the point of despair or frenzy.

The painless intervals are clear and blithe. Their alternation with bouts of illness leads to his view of life as a harmony of pain and pleasure, which alike are necessary to happiness. In short, hard as his initiation has been, he finds himself much better off than countless healthy men. Never before has he shown such complete confidence; never from now on will he lose it.

He does not forget our limitations; but having demonstrated

them with thoroughness and *brio,* he is ready to discuss our resources. Now he reveals that the philosophy he had so derided is not
the real thing but a prevalent counterfeit. True philosophy is the
road to wisdom and happiness, a road open to all. The soul in which
it dwells should make even the body healthy. "It should make its
contentment, tranquillity, and gladness shine out from within;
should form in its own mold the outward demeanor, and consequently furnish it with graceful pride, an active and joyous bearing,
and an equable and good-natured countenance. It is *Baroco* and
Baralipton* that make their disciples so wretched and grimy, and not
philosophy; they know her only by hearsay. Why, she makes it her
business to calm the tempests of fortune and to teach hunger and
fevers to laugh." In short, where at first to philosophize had meant
to learn to die, now, Montaigne writes, "It is philosophy that teaches
us to live."

One of Montaigne's main aims from now on is to avoid artificiality and be natural. In this he is of his time. The same aim is
prevalent among contemporary primitivists and those who oppose a
pleasure-seeking "Epicureanism" to the more established, virtue-
directed "Stoicism." Montaigne is one of the leading spokesmen for
"nature" against "art."

The distinction in his mind is rather constant though mainly
implicit, and more clearly felt than closely analyzed. There seem to
be two chief criteria: whatever makes us happy, whatever is found
in other living creatures, is natural. In a sense the two are one, since
all creatures naturally seek happiness. In man Montaigne regards as
natural the body, most emotions, the necessary appetites, common
sense, and judgment. Usually unnatural, and always subject to unnatural use, are imagination, irresponsible reasoning, and their feck-
less progeny ambition, presumption, avarice, insatiability, anxiety,
and apprehension.

Montaigne had rejected Stoical humanism as antinatural, setting
man apart from nature, ordering him to conquer natural impulses
and wrongly assuming that he can and should. Now as his arguments
for nature against art grow fuller, they grow more solid and less
sweeping, more a matter of measured conviction and less of paradoxical sally. In a passage placed immediately before the "Apology,"

* Artificial words in scholastic logic whose vowels represent forms of syllogisms.

he now speaks with marked detachment about our supposed equality with the animals. "But when . . . I meet with arguments that try to show the close resemblance between us and the animals . . . and with how much probability they are likened to us, truly I beat down a lot of our presumption and willingly resign that vain and imaginary kingship that people give us over the other creatures." Now, as his new-found confidence reaches out beyond himself to all mankind, he seeks his models no longer among the animals but among natural men.

In the chapter "Of Cannibals" (I: 31) he describes a tribe of Brazilians encountered by Villegagnon's expedition in 1557. Montaigne talked with one of them at Rouen in 1562 and long had a servant who had spent years among them. It may be he who led La Boétie to toy with the notion of fleeing the corrupt Old World for the New. But despite a few scattered allusions in the early essays, it is only now, sixteen years later, that Montaigne uses them to belittle human art and show the dignity of human nature.

There is nothing wild or barbaric about these people, he says, except to our distorted vision that sees perfection only in our own ways:

They are wild, just as we call wild the fruits that Nature has produced by herself and in her normal course; whereas really it is those that we have changed artificially . . . that we should rather call wild. . . . It is not reasonable that art should win the place of honor over our great and powerful mother Nature. We have so overloaded the beauty and richness of her works by our inventions that we have quite smothered her. Yet wherever her purity shines forth, she wonderfully puts to shame our vain and frivolous attempts. . . .

These nations, then, seem to me barbarous in this sense, that they have been fashioned very little by the human mind, and are still very close to their original naturalness. The laws of nature still rule them, very little corrupted by ours.

Plato and Lycurgus should have known the admirable simplicity that Montaigne describes in terms later borrowed by Shakespeare in *The Tempest*. Letters and mathematics, magistrates, political superiors, and servants, trade, riches, and poverty, successions and partitions, are unknown in the cannibal commonwealth; there are "no occupations but leisure ones, no care for any but common kinship, no clothes, no agriculture, no metal, no use of wine or wheat. The very words that signify lying, treachery, dissimulation, avarice, envy, belittling, pardon—unheard of." By the rules of reason, we are right to call them barbarous; but we are far worse. Our judicial torture, practiced in the name of religion, is more savage than their cannibalism.

Montaigne's cannibals have many good qualities that are not specifically natural: temperance, fairness, sense, and above all courage. But the unifying trait is their filial obedience to nature. They are content to accept her bounty and satisfy their actual needs; the very wisdom of happiness is in them. One statement of Montaigne's final ideal was to be that "It is an absolute perfection and virtually divine to know how to enjoy our being rightfully"; already he finds this perfection in his cannibals, who lack nothing, not even "that great thing, knowing how to enjoy their condition happily and be content with it." These qualities they owe not to mere instinct or custom, but to reasoning and judgment: witness the natural art, quite Anacreontic, of one of their love songs, and the things that amazed them most in France: a child ruling grown men, and some men gorged while others—"their halves," as the cannibals call them—starve. "All this," Montaigne concludes ironically, "is not too bad—but what of it? They don't wear breeches."

Montaigne uses the cannibals to symbolize the candor he strives for in his book when he tells the reader he wishes he could go them one better: "Had I been placed among those nations which are said to live still in the sweet freedom of nature's first laws, I assure you I should very gladly have portrayed myself here entire and wholly naked."

But if nature is our best guide, we must be her followers, not her slaves. Having established the limitations of reason, Montaigne now shows its strength (in its best sense and use) as the faculty that sets man above the rest of creation: "Since it has pleased God to give us some capacity for reason, so that we should not be, like the animals, slavishly subjected to the common laws, but should apply ourselves to them by judgment and voluntary liberty, we must indeed yield a little to the simple authority of Nature, but not let ourselves be carried away tyrannically by her; reason alone must guide our inclinations."

By this view man has a chance to progress—as an individual at least—and to improve on nature. The central antithesis is not simply nature versus art, but human nature versus misguided human art. This suggests three levels of behavior: natural simplicity, rationalistic art or artificiality, and a higher human naturalness that is beyond art.

In the early essays Montaigne deals mainly with levels two and three (the bottom two), art and nature. When we glimpse them all, one and three are closely linked. The humble are as brave as the philosophers, the ignorant as wise as the learned. The simple take heaven by storm; the learned are headed for hell; the Pyrrhonists, who know their ignorance, are on the first level and ready, if God wills, to be raised above all human levels. The chapter "Of Vain Subtleties" (I: 54) is full of examples of extremes that meet, one of which well illustrates Montaigne's point:

Stupidity and wisdom meet at the same point of feeling and of resolving to endure human accidents. The wise curb and command misfortune; the others are not aware of it. The latter are, so to speak, short of the accidents, the former beyond them. The wise . . . disdain them and trample them underfoot, having a strong and solid soul against which the arrows of fortune . . . must necessarily bounce off. . . . The ordinary and middle condition of men lodges between these two extremes: which is that of those who perceive evils, feel them, and cannot endure them.

Montaigne's fullest treatment of the three moral levels appears in "Cruelty" (II: 11), in a sort of inner dialogue that seems to follow the order of his thinking since he retired. Virtue, he begins, must be more than some innate inclination to goodness: to master wrath by reason is greater than not to feel it: "The one action might be called goodness, the other virtue: for it seems that the name of virtue presupposes difficulty, combat, and contrast, and that it cannot exist without opposition." Hence we call God good, not virtuous; hence Stoics, Epicureans, and others have sought out pain as a test: "Virtue refuses facility as a companion. . . . It demands a rough and thorny road."

Now Montaigne completely reverses himself. "I have come thus far quite at my ease. But at the end of this discourse it comes into my mind that the soul of Socrates, which is the most perfect that has come to my knowledge, would be, by my reckoning, a soul with little to recommend it: for I cannot conceive in that person any power of vicious lust." Then is Socrates not virtuous? Is virtue impossible without vice? What if it enjoys pain as Cato the Younger must have enjoyed his suicide, as an athlete enjoys a test of strength?

Both these men left no room in themselves for vice; they made virtue a habit, "the very essence of their soul, its natural and ordinary gait." Obviously this is as far above ordinary virtue as that is above innocence. Socrates took death without strain, simply, gaily, in his stride. "Cato will pardon me, if he please; his death is more tragic and tense, but the other is still, I know not how, more beautiful."

There are some curious things about these levels: God's presence on the "lowest," the contrast between Socrates and Cato on the highest, and certain ambiguities about Montaigne's own place. Naturally he sets this at the bottom. His virtue (or rather innocence) is accidental; he was simply born hating most vice. However, he has not let his vices become great or corrupt his judgment; though he has not fought them hard enough, he has managed "to regulate them and keep them from mixing with other vices," since they support one another. "Mine I have cut down and constrained to be as solitary and simple as I could." In short, his is no mere passive innocence; he is nearer the upper levels than he claims.

The athlete of virtue, Cato, seems not far above the middle level; his death is tense and tragic. Socrates is immune to tragedy and tension. If Montaigne rates the virtue of human art above the innocence of nature, still man's highest virtue is beyond art, compounded of nature and habit. And habit is on the side of nature; soon Montaigne—after Aristotle and others—will call it a second nature.

In the essays of 1578–80 Montaigne's ideal is no longer simply nature, but something more self-directed, human nature. Reason must keep man unenslaved by the natural law. Hard as it is to force our inclinations, we can train them by habit and control them by judgment. More and more judgment is man's key faculty, by which he can and should rise above mere nature.

In the "Apology" Montaigne writes about man with apparent disdain. Now he shows detachment toward this attitude too. "Of all the opinions antiquity has held of man," he writes, "the ones I embrace most willingly and adhere to most firmly are those that despise, humiliate, and nullify us most. Philosophy seems to me never to have such an easy game as when she combats our presumption and vanity, when she honestly admits her uncertainty, weakness, and ignorance. It seems to me that the nursing mother of the falsest opinions we have, both public and private, is the overgood opinion man has of himself." No misanthrope, the spectacle of man's cockiness often makes him sound like one. However, he has examined in detail such human limitations as (in random order) susceptibility to fear, imagination, custom, natural inclinations, impulsion from without and within, wine, illness, conscience, the stars, insects, sense impressions, fortune, and so forth; our impotence to achieve knowledge, goodness, and happiness; our inelasticity even for aspiration. Now he begins to dwell on the qualities of our defects.

Many of our weaknesses can be sources of strength. Our capacity for diversion, which Montaigne has used though not yet discussed, is a benefit of our inconstancy. Those tyrants custom and habit can be helpful; they can conquer the fear of death better than philosophy, and lead to the highest virtue. The mutability of our judgment is a cause for skepticism; but awareness of it is wisdom, for wisdom is knowledge of ourselves and of our place in the scheme of things.

In the realm of enjoyment especially our resources are many. Our ephemerality is a condition of our pleasure. Ignorance may lead to happiness as well as to virtue. The arbitrariness of the soul gives hope of contentment. The soul no longer needs assistance from the body, but should help it, control it, be a good husband to it. Even the difficulty of knowing others makes us our own best judges; which is a great freedom. Once Montaigne had listed contempt as a thing to fear; now he does not. Self-knowledge can replace anxiety about other people's opinions of us with the security of free men.

Montaigne's awareness of the possibilities of human nature shows most clearly in his faith in education. If the negativism of the "Apology" is permanent and in earnest, why try to educate? If we can know nothing, what can we learn or teach? Where "Pedantry" (I: 25) had been mainly destructive, "The Education of Children" (I: 26) shows what proper training can do. Without Rabelais's vast faith in learning, Montaigne shares his optimism and concern for the training of mind, body, and character. Unlike his reluctant admirer Rousseau much later, he does not believe that infants are angels and that education must be negative; but he anticipates his concern with the child as an entire person and with his active participation in his own education—with learning by doing and the lessons of things, not only of books. He has many affinities with the modern theories— in their unadulterated form—of John Dewey.

His educator is a tutor, who should be marked by "a well-made rather than a well-filled head" and distinguished in character and understanding even more than in learning. He must listen as well as talk, and develop the boy's faculties, training him through habit for toughness in body, modesty in knowledge, readiness to learn, and the freedom of adaptability. History will give experience in time; travel, in space. These, practice, and attention to meaning rather than rote, will help fashion judgment, which is the main aim of education. Philosophy will be the guide, virtue the goal; both lead to happiness and wisdom. Taking nothing on authority but judging everything by himself, the pupil will learn to love virtue and hate vice for their own sakes, not out of impotence or fear of punishment. A sound education will produce not a donkey laden with books but a mature, morally independent man. This education of the judgment, difficult but essential, can train apparently all but a few to be free, versatile, judicious, wise, and happy.

Montaigne's awareness of our potentialities gives him much to live for even in his painful illness. Free from anxiety, knowing from self-study what to expect of himself, he can make the most of life. "I welcome health with open arms," he writes, "free, full, and entire, and whet my appetite to enjoy it, the more so as it is rarer and less ordinary with me. . . . I am at grips with the worst of all maladies, the most sudden, the most painful, the most mortal, and the most irremediable. . . . Yet I have kept my mind, up to now, in such a state that, provided I can bring constancy to it, I find myself in a considerably better condition of life than a thousand others, who have no fever or illness but what they give themselves by the fault of their reasoning." To enjoy life is a legitimate aim for him. Only nobler beings have the right to despise our being; self-contempt is a malady peculiar to man. It is equally vain to try to be other than we are. If we accept ourselves as we are and life as it is, we have much to enjoy.

When Montaigne publishes the first edition of the *Essays* in 1580, he has stated or suggested all his key ideas but one—human unity and solidarity. He is still very individualistic in his concern with himself and his sense of the difference between men.

He is becoming less so. Often he generalizes about man's limita-

tions and possibilities. He sees the unity of kings and peasants, cannibals and Frenchmen. He foreshadows his final plan when he calls man
the subject of his study and qualifies himself as model and portraitist
by his typicality and judgment. Sympathy and insight have made
him a cosmopolite who embraces a wide range of friends and kindred:
La Boétie, Cato, Socrates, Seneca, Plutarch, the ignorant, cannibals,
even animals.

However, he seems still concerned with the individual alone; he
has offered no modification yet to his self-centered early statement
that "The greatest thing in the world is to know how to belong to
oneself."

And where later he will find a balance, now he sees little but
diversity. With this theme the *Essays* of 1580 begin and end. Montaigne's first chapter defines man as "a marvelously vain, diverse, and
undulating object," on which "it is hard to found any constant and
uniform judgment." Book II begins with "The Inconsistency of Our
Actions," which shows that we are utterly different even from ourselves, and ends on the diversity of human opinions: "I do not at all
hate opinions contrary to mine. I am so far . . . from making myself incompatible with the society of men because they are of a different sentiment than mine, that on the contrary, since variety is
the most general fashion that nature has followed, I find it much
more novel and rare to see our humors and opinions agree. And perhaps there were never in the world two opinions entirely and exactly alike, any more than two faces. Their most intrinsic quality is
diversity and discord."

Though human diversity does not dismay Montaigne, it is what
strikes him most. He still thinks and feels as one man alone, not as a
member of a homogeneous group; his portrait is still mainly that of
an individual. He has yet to gain an important element of his final
thought.

Chapter 12: Travel in Italy [1580–1581]

INE YEARS OF RETIREMENT is a long time at Montaigne's age. From his thirty-eighth birthday and the Latin inscription on his wall to the day after his forty-seventh (March 1, 1580), when he signed the preface introducing the reader to the *Essays*, he had found his function and produced a book. Writing at first to make his wandering mind behave, he had moved from compiling anecdotes to probing the ills that menace man and their possible remedies; from this to a skeptical rejection of presumptuous faith in reason; and from this to the study and portrayal of self, for which he developed the essay as a form and a method. After exposing his and our limitations, he had displayed our resources. If he had written nothing more thereafter, he would still have created an important and original book.

He may have had little thought in 1580 of enlarging it later. His sense of its worth is as tentative as its title. Now it is merely "for a nook in a library, and to amuse a neighbor, a relative, a friend"; he has found his subject "so barren and so meager that no suspicion of ostentation can fall upon my plan." His manner, as we have noted, is constantly deprecatory: "If strangeness and novelty

. . . do not save me," he writes, "I shall never get out of this stupid enterprise with honor." Though of course he really thinks better of it than this, he feels no assurance that others will. His address to the reader is as much a farewell as a greeting: "I am myself the matter of my book; you would be unreasonable to spend your leisure on so frivolous and vain a subject. So farewell."

Next on Montaigne's agenda was a seventeen-month trip (June 22, 1580–November 30, 1581) which would have been longer if he had not been called back to France. It took him to mineral baths and points of interest in France, Switzerland, Germany, Austria, and especially Italy, to visits of at least several days at Augsburg, Venice, Florence, Loreto, Siena, Pisa, and Lucca, and long ones at the baths of La Villa near Lucca and at Rome. Though there have been theories of a secret diplomatic mission or the hope of becoming ambassador to Venice, the evidence does not support them. He had five strong reasons for the trip: health, heartsickness over France, weariness of domesticity, desire to see Venice and Rome, and sheer love of travel.

Suffering intensely from the kidney stone, he had found some relief at the baths of Aigues-Caudes and Bagnères. Now he tries such foreign spas as Plombières, Baden, and La Villa, and assesses others along the way. His journal is in part a record of treatment and effect, even to the volume of mineral water drunk and voided, the size, shape, and circumstances of stones and gravel passed. Deeply mistrustful of medicine, he believed that experience should make an intelligent man his own best doctor. A natural, hence harmless, way to try to purge his stones was drinking and bathing in mineral waters. Finding conflicting theories on their proper use, he prescribed his own treatment and carefully noted the results. At times he sounds almost like his friend who made his life known "only by the workings of his belly. You would see on display at his home a row of chamber pots, seven or eight days' worth. That was his study, his conversation; all other talk stank in his nostrils." However, the journal is much more than a case history, and Montaigne seems to have a wry smile for his notations when he remarks: "It is a stupid habit to keep count of what you piss."

The *Essays* record Montaigne's heartsick indignation at the state of France in the civil wars. Evil men are using religion as a pretext for evil deeds; if anyone picked out of even the loyalist army those who serve simply for the sake of religion, their king, or the country's laws, he could not make up even one complete company of soldiers. "I see not one action, or three, or a hundred, but morals in common and accepted practice, so monstrous, especially in inhumanity and treachery, that I have not the heart to think of them without horror; and I marvel at them almost as much as I detest them." A thousand times Montaigne has gone to bed in his own home expecting to be betrayed and slaughtered that very night. Where a man of good will can be of no use, he may as well leave:

> The other thing that invites me to these excursions is that the present moral state of our country does not suit me. . . .
> I find no man . . . to whom the defense of the laws costs more. . . . I escape; but . . . more by good luck, and even by my prudence, than because of justice. . . . I live more than half by others' favor, which is a harsh obligation. . . .
> I ordinarily reply to those who ask me the reason for my travels, that I know well what I am fleeing from, but not what I am looking for. If they tell me that among foreigners there may be just as little health, and that their ways are no better than ours, I reply, first, that that is not easy. . . . Second, that it is always a gain to change a bad state for an uncertain one, and that the troubles of others should not sting us like our own.

Even Montaigne's journal shows his annoyance with France when his secretary writes, presumably at his dictation: "In truth there entered into his judgment a bit of passion, a certain scorn for his country, which he regarded with hatred and indignation for other considerations."

We have already noted his impatience with unbounded domesticity. The pressure was strong to stay home and be sensible; parts of his chapter "Of Vanity" are like a dialogue with his wife in defense of his right to travel.

> Some people complain of my taking pleasure in continuing this exercise, married and old as I am. They are wrong. . . .
> We have not made a bargain, in getting married, to keep continually tied to each other by the tail. . . . And a wife should not have her eyes so greedily fixed on the front of her husband that she cannot see the back of him, if need be. . . .
> "But at such an age you will never return from so long a journey." What do I care? I undertake it neither to return from it nor to complete it; I undertake only to move about while I like moving. . . .
> Death is the same to me anywhere. However, if I had the choice, it

would be, I think, rather on horseback than in a bed, and out of my house, away from my people. . . . Let us live and laugh among our friends, let us go die and look sour among strangers. . . .

"But on such a long journey you will be forced to stop miserably in some hovel where you will lack everything." . . . I need nothing extraordinary when I am sick; what nature cannot do for me, I do not want to have done by a pill. . . .

"Have you no more comfortable pastimes? What do you lack? . . . Reform yourself alone, for in that your power is complete. . . ."

I see the reasonableness of this admonition, and see it perfectly well; but it would have been quicker and more to the point to tell me in a word: "Be wise." This resolution is beyond wisdom; it is wisdom's work and product.

Domestic matters, for Montaigne, are no less importunate because they are less important; he would discard them entirely if he could, and at least wants long vacations from them: "In the midst of the job . . . a thousand things give me reason to desire and fear. . . . Absent from home, I strip off all such thoughts; and I should then feel less the ruin of a tower than I feel, when present, the fall of a tile. . . . At home I am responsible for all that goes wrong. . . . When I travel, I have only myself and the use of my money to think about."

One of Montaigne's aims is to see Rome, his spiritual home since infancy. For one thing, he worries less there: Rome's endurance gives hope for France, and its distance lends perspective. There, without anxiety, he can watch "my walls, my trees, and my revenue grow and decrease, within two inches," just as if he was there. For another, it symbolizes the entire past, everything we know. He associates its heroes piously with his own father:

I could not revisit the tomb of that great and mighty city so often that I would not marvel at it and revere it. . . . I was familiar with the affairs of Rome long before I was with those of my own house. I knew the Capitol and its location before I knew the Louvre, and the Tiber before the Seine. I have had the abilities and fortunes of Lucullus, Metellus, and Scipio more in my head than those of any of our men. They are dead. So indeed is my father, as completely as they. . . . Nevertheless I do not cease to embrace and cherish his memory, his friendship, and his society, in a union that is perfect and very much alive.

Republican Rome is his ideal homeland; he delights in the chance to see and touch it: "I cannot revisit so often the site of their streets and houses and those ruins stretching deep down to the Antipodes, that I do not muse over them. . . . The sight of the places we know were frequented and inhabited by people whose memory is held in honor somehow stirs us more than hearing the story of their deeds or reading their writings."

It is no surprise that once within range, though after a sleepless night, Montaigne got his party off three hours before daybreak, "so eager was he to see the pavement of Rome." Nor that once there he used "all my five natural senses" to obtain the title of Roman citizen and later reproduced the document in full in the *Essays*. He loved to explore the ancient city. "All these days," his secretary writes, "he spent his time only in studying Rome. At the beginning he had taken a French guide; but when this man quit . . . he made it a point of pride to learn all about Rome by his own study, aided by various maps and books that he had read to him in the evening; and in the daytime he would go on the spot to put his apprenticeship into practice; so that in a few days he could easily have guided his guide." The grandeur of the Rome that had been, though conceivable only through inference, filled him with eloquent awe:

He said that one saw nothing of Rome but the sky under which it had stood and the plan of its site . . . : this was nothing but its sepulcher. The world, hostile to its long domination, had first broken and shattered all the parts of this wonderful body; and because . . . it still terrified the world, the world had buried its very ruin. . . . The buildings of this bastard Rome which they were now attaching to these ancient ruins, although fully adequate to carry away the present age with admiration, reminded him precisely of the nests which sparrows and crows in France suspend from the arches and walls of the churches that the Huguenots have recently demolished.

But he loves the modern city too as "a pleasant place to live in," most entertaining, the one true cosmopolis: "the most universal city in the world . . . pieced together out of foreigners; everyone is as if at home."

Montaigne's love of Venice is almost as strong though less obvious. Its prestige was great, though no longer fully merited, as a locus of political intelligence and power, a seat of learning, and a truly democratic republic where thought and expression were free. La Boétie had made it his symbol of liberty in the *Voluntary Servitude;* Montaigne had said that his friend would rather have been born there than in Sarlat—adding, after his trip, "and with reason."

It was the day before what would have been La Boétie's fiftieth birthday (October 31, 1580) that Montaigne entered Venetian territory; he reached Venice itself five days later; the timing suggests a memorial tribute. However, it was his own eagerness that prompted his hasty visit preparatory to a long stay later. "What had made him undertake it," his secretary writes, "was his extreme hunger to see that city. He said that he could not have stayed peacefully in Rome or anywhere else in Italy without having had a look at Venice."

He was cordially welcomed by the French ambassador, Arnaud du Ferrier (a Protestant sympathizer, as he noted), who had him to dinner twice. When this veteran sought to warn him against over-enthusiasm, he was puzzled: "Among other remarks of the said ambassador, this one seemed strange to him: that he had no dealings with any man of the city, and that they were such a suspicious sort of people that if one of their gentlemen spoke to him twice, they would hold him suspect."

Montaigne found the city "different from what he had imagined, and a little less wonderful." He studied it diligently, and later judged other cities by its standard. He found Florence on his first visit "incomparably inferior to Venice"; Rome was at first less free, and only later seemed to match it. Ancona made him think of an excursion there. Tiring of La Villa, he noted that there were other good baths on the way both to Rome and to Venice. The only criticism he ever offered is this: "Those beautiful cities Venice and Paris weaken my fondness for them by the acrid smell of the marshes of the one and of the mud of the other." For decrepitude he considered it ideal: "I should be prone to recommend Venice to myself for retirement in such a feeble condition of life."

Montaigne's longing for Venice was so great that in 1588 he tried to persuade de Thou to accept the post of ambassador there. "He himself was thinking about Venice," his friend writes, "and declared he would not leave his [de Thou's] company for the entire time that de Thou should be in that city." He never did go there again; but he probably never ceased to wish he might.

For all the attractions of Venice and Rome, Montaigne's main aim was simply to travel, as an excellent exercise for both body and mind. He had recommended this for his ideal pupil; now he says that "I know no better school . . . for forming one's life, than to set before it constantly the diversity of so many other lives, ideas, and customs, and to make it taste such a perpetual variety of forms of our nature." But travel is not only a schooling; it is also a delight:

> I . . . travel most often for my pleasure. . . . If it looks ugly on the right, I take the left; if I find myself unfit to ride my horse, I stop. . . . Have I left something unseen behind me? I go back; it is still on my road. . . . Do I fail to find what I have been told about, in the place I go? . . . I do not regret my trouble; I have learned that what they told me about was not there. . . .
>
> I know well that . . . this pleasure in traveling is a testimony of restlessness and irresolution. And indeed these are our ruling and predominant qualities. Yes, I confess, I see nothing, even in a dream or a wish, that I could hold myself to; variety alone satisfies me, and the enjoyment of diversity, at least if anything satisfies me.

Montaigne's boundless curiosity revels in the adventures offered by new vistas. Sainte-Beuve, who once wrote a fine epitome of disillusionment in his remark "there is nothing on the other side of the hedge any more," enjoyed him especially as a traveler, whom he calls "the wisest Frenchman who ever lived." He delights in Montaigne's zest as he goes "sprinkling his stones and gravel over the roads" and managing "still to be gay and happy on top of all that." As he rightly says, Montaigne "loved travel for the travel itself—to go for the sake of seeing and seeing still more." Much as Montaigne wanted to see Italy and Rome, at times he would have preferred almost any place less familiar and more remote. His secretary summed it up thus in the *Travel Journal:*

> I truly believe that if Monsieur de Montaigne had been alone with his own attendants he would rather have gone to Cracow or toward Greece by land than make the turn toward Italy; but the pleasure he took in visiting unknown countries, which he found so sweet as to make him forget the weakness of his age and of his health, he could not impress on any of his party, and everyone asked only to return home. Whereas he was accustomed to say that after spending a restless night, he would get up with desire and alacrity in the morning when he remembered that he had a new town or region to see. I never saw him less tired or complaining less of his pains; for his mind was so intent on what he encountered, both on the road and at his lodgings, and he was so eager on all occasions to talk to strangers, that I think this took his mind off his ailment.
>
> If someone complained to him that he often led his party, by various roads and regions, back very close to where he had started (which he was likely to do, either because he had been told about something worth seeing, or because he had changed his mind according to the occasions), he would

answer that as for him, he was not going anywhere except where he happened
to be, and that he could not miss or go off his path, since he had no plan
but to travel in unknown places; and that provided he did not fall back
upon the same route or see the same place twice, he was not failing to
carry out his plan. And as for Rome, which was the goal of the others, he
desired less to see it than the other places, since it was known to every
man, and there was not a lackey who could not tell them news of Florence
and Ferrara. He also said that he seemed to be rather like people who are
reading some very pleasing story and therefore begin to be afraid that soon
it will come to an end, or any fine book; so he took such pleasure in
traveling that he hated to be nearing each place where he was to rest, and
toyed with several plans for traveling as he pleased, if he could get away
alone.

Our only record of Montaigne's trip is the diary he kept, dictating about half of it to his secretary, apparently a man of intelligence and breeding who had worked for him before. After dismissing
him in Rome in February, Montaigne wrote the other half himself—
half in French, half in Italian.

The document has a curious history. Never intended for publication, it was discovered in 1770 by Canon Prunis, a historian of
Périgord in quest of materials, in an old coffer in Montaigne's château.
The first two of its 180 pages were missing and have never been
found. Its authenticity was established from the first. Prunis planned
to publish it but was outmaneuvered by the littérateur Meusnier de
Querlon, who brought out three simultaneous editions, in Rome and
in Paris, in 1774, and two more later in that year and the next. The
manuscript, apparently deposited in the (then) Bibliothèque du Roi,
has been lost without a trace. Querlon's readings are neither always
satisfactory nor identical in all his five editions; but we can check
their accuracy almost solely against each other.

Both the *Travel Journal* and the *Ephemeris* show Montaigne
leaving home on June 22, 1580, for the siege of La Fère in Normandy by his future co-worker Marshal Jacques de Matignon. It was
probably at court in Paris on the way that Montaigne was complimented on his *Essays* by Henry III, and replied that if his Majesty
liked them he should like him too, since they were simply an account
of his life and actions. On June 15 the king had declared his resolve
to retake La Fère; the siege began on July 7 and ended successfully on
September 12.

It was not duty alone that led Montaigne to heed the king's

call for volunteers. Although he regarded war as a "human disease," he found the military life noble both in its cause, the protection of the country's peace and greatness, and in the zest of its execution: "You enjoy the company of so many noble, young, active men, the regular sight of so many tragic spectacles, the freedom of that artless relationship, a manly and unceremonious way of life, the variety of a thousand diverse actions, the brave harmony of martial music which delights your ears and arouses your soul, the honor of this exercise, even its severity and hardship. . . . A volunteer, you assign yourself specific roles and risks . . . and you see when life itself may be justifiably devoted to them." He was probably at the siege for much of July, possibly from the start. On August 2 his friend Philibert de Gramont, one of the king's *mignons,* seneschal of Béarn and husband of Diane d'Andoins, was mortally wounded there and died four days later. Montaigne was one of several friends who escorted his body to Soissons, noting later that "everywhere we passed, the people were moved to tears and lamentations by the mere solemn pomp of our convoy."

Just when the trip itself began we do not know, because of the two missing pages at the start of the *Journal;* but September 5, 1580 finds the party just north of Paris at Beaumont-sur-Oise, where young Charles d'Estissac rejoins the group. About seventeen, he was a grandnephew of Rabelais's protector Geoffroy and son of that paragon of mothers, Louise, to whom Montaigne had dedicated his chapter "Of the Affection of Fathers for Their Children" (II: 8). A second companion was Montaigne's youngest brother, Bertrand de Mattecoulon, aged twenty, the future duelist; a third, Monsieur de Cazalis, is probably the Bernard (or Bertrand) de Cazalis who had married Montaigne's youngest sister, Marie, a year before and may already have lost his wife. A fourth was a Monsieur du Hautoy, a Barrois, apparently a friend of d'Estissac, probably the gentleman mentioned as joining the party with him. All four were probably not over twenty, lively but unconcerned with thought or letters. The group included about a dozen servants.

Cazalis left the party at Padua on November 12 apparently to study at the university. Mattecoulon seems to have accompanied Michel until his final departure from Rome, where he remained in a nice little low-priced room with forty-three gold crowns which would allow him to stay and learn fencing for five months. D'Estissac and du Hautoy also remained in Rome then; it is not clear whether they had stayed there from the first or gone touring and bathing with Montaigne.

Here are some basic statistics on the trip.* It may be divided into eleven stages: (1) Across France toward Switzerland (September 5–28, 1580), about 225 miles southeast by south from Beaumont through Meaux, Epernay, Châlons, Bar-le-Duc, Domrémy, Epinal, with an eleven-day stay at the baths of Plombières. (2) Switzerland (September 28–October 7), about seventy-five miles east, from Mulhouse to Schaffhausen, with two days at Basel and five at the baths in Baden. (3) Germany, Austria, and the Alps (October 8–27), going east from Constance beyond Kempten, north to Augsburg (four days), then south through Munich, Innsbruck, and the Brenner Pass to Bolzano. (4) Italy on the road to Rome (October 28–November 30)—about 350 miles south—via Trent, Lake Garda, Verona, Vicenza, Padua, Venice (one week), Ferrara, Bologna (three days), Florence and Siena. Stage 5 is nearly five months in Rome (November 30, 1580–April 19, 1581). Stage 6 (April 19–May 7) took Montaigne about 125 miles northeast to Loreto (three days), northwest to Sinigaglia, west about 115 miles via Urbino and Florence to Lucca (three days) and the nearby baths of La Villa for his first stay (Stage 7, May 7–June 21). For over half the summer (Stage 8, June 21–August 14) he traveled, east to Florence (ten days), west to Pisa for twenty-four and Lucca for seventeen, and then returned for his second stay (Stage 9, August 14–September 12) at La Villa, which he left when summoned back to Bordeaux to take up his duties as mayor. He went back to Rome (Stage 10, September 12–October 1), about 170 miles south, spending eight days in Lucca, three in Siena, and three in Viterbo; and after two weeks in Rome winding up his affairs, he returned rapidly home to Montaigne (Stage 11, October 15–November 30; about 750 miles north, northwest, and west) via Siena, Lucca, Piacenza, Pavia, Milan, Chambéry, Lyons (eight days), Clermont-Ferrand, Limoges, and Périgueux.

Of his 451 days on the trip he had spent just over half in Rome and La Villa: 154 in Rome (140 + 14), 74 in La Villa (45 + 29); about one quarter in stays totaling three days or more at thirteen other cities: Lucca 29 days in all, Pisa 14, Florence 13, Plombières

---

* For a map of the trip, see the end papers.

11, Lyons 8, Venice 7, Baden 5, Siena 5, Augsburg 4, and 3 each at Bologna, Loreto, Viterbo, and San Chirico; the remaining quarter stopping at more than a hundred towns and villages, sometimes for two days, mostly for one. He covered between 2,500 and 3,000 miles in all, on horseback, mostly in about 120 days of travel, at a pace of twenty or twenty-five miles a day. About one fifth of his time he spent at mineral baths (mainly La Villa) seeking relief from his stone.

The *Travel Journal* disappointed many of its first readers, who had hoped for something polished and profound, or at least daringly skeptical. Even today, when we treasure every document, we learn more than we may wish of waters drunk and voided and of meals, prices, and accommodations. Many of these items, however, are strokes in a kind of portrait. Intimate knowledge, Montaigne knew, is rarely accessible to the tourist; since every movement reveals us, externals are better than nothing. From the many details the *Journal* records in Basel about churches, houses, interiors, furniture, clocks, scrubbed and polished woodwork and floors, ingeniously wrought spits, meals of three or four hours at groaning tables, there emerges a sketch of a hard-working, tidy people, fond of food and comfort. The meaning Montaigne found in such particulars is shown by his remark about the Inn of the Rose at Innsbruck: "Around some of the beds there were curtains; and to show the character of the nation, they were beautiful and rich, of a certain kind of linen, cut and open-worked, for the rest short and narrow, in short no use for what we use them for."

Montaigne's interest in machines and even gadgets is surprising. He describes in detail systems of water supply at Neufchâteau, Constance, and Augsburg, a clipped and trained tree at Schaffhausen, a postern gate at Augsburg that lets travelers into the city by night for a fee with elaborate precautions, and the pleasure houses and gardens of the Fuggers at Augsburg, the duke of Florence at Pratolino and Castello, and the cardinal of Ferrara at Tivoli. Since the accounts of all but the last of these are recorded by the secretary and some of the enthusiasm may be his, let us see what Montaigne himself tells us of the Villa d'Este at Tivoli. Though published materials make a full account unnecessary, he spends about 900 words describing the palace and garden and comparing them with Pratolino. Examining everything closely, he takes special delight in the water music and the fountains:

The gushing of an infinity of jets of water checked and launched by a single spring that can be worked from far off, I had seen elsewhere on my trip. . . . The music of the organ . . . is effected by means of the water, which falls with great violence into a round arched cave and agitates the air that is in there and forces it, in order to get out, to go through the pipes of the organ and supply it with wind. Another stream of water, driving a wheel with certain teeth in it, causes the organ keyboard to be struck in a certain order; so you hear an imitation of the sound of trumpets. In another place you hear the song of birds, which are little bronze flutes that you see at regals; they give a sound like those little earthenware pots full of water that little children blow into by the spout, this by an artifice like that of the organ; and then by other springs they set in motion an owl, which, appearing at the top of the rock, makes this harmony cease instantly, for the birds are frightened by his presence; and then he leaves the place to them again. . . .

Elsewhere there issues a noise as of cannon shots; elsewhere . . . as of harquebus shots. This is done by a sudden fall of water into channels; and the air, laboring . . . to get out, engenders this noise. . . .

There are ponds or reservoirs, with a stone margin all around and many tall freestone pillars above this parapet, about four paces apart. . . . From the head of these pillars water comes out. . . . The mouths . . . facing one another, cast and scatter the water into this pond with such force that these shafts of water come to meet and clash in the air, and produce a thick and continual rain falling into the pond. The sun, falling upon it, engenders, both at the bottom of this pond and in the air and all around this place, a rainbow so natural and vivid that it lacks nothing of the one we see in the sky.

Montaigne is fascinated by all signs of human ingenuity. His favorite landscapes are those cultivated against odds. A typical example is near Thann, where "we found a very beautiful big plain, flanked on the left hand by hillsides covered with vineyards of the most beautiful and best cultivated sort and of such extent that the Gascons who were there said they had never seen so many in succession." Another is near Foligno:

. . . We had for some time a very handsome view of a thousand varied hills, clad on all sides with all kinds of beautifully shady fruit trees and the finest wheat fields possible, often in a place so steep and precipitous that it was a miracle that even horses could get to them; the most beautiful valleys, an infinite number of streams. . . . Often, very far above our heads, we would see a beautiful village, and below our feet, as if at the

Antipodes, another, each one having many and various attractions. This fact itself gives them no mean luster, that among such fertile mountains as these the Apennines show their frowning and inaccessible peaks, from which you see many torrents rolling down, which, having lost their first fury, soon after, in these valleys, turn into very pleasant and very gentle streams. Among these summits you discover, both on the heights and down below, many fertile plateaus, sometimes so large as to extend out of sight. . . . It does not seem to me that any painting can represent so rich a landscape.

The same love of nature shows in Montaigne's choice of a room at La Villa. After inspecting the houses, he "settled on the finest, especially for the view, which overlooks . . . all this little valley, and the river Lima, and the mountains . . . all well cultivated and green all the way to the summit. . . . All night from my room I heard, very soft, the sound of the river." Or again, at the view of Narni rising above the plain among "highly cultivated inhabited hillsides," he remarks: "I had my colic very badly, and it had gripped me for twenty-four hours and was then in its last effort; however, I did not fail for all that to enjoy the beauty of that place."

Religion is the strongest interest that the trip reveals in Montaigne. Again and again when he stops he seeks out the local priest or minister and corners him for a talk. He is especially curious about other faiths. We have mentioned his attending synagogues and describing a circumcision sympathetically and at length. In Protestant Mulhouse the secretary writes: "Monsieur de Montaigne went to see the church; for they are not Catholics here." At Basel, Baden, Lindau, Isny, Kempten, and Augsburg he visits the churches of the Protestants and discusses their views. He is struck by the disputes between Zwinglians, Calvinists, and Lutherans. At Lindau he makes a note used later in the *Essays*, that "under the authority of Martin [Luther], whom they accept as their chief, they get up many disputes over the interpretation of the meaning of Martin's writings." In Kempten he attends a Lutheran service, makes careful notes, and has a long talk with the minister afterward. At Isny, Montaigne, "as was his custom, promptly went and found a doctor of theology of this town, to pick up information, and this doctor dined with our party." After showing them the Lutheran church, he went to a monastery with them and watched "without taking off his bonnet" until d'Estissac and Montaigne had finished their prayers. Montaigne quizzed him about the Calvinist charge of Lutheran Ubiquitism, the belief "that the divinity was inseparable from the body, wherefore, the divinity being everywhere, the body was everywhere also; and second, that since Jesus Christ had always to be at the right hand of the Father, he was everywhere, inasmuch as the right hand of God, which is the power, is everywhere." Montaigne is hard to satisfy and less diffident about theology than he sometimes sounds. "This good doctor loudly denied this imputation . . . but in fact it seems to Monsieur de Montaigne that he did not defend himself very well."

Naturally we find him oftener at Catholic services. He is dismayed at Italian casualness: at High Mass in Verona the men "were talking right in the choir of the church, covered, standing, their backs turned toward the altar, and looking as if they were not thinking of the service except at the elevation"; and in Rome at the Pope's Mass in Saint Peter's on Christmas Day "it seemed novel to him [Montaigne], both at this Mass and others, that the Pope and cardinals and other prelates are seated, and, almost all through the Mass, covered, chatting and talking together." He finds these ceremonies "more magnificent than devout" and concludes that the people in general seem "less devout than in the good towns in France," though extremely ceremonious. His opinion is confirmed by his Jesuit friend Maldonado, who finds the common people "incomparably more devout in France than here; but the rich, and especially the courtiers, a little less."

An impartial observer, Montaigne comments quizzically that Rome is "all court and all nobility: every man shares in the ecclesiastical idleness." He seems mainly perplexed by the flagellant Penitents. He reports a miraculous cure with the same detachment as an ugly squabble among friars. Noncommittally he tells in Loreto how the house where Jesus was born was miraculously transported "first to Sclavonia, and then near here, and finally here." Here is his account of a Roman priest driving out an evil spirit. After reading many prayers and exorcisms, he turned to the possessed man ("a melancholy man and as if half dead," bound and held on his knees before the altar), "now speaking to him, now speaking to the devil in his person, and then insulting him, beating him with great blows of his fist, spitting in his face." With the pyx and the host in one hand and a taper in the other, he threatened the devil "in the loudest and most magisterial voice he could"; and finally, in normal tones, sent the man home with his relatives. Questioned later, he said this was an obstinate devil who would be hard to cast out. "He told several stories about this science and his ordinary experience of it, notably that the day before he had rid a woman of a big devil who, in coming out, had pushed nails, pins, and a tuft of his hair out of this woman through her mouth. And because someone answered him that she was not yet completely recovered, he said that this was another sort of spirit, lighter and less harmful, who had returned into her that morning; but that this sort (for he knows their names, their divisions, and their most particular distinctions) was easy to conjure. That is all I saw."

Generally, however, Montaigne seems well impressed by Catholic practice. One of his greatest pleasures in Rome during Lent was the sermons of such excellent speakers as "that renegade rabbi" (whom we saw in chapter 2) who preached to the Jews every Saturday, using their own arguments and texts to combat their belief; Father Toledo, outstanding "in depth of learning, in pertinence, and in readiness," who preached to the Pope and the cardinals; and an unnamed third, "very eloquent and popular, who was preaching to the Jesuits, with much ability, besides his excellent language; the last two are Jesuits." He has great admiration for the young Society of Jesus and marvels at the place it has attained in Christendom: "I believe there never was a brotherhood and body among us that held such a rank, or, to sum up, that produced such results as these men will, if their plans continue. They will soon possess all Christendom: it is a nursery of great men in every sort of greatness. It is the one limb of our Church that most threatens the heretics of our time."

On the previous page we noted a conversation between Montaigne and one of the ablest theologians of his day, his good Jesuit friend Juan Maldonado. A younger contemporary, Pierre de Lancre, says he was Montaigne's actual spiritual director: "Maldonado was the heart and soul of the sieur de Montaigne, who considered him so able that when they were in Rome together, when the said lord maintained some opinion or point in religion that he could not defend well, he thought that he was getting out of it well by saying that this was the opinion of Father Maldonado. He thought him the ablest theologian of his time and of his acquaintance, and his own intimate friend; he rested his own belief entirely on Maldonado's opinions."

Maldonado had helped in the first conversion of Henry of Navarre in 1572; twenty years later Navarre, then Henry IV, contemplating his second and final conversion, asked for him, learned with regret of his death, and ordered the Jesuits to publish his complete writings. Montaigne probably met him no later than 1579, when Maldonado was inspecting a new school in Bordeaux. They thought much alike in general, on the value of the sacraments, and on the dangers of allowing the untrained to argue theology and of Protestantism leading to atheism. Montaigne mentions him only in the *Travel Journal*, to tell of their two meetings. The second of these we have just seen. Of the first, at Epernay (September 8, 1580), the secretary writes: "In the said church after Mass, Monsieur de Montaigne spoke to Monsieur Maldonado, a Jesuit whose name is very famous because of his erudition in theology and philosophy, and they had several talks together on learned matters, both then and after dinner, at the said Monsieur de Montaigne's lodgings, where the said Maldonado came to see him." This is all we hear about the learned matters, though the secretary enlarges on the baths at Liége where Maldonado, who also suffered from the stone, had just been. Their conversations show that they were on cordial terms; for their intimacy we have only the word of de Lancre.

In a century when pontiffs were as often magnificent and bellicose as devout, Montaigne's comments on Pope Gregory XIII (Ugo Buoncompagno, 1572–85, who publicly celebrated the Massacre of Saint Bartholomew's Day) are judicious and respectful. He finds him majestic, assured, vigorous, passionately devoted to his son, and concerned with building, giving alms, and winning back young foreigners to the Church. "In truth," Montaigne concludes, "his life and his conduct have nothing very extraordinary about them one way or the other, but incline much more to the good." When Montaigne and his companions were given an audience (December 29, 1580), he believes that the pontiff raised his foot a bit for him to kiss. Before his final benediction the Pope, "with a courteous countenance, admonished Monsieur d'Estissac to pursue study and virtue, and Monsieur de Montaigne to continue in the devotion he had always borne to the Church and the service of the Most Christian King, and said that he would gladly be of service to them whenever he could." Later his authority, Montaigne believes, helped him become a citizen of Rome.

The *Travel Journal* reveals many details of Montaigne's religious practice, but the total picture is inconclusive. We find him often going to Mass, but often appearing to miss it, even on Sunday. Only at Loreto is there mention of his taking communion, and with it confession. However, he obviously does not trouble to record every religious function, and we cannot tell how much assiduity was expected of him on his travels. All we can safely say is that he shows himself a stanch practicing Catholic. Typical and apparently spontaneous is one exclamation in alarm over his health: "God knows! His will be done!"

Of especial interest is Montaigne's report of the criticism of the 1580 *Essays* by the papal censor, Master of the Sacred Palace, Sisto Fabri (1541–94), professor of theology at the University of Rome and soon (1583) to be general of the Dominican Order. What happened was this. When Montaigne reached Rome, he was surprised to have his books taken from him at the customs, as was the practice. Dismayed to learn that their prospective examiners had censured some German books for mentioning the Protestant heresies they were combating, he was relieved that by luck he had no condemned books with him. When his *Essays* were returned four months later they had been studied with great care, but the criticism was mild, the fideism of the "Apology" tacitly accepted, and the interview a duel in politeness:

On this day in the evening my *Essays* were returned to me, corrected according to the opinion of the learned monks. The Master of the Sacred Palace had been able to judge them only by the report of some French friar, since he did not understand our language at all; and he was so content with the excuses I offered on each objection that this Frenchman had left him that he referred it to my conscience to redress what I should see was in bad taste. I begged him on the contrary to follow the opinion of the man who had made the judgment, admitting in certain things—such as having used the word "fortune," having named heretic poets, having excused Julian, and the objection to the idea that anyone who was praying should be free from evil impulses at the time; *item*, esteeming as cruelty whatever goes beyond plain death; *item*, that a child should be brought up to do anything; and other things of that sort—that this was my opinion, and that they were things I had put in, not thinking they were errors; in other matters denying that the corrector had understood my thought. The said Master, who is an able man, was full of excuses for me, and wanted me to realize that he was not very sympathetic to these revisions; and he pleaded very ingeniously for me, in my presence, against another man, also an Italian, who was opposing me.

They kept one book, a Swiss history, simply because the anonymous translator was a heretic and the preface condemned. Montaigne concludes by marveling "how well they know the men of our countries."

When about a month later Montaigne went to take leave of his friendly critic, the consideration was even more marked:

On April 15th I went to say good-by to the Master of the Sacred Palace and his colleague, who urged me not to make use of the censorship of my book, in which censorship some other Frenchmen had informed them there were many stupid things; saying that they honored both my intention and affection for the Church and my ability, and thought so well of my frankness and conscience that they left it to myself to cut out of my book, when I wanted to republish it, whatever I found too licentious in it, and among other things the uses of the word "fortune." It seemed to me that I left them well pleased with me; and to excuse themselves for having scrutinized my book so attentively and condemned it in certain details, they cited me many books of our time by cardinals and churchmen of very good reputation, censured for a few such imperfections which did not affect in the least the reputation of the author or of the work as a whole. They urged me to help the Church by my eloquence (those are their courteous formulas) and to make my abode in this city, at peace and without interference from them. These are persons of great authority and potential cardinals.

With due allowance for courtesy, Montaigne had been ably defended by a churchman of the highest authority; a tribute had been paid to his integrity; only a few criticisms remained. An amateur in theology, he had come off as well as most professionals. He had reason to be pleased with this first searching scrutiny of the *Essays*.

It is the *Journal* that reveals Montaigne's desire to live the life of the people he visits. After a month on the road the secretary remarks on this: "Monsieur de Montaigne, to essay completely the diversity of manners and customs, let himself be served everywhere in the mode of each country, no matter what difficulty this caused him. . . . In Switzerland he said he suffered no inconvenience, except for having at table only a little cloth half a foot square for a napkin." In Germany a few days later he reports that Montaigne "preferred the conveniences of this country to the French, beyond comparison, and conformed to them even to drinking wine without water." Augsburg brings a big disappointment. Plagued by a cold, Montaigne holds his handkerchief to his nose in church, hoping to pass unnoticed since he is simply dressed and unattended; later he learns that this was remarked on: "At last he had fallen into the fault that he most avoided, that of making himself noticeable by some mannerism at variance with the taste of those who saw him; for as far as in him lies, he conforms and falls into line with the ways of the place where he happens to be, and in Augsburg he wore a fur cap around the town." Especially noteworthy is his decision to write his *Journal* in Italian for the last six months of his stay in Italy (May 13– November 1). Fluent as he was, he could not express himself fully and personally in the language. This constraint, for a man bent on expressiveness, was a significant sacrifice for the sake of trying to "live Italian."

Montaigne finds much to enjoy and admire wherever he goes. He is vexed at the silly reports he has read that the countries he visits are wild and uncomfortable. He likes the people and places he sees. "They are a very good nation," he writes of the Swiss, "especially to those who conform to them." The Lorrains near Plombières are also "a good people, free, sensible, considerate." Before leaving Germany he writes to François Hotman how much he has enjoyed his stay and how sorry he is to go. He finds the Roman upper classes "as courteous and gracious as possible, whatever the common run of Frenchmen say, who cannot call people gracious who find it hard to endure their excesses and their ordinary insolence." On his third visit to Florence he admits that it is rightly called "the beautiful"; and a little later in Lucca, that he has been well lodged in Italy and lacks only a good friend.

Montaigne's friendliness is returned in kind. He is readily admitted to the Vatican Library, though the French ambassador is not. The papal censor treats him with cordial respect. The Pope—raised slipper or no—greeted him graciously and helped him become a Roman citizen. One tribute must have delighted him. An inveterate scoffer at medicine with a keen sense of what it needed, he found himself called on more than once to arbitrate between the grave sons of Aesculapius: "Thus today certain doctors who had to hold an important consultation for a young lord, Signor Paolo Cesi (nephew of Cardinal Cesi) . . . came to ask me, at his behest, to be good enough to hear their opinions and arguments, because he was resolved to rely wholly on my judgment. I laughed about this to myself. Many other similar things have happened to me, both here and in Rome."

When Montaigne left the baths of La Villa after his first stay, it was "after receiving . . . all the indications of friendliness that I could desire." When he returned two months later, "I received a warm welcome and greetings from all those people. In truth it seemed

that I had come back to my own home." For in the month and a
half of his first stay, the man who feared that La Boétie had spoiled
him for ordinary acquaintanceships had shown himself a very good
mixer. Besides making friends as he went along, he had given two
parties. On May 14, 1581, "After dinner I gave a dance for the
peasant girls, and danced in it myself so as not to appear too reserved." A week later he offered a big dance ("I wanted to give the
first one of this year"), had it announced several days ahead, sent to
Lucca for the customary prizes (two for the men, nineteen for the
women; six crowns' worth), hired five fife players (a crown and a
day's food for the lot; a bargain), and invited all the ladies and
gentlemen at the baths to the dance and supper after. Though he
feared at first that "we would be left alone," over a hundred people
came, besides the natives. Late in the afternoon, when it was time to
award the prizes, he cut his way through ceremony to good purpose:

I addressed myself to the most important ladies, saying that since I lacked
sufficient skill and boldness to judge such beauties and graces and nice
manners as I saw in these girls, I begged them . . . to distribute the prizes
to the company according to their merits. We were held up on ceremony
for a bit because they refused to assume this charge, which they took to
be too much courtesy to them. Finally I added this condition, that if they
would be good enough to take me into their counsel, I would give my
opinion. And this was the result, that I picked out with my eyes now this
one, now that; wherein I did not fail to have some regard for beauty and
grace, pointing out that the charm of the dance depended not only on the
movement of the feet, but also on the carriage and grace and charm and
elegance of the whole person. . . . One of the girls refused the prize. She
sent to beg me that for her sake I should give it to another girl; which I
did not consent to do. The other was not one of the most attractive.
     . . . I would give the present that seemed right to me to the lady,
kissing it, and she, taking it, would give it to the girl, saying graciously:
"Here is this lord knight who is giving you this fine present: thank him."
"On the contrary, you are obliged to her ladyship, who out of so many others
has judged you worthy to receive a prize. I am very sorry that the present is
not more worthy of such-and-such a quality of yours"—and I named these
according to what they were. The same thing was promptly done with the
men.

Montaigne found it a rare treat "to see these peasant girls, so
elegant, and dressed like ladies, dance so well." He invited everyone
to supper, he reports candidly, "for the banquets in Italy are nothing
but a very light meal by French standards—a few cuts of veal and
one or two brace of chicken is all." Among others at his table (with
the colonel of the vicariate, "who is like a brother to me") he had

an ugly peasant woman of thirty-seven, Divizia, unable to read or write but brought up on Ariosto, who had a knack for impromptu verse and delivered some in Montaigne's honor. ("To tell the truth," he confides, "they are nothing but verses and rhymes.") All in all, guests and host seem to have had a delightful time.

Not all the trip was pleasant. The *Journal* also offers our only direct glimpses of the suffering Montaigne. Sometimes he passed several stones in a few days; sometimes he was in great pain for weeks without respite. One of his worst attacks culminated on August 24, 1581, during his second stay at La Villa. For about ten days the stone, together with stomach trouble, headaches, and toothaches, gave him pain that rose to agony. At last the stone passed.

On the 24th, in the morning, I pushed down a stone that stopped in the passage. I remained from that moment until dinnertime without urinating, in order to increase my desire to do so. Then I got my stone out, not without pain and bleeding, both before and after: as big and long as a pine nut, but as thick as a bean at one end, and having, to tell the truth, exactly the shape of a prick. It was a very fortunate thing for me to be able to get it out. I have never ejected one comparable in size to this one. I had guessed only too truly from the quality of my urines that this would be the result. I shall see what is to follow.

There would be too much weakness and cowardice on my part if, finding myself every day in a position to die in this manner, and with every hour bringing death nearer, I did not make every effort toward being able to bear death lightly as soon as it surprises me. And in the meantime it will be wise to accept joyously the good that it pleases God to send us. There is no other medicine, no other rule or science, for avoiding the ills, whatever they may be and however great, that besiege men from all sides and at every hour, than to make up our minds to suffer them humanly, or to end them courageously and promptly.

This is Montaigne's final philosophy, balanced and receptive. Accept God's gifts joyously; prepare to bear death lightly; if the pain grows extreme, end it promptly or—better—suffer it humanly (*umanamente*). The adverb is significant; henceforth "human" is an expression of Montaigne's highest praise.

The influence of Montaigne's trip on his thought has been well assessed by Imbrie Buffum, who finds it in five main areas: the role of experience; pain, pleasure, and virtue; solitude and society; custom; and unity and diversity. In each of these the *Essays* of 1588 reveal a considerable change—already prepared in 1578–80—from those published in 1580, and the *Journal* shows an important step in that change.

Before 1580 Montaigne had sensed the power of experience and the experimental method; on his trip he gives it a real test; henceforth, as we see in his final chapter, it is to be his main guide. He had first seen virtue as power, achieved through struggle, over vice, weakness, and pain. By 1578–80 he had reduced the premium on effort, placing the easy goodness of Socrates above the heroic tension of Cato. His trip helped him see that our best resource against pain is diversion, which he practiced for a year and a half before making it a part of his final philosophy.

He had moved a long way already from the solitary shell he had recommended at first; the trip draws him much farther still. Custom he had presented originally as mainly absurd and tyrannical; on the trip he finds conformance to it well worthwhile; hereafter he will emphasize its utility more and more.

The greatest change in Montaigne's outlook between the *Essays* of 1580 and those of 1588 concerns unity and diversity. The trip made him more aware of his own particularity, both in using the baths and in confronting the infinite variety of custom, and at the same time of the basic human nature underlying the varied patterns of our behavior.

Thus the trip, and the play of his mind upon it, carried him forward on the meditative journey of his life, farther from book learning and theory into convictions of his own learned from life.

His most important gain is his heightened confidence in himself and others. He had worried a bit about the eccentricity of his *Essays;* now he sees the first signs of their acceptance and success. He had had one true friend, and never ceased to mourn him; but wherever he went he was well received and made cordial contacts easily, with Swiss, Germans, and Italians, Calvinists, Lutherans, and Jews, as well as with Frenchmen and Catholics. The earlier *Essays* had not suggested that he would like these ordinary people so much; but he does, and quite unabashedly. Trying out their ways and making friends with them enhances his confidence in others and his sense of human solidarity.

The trip helped make him not merely a citizen of Rome but in the fullest sense a citizen of the world, a representative man, aware of this fact, confident and ready to speak to and for all men.

N SEPTEMBER 1, 1581, a week after the night of agony noted in our last chapter, Montaigne had still not recovered. "I began," he wrote in his *Journal,* "to find these baths unpleasant. And if news had come from France, which I was expecting, having been four months without receiving any, I would have been ready to leave at the first opportunity, and do my autumn cure at any other baths whatever." Less than a week later he had unexpected news from France: "This same morning they delivered into my hands, by way of Rome, letters from Monsieur de Tausin, written in Bordeaux on August 2nd, by which he advised me that the day before, by general consent, I had been made mayor of that city; and he urged me to accept this charge for the love of my country."

Montaigne left five days later (September 12) and took almost three weeks, where he needed one, to return to Rome. On arrival (October 1) "I received the letters from the jurats of Bordeaux, who wrote me very courteously about the fact that they had elected me mayor of their city, and urgently requested me to join them." His two weeks there were busy with preparations and good-byes.

On the way home he indulged in only a few delays: two days each in Siena, Milan, and Limoges, eight in Lyons. The *Journal* becomes terse and meager; as Montaigne says, "I had nothing but my return home on my mind." He arrived on November 30, five days after his king had written him from Paris:

> Monsieur de Montaigne, because I hold in great esteem your fidelity and zealous devotion to my service, it was a pleasure to me to understand that you were elected mayor of my city of Bordeaux; and I have found this election very agreeable and confirmed it, the more willingly because it was made without intrigue and in your remote absence. On the occasion of which my intention is, and I order and enjoin you very expressly, that without delay or excuse you return as soon as this is delivered to you and take up the duties and services of the responsibility to which you have been so legitimately called. And you will be doing a thing that will be very agreeable to me, and the contrary would greatly displease me.

Montaigne says little about how all this struck him: "Messieurs of Bordeaux elected me mayor of their city when I was far from France and still farther from such a thought. I excused myself, but I was informed that I was wrong, since the king's command also figured in the matter." His election, it appears, was a surprise, flattering but not wholly pleasing; he probably demurred to no avail in a letter from La Villa, but left for Rome, where he could confer with an expert like Paul de Foix; friends and the jurats' letter may have helped convince him that he could not lightly decline; the king heard of his demurrer and wrote him on November 25, thinking he was still in Rome; in fact he was nearly home. Before he got the king's letter he may have learned his intent from his neighbor the marquis de Trans.

He seems convinced that he owed his election entirely to the jurats, whose "knowledge of my late father had alone incited them to this"; but in all probability he was selected late in 1580 at the conferences of Le Fleix, where Trans was host. Henry III and his mother, Catherine, sent his brother François, duke of Anjou, to arrange peace with Henry of Navarre. Montaigne was highly regarded by all three principals, as well as by Margaret of Valois, sister of the king and wife of Navarre, who had read his translation of Sebond and asked him to compose his "Apology." Their combined support probably persuaded the six jurats and twenty-four worthies to elect Montaigne—perhaps unanimously—on August 1, 1581.

The political situation was normally tense and complex, and

personalities made it no simpler. Henry of Navarre, leader of the rebellious Protestants, was also brother-in-law and distant cousin to the king, second in line (after Anjou) to succeed him, one of his great vassals, responsible to him for order in the southwest. Far more political than religious, his relations with his ardent coreligionaries were uneasy; yet they needed each other and generally knew it. He had mistrusted the king and queen mother ever since his forced abjuration during the Saint Bartholomew's Day Massacre (1572), just after his marriage, and his virtual captivity at court until in 1576 he escaped, returned to Protestantism, and took command of the Reformists in the southwest. A determined and magnetic leader and astute politician, he never lost his weakness for women.

His wife, Margaret, was attractive, intelligent, romanesque, and headstrong. Her marriage had of course been no love match; she had once been fond of Henri de Guise, never of Protestantism. Navarre skipped court without her, and she did not join him for two years. When she did, the south of France was in virtual anarchy; the queen mother's triumphal tour of pacification proved more showy than effective. With Margaret's arrival, Navarre's court at Nérac changed from warlike to idyllic. Almost as fond of men as her husband was of women, she soon took to his captains as he did to her ladies-in-waiting. At the women's instigation, the "Lovers' War" broke out for over a year; the recapture of La Fère was one of its final actions.

Catherine de' Medici, now just over sixty, was still vigorous, alert, and intelligent, fond of eating, riding, negotiations, splendor, and the arts. After twenty-six years of a humiliating marriage to a king (Henry II) in love with a much older woman (Diane de Poitiers), her twenty years as Regent and queen mother had brought her about as many cares as satisfactions. Her original policy of tolerance and balance of power had led to humiliation; the bloodshed of Saint Bartholomew's Day had failed; she had buried four daughters and three sons, including two kings of France. Two sons remained, Henry III and the mercurial Anjou, who seemed driven to make trouble for his brother and who, ironically, succeeded best at this in death.

The last Valois king, Henry III, had many remarkable gifts but not that of ruling. Learned and highly cultivated, a born orator and a connoisseur of arts and letters, he lacked the desire and will for politics. His early love affairs led to transports as excessive as were his religious practices, which included nocturnal processions and penitential flagellation. In an age of virile vices, he alienated his people by his devotion to his *mignons,* his darlings—handsome young noblemen, fierce duelists, whom he showered with honors and who strutted the streets as bedecked and made up as any women, even as the king loved to dress up in women's clothing. The further he went, the more spasmodically he applied himself to affairs of state. His behavior in 1588 at the Estates General of Blois, culminating in the assassination of his rival Guise, was extreme but not atypical.

The third power, Guise (1550–88), was the most consistent and —until his death—the most successful of the three Henrys. No prince of the blood like Navarre, he came from a noble Lorrain family risen to eminence under Henry II as foes of Protestantism. His father, François, a great general, directed the "Vassy Massacre" of 1562 that set off the religious civil wars. If Montaigne was right, Guise cared no more than Navarre about religion, but found his support among the Catholic extremists of the Holy League. When a Protestant fanatic assassinated his father in 1563, Guise had a clear role and mission: to succeed him and avenge him. He was a leader in the 1572 massacre and from 1576 head of the League. After the massacre he sought the friendship of Navarre, who understandably had none to offer him. His militant anti-Protestantism in an overwhelmingly Catholic country, coupled with the king's unpopular vices and moderation, made him the national hero of the 1580's and in his last few years the uncrowned ruler of France.

The rivalries and enmities were of course unofficial. Just as Navarre was the king's administrator and potential successor, so Guise was his leading general, and Guise's Holy League claimed merely to be defending the Most Christian King against excessive influence contrary to the true faith. All the rival leaders were for law and order— on their own terms—and of course were never all contented at the same time.

Bordeaux was a trouble spot in a troubled kingdom. The League had strong supporters there. The Parlement, mayor and jurats, and most of the people were Catholic loyalists. All around, however, especially to the south and southeast, were Protestant strongholds and troops. Both Navarre and Condé were formally refused admittance for fear of a coup.

Two key figures in keeping the city peaceable and loyal were the mayor and the king's lieutenant general in Guienne. The latter, responsible also to Navarre, often had to oppose him—tactfully if possible; the mayor's position was somewhat similar. Sometimes the same man filled both posts. Montaigne's predecessor, Arnaud de Gontaut, baron de Biron (1524–92), Marshal of France and lieutenant general in Guienne, a stalwart loyalist, had treated Navarre as an enemy, fought him vigorously, and once fired his cannon on Nérac while Margaret was there. She never forgave the insult, and for once made common cause with her husband. A year later Biron was replaced as mayor by Montaigne and as lieutenant general by an able soldier who was also an astute diplomat, Jacques de Goyon, marshal de Matignon (1525–97).

As far back as the early thirteenth century the jurats had elected the first mayors of Bordeaux. From 1261 to 1279 and from 1287 to 1451 the mayors were appointed by the king of England, and then for another century by the king of France. In 1550 Henry II restored most of the privileges taken from the city after the salt-tax riots. He reduced the number of jurats to six, three elected each year for a two-year term; assigned to them and the mayor jurisdiction over the city and suburbs, subject to appeal to the Parlement; and once again allowed the jurats to elect their mayor, though limiting the term of office to two years, renewable. The jurats respected the tradition set by Charles VII of electing only a sword-bearing nobleman —such as Pierre de Montaigne. Both offices were unpaid; each year the mayor received two robes with the city's colors.

The mayor, says chronicler Jean Darnal, has always been elected "from the most noble, valiant, and capable lords of the region." He had a company at his disposal to maintain order, and often led the armies as well as the nobles in war. Concerned with policy, he left detail to the jurats as he often had to travel to represent the city before the powers of the realm. "The entire city relied mainly on him."

The jurats too were men of consequence, normally two nobles, two lawyers, and two businessmen; they and the mayor were known as the "governors" of Bordeaux. In no other city in France, says Darnal, did the people's magistrates have fuller jurisdiction or make a finer public appearance. When they marched as a body, they were led by forty archers of the watch in scarlet cassocks, then by the city officers—Treasurer, Assessors, Notary, Gatekeeper, Horseman,

Trumpeters, Weigher of Bread, Guardians of Weights and Measures, Markers and Gaugers of Wine, Taxers of Fish, Inspectors of Fish, Taverns, River, and Port, Superintendents of Public Works, and various lesser fry. After all these, sumptuously gowned, came the nine real authorities: the Public Attorney and Town Clerk in the rear, the six Lord Jurats two by two, and, a few paces ahead, in a robe of red-and-white velvet with brocade trimmings, his Lordship the Mayor.

Though chosen, as he thought, for the wrong reasons, and in no condition to accept, Montaigne was duly impressed: "It is an office that must appear all the handsomer for this, that it has no remuneration or gain other than the honor of its execution. The term is two years; but it can be extended by a second election, which happens very rarely. This was done in my case, and had been done only twice before." He took pains to tell the jurats exactly what to look for: "I deciphered myself to them faithfully . . . without memory, without vigilance, without experience, and without vigor; also without hate, without ambition, without avarice, and without violence; so that they should be informed and instructed about what they were to expect of my service." He feared they might be counting on another Pierre de Montaigne, utterly devoted to the cares of office, forgetting health and home and nearly losing his life in arduous journeys for his city. "He was like that . . . there was never a more kindly and public-spirited soul." Though Montaigne admired his father's way, he neither approved of it nor planned to follow it.

His first term as mayor was very calm. We do not know when he received Henry III's order to duty or when he acted on it. Since the second edition of the *Essays* was published in 1582 with some additions, he probably worked on it soon after his return. February 8, 1582 finds him paying his respects to the king and queen of Navarre at Cadillac, about twenty-five miles southeast of Bordeaux, on a trip as friendly as it was official; for queen Margaret was godmother at the baptism of the daughter of Montaigne's close friends Diane de Foix-Candale and Louis de Gurson, whose marriage he had served well. His first official appearance that we know of had come two weeks earlier (January 26) at the opening in Bordeaux of the Court of Justice of Guienne, constituted at the conferences of Le Fleix to combat partisanship, with jurisdiction over all cases arising out of the latest edict of pacification. This was a distinguished group of four-teen men drawn from the Parlements and the Grand Council and numbering several able writers. Pierre Pithou, poet and future col-laborator in the anti-League *Satire Ménippée,* became a good friend. The magistrate and historian de Thou formed an even closer bond and "learned many things from Michel de Montaigne, a man free in spirit and foreign to factions, who was then performing the very honorific function of mayor in that town [Bordeaux] and who had great and certain knowledge of our affairs, and especially of those of his own Guienne." A third new friend was Antoine Loisel. After Montaigne had praised his opening speech on the need for rule by law, Loisel replied in his closing address seven months later (August 22) with a charming tribute. When it was printed he sent a copy to Montaigne, who had missed it, with an inscription saying he hoped that Montaigne would enjoy this as much as the opening one, and that it could not be better addressed than to "the man who, being mayor and one of the first magistrates of Bordeaux, is also one of the principal ornaments not only of Guienne, but also of all France." Over a year later Montaigne received a book of Loisel's. He showed his appreciation in his inscription on a copy of the 1588 *Essays:* "This is a poor return for the handsome presents you have made to me of the fruits of your labors, but the fact is that it is the best return I can make. In God's name, sir, take the trouble to leaf through some part of this in some leisure hour and tell me what you think of it, for I fear I am getting worse as I go on."

On March 13, 1582, Montaigne and the jurats, having received serious complaints, examined the affairs of the Saint-James priory, a recent bequest to the Jesuits, who had farmed out the care and feed-ing of foundlings to one Noël Lefèvre. His contract, register, and records were confused and doctored, his nurses so grossly underpaid that they could balance their accounts only by starving their nurs-lings. He claimed that the Jesuits would not pay him enough to pro-vide proper care.

On this the mayor and jurats supported him, noting that the cost of living had risen by half in nine years, and making the follow-ing rulings. The children's expenses must come out of the priory's revenue, which the Jesuits must make known; exact records must be kept; the nurses must be reliable Bordelaises decently paid to feed and raise the children; when a child died it must be brought to the town hall for an inquest; any death from other than natural causes would lead to vigorous prosecution.

This action seems banal today, but it was not so then. The conviction that charity is a responsibility not merely of the Church but of the civil authorities reveals a keen social conscience in the mayor and jurats.

We have only a few other glimpses of Montaigne in his first term: two inconsequential letters; the birth (February 21, 1583), baptism, and death a few days later of his sixth daughter—the fifth to die in infancy; and a mission to Paris in August, 1582 "on the city's business, with ample memoranda and instructions." He was probably seeking confirmation of the city's privileges, which Henry III approved, at the request of the mayor and jurats, a year later.

Montaigne's second term (August 1, 1583–August 1, 1585) was as busy as his first was calm. Even his re-election was disputed. There had long been antagonism and litigation between the mayor and jurats and the governors of the king's two fortresses in Bordeaux, the Château du Hâ and the Château Trompette. The commander of the former, Jacques d'Escars, sieur de Merville, Grand Seneschal of Guienne, hoped to replace Montaigne as mayor and had strong support from his lieutenant Thomas de Ram, the archbishop of Bordeaux Antoine Prévost de Sansac, and a large faction in the Parlement including Montaigne's brother-in-law Richard de Lestonnac, his cousin Geoffroy de Montaigne, and his mother's cousin President Jean de Villeneuve. When the jurats and twenty-four worthies re-elected Montaigne and chose three jurats opposed to Merville, Villeneuve threatened reprisals, and Ram appealed to the Parlement, claiming that the election violated the royal ordinance of 1550 and that the nobility had not been properly consulted about the jurats. Montaigne and the jurats replied by challenging about fifty counselors of the Parlement who had campaigned against them. The opponents complained to the king. On February 4, 1584, though the status of the jurats remained in doubt, Montaigne's re-election was once for all confirmed.

Early in Montaigne's second term (August 31, 1583) the mayor and jurats of Bordeaux sent a letter of remonstrance to king Henry III. The burden of taxes, they claim, has become crushing; all appeals have been in vain. The royal ordinances, and reason itself, dictate that "all impositions must be made equally upon all persons, the strong supporting the weak, and . . . those who have the greater means should feel the burden more than those who live only precariously and by the sweat of their body." Yet more and more officers, magistrates, and their families, even children of counselors in the Parlement, have been exempted, so that any new taxes "will have to be borne by the least and poorest group of the inhabitants of the cities, which is quite impossible." They request a ruling on the dispute with the fortress commanders; a curb on the multiplication of licenses to sell wine; and provision for the pilgrims who turn beggars on their way to Santiago de Compostela. They protest the costs that often deny justice to the poor:

> As kings rule by justice and all states are maintained by it, so it is necessary that it be administered gratuitously and with as little burden on the people as possible. Your said Majesty . . . has by your very sacred edict forbidden all venality in judiciary offices. However, through the fault of the times, the multiplicity of offices has persisted, by which the poor people is very grievously burdened. . . . For what used to cost only one sou now costs two, and for one court clerk that you had to pay you have to pay three, to wit, the clerk, the assistant clerk, and the assistant clerk's clerk; with the result that the poor, not having the means to meet so many expenses, are most often constrained to abandon the pursuit of their rights; or, what should be used to support their families or to meet public necessities is by this means paid out to assuage the ambition of certain private persons, to the detriment of the public.

The remonstrance also requests repairs on the Cordouan Tower, an old brick edifice on an islet in the Garonne, now too dilapidated to serve its purpose—important to Bordeaux for the revenue—as a toll station for river traffic. Henry III had moved in 1581 and 1582 to have it examined and repaired by the able engineer Louis de Foix; but those designated to raise the money dragged their heels; and in January, 1583, to expedite matters, he appointed a three-man commission of Montaigne as mayor, treasurer Ogier de Gourgues, and Parlement president François de Nesmond. Presumably they had not even officially met; for the remonstrance states that although most of the money has been raised, "there has not been a finger lifted for this repair, nor provision made for preparing for it." It asks that the commission keep control of the money, that the receiver be forbidden to use it for any other purpose, and that his Majesty be pleased "to provide that the said repair shall be started." Neither

Montaigne nor Louis de Foix lived to see the work finished; but a contract signed on March 2, 1584, put Foix and his men to work and started the project toward completion.

From November, 1583 to January, 1584, we have eleven glimpses of Montaigne. Two are random: Elie Vinet writes (November 26) to an unknown addressee that Montaigne is in Bordeaux and has received Loisel's book; and on December 22 Montaigne serves as godfather to a marrano of Portuguese descent. Two others show Montaigne conferring with Margaret of Valois (December 2) and in contact with Matignon (January 21).

More enlightening are five letters to Montaigne from Philippe de Mornay (Duplessis-Mornay), a leading adviser to Navarre, explaining the Protestant seizure of Mont-de-Marsan and urging him to make their case known to their adversaries. In the midst of these, Montaigne and the syndic and chronicler Gabriel de Lurbe were chosen to present a letter of remonstrance to Henry of Navarre from the mayor and jurats of Bordeaux (December 10, 1583) complaining that Protestant troops in the Mas-de-Verdun (on the Garonne) had been stopping Bordeaux river traffic on the pretext that their pay was overdue. On December 14 he wrote to Matignon from Mont-de-Marsan that he had seen Navarre and would try again: "For the first attempt, we did not come away with much hope in the matter of your request. He wants to use all possible means to be paid. We shall see tomorrow whether we can bring him down a bit." Three days later Navarre wrote angrily to Matignon urging him to get the soldiers paid, and amicably to the mayor and jurats that he can do little until his men receive their due.

At this time Navarre was furious with Matignon, whose delays in delivering Mont-de-Marsan had led him finally, in time of peace, to take it by storm on the night of November 21. Matignon had countered by putting strong garrisons in Bazas, Condom, and Agen, threatening Navarre's capital of Nérac. Mornay's letters to Montaigne go back further, to November 9. Margaret of Valois, expelled from court by her brother, was on her way to join her husband. When Navarre protested this affront, Henry III merely sent Bellièvre to urge him to take back his wife. The summer before, Navarre had fallen in love with Diane (Corisande) d'Andoins, who joined him at Mont-de-Marsan in November as his reigning mistress.

Mornay's first letter deals mainly with Margaret and Matignon.

"This prince [Navarre] judged that they wanted to lead him by force to their purposes; and that these two [Matignon and Bellièvre], although by different routes, were moving toward the same goal. You know his profession of courage: *flectatur fortè facilè, at frangatur nunquam.* * Thus he asked M. de Bellièvre to put off proposing his main mission until these battle alarms were quieted." Mornay's friendly greeting refers to earlier correspondence: "Sir, if my letters give you pleasure, yours give me profit; and you know how far profit surpasses pleasure."

The next letter (November 25) reveals that "the king of Navarre has written you how he entered his town of Mont-de-Marsan" and explains that his patience was exhausted by "the extreme insolence of his subjects and the marshal's endless delays." "To you who, in that tranquillity of mind of yours, are neither agitating, nor agitated without good cause, we are writing for another purpose, not to assure you of our intent, which is well known to you and cannot be concealed from you (whether because of our frankness or because of the keenness of your mind), but to make you pledge and witness of it, if need be, to those who judge us ill because they do not see us and because they see rather with the eyes of others than with their own." Mornay's conclusion is most friendly: *"Haec tibi, et tuo judicio.*† For the rest, depend on our friendship as very old and yet always fresh; and with the same faith I shall think the same of yours, which I think I know through my own better than in any other way. You shall prove this when and where you like."

Mornay's third letter (December 18), shortly after Montaigne's visit with the remonstrance, is indignant at Matignon. "They are surrounding us with garrisons. . . . This prince thinks only of peace; and I greatly desire that they should not press him beyond measure: you know him. Even when he should fear, he will not." By December 31 Mornay sounds discouraged. An appeal to the German Protestants has failed, and he writes to justify it: "Our purpose was only to show that our peaceful conduct was caused not by necessity but by good will. This prince learned that his patience was being interpreted as lack of means." Their situation is not bright: "Sir, our counsels depend in part on the places where you are; for we are merely parrying the blows." He concludes again most cordially: "I

* Let him easily be strongly persuaded, but broken never.

† This much to you, and to your judgment.

write you frankly in my own way. . . . I know that you are doing what good you can."

A final letter of January 25, 1584 finds most of the problems solved. (Montaigne had written Matignon on the 21st that his neighbors had returned from meeting Navarre "with only peaceful inclinations.") Navarre has retained Mont-de-Marsan and consented to take back his wife in return for Matignon's reducing the garrison at Bazas and withdrawing those at Agen and Condom. Mornay, still trying to win Montaigne, praises Navarre's forbearance in taking Margaret back without proper satisfaction from the king. Here the correspondence as we have it ends.

By May, 1584 Navarre is well disposed toward Matignon. Again Montaigne is a trusted intermediary; he brings the marshal Navarre's letter of the 10th, which reads in part: "I fully recognize your good will for the repose of this kingdom and in particular toward me. . . . No accidents, good or bad, will ever change my good inclinations; but Monsieur de Montaigne will tell you the rest." Two months later (July 12) Montaigne's greeting to Matignon suggests that there has been a loss of contact; Matignon may have thought him too sympathetic to Navarre: "Sir, I have just now received yours of the 6th, and I very humbly thank you for showing a sort of sign, by the command you give me to come back to you, that you do not find my assistance disagreeable. This is the greatest benefit that I can expect from this public office of mine, and I hope to go to see you on my first day there [in Bordeaux]." He gives news of the Protestant gatherings at Sainte-Foy. Epernon is on his way from Henry III to urge the conversion of Navarre, who is considering an invitation by the Dutch to succeed Anjou as their protector.

For the duke of Anjou, the last possible Valois successor, had died of consumption (June 10, 1584), making the Protestant Navarre heir to the throne of Catholic France. The tension was acute. The League became more openly a third party, named its own candidate for the royal succession, and forced the king to become its nominal leader and send armies against Navarre even while he favored his claim and urged his reconversion.

Montaigne writes to Matignon on August 19 that he has little to report: a poor neighborhood tailor robbed and stabbed to death by "some good people of the Reformation from Sainte-Foy-la-Grande." He has just returned home, apparently from Bordeaux.

"The favors you show me and the intimacy you grant me with you" have emboldened him to write "merely to inform you of my health, which has improved a little from the change of air."

December, 1584 finds Montaigne entertaining royalty for the first time. A letter of the 10th from his château urges the jurats to reach their own decision about some letters and promises to come and confer with them as soon as he can. "This whole court of Sainte-Foy-la-Grande is on my hands, and they have come to see me by appointment. When this is over, I shall be more at liberty." Sainte-Foy, on the Dordogne about ten miles east of Montaigne, was a gathering place for Reformists. Montaigne was expecting a visit from Navarre and his suite, which he later wrote up in his *Ephemeris:*

December 19.   1584. The king of Navarre came to see me at Montaigne, where he had never been, and was here for two days, served by my men without any of his officers. He would have neither tasting nor covered dishes,* and slept in my bed. He had with him my lords the prince of Condé, de Rohan, de Turenne . . . [Montaigne lists thirty-two others individually]. These and about ten others slept here, besides the valets, pages, and soldiers of his guard. About as many again went and slept in the villages. When he left here I had a stag started in my forest, which led him a chase for two days.

Montaigne's account seems to show mild relief and satisfaction that the visit has gone well. A letter to Matignon a month later suggests that he found little opening for any advice but was still trying to persuade Navarre to trust and meet with Matignon and not let his passion for Corisande becloud his role as heir apparent. It also fore-shadows what we hear in 1588 from the English and Spanish ambassadors of his influence on Corisande and through her on Navarre. He writes to Matignon in part:

Sir, on the strength of several accounts that Monsieur de Bissouse has given me, on behalf of Monseigneur de Turenne, of his judgment of you and of the confidence this prince has in my advice (though I do not build much on courtly phrases), I decided at dinnertime to write to Monseigneur de Turenne, to this effect:
That I was saying good-by to him by letter. That I had received the letter from the king of Navarre, who seemed to me to be taking good advice by trusting in the affection that you offered him to do him service. That I had written to Madame de Guissen [Corisande] to make use of time to further her enterprise, and that I would urge you to assist in this. That I had advised her not to engage the interest and fortune of this prince

* Both of these are traditional princely safeguards against poison.

in her passions, but, since she had so much power over him, to look more to his advantage than to her personal inclinations. That you were talking about going to Bayonne, where I might perhaps offer to follow you if I thought that my presence could be of even the slightest use to you. That if you went there, the king of Navarre, knowing you were so near, would do well to invite you to see his beautiful gardens at Pau.

An undated letter from Turenne to Montaigne, which must be of about this time, confirms his friendly esteem and Montaigne's role as mediator. They are leaving, he writes, to see a prince (presumably Condé): "On his return, the king of Navarre has made up his mind to see Marshal de Matignon; I beg you to keep a hand in this, for it is well known that by your persuasion and according as you press it, this can happen, for the good of the king's service, the repose of the government, and the satisfaction of all good people. . . . I beg you to believe that I have infinite affection for your friendship, and you may make use of me as your humble friend, certain to obey you."

Seven letters in the following month from Montaigne in his château to the jurats (February 8, 1585) and to Matignon (January 26, February 2, 9, 12, 13, and undated) reveal his involvement and vigilance during his "vacations" at home from his mayoralty. He shares the jurats' satisfaction in "the successful expeditions that have been reported . . . by your deputies" and hopes to rejoice with them soon in person. The background is this. The winegrowers upstream on the Dordogne and Garonne were forbidden to bring each year's wines to Bordeaux until Christmas; but infringements were increasing. Montaigne had probably gone to Bordeaux in late December or early January, at the jurats' request, to help them draw up a remonstrance to the king. They sent deputies, who must have reached Paris by mid-January, and on the 17th the king's letters patent promised enforcement. Montaigne's letters to Matignon on January 26 and February 9 show his interest and the role he probably played.

The six letters to Matignon are full of business and news of Protestant doings. The gathering at Sainte-Foy has broken up, he reports on January 26; Mornay assures him of Henry's reconciliation with Margaret, but in fact "there is nothing so distasteful to the husband as to see people on terms of good understanding with the wife." On February 2 he has heard from Le Fleix: du Ferrier (the former ambassador to Venice) and La Marsillière are still at Sainte-Foy, and Navarre will be longer in Béarn than had been thought. Another source reports Navarre heading for Bayonne and Dax. On February 9 Montaigne has news of Protestant stirrings, a skirmish between vagabond groups nearby, and the seizure on Navarre's orders of one Ferrand carrying letters from Margaret to the queen mother and others at court. He has his boots on to go to Le Fleix to see du Ferrier and La Marsillière. The jurat Lamothe needs to see him alone on business and may come to Montaigne. He hopes that Matignon has voided a stone he had mentioned, as he himself has recently done. He is eager to confer with him: "As for the command that you are pleased to give me, to come to see you, I very humbly beg you to believe that there is nothing I would do more willingly; and I shall never cast myself back into solitude so far or unburden myself of public affairs so thoroughly as not to retain a singular devotion to your service and a fondness for being wherever you may be."

On February 12 Montaigne has just come back from Le Fleix. The Ferrand incident reveals the bitter mistrust between Navarre and his queen. Margaret had felt slighted and thought of returning north; Henry had been led to suspect that Ferrand was in effect a spy. At Sainte-Foy on his way back Montaigne had seen the sick and aging du Ferrier, who promised a return visit; Montaigne doubts he is well enough to come, but will wait a few days for him and not join Matignon until next week. The next day Montaigne has heard from du Ferrier that Navarre plans to go to Montauban. There are disturbing reports of troop movements, apparently Protestant, in the neighborhood. Presumably of the same month is an undated letter relaying reports from Pau that Corisande is still quite ill and that Navarre is on his way to Bayonne, Nérac, Bergerac, and Saintonge. Montaigne has two letters from Matignon and hopes to leave the next day to see him; President d'Eymar of the Parlement has borrowed his horses, which he expects back that evening. Because of floods, he will need two days for the trip to Bordeaux; and he specifies his route in case Matignon leaves town and their paths cross.

Matignon's pressure on Montaigne to return to Bordeaux in February may already reflect concern over ominous stirrings. On March 30 the League, by the Péronne Manifesto, declared the resolve of their leaders and their candidate for heir apparent, the Cardinal de Bourbon, "to oppose those who seek in every way to subvert the Catholic religion and the state." Now they raised armies and moved to take over the chief cities, successfully except in the south and west. Their man in Bordeaux was Louis Ricard Gourdon de Genouillac, baron de Vaillac, commander of the Château Trompette. Soon after mid-April Matignon made his move. The city, his biographer writes, was full of Leaguers; Vaillac had promised Guise to take it over. To deliver a communication from the king, Matignon "assembled in his residence the presidents and king's men of the Parlement, Michel de Montaigne, then mayor, the jurats . . . and principal officers of the city . . . without forgetting Vaillac himself." When all were there, Le Londel d'Auctoville, captain of Matignon's guards, seized all approaches to the building. Matignon informed the company of the threats to the city. "Then, turning his eyes upon Vaillac, who was seated with the others, he told him that his fidelity was suspect to the king and that His Majesty, to rid himself of this anxiety, desired him to turn over the Château Trompette into Matignon's hands." When Vaillac asked to justify himself and avoid the shame of removal, Matignon replied "that the way to die was to resist the king's orders; that if he made any further delays, he would consider him guilty; that if he did not make him master of the place, he would have his head cut off before the eyes of his garrison." He had Le Londel disarm and guard Vaillac, and "ordered the mayor [Montaigne] to make known the king's intentions and his own to the entire city, in order to dispose the townsmen who were true and faithful servants of His Majesty to join with his troops and overpower the soldiers of the garrison, if Vaillac's punishment did not force them to surrender." After many pleas and long hesitations, Vaillac turned over the fortress without a blow.

Apparently Montaigne reported the affair in person to Navarre, who wrote to Matignon on April 24 from Bergerac: "I was very pleased to have learned such particular news of you from Monsieur de Montaigne. I have commissioned him to tell you mine and to assure you more and more of my entire friendship. So, relying on him, I will ask you to believe him as you would myself."

The time came probably a few weeks later for a general review of the troops in Bordeaux. There was fear of an attempt to assassinate the city's leaders. Matignon was away. Montaigne remembered, as a youth, seeing the king's lieutenant Moneins murdered in the salt-tax

rioting when he lost his nerve and the mob saw it. He urged the opposite course and prevailed:

Once it was planned to have a general review of various troops under
arms. That is an excellent occasion for secret vengeances; never can they
be executed with greater security. There were public and notorious evidences
that things would go badly for some who had the principal and necessary
responsibility for the reviewing. Various plans were proposed, since the
matter was difficult and had much weight and consequence. Mine was that
they should above all avoid giving any sign of this fear, and should show
up and mingle in the ranks, head high and countenance open, and that instead of cutting out anything (as the other opinions mostly aimed to do),
they should on the contrary urge the captains to instruct their soldiers to
make their volleys fine and lusty in honor of the spectators, and not spare
their powder. This served to gratify the suspected troops, and engendered
thereafter a useful mutual confidence.

On May 22, 1585, from Bordeaux, Montaigne sends Matignon
a long letter full of news, mainly of League armies under Mayenne,
Mercoeur, and Elbeuf. The city is quiet, but its governors are vigilant.

We are busy with our gates and guards, and are watching them a
little more attentively now in your absence, which makes me fear not only
for the preservation of this city but also for your own. . . .

I fear that affairs will come upon you from so many sides in the region
where you are that you will be busy a long time. . . . If anything new
and important comes up, I will promptly dispatch to you a man especially
to let you know about it; and you are to suppose that nothing is stirring if
you have no news from me. I beg you also to consider that this sort of movement is usually so unexpected that if it should happen they will have me
by the throat without giving me warning. I will do what I can to get news
from all parts, and to that purpose will visit all sorts of men and see what
their feeling is. Up to this moment nothing is stirring. . . .

I am telling you what I hear, and mingling the news of town rumors
which I do not consider likely with truths, so that you may know everything; very humbly entreating you to come back as soon as your affairs will
allow; and I assure you that we will meanwhile spare neither our labors,
nor, if necessary, our life, to keep everything in obedience to the King.

Five days later (May 27) Montaigne writes that Vaillac is still near by.
He hopes Matignon may return the next day. Meanwhile they are
on guard:

The proximity of Monsieur de Vaillac fills us with alarms, and there is not
a day that does not bring me fifty urgent ones. We very humbly entreat
you to come here just as soon as your affairs may permit. I have spent every

night either around the town in arms or outside of town at the port, and before your warning I had already kept watch there one night on the news of a boat loaded with armed men which was due to pass. We saw nothing; and the evening before last we were there until after midnight . . . but nothing came.

Ten days later (June 6) Montaigne is with Navarre at Sainte-Foy, about to bear greetings and a letter to Matignon. He may have done more; for a week later his long efforts had borne fruit: Navarre and the reluctant Matignon had at last met. Montaigne learned this in a cordial letter from Matignon at Marmande (June 13) commending himself affectionately to his good graces, and signing himself "entirely your very perfect friend." The letter was to go to the jurat Lamothe in case Montaigne was absent; which suggests that he had now gone home.

After his long vigilance he had earned a rest. June had brought Bordeaux a heat wave and with it, on the bad air from the adjoining marshes, a murderous attack of the plague. From June to December more than 14,000 people died—almost a third of the normal population, more than half of those remaining in the city. As early as June 17 the jurats ordered strenuous emergency measures. On June 30, Matignon wrote to the king that only a few officials were still there. "The plague is spreading so in this city that there is no one having the means to live elsewhere who has not abandoned it." In July things were even worse. Outsiders were not allowed to enter; a skeleton Parlement and two jurats out of six remained.

Montaigne's second term as mayor was to end on August 1. On July 30 he is at Libourne and has seen Matignon, who has told him of—or shown him—Lamothe's report of the 28th that "the malady has gotten so furious that we can no longer keep it in control, because every one of the inhabitants has abandoned the city, I mean those who can bring some remedy to it; for as for the little people who have stayed, they are dying like flies." Lamothe fears trouble assembling the delegates for the coming election, and hopes to take a week's vacation afterward.

It was probably an open secret that Matignon would succeed Montaigne, who was with him and may have been following his advice when on July 30, 1585, he wrote to the jurats:

Gentlemen, I found news of you here by chance, which the marshal communicated to me. I will spare neither my life nor anything else for your service and will leave you to judge whether the service I can render you by my presence at the coming election is worth my risking going into the city in view of the bad condition it is in, especially for people coming from as pure an air as I do. On Wednesday I will come as close to you as I can, to Feuillas if the disease has not reached there; at which place, as I am writing to Monsieur de Lamothe, I shall be very happy to have the honor of seeing some one of you to receive your commands and to discharge myself of the messages that the lord marshal will give me for the company.

Whereupon I very humbly commend myself to your good graces and pray God, gentlemen, to give you a long and happy life.

From Libourne, July 30th, 1585.

Your humble servant and brother,

Montaigne

The next day accordingly finds him at Feuillas, just across the river from Bordeaux. The jurats have sent no delegate but a letter which he has communicated to Matignon, whose instructions he transmits in return. In his last act as mayor, Montaigne has some instructions of his own: "As for that bad example and the injustice of taking women and children prisoners, I do not at all think that we should imitate it as others have done. I have said this also to the said lord marshal, who has instructed me to write you not to make a move in this matter until you have fuller word."

Montaigne's letter of July 30, 1585, raised a storm of criticism when first published about a century ago. Even such admirers as Sainte-Beuve placed him in dismal contrast with such heroes as Rotrou at Dreux and Belzunce at Marseilles. His action—or abstention— appears, however, to have drawn no notice from his contemporaries, nor to have struck him as needing defense; for he offers none in either letter to the jurats or in the chapter on his mayoralty. After all, when he wrote, he was staying with his successor, who may well have urged him not to go. It might have been heroism to re- turn; to Montaigne it would presumably have seemed false heroics.

When Montaigne reflects on his mayoralty in the *Essays*, he takes pains to refute two related criticisms: that "I went about it like a man who exerts himself too weakly and with a languishing zeal," and that "my administration passed without a mark or a trace." The second of these, he thinks, mistakes ostentation for effectiveness: "It is acting for our private reputation and profit, not for the good, to put off and do in the public square what we can do in the council chamber, and at high noon what we could have done the night before, and to be jealous to do ourselves what our colleague does as well. . . . I have not had that iniquitous and rather common disposition of wanting the trouble and sickness of the affairs of this city to exalt and honor my government; I heartily lent a shoulder to make them easy and light." The first criticism has more substance; but his reply to it fills his chapter "Of Husbanding Your Will" (III: 10).

He has trouble enough with his own pressures, he says, without inviting others. When pushed into managing others' affairs, he has promised "to take them in hand, not in lungs and liver; to take them on my shoulders, not incorporate them into me; to be concerned over them, yes; to be impassioned over them, never." Most people do just the opposite: "Men give themselves for hire. Their faculties are not for them, they are for those to whom they enslave themselves; their tenants are at home inside, not they. . . . They seek business only for busyness. It is not that they want to be on the go, so much as that they cannot keep still. . . . Occupation is to a certain manner of people a mark of ability and dignity. Their mind seeks its repose in movement, like children in the cradle. They may be said to be as serviceable to their friends as they are importunate to themselves."

Montaigne has several reasons for opposing this habit. Men are wrong to confuse altruism with what today we might call other-directedness. "Those who know how much they owe to themselves . . . find that nature has given them in this a commission full enough and not at all idle. You have quite enough to do at home; don't go away. . . . The main responsibility of each of us is his own conduct; and that is what we are here for."

Extreme involvement hampers efficient action: "We never conduct well the thing that possesses and conducts us." Its excessiveness makes it unjust and divisive; it sharpens anger and hostility:

People adore everything that is on their side; as for me, I do not even excuse most of the things that I see on mine. . . .

I adhere firmly to the healthiest of the parties, but I do not seek to be noted as especially hostile to the others and beyond the bounds of the general reason. I condemn extraordinarily this bad form of arguing: "He is of the League, for he admires the grace of Monsieur de Guise." "The activity of the king of Navarre amazes him; he is a Huguenot." "He finds this to criticize in the king's morals: he is seditious in his heart."

The overinvolved make themselves miserable to no purpose; for we cannot always have our way. Our center of gravity must remain in ourselves: if a man "desires the good of his country as I do, without getting ulcers and growing thin over it," he will be "unhappy, but not stunned, to see it threatened." Montaigne seeks not refusal or abdication, but merely judicious separation of roles: "I do not want a man to refuse, to the charges he takes on, attention, steps, words, and sweat and blood if need be. . . . But this is by way of loan and accidentally. . . . I have been able to take part in public office without departing one nail's breadth from myself, and to give myself to others without taking myself from myself. . . . We must play our part duly, but as the part of a borrowed character. . . . I see some . . . who are prelates to their very liver and intestines, and drag their position with them even into their privy. . . . The mayor and Montaigne have always been two, with a very clear separation."

In general he is satisfied with his performance. He had been ready to work himself "a bit more roughly" if necessary, but found that not all important offices are difficult. In his quiet way, he has been effective. "I could easily check a disturbance without being disturbed, and punish a disorder without losing my temper. Do I need anger and inflammation? I borrow it and wear it as a mask." He neither sought to do what "ambition mixes up with duty and covers with its name," nor left undone, as far as he knows, "any action that duty genuinely required of me." Thus he sums up his tenure with composure, thankful that he could meet the demands of his office adequately with his abilities, temperament, and good fortune: "I had nothing to do but conserve and endure, which are noiseless and imperceptible acts. . . . Abstention from doing is often as noble as doing . . . and the little that I am worth is almost all on that side. In short, the occasions of my term of office were suited to my disposition, for which I am very grateful to them. . . . Anyone who will not be grateful to me for the order, the gentle and mute tranquillity, that accompanied my administration, at least cannot deprive me of the share of it that belongs to me by right of my good fortune." In an unsought task for which he felt ill suited he had done as well as he expected and much better than he had promised:

I had published elaborately enough to the world my inadequacy in such public management. I have something still worse than inadequacy: that I hardly mind it, and hardly try to cure it, in view of the course of life that

I have designed for myself. I did not satisfy myself either in this undertaking, but I accomplished about what I had promised myself, and far surpassed what I had promised those whom I had to deal with. . . . I am
sure I left no cause for offense or hatred. As for leaving regret and desire,
at the very least I know this well, that I did not greatly care about that.

Montaigne was not the most dedicated of public servants; but he
was not as casual as his counterattack against overinvolvement makes
him sound. He passed up a chance to be heroic; he was not passionately involved; but he was vigilant, conscientious, and quietly
effective. His job was to preserve loyalty and peace; he did it well.

His experience as mayor increased his confidence in himself and
others. Until then he had little but his *Essays* to be proud of; and
though to us this may well seem enough for anyone, we have the
perspective of nearly four centuries; he did not. His hankering to
be a man of action is revealed when he says that a given man "produces Essays, who cannot produce results." Suddenly and unexpect-
edly there was a demand for his unglamorous but solid virtues. Since
he idolized his father and admired his public career, it enhanced
his image of himself to be called, unsoliciting and even unawares,
to the highest office his father had held, and then re-elected to it—
as his father had not been and few had. Finally, he knew that whatever the appearances, those who could judge—Henry III, Navarre,
and Matignon in particular—knew that he had done his job well.
His uneasy awe of men of action changes to an unillusioned but
sympathetic understanding. He has dealt with them man to man;
he has taught them things about each other; in a modest way he has
been one of them.

His confidence in others is shown particularly toward the people
of Bordeaux. In the remonstrance to Henry III we saw his concern
with their plight in the face of high taxes and expensive justice. He
not only likes but respects them. His natural languor, he says, must
not be taken as proof of impotence, insensibility, or ingratitude toward them:

The people of Bordeaux . . . did everything in their power to gratify me,
both before they knew me and after, and did much more for me by giving
me my office again than by giving it to me in the first place. I wish them
all possible good, and certainly, had an occasion arisen, there is nothing I
would have spared for their service. I bestirred myself for them just as I
do for myself. They are a good people, warlike and idealistic, yet capable

of obedience and discipline and of serving some good purpose if they are well guided.

This tribute shows how far Montaigne has moved from his early humanistic disdain for the vulgar. He had come from animals to cannibals to foreigners, always less paradoxically and perversely; now he shows affectionate respect for ordinary citizens. Nor does he praise them to spite the great, into whose problems his insight has grown. More and more the people have his sympathy and admiration; but his good will is not confined to any class. Now those with whom he feels solidarity are the great majority, and the exceptions are few.

Chapter 14: *The* Essays *of* 1588 [1585–1588]

HE FIRST YEAR after his mayoralty (August, 1585–July, 1586) Montaigne apparently spent quietly at home, working over his first two books of *Essays* and preparing the new Book III. He had probably written almost twelve of its thirteen chapters when disaster struck. In July, 1585, Henry III had capitulated to the League by signing the Treaty of Nemours and sponsoring their war on the Protestants. A large League army under Mayenne joined Matignon's troops in December, captured some minor Protestant towns, paused for two months in Bordeaux, and on July 10, 1586, somewhere between 15,000 and 25,000 strong, laid siege to Castillon, on the Dordogne, about five miles southwest of Montaigne. Well fortified and manned, the town held out stoutly. Some of the action bordered on Montaigne's estate; some besiegers camped on his land and pillaged him and his tenants.

I was writing this about the time when a mighty load of our disturbances settled down for several months with all its weight right on me. I had on the one hand the enemy at my door, on the other hand the freebooters, worse enemies . . . and I was sampling every kind of military mischief all at once. . . .

The people suffered very greatly at that time. . . . The living had to suffer; so did those who were not yet born. They pillaged them, and consequently me too, even of hope, snatching from them all they had to provide for their living for many years.

After years of living on Protestant sufferance, surrounded by their strongholds, Montaigne was suspect to the League. He had one brother serving Navarre, and a Protestant brother and sister; Mornay and Turenne were his friends, as was Navarre himself, who had made him gentleman of his chamber, stayed in his château, and slept in his bed. He had not volunteered, as he might have, to serve in the besieging royal army. Besides this shock, he writes, "I incurred the disadvantages that moderation brings in such maladies. I was belabored from every quarter; to the Ghibelline I was a Guelph, to the Guelph a Ghibelline. . . . The situation of my house, and my acquaintance with men in my neighborhood, presented me in one aspect, my life and my actions in another. There were no formal accusations. . . . It was mute suspicions that were current secretly." Finding no help around him, he sought the strength he needed in himself. His conscience "bore itself not only peaceably but proudly"; his health was unusually good; he found he would need "a great shock to throw me out of my saddle."

Then the second blow struck. Late in August the plague broke out among the besiegers, spread to the neighborhood, and made a shambles of Castillon, which was captured on September 1. The healthy air of Montaigne's estate was poisoned; he had to take his family away for six months (September, 1586–March, 1587), seeking a place to stay. "I, who am so hospitable, had a great deal of trouble finding a retreat for my family: a family astray, a source of fear to their friends and themselves, and of horror wherever they sought to settle, having to shift their abode as soon as one of the group began to feel pain in the end of his finger." The worst of it was the anxiety for the others; alone, Montaigne would have been gayer and gone farther. He was still on the road when summoned by Catherine de' Medici to her conferences with Navarre at Saint-Brice.

If the plague was troublesome for Montaigne, it was murderous for his peasant neighbors, who had no escape. Already earlier he had

praised their courage; when he returns to his book his admiration
abounds:

Now, what example of resoluteness did we not see then in the simplicity
of this whole people? Each man universally gave up caring for his life. The
grapes remained hanging on the vines, the principal produce of the country,
as all prepared themselves indifferently, and awaited death that evening or
the next day with face and voice so little frightened that it seemed that
they had made their peace with this necessity. . . . I saw some who feared
to remain behind, as in a horrible solitude. . . .
    Here a man, healthy, was already digging his grave; others lay down
in them while still alive. . . . In short, a whole nation was suddenly, by
habit alone, placed on a level that concedes nothing in firmness to any studied
and premeditated fortitude.

Their heroism leads him to repudiate premeditation of death as an
example of misguided human art. We have abandoned nature, he
finds, and are trying to improve on her; yet every day we must seek
models of serene constancy in the traces of her image that ignorance
has imprinted on the life of the "rustic, unpolished mob."

If you don't know how to die, don't worry; Nature will tell you what to
do on the spot, fully and adequately. . . .
    I never saw one of my peasant neighbors cogitating over the counte-
nance and assurance with which he would pass this last hour. Nature teaches
him not to think about death except when he is dying. And then he has
better grace about it than Aristotle, whom death oppresses doubly, both
by itself and by such a long foreknowledge. . . .
    Isn't that what we say, that the stupidity . . . of the vulgar gives
them this endurance of present troubles and this profound nonchalance about
sinister accidents to come . . . ? For Heaven's sake, if that is so, let us
henceforth hold a school of stupidity.

    Our natural resources are almost infinite: "We are each richer
than we think, but we are trained to borrow and beg. . . . We need
hardly any learning to live at ease. And Socrates teaches us that it is
in us, and the way to find it and help ourselves with it. . . . He did a
great favor to human nature by showing how much it can do by itself."
    The success of Montaigne's first two books encouraged him to
write his third. We have noted Henry III's compliment, the respectful treatment by the papal censor, and the demand for a second
edition within two years. A third seems to have come out in Rouen
by 1584, though no copy of it is now known. By 1587 Montaigne

was to be published in Paris, and there again in 1588 in three books. It was a joke in Gascony, he says, to see him in print; there he buys printers, elsewhere they buy him.

On May 23, 1583 the great Belgian scholar Justus Lipsius, having enjoyed the *Essays* of "the French Thales," wrote that "certainly the like of his wisdom does not dwell among us." He published the letter three years later with a note explaining that he referred to a book by Montaigne in French, "honorable, wise, and very much to his taste." Since his letters circulated widely, Montaigne probably soon knew of his judgment. Lipsius was prone to adulation, and his note shows that the *Essays* were not yet well known among the learned; but this was high praise to receive so soon, from a Latinist for a book in French, from a foreigner who was one of the leading erudites of Europe.

There had been borrowing from the start: by Montaigne's brother-in-law Geoffroy de La Chassaigne de Pressac in "Cleander, or Honor and Valor" (1582), and two years later in Matthieu Coignet's *Instruction for Princes* and Guillaume Bouchet's *Evenings*. More was soon to follow.

Also in 1584 came recognition in the *French Bibliographies* of Antoine du Verdier, who quotes a long passage from "Books" (II: 10), and La Croix du Maine in a long, intelligent, laudatory article. Montaigne's great learning, wide reading, and marvelous judgment, he writes, are fully evident to readers of his fine book, whose title he discusses perceptively; its three editions attest its warm reception "by all men of letters." His concluding comparison makes Montaigne seem imitative but must have pleased him:

> And to say what I think of the book in a word, I will say that if Plutarch is so esteemed for his fine works, Montaigne should be for having imitated him so closely, principally his *Moral Essays*. And if Plutarch has been esteemed the only one of the learned whose works should survive (if it happened that all other authors were lost), I say that the man who has followed and imitated him most closely must be the most commendable after him.

In short, the *Essays* were a success from the first, and Montaigne soon knew it. If their real originality, the self-portrait, was not their main attraction, at least it aroused neither repulsion nor ridicule. This added to his confidence, led to publication in Paris, and encouraged him to add a third book that would portray him more fully and be more his own.

The publisher of the 1588 edition, Abel L'Angelier, was one of the best in France. The title page announced it as "fifth edition, enlarged by a third book and by six hundred additions to the first two"; the royal privilege, dated June 4, 1588, calls it "amplified in more than five hundred passages." (Villey's count of the additions falls between these two.) Book III is longer than I, shorter than II; the new material—Book III plus the 500-odd additions to I and II—is about three quarters as long as the old, making the *Essays* of 1588 nearly twice the length of those of 1580.

Montaigne probably did little or no work on his book while he was mayor. All the quotations and allusions date the new material at 1585 or later; and the 1587 Paris edition merely reproduces that of 1582. Few passages seem to have been added after Montaigne came to Paris in February, 1588. Thus he composed the new material in two stages of less than a year each: from the end of his mayoralty to the siege of Castillon (August, 1585–June, 1586) and from his return home after the plague to his departure for Paris (April, 1587–January, 1588).

Montaigne is still skeptical, but now less strenuously so. He still has his sense of diversity but now sees unity too, both in the individual and in mankind. If perfect truth is unattainable, experience has taught him the value of the practical moral truths by which we live. Much as he still finds baffling in himself, he understands enough to have insight into others too. Though still concerned with himself, he speaks more and more to and for the race as well; though he still favors private life, he sees man as a social being as well. He speaks out more about himself, his book, the problems of youth and age; but always in the context of his two major concerns: human nature and human conduct.

The 1588 material, written in a few years by a fully mature mind, shows none of the internal change that we find within that of 1580. There are changes of mood: "Vanity" surveys the human condition wryly, "Experience" triumphantly; but the two chapters complete each other and do not clash. The one development is in Montaigne's boldness, which continues to grow as he writes.

With his heightened confidence, he writes faster now and demands more attention from his reader. He has much to say, and everything holds together; he needs space to show the movement of his thought as well as its substance. So he makes the chapters longer; the thirteen of Book III contrast with fifty-seven in Book I and thirty-seven in Book II. "The Useful and the Honorable" (Chapter 1; fifteen pages in the Pléiade *Œuvres complètes*) studies the problem of public morality and speaks out for decency against expediency. "Repentance" (fourteen pages) defends Montaigne for rarely repenting, shows how little that goes by that name deserves it, and rejects it as inappropriate to the examined life unless it comes from God. "Three Kinds of Association" (twelve pages) discusses Montaigne's favorite company—attractive men, attractive women, and books. "Diversion" (ten pages) is shown to be our best resource against pain and grief. "On Some Verses of Virgil" (fifty-eight pages) deals with sex—its vast importance, the need for frank discussion of it, the false standards that equate chastity (in women alone) with goodness. "Coaches" (eighteen pages) is an indictment of European cruelty in the New World. "The Disadvantage of Greatness" (five pages) brings out just that.

In "The Art of Discussion" (Chapter 8; twenty-three pages) Montaigne treats his favorite occupation and what it requires. "Vanity" (fifty-eight pages) dwells on the *Essays* and on impractical moral codes, but mainly on Montaigne's love of travel and the vanity it illustrates. "Husbanding Your Will" (twenty-two pages) deals with Montaigne's mayoralty and the dangers of passionate involvement. "Cripples" (twelve pages) is a skeptical analysis of supposed miracles and an attack on witch hunting. "Physiognomy" (twenty-eight pages) praises the heroism of the peasants and the perfection of Socrates' simple humanity. "Experience" (Chapter 13; fifty-six pages) discusses the problem of diversity and unity and that of knowledge, to which experience leads more surely than reason; portrays Montaigne by his physical regimen; and comes to a triumphant conclusion on the joy and dignity of life lived naturally according to our mixed condition.

Montaigne's sense of unity, never more than implicit before, is now clear already in his second chapter. He first notes that of mankind: "I set forth a humble and inglorious life; that does not matter. You can tie up all moral philosophy with a common and private life

just as well as with a life of richer stuff. Each man bears the entire
form of man's estate. (*Chaque homme porte la forme entiere de
l'humaine condition.*)" A few pages later, apropos of superficial re-
forms that do not correct and may increase our essential vices, he
points out, as he had earlier, that natural inclinations are strengthened
by education but can hardly be changed or suppressed. Now he infers from this a bedrock unity and stability in each individual: "Just
consider the evidence of this in our own experience. There is no one
who, if he listens to himself, does not discover in himself a pattern all
his own, a ruling pattern (*une forme sienne, une forme maistresse*),
which struggles against education and against the tempest of the
passions that oppose it." He has come far from his early statements
that we are more different from ourselves than from others and some
men more different from some others than from some animals. His
new sense of unity balances his sense of diversity. Events, he says, are
too dissimilar for us to draw any certain inference from their similarity: "Resemblance does not make things so much alike as difference makes them unlike." However, even as no two things are entirely alike, so no two are entirely different. "An ingenious mixture
on the part of nature. If our faces were not similar, we could not
distinguish man from beast; if they were not dissimilar, we could
not distinguish man from man."

Montaigne's greater confidence is seen throughout Book III in
greater boldness: not only in the type of essays he writes, but also in
freer self-revelation, in what he says of his book and his plan, and in
his opinions about himself and man.

In 1580 his note to the reader had indicated respect for the
public as his greatest obstacle in self-revelation. Now that his years
allow him more freedom to prattle about himself, "I speak the truth,
not my fill of it, but as much as I dare speak; and I dare to do so a
little more as I grow old." It is not just a matter of age, however;
pleased with the praise his book has received, Montaigne knows that
"the favor of the public has given me a little more boldness than I
expected." He wants to be known just as he is; finds it painful to
dissemble; and dislikes "even thoughts that are unpublishable." He
blames Tacitus for apologizing over mentioning an honorable office
he held: "For not to dare to speak roundly of oneself shows some
lack of heart." Montaigne speaks less roundly of himself than he says

we should or than he will later, but more so than he had before. "On Some Verses of Virgil," for example, is outspoken not only about sex in general but also about its role, past and present, in Montaigne's life. "Experience" describes his physical life in prosaic detail, from his taste in fruit and meat to his habits in sleeping and defecation.

Montaigne's remarks about his *Essays* are more frequent and candid now. In a "humorous and familiar style" and a rich but unformed language, he writes his book "for few men and for few years." He avoids reading as he writes for fear of its influence, and is glad to work "in a backward region" where no one helps or corrects him, since the book, even if weaker, is more his own. "I go out of my way," he says, "but rather by license than carelessness. My ideas follow one another, but sometimes it is from a distance, and look at each other, but with a sidelong glance." He adds but does not correct, for an author has no right to suppress what he has mortgaged to the public.

He studies himself more than any other subject; that is his metaphysics and his physics. "I would rather be an authority on myself than on Cicero. In the experience I have of myself I find enough to make me wise, if I were a good scholar." Fortune has placed him too low to keep a record of his life by his actions; he keeps it by his thoughts. He makes no claim to learning: "I speak ignorance pompously and opulently, and speak knowledge meagerly and piteously."

He now calls his writings "the essays of my life," "this essay of myself," "this third extension of the other parts of my painting." His sense of his own technique is clearer. His chapter titles are often more allusive than expository; he loves the free, gamboling "poetic gait"; he has no patience with artificial signposts: "I want the matter to make its own divisions. It shows well enough where it changes, where it concludes, where it begins, where it resumes, without my interlacing it with words, with links and seams introduced for the benefit of weak or heedless ears, and without writing glosses on myself." He wants a heedful reader or none at all:

It is the inattentive reader who loses my subject, not I. Some word about it will always be found off in a corner, which will not fail to be sufficient, though it takes little room. . . .

Because such frequent breaks into chapters as I used at the beginning seemed to me to disrupt and dissolve attention before it was aroused . . . I have begun making them longer, requiring fixed purpose and assigned leisure. In such an occupation, if you will not give a man a single hour, you will not give him anything.

He warns us against his own paradoxes even as he once warned one of the great that feeling him prepared in one direction, he earnestly proposes the other side to him, to enlighten, but not to compel, his judgment. He has many opinions that he would gladly make his son dislike, if he had one.

Though he knows the dangers of filling his book with talk about itself, he does so anyway as part of his self-portrait, and now with less self-depreciation than candor. He finds his own work harder to judge than anyone else's, and places the *Essays* "now low, now high, very inconsistently and uncertainly." He regrets having been persuaded to quote as freely as he has; his own preference would have been to speak only in his own person. He fears he may repeat himself, for his memory weakens cruelly every day. Though no man ever knew his subject better, the main thing he has learned is how much he still has to learn: "I have seen no more evident monstrosity and miracle in the world than myself. . . . The more I frequent myself and know myself, the more my deformity astonishes me, and the less I understand myself." Still he has thoroughly exposed his subject: "I leave nothing about me to be desired or guessed."

By mirroring his life in that of others, he has come to know others well. He often understands their characters better than they do and reveals their motives to them from their actions; he has astonished at least one by his pertinent description and taught him things about himself.

The honesty needed for self-portrayal has been a moral discipline: "I have ordered myself to dare to say all that I dare to do. . . . Everyone is discreet in confession; people should be so in action." Finally, the publication of his behavior has helped by serving him as a rule and obliging him not to belie his portrait.

Book III of the *Essays* is full of Montaigne's reflections about man: his nature, his relation to himself, his fellows, and life itself, the way to wise and happy living. Whatever else he treats, the pathways of his mind lead out from these and always back to them. He has much to say about man and society, the whole man, a morality made for man, nature and human nature, and the joy of living.

Our last chapter showed his search for a balance between duty

to others and to self. The most honorable occupation, he believes, is
to serve the public and be useful to many. However, he adds, "I stay
out of it; partly out of conscience . . . partly out of laziness."
What he means by "laziness" is temperament; he dislikes mastery,
"both active and passive." Though not without ambition, he finds
public life distasteful and morally debilitating. His little experience
of it has left him "just that much disgusted with it." He could
probably adapt himself to it if he had to, but would rather leave it
to those who enjoy it and are no worse for it.

> The virtue assigned to the affairs of the world is a virtue with many
> bends, angles, and elbows, so as to join and adapt itself to human weakness;
> mixed and artificial, not straight, clean, constant, or purely innocent. . . . I
> once tried to employ in the service of public dealings ideas and rules for liv-
> ing as crude, green, unpolished—or unpolluted—as they were born in me or
> derived from my education, and which I use . . . conveniently . . . in
> private matters. . . . I found them inept and dangerous. . . . He who
> walks in the crowd must step aside, keep his elbows in, step back or advance,
> even leave the straight way, according to what he encounters. He must live
> not so much according to himself as according to others, not according to
> what he proposes to himself but according to what others propose to him,
> according to the time, according to the men, according to the business.

Private life is less glamorous but more demanding. In public we
wear a mask, play a part, display our "art"; we need the semblance
of goodness. In private we reveal our face, our self, our nature; we
need goodness itself.

> To win through a breach, to conduct an embassy, to govern a people, these
> are dazzling actions. To scold, to laugh, to sell, to pay, to love, to hate, and
> to deal pleasantly and justly with our household and ourselves, not to let
> ourselves go, not to be false to ourselves, that is a rarer matter, more diffi-
> cult and less noticeable.
>
> Therefore retired lives, whatever people may say, accomplish duties as
> harsh and strenuous as other lives, or more so. . . . I can easily imagine
> Socrates in Alexander's place; Alexander in that of Socrates, I cannot. If
> you ask the former what he knows how to do, he will answer, "Subdue the
> world"; if you ask the latter, he will say, "Lead the life of man in con-
> formity with its natural condition"; a knowledge much more general, more
> weighty, and more legitimate.

Public persons depend on the opinions of others, who cannot truly
know us and can only guess at our nature. The moral is obvious:
"do not cling to their judgment; cling to your own." For moral inde-

pendence we should, like Montaigne, have our own laws and court to judge us.

Montaigne's preference for private life no longer means withdrawal. His ideal is proper self-possession: giving ourselves to others, but not giving ourselves away. He thinks it only just that we include ourselves in the golden rule, and do our duty to society, but apply even this experience to our own lives. We owe friendship to ourselves as well as to others: not an "overindulgent and undiscriminating" one which, like the ivy, decays the wall it clings to, but a "salutary and well-regulated" one, "useful and pleasant alike." The true point of this friendship is a mystery of the temple of Pallas. "He who knows its duties and practices them, he is truly of the cabinet of the Muses; he has attained the summit of human wisdom and of our happiness."

In every way Montaigne values and seeks wholeness. Although only fools fail to recognize our natural limitations, he wants no others. True to his time, he believes in living richly and fully. Already before 1580 he had sought to train a rounded man who can do all things and does good only by choice. Now an important concern is to resist the encroachment of age. The decaying body needs as much control as the lusty one of youth. His own flees disorder and tries "roughly and imperiously" to dominate. "I defend myself against temperance as I once did against sensual pleasure. . . . Wisdom has its excesses, and has no less need of moderation than does folly." Of course the term "wisdom" here is ironic: "We call 'wisdom' the difficulty of our humors, our distaste for present things. But in truth we do not so much abandon our vices as change them, and, in my opinion, for the worse. . . . Old age puts more wrinkles in our minds than on our faces; and we never, or rarely, see a soul that in growing old does not come to smell sour and musty. Man grows and dwindles in his entirety." Montaigne will never be grateful to impotence for any such "sluggish and rheumatic virtue." To keep his mind free and whole, he urges it to rescue itself from old age: "Let it grow green, let it flourish meanwhile, if it can, like mistletoe on a dead tree."

Above all, we must not let these changes corrupt our judgment; it must retain the eyes of youth as well as of age. The young Montaigne could see the face of vice in voluptuousness; now he still sees the face of voluptuousness in vice, and judges his earlier state as though he were in it. Only thus can we be all that we have been, neither merely young nor merely old, but whole.

The other aspect of wholeness that most concerns Montaigne is versatility, by which he usually means the ability to relax and enjoy a full life. The great power here is habit, which may either immobilize us or make us adaptable; we must use it wisely. "The fairest souls are those that have the most variety and adaptability. . . . I would admire a soul with different levels, which could both be tense and relax, which would be well off wherever fortune might take it, which could chat with a neighbor about his building, his hunting, and his lawsuit, and keep up an enjoyable conversation with a carpenter and a gardener." The conclusion of Montaigne's final chapter is full of this theme. Caesar and Alexander, both Catos, Epaminondas, and Scipio the Younger took delight in natural and even childish pleasures in the midst of more momentous occupations. As usual, Socrates is our best model. Brave in the face of hardship and death, given to day-long trances when deep in thought, he could also, when that was appropriate, drink the rest of the army under the table or play games gracefully and happily with children. "We should never tire of presenting the picture of this man as a pattern and ideal of all sorts of perfection."

Montaigne is a basically earnest moralist whose great concern is conduct. He finds men addicted to lofty professions and overready, when they cannot live up to them, to abandon all effort and fall back lower than before. "Instead of changing into angels, they change into beasts; instead of raising themselves, they lower themselves." All such moral codes are perverse products of our restless, presumptuous mind: "What is the use of these lofty points of philosophy on which no human being can settle, and these rules that exceed our use and our strength? . . . A goal that we cannot reach seems unjust. . . . Human wisdom has never yet come up to the duties that she has prescribed for herself; and if she ever did come up to them, she would prescribe herself others beyond, to which she would ever aim and aspire, so hostile to consistency is our condition."

Unjust self-condemnation, the other side of the coin of presumption, is another perverse affliction and one of our worst. "Alas, poor man! You have enough natural ills without increasing them by your invention, and you are miserable enough by nature without being so by art." In an early essay Montaigne had noted the near impossibility of even wishing to be other than we are. Now, convinced that we can do little to change our ruling pattern, he confirms the same lesson: "I may desire in a general way to be different; I may condemn and dislike my nature as a whole, and implore God to reform me completely and to pardon my natural weakness. But this I ought not to call repentance, it seems to me, any more than my displeasure at being neither an angel nor Cato. My actions are in order and conformity with what I am and with my condition. I can do no better."

Montaigne finds none of this impracticality in Christianity. For him its ethic is based on submission and acceptance. God made nature what it is and us what we are; he interferes little with his creation, but leaves us to work out our own earthly salvation. It is surprising that such a stanch believer as Montaigne makes no use of the Gospel in his moral code; it seems possible that, without going against it at all, he is bypassing it as a moral force proven ineffective by the religious wars; but he clearly finds his wholly human ethic compatible with his just, benign, *laisser-faire* God. He takes for granted two ways of thinking: his own, merely human but well-intentioned, and the true, authoritative way of the Church. When he says he rarely repents, he is quick to go on: "always adding this refrain, not perfunctorily but in sincere and complete submission: that I speak as an ignorant inquirer, referring the decision purely and simply to the common and authorized beliefs." How far he is from any revolt is seen when he joins two apparently contrasting statements that clearly, for him, are simply complementary: "God must touch our hearts. Our conscience must reform by itself through the strengthening of our reason, not through the weakening of our appetites."

The important thing, however, is his sturdy insistence that man not be judged by standards not meant for him. Human ethics must be grounded securely in human psychology. The only useful and acceptable human morality must be a morality made for man.

Montaigne's basic conviction about the human condition is that man is made up of body and soul and that these two parts are equal. Most moral philosophy, especially since Plato, has considered the soul a likelier candidate for immortality, and therefore better, than the body. Often it has declared the body bad, the soul good, or even seen the body as the prison of the soul. Christianity, believing in the resurrection of the body, the gift and temple of God, has generally been more balanced. Montaigne sees the Christian attitude entirely in this light.

He had emphasized the body from the first, rejecting Plato's belief in the immortality of the soul alone because its disjunction from the body is the destruction of our being, and proclaiming that "these parts must not be separated." Now his stress becomes more urgent. He finds nothing in us here on earth that is purely either corporeal or spiritual, attacks our attempts to "dismember by divorce a structure made up of such close and brotherly correspondence," and constantly seeks to correct our one-sided view of our make-up: "It is still man we are dealing with, and it is a wonder how physical his nature is. . . . Life is a material and corporeal movement." To ignore this is to ignore the full truth about man.

Montaigne regards the body as sane, simple, solid, earthy, and slow to change. Fortunately, it seems to be entirely subject to nature, which has placed our greatest pleasures in the satisfaction of its needs. Thanks to this and to its stability, it can sometimes help the soul.

He finds the soul very complex and volatile. Properly directed, it can do wonders for us; normally it spoils our happiness by trying to improve on nature. It is centrifugal, ambitious, erratic, never at rest.

Its parts or functions are not always clear. Mind (*esprit*) sometimes represents the entire soul, sometimes its knowing and reasoning faculties. The flightiest part is imagination, which often needs to be corrected and consoled by the mind. Reason has at least two separate meanings, that of *reasoning,* which is specious, presumptuous, and irresponsible; and (especially in matters of conduct) that of *reasonableness,* which is always excellent. Understanding (*entendement*) and judgment are so closely related—the former leading naturally to the latter—as to seem often almost synonymous. They test new appearances against past experience and assign them their share of good or evil, truth or falsehood. Conscience is also paired with judgment, but often appears as a function of it. Judgment is the master quality; if it is weak, mind and soul are dangerous even to their possessor; where it rules harmoniously, all is well.

Not until after 1588 will Montaigne draw the full lesson of the soul's infinite power to make us happy; but already he is close to it. We have in us all we need to live wisely and comfortably. We can divert the ailments of the soul; direct our mind to help the body, to fool the imagination, and to make us happy even about pain; and train our soul to view pain and pleasure serenely as necessary parts of our life.

The soul should be a good husband to the body, not always clinging closely to it, for fear of contagion when the body is ill, but taking part in its natural pleasures, moderating them if necessary, and enjoying them conjugally.

Do I find myself in some tranquil state? Is there some voluptuous pleasure that tickles me? I do not let my senses pilfer it, I bring my soul into it, not to implicate herself, but to enjoy herself, not to lose herself but to find herself. And I set her, for her part, to admire herself in this prosperous estate, to weigh and appreciate and amplify the happiness of it. She measures the extent of her debt to God for being at peace with her conscience and free from other inner passions, for having her body in its natural condition, enjoying controlledly and adequately the agreeable and pleasant functions with which he is pleased to compensate by his grace for the pains with which his justice chastises us in its turn; how much it is worth to her to be lodged at such a point that wherever she casts her eyes, the sky is calm around her: no desire, no fear or doubt to disturb the air for her, no difficulty . . . over which her imagination may not pass without hurt.

Here as elsewhere Montaigne seeks a balance. He hates "that inhuman wisdom" that disdains the cultivation of the body. For our being is a gift of God; no part of it is unworthy of our care. "And it is not a perfunctory charge to man to guide man according to his nature; it is simple, natural, and the Creator has given it to us seriously and expressly." Those who aim above our condition fall below it: "They want to get out of themselves and escape from the man. That is madness." To enjoy our being rightfully is "an absolute perfection and virtually divine."

Man is full of absurdity, inanity, or, as Montaigne usually terms it, vanity: as much beast as angel, rooted in creation not above it, incapable of true knowledge; his senses and imagination gullible, his soul irresponsible, his soon-decaying body seeking to dominate. We are far from the usual bright Renaissance picture of man as the little universe, the microcosm, regent and masterpiece of God's creation. Evil too is natural to man: ambition, envy, jealousy, vengefulness, cruelty, superstition, despair, are rooted in us; extirpate them and you destroy the conditions of our life. However, we have some control over vice: to know it is to hate it; repentance follows it as the night the day. Vanity remains the keynote, as it had been from the first. "I do not think there is as much unhappiness in us as vanity, nor as much malice as stupidity. We are not so full of evil as of inanity."

It is vanity, he now points out, that we most enjoy. Aware as he is, and as few others are, of the value of pleasure, play, and pastime, he is content to make use of "vanity itself, and asininity," if he finds it enjoyable. "Our humors are not too vain if they are pleasant."

Book III of the *Essays* is full of this theme. "Our follies do not make me laugh, our wisdom does," he writes in chapter 3; in 4, "Is there anything besides ourselves in nature that feeds on inanity and is subject to its power?" Chapter 5 shows the whole world revolving about the urge for copulation, which of all our actions most comically reveals us as the plaything of the gods. Chapter 10 exposes vanity in our motivation for public affairs; 11, our love of vain speculation; 12, the vanity of knowledge as a preparation for death. Chapter 13 is permeated by the theme. Chapter 9, "Of Vanity," is well named. There is vanity, Montaigne admits, in his love of travel. "But where is there not? And these fine precepts are vanity, and all wisdom is vanity." It is our very essence, and we should recognize it as such:

If others examined themselves attentively, as I do, they would find themselves, as I do, full of inanity and nonsense. Get rid of it I cannot without getting rid of myself. We are all steeped in it, one as much as another; but those who are aware of it are a little better off—though I don't know. . . .

It was a paradoxical command that was given us of old by that god at Delphi: "Look into yourself, know yourself, keep to yourself. . . . It is always vanity for you, within and without; but it is less vanity when it is less extensive. Except for you, O man . . . each thing studies itself first, and, according to its needs, has limits to its labors and desires. There is not a single thing as empty and needy as you, who embrace the universe; you are the investigator without knowledge, the magistrate without jurisdiction, and all in all, the fool of the farce."

Our essence, then, is vanity; but the equation works both ways. Vanity is our essence; and we are fools if we despise our essence. From the first Montaigne had spoken his mind about this: "Things that have a nobler and richer being may accuse ours; but it is against nature that we despise ourselves." Instead we should accept our condition. "There is . . . no knowledge so hard to acquire as the knowledge of how to live this life well; and the most barbarous of our maladies is to hate and disdain our being."

This is the final message of Book III and of the *Essays*. Far from ignoring our frailties, it includes them in its sense of what it is to be a man. Our absurdity in no way precludes a certain dignity. If we accept our great limitations, our resources for wise and happy living will be greater still.

Montaigne is often portrayed as a moralist so permissive as to be almost flabby; and he sometimes sounds that way: "We must slide over this world a bit lightly and on the surface. . . . Oh, what a sweet and soft and healthy pillow is ignorance and incuriosity, to rest a well-made head!" He is so concerned with self-acceptance that he often seems uninterested in self-improvement. "Nature," he says, "is a gentle guide, but no more gentle than wise and just. . . . We cannot go wrong by following nature."

He has not attained that "disdainful vigor" which relies wholly on itself and which nothing can either aid or disturb; he is "a peg lower." He mistrusts the "inimitable straining for virtue" of both Catos, and finds their disposition severe, even troublesome. He lets himself follow his inclinations: "I have not, like Socrates, corrected my natural disposition by force of reason. . . . I let myself go as I have come. I combat nothing."

Yet amid these disclaimers of resistance to vice we find evidence of control. If he does not know "how to foster quarrels and conflict" in himself, if his virtue is mere accidental innocence and his resistance slight, still he condemns his vices, will not let them infect his judgment, and does "regulate them and keep them from mixing with other vices, which for the most part hold together and intertwine, if you are not careful. Mine I have cut down and constrained to be as solitary and simple as I could."

In short, he seeks control as well as acceptance. Already in 1578–80 he had warned that we must not be slaves to nature but be guided by reason alone. Now he wants the complete self-mastery, in every direction, that alone gives true freedom; he must be a slave only to reason—and can scarcely manage that. His obedience to nature is largely a reasoned distrust of "the inventions of our mind, of our science and art, in favor of which we have abandoned nature and her rules, and in which we know not how to maintain either moderation or bounds."

His plan, as we have seen, helps him achieve a certain firmness. Self-portrayers must practice what they preach; he must "go the same way with my pen as with my feet." His method is habit, whose power for good he stresses more and more. After Aristotle, he calls it "a second nature"; and he adds: "and no less powerful." It has made him what he is, turning "this form of mine . . . into substance, and fortune into nature." We have only to choose the best form we can, such as versatility, and habit will make it easy: "It is for habit to give form to our life, just as it pleases; it is all-powerful in that." Thus Montaigne can make the apparently perplexing statement: "What those men [the Stoics] did by virtue, I train myself to do by disposition [*complexion*]"—meaning that he does this by habit, which forms a second nature or *complexion*.

Even in "Physiognomy" (III: 12), where he urges us to abandon premeditation of death, put our trust in nature, and hold a "school of stupidity," the peasants are not his real heroes. They are a corrective; Socrates is a model. He can teach us to find in ourselves the little learning we need for happy living. By our artificial standards his simplicity is low and backward; and Montaigne sharpens this paradox with relish: "He . . . raised himself, not by sallies but by disposition [*complexion*], to the utmost point of vigor. Or, to speak more exactly, he raised nothing, but rather brought vigor, hardships, and difficulties down and back to his own original and natural level, and subjected them to it. . . . By these vulgar and natural motives, by these ordinary and common ideas . . . he constructed not only the best-regulated but the loftiest and most vigorous . . . actions and morals that ever were. . . . Even the simplest can recognize in him their means and their strength." Socrates accepts our human condition and follows nature; but he has also improved his nature by reason and habit. The peasants are surprisingly good; he is perfect. Their virtue is natural; his is fully human.

Montaigne is more like Socrates than he likes to claim. Though he lacks his vigor, he adopts his "refrain and favorite saying," the phrase "according to one's power." He strives for self-mastery. His defense of the examined life shows how much it demands beyond obedience to impulse: "Those of us especially who live a private life . . . must have a pattern established within us by which to test our actions, and . . . now pat ourselves on the back, now punish ourselves. I have my own laws and court to judge me . . . I restrain my actions according to others, but I extend them only according to myself."

In Book III Montaigne's favorite term of praise is not "natural" but "human." The opinions he embraces are "those that are most solid, that is to say, most human and most our own." Epaminondas is one of the very best of men because, to the most violent actions, "he wedded goodness and humanity." Even for a god this is Montaigne's highest praise: Vulcan's generosity to the unfaithful Venus manifests "a humanity truly more than human." The concept is central in his final formulations of his ideal: "There is nothing so beautiful and legitimate as to play the man well and properly."

Until his illness Montaigne had appeared wary of life. Extreme but otherwise typical is the statement noted earlier: "Our well-being is but the privation of being ill." In 1578–80 he had shown more optimism. Now his constant stress is on the chances life offers for happiness.

Much of this we have noted already. We need little learning to live at ease; diversion is a benefit of our inconstancy; Nature gently leads us almost imperceptibly out of life when the time comes; we can control the way things strike us, cozen our imagination, and learn much, if we will, from experience. Virtue is no longer a struggle, but pleasant and gay, like the wisdom Montaigne loves. He has a new sense of the relation between pleasure and pain, which resembles Socrates' meditation early in the *Phaedo* and may be derived from it: "Our life is composed, like the harmony of the world, of contrary things, also of different tones, sweet and harsh, sharp and flat, soft and loud. If a musician liked only one kind, what would he have to say? He must know how to use them together and blend them. And so must we do with good and evil, which are consubstantial with our life. Our being is impossible without this mixture, and one element is no less necessary for it than the other."

The concluding pages of the *Essays* are a hymn of gratitude for the legitimate joys of life. Some "wise folk," he says, "pass the time" as if life was something irksome and contemptible. "But I know it to be otherwise and find it both agreeable and worth prizing, even in

IVLIVS   IO METAΓEITNIΩN

V I. ID. IV L.   δεκάτη

ΕΠΗΦΙ   16   תמוז

A N N O *post nat.Chr.*140, *Deceßit Adrianus Imp. apud Ba= iae,aetatis anno* 72,*mense* 6, *Sepultus est Puteolis. Praefuit Im perio annos penè* 22. *AElius Spartian.*

A N N O *post nat.Chr.*1376, *mortuus est Eduardus V valliae Princeps,Eduardi* I I I, *Angliae Regis filius: is qui antè in a= gro Pictauiensi Ioannem Franciae Regem in acie superatum er captum cum filio Philippo,in Angliã abduxerat . Lilius.*

1588 entre trois et quatre apres midy
estant logé aus fausbourgs germein a Paris
et malade d'un espece de goutte qui lors
premierement m'auoit sesi il y auoit iustemant
trois iours iefus pris prisonier par les capitenes
et peuple de Paris c'estoit au temps que le Roy
en estoit mis hors par monsieur de guise fus
mené en la bastille et me fut signifié qu'il c'estoit
a la sollicitation du duc d'Elbœuf lequel par
droit de represailles et au lieu d'un sien parant
gentilhome de normandie que le Roy tenoit
prisonier a Roan. La roine mere du roy auertie
par mr pinard secretere d'estat de mon enpriz
sonemant obtint de mosieur de guise qui estoit
lors de fortune aueq elle et du preuost des
marchans uers le qul elle onuoia (mosieur de
uilleroy secretere d'estat s'en souignant aussi
bien for en ma faueur) que sur les huit heures
du soir du mesme un maistred'hostel de ma dicte
damageste me uint faire mettre en liberté
moienant les reserits dudit seigneur duc et
dudit preuost adressas au clerc capitene
pour lon de la Bastille

A page from Montaigne's Ephemeris: *Montaigne in the Bastille*

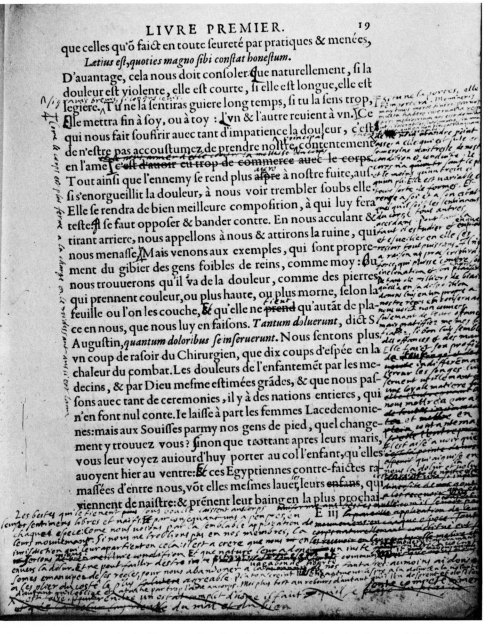

que celles qu'õ faiɕ en toute ſeureté par pratiques & menées,

Lætius eſt, quoties magno ſibi conſtat honeſtum.

D'auantage, cela nous doit conſoler. Que naturellement, ſi la douleur eſt violente, elle eſt courte, ſi elle eſt longue, elle eſt legiere. Tu ne la ſentiras guiere long temps, ſi tu la ſens trop, Elle mettra fin à ſoy, ou à toy : l'vn & l'autre reuient à vn. Ce qui nous fait ſouffrir auec tant d'impatience la douleur, c'eſt de n'eſtre pas accouſtumez de prendre noſtre contentement en l'ame, ~~c'eſt d'auoir eu trop de commerce auec le corps~~. Tout ainſi que l'ennemy ſe rend plus aſpre à noſtre ſuite, auſſi s'enorgueillit la douleur, à nous voir trembler ſoubs elle. Elle ſe rendra de bien meilleure compoſition, à qui luy fera teſte. Il ſe faut oppoſer & bander contre. En nous acculant & tirant arriere, nous appellons à nous & attirons la ruine, qui nous menaſſe. Mais venons aux exemples, qui ſont proprement du gibier des gens foibles de reins, comme moy : Ou nous trouuerons qu'il va de la douleur, comme des pierres qui prennent couleur, ou plus haute, ou plus morne, ſelon la feuille ou l'on les couche, & qu'elle ne ~~prend~~ qu'autát de place en nous, que nous luy en faiſons. *Tantum doluerunt*, dict S. Auguſtin, *quantum doloribus ſe inſeruerunt.* Nous ſentons plus vn coup de raſoir du Chirurgien, que dix coups d'eſpée en la chaleur du combat. Les douleurs de l'enfantemét par les medecins, & par Dieu meſme eſtimées grádes, & que nous paſſons auec tant de ceremonies, il y à des nations entieres, qui n'en font nul conte. Ie laiſſe à part les femmes Lacedemoniennes : mais aux Souiſſes parmy nos gens de pied, quel changement y trouuez vous ? ſinon que trottant apres leurs maris, vous leur voyez auiourd'huy porter au col l'enfant, qu'elles auoyent hier au ventre : & ces Egyptiennes contre-faiɕtes ramaſſées d'entre nous, võt elles meſmes lauer leurs enfans, qui viennent de naiſtre : & prénent leur baing en la plus prochai-

E iij

A page of the Essays *showing Montaigne's handwritten additions*

Frontispiece of the Bordeaux Copy with Montaigne's corrections

Pierre Charron

Marie de Gournay

its decadence, in which I now possess it; and nature has placed it in our hands adorned with such favorable conditions that we have only ourselves to blame if it weighs on us and if it escapes us unprofitably. . . . It takes management to enjoy life. I enjoy it twice as much as others, for the measure of enjoyment depends on the greater or lesser attention that we lend it."

Most men reject proper pleasures for vain ambitions, and seek other conditions because they do not understand the use of their own. The wise man accepts his life with gratitude:

As for me, then, I love life and cultivate it just as God has been pleased to grant it to us. I do not go about wishing that it should lack the need to eat and drink . . . nor that we should beget children insensibly with our fingers or our heels; nor that the body should be without desire and without titillation. Those are ungrateful complaints. I accept with all my heart what nature has done for me, and I am pleased with myself for this and thank her for it. We wrong that great and all-powerful Giver by scorning his gift, altering it, and disfiguring it.

Some time in the last four years of his life he was to add: "Himself all good, he has made all things good."

HOUGH HIS MAIN ACHIEVEMENT was his *Essays,* Montaigne played more of a role in the affairs of his time than most authors. A complete picture of him must show not only the introspective in his tower, the squire in his manor, and the traveler on his horse, but also the man of judgment in the councils of the great.

This public Montaigne has appeared often in these pages—at court as early as 1559, receiving the Order of Saint Michael in 1571, negotiating with Guise and Navarre between 1572 and 1576, gentleman of the king's chamber by 1573 and of Navarre's chamber in 1577, urged by Margaret of Valois to defend Sebond, congratulated by Henry III on his *Essays,* chosen to be mayor of Bordeaux by Catherine de' Medici, Margaret of Valois, Henry III, and Henry of Navarre, and politely ordered by the king to take up the duties of his office. As mayor we have seen him in contact twice with Margaret and almost constantly with her husband, Navarre, who chose him to present his case to the Catholics (writing him and having Mornay write him repeatedly), sent messages by him to Matignon, and visited him late in 1584.

His involvement did not end with his mayoralty. Late in 1586 the pressure on Henry III was very heavy; the League opposed his support of Navarre as heir; a German and Swiss army was being raised to aid Navarre; the treasury was empty; he wanted peace. Catherine de' Medici resolved to press her son-in-law personally to abjure and return to court, or at least sign a one-year truce. She sought him close to his own grounds, at the château of Saint-Brice near Cognac; the meetings lasted sporadically from December, 1586 to early March, 1587.

On December 31, 1586 she wrote from Cognac to one of her treasurers, Raoul Féron:

Because I am writing to Montaigne for him and his wife to come and join me, I want, and I order you, to furnish him, besides the 100 crowns that you have already paid out to him in these last few days, with a hundred and fifty crowns more, partly to replace one of the horses for his wagon,* partly to meet their extraordinary expenses, coming across country, and also for the purchase of some clothes that they need. . . .

A month and a half later (February 18, 1587), she wrote to her son Henry III from Niort:

Meanwhile I will tell you also, my son, that, pursuant to your intention, I have told and commanded the sieur de Malicorne † what you wanted to have done with Montaigne; and I shall keep my hand on this matter and on everything else that concerns your service, according to your intention, in the provinces down here.

Now it is possible that the Montaigne in question is not Michel. Among the queen mother's 108 secretaries was a François Montaigne, whose name appears four times in her letters between 1563 and 1584; a married man, like the Montaigne summoned to Saint-Brice, a trusted member of her staff, close enough to her and to the king for them both to take an interest (apparently humorous) in a letter of his to his wife.

However, Roger Trinquet has shown that it was probably Michel de Montaigne who was summoned to Saint-Brice. Catherine's references to "Montaigne" without a title do not rule him out, since she often speaks of titled persons by their name alone; her term "*hardes*" for the clothes they need to buy was not pejorative at that

---

* "*Chariotte*," which in 1611 Cotgrave defines as "a kind of litter, borne up by an axletree, and two wheeles."

† Jean de Chourses, seigneur de Malicorne, governor of Poitou.

time; a *"chariotte"* was not too plebeian a vehicle for the Montaignes, since Bordeaux boasted only three carriages before 1589;
the travel money issued (250 crowns, or 750 livres) is appropriate for a nobleman but would amount to almost two years' worth
of François Montaigne's annual wages of 400 livres. Michel would be
much likelier than François to elicit such concern and command such
expenses. It was natural for Catherine to seek his aid in dealing with
the reluctant Henry of Navarre. Moreover, the conferences were held
during Montaigne's flight from the plague, which probably led him
north in the general direction of Cognac and, after three months,
may have left him sartorially and financially ill equipped to make a
proper appearance before the queen mother, the king of Navarre,
and their entourages.

Catherine's second letter (February 18, 1587), which M. Trinquet did not mention, adds to the strong probability in favor of
Michel; for the association with "the provinces down here" fits him
and not François, and the king was hardly likely to send his mother
careful instructions about one of her many secretaries, nor she to call
on the governor of Poitou to carry them out.

Two passages in the *Essays* seem to refer to participation in these
conferences. One is a sketch (without naming him) of Henry of
Navarre, written between 1582 and 1588: "I know a man . . .
whose fine career is being corrupted every day by such persuasions:
that he should stay in close among his own people; that he should
hear of no reconciliation with his former enemies, should keep apart
and not trust himself to hands stronger than his own, whatever
promise may be made him, whatever advantage he may see in it. . . .
Such tender and circumspect prudence is a mortal enemy of lofty
actions." The second, coming just after Montaigne's account of his
flight, was probably written upon his return: "I still listen without
frowning to the seductions that are held out to me to draw me into
the market place, and I defend myself so softly that it looks as if I
would prefer to succumb to them." Trinquet infers that the sub-
orner is Catherine, who probably offered Montaigne a permanent
place in her council; that he asked for time to consider; and that she
was finally unable to use him, because League pressure led Henry III
to insist that she take on as negotiators only men not suspected of
being friendly toward the Huguenots.

Though the offers are only conjecture, it seems almost certain
that the man she called on to try to win over the wary Navarre was

the ex-mayor of Bordeaux, whom he had known, respected, and trusted for many years.

As Montaigne, back home again, worked on his *Essays* in the spring and summer of 1587, the German Protestant army made ready and began to move. Henry of Navarre, with a few minor successes in Poitou under his belt, planned to join with the Germans in Lorraine and try to crush Guise once for all. Henry III, shrewdly, sent Guise with one army to protect the frontier of Lorraine against the Germans, his own pro-League *mignon* Joyeuse southwest with another army to join Matignon and check Navarre, and kept most of his troops under his own command on the Loire to make sure that the two Protestant armies could not join forces. He hoped that Joyeuse would contain Navarre and that Guise would weaken the invaders in a hard battle but be beaten by them, leaving himself once again master in France.

On October 20, 1587, Joyeuse, not content to wait for help from Matignon or merely to contain Navarre, pursued his troops as they drew back to the south from La Rochelle and attacked them at Coutras, where Navarre's veterans, with almost no losses, destroyed his army, killing hundreds of nobles including Joyeuse and his brother Saint-Sauveur. Hitherto courageous in defeat, Navarre showed grace and magnanimity in victory, publicly deploring the loss of so many brave Frenchmen, treating his prisoners humanely, holding a Catholic funeral service for Joyeuse and his brother, and sending their bodies to Matignon for transmittal to the bereaved family. Even with this great obstacle removed to a juncture with the Germans, he made no move to follow up his advantage. This caused such surprise that when two months had passed, a rumor spread in Paris that Navarre was dead and led to the following exchange:

Even the greatest, unable to get any news of what he was doing or where he was, did not know what to think of it; to such a point that one day the duke de Guise, in this uncertainty (halfway believing it because he wanted it), approaching the king (who was warming himself by the fire) and wanting to learn news of him [Henry of Navarre], asked him if he had not received any, and how he was. Whereat the king broke out laughing and said to him: "I know the rumor that is current here and why you ask me this. He is as dead as you are; he is in good health and is with his whore!"

The king's information was precise; the woman in question was Navarre's mistress Diane ("Corisande") d'Andoins. After his vic-

tory, Henry had made his way far south to Navarrenx, near the
Spanish border, to present her with the banners won at Coutras. It
was his first glimpse of her in over a year and a half. For almost a
month, from November 9 to December 4, at Navarrenx, Pau, and
Hagetmau, the two were together. Apparently Navarre was once
again the thrall of a fair charmer.

But this was a curious idyll. He had just acquired a younger
mistress, Esther Ymbert of La Rochelle. Much of the month he
spent away from Corisande out hunting and on trips to Pau. When
he left, though there was no break, they were to be parted for over
six years, and their liaison was over.

However, if Corisande had lost some of her charm for Navarre,
she remained a wise counselor. To take the road thrown open by his
victory would mean confronting the king of France in the field on
the way to a juncture with an invading foreign army, and thus
abandoning his defensive role for that of rebel against the crown
he hoped to inherit. His present of the banners to Corisande seems
a symbolic tribute to the loyalist policy which she had long urged
and which he now accepted.

What makes this the more likely is the first visit Navarre made
after Coutras, to a man known for both his conciliatory loyalism and
his influence on Corisande: Michel de Montaigne. On October 23,
1587, just three days after the battle, Navarre spent the night—for
the second time only—at Montaigne. His host recorded the first visit,
but not this one, presumably because important and confidential
matters were discussed. Raymond Ritter has argued that Matignon's
delay in joining Joyeuse before Coutras, which may have been decisive, was due to Montaigne's advice to avoid a pitched battle against
Navarre, and that Navarre came to thank him and ask for further
services. Montaigne probably urged him to consolidate his position
as heir to the throne by abjuration and offered to discuss a firmer
accord with Henry III. Navarre's principal counselors were Protestants first and loyalists—if at all—later; Montaigne was a natural intermediary and negotiator. Within three months he was on his way to
Paris on a mission, sponsored by Matignon, from Navarre to Henry
of France. If such a trip was not yet under discussion, means of
reconciliation probably were.

The following January, 1588, found Montaigne in Moissac
with Matignon, and presumably conferring with Henry of Navarre

in Montauban, about fifteen miles to the east, before setting out for the court of France. The interest in his trip among Catholics and Protestants alike is attested by seven documents written by five different persons.

On January 24, 1588, Philippe de (Duplessis-) Mornay, influential Protestant adviser to Henry of Navarre and old friend of Montaigne, wrote from Montauban to his wife in Nérac:

Above all don't be troubled in your mind, for there is no reason to be. . . . Our army is coming along well in Germany.* Monsieur de Montaigne has gone to court. We are told that peace overtures will soon be made to us by neutral persons.

On February 1, 1588,† Sir Edward Stafford, the English ambassador to France, reported from Paris to his chief, Principal Secretary Sir Francis Walsingham:

There is news come today that the Marshal Matignon's son is coming hither, and is looked for every hour; that he bringeth with him one Montigny, a very wise gentleman of the king of Navarre, whom he hath given his word to present unto the King. I never heard of the man afore in my life.

From Orléans on the morning of February 16, 1588, Montaigne wrote to Matignon:

Sir, you have learned that our baggage was seized before our eyes in the forest of Villebois, and then, after a long time and much confused discussion, the seizure was judged unjust by his Highness the Prince.‡ Meanwhile we did not dare go on, because of the uncertainty over our personal security, about which we were to be enlightened in writing on our passports. This raid was occasioned by the same Leaguer who had seized Monsieur de Barrault and Monsieur de La Rochefoucauld.§ The tempest fell upon me, who had my money in my strongbox. I have not recovered any of it, and most of my papers and clothes also remained with the men. We did not see his Highness the Prince. Monsieur de Thorigny ‖ lost fifty-odd crowns, a silver water pitcher, and some odds and ends of clothes. He turned out of his way in great haste to go to see the mourning ladies at

---

* The first German army had been routed and a second was being recruited.

† Dated January 22, 1587. The English still clung to both "old styles," rejecting the new Gregorian calendar that moved the date ten days ahead, and still beginning the new year only at Easter.

‡ Henry I, prince de Condé, second to Navarre as a Protestant leader, who died a month later.

§ The text may be faulty here; our only source is a bad copy of a lost original. If indeed "Leaguer" is what Montaigne wrote, the holdup was apparently a Protestant reprisal for two earlier ones by Leaguers.

‖ Odet de Matignon, comte de Thorigny (1557–95), son of the marshal.

Montrésor,* where the bodies of the two brothers and of the grandmother are, and picked us up again yesterday in this city, which we are leaving presently.

The trip to Normandy is put off.

The King has sent Messieurs de Bellièvre and de La Guiche to Monsieur de Guise to summon him to come to court. We shall be there Thursday.†

Four days later, on February 20, Stafford wrote from Paris to his chief sponsor, William Cecil, Lord Burghley, Lord Treasurer of England:

I [have] written to Mr. Secretary in a letter in cipher—I cannot tell whether he will show it—of the coming of one Montaigne here from the King of Navarre, sent with Matignon's son; and how all the King of Navarre's servants here are jealous of his coming, being neither addressed to them nor knowing ‡ any tittle of the cause, and besides (to your lordship I may write it, for I know it shall not be spoken of and so I beseech you) they suspect it the more because he is a great favourite of the Countess of Bishe,§ who they say governeth the King of Navarre as she listeth, and is a very dangerous woman; and who marreth the King of Navarre's reputation throughout all the world; for he is altogether assotted, as they say, upon her. They fear, and so do I too, that he is come to treat with [*sic*] some private matter with the King, unknown to all of them of the Religion; for sure no man knoweth anything of it, and think that neither Du Plessis, Vicomte Turene [*sic*] nor any affected in religion are anything acquainted with it. Besides, the man is a Catholic, a very sufficient man; was once Mayor of Bordeaux, and one that would not take a charge to bring anything to the King that should not please him. Nor the Marshal Matignon would not have taken upon him to have given him to conduct to his son, without he had been very sure his commission should please and not displease the King. I did not write in my long letter by Mr. 'Hacklytt' ‖ without purpose that I feared the King of Navarre would be constrained either willingly or against his will to content the King; which I would fain not have done without the Queen's knowledge, and she had in some kind still an oar in their boat.

On February 25 Don Bernardino de Mendoza, the Spanish ambassador to France, wrote from Paris to King Philip II:

* A little town about thirty-five miles southeast of Tours. The brothers are Joyeuse and Saint-Sauveur, the ladies their mother and Joyeuse's wife. The Joyeuses and Matignons were related.

† February 18.

‡ Neither [he] being addressed to them nor [they] knowing.

§ Diane ("Corisande") d'Andoins, comtesse de Guiche. Puns and mistakes about her name were very common.

‖ The geographer Richard Hakluyt, then chaplain and secretary in Stafford's embassy.

And here, they say, has arrived Monsieur de Montaigne, who is a Catholic gentleman and a follower of the man from Béarn * under the direction of Matignon; and because those who handle the affairs of the man from Béarn do not know the reason why he has come, they suspect that he is on some secret mission. . . .

On February 28 Mendoza again wrote to his king from Paris:

Monsieur de Montaigne, about whom I wrote to your Majesty in one of my letters of the 25th, is considered to be a man of understanding, though somewhat addle-pated. They tell me that he controls the countess of La Guisa,† who is a very beautiful lady and lives with the sister of the man from Béarn, since she is the brother's lady. They say that the man from Béarn has dealings with him; and therefore they judge that he [Montaigne] is entrusted with some commission and that the King wants to make use of Montaigne so that he [Montaigne] may intercede with the said countess of La Guisa, that she may persuade the man from Béarn to come to what the King desires.

In her "Life of the Demoiselle de Gournay" (1641), writing of herself in the third person, Montaigne's *fille d'alliance* tells of Montaigne's trip and its sequel. She had read the *Essays* when she was eighteen or nineteen and been so struck with them that more than anything in the world she wanted to know the author as a friend:

So much so that near the end of the two- or three-year period that passed between her first sight of the book and of the author, having received, as she was wanting to write him, a false report that he was dead, she was smitten with intense grief; for it seemed to her that her soul's entire glory, felicity, and hope for enrichment were nipped in the bud by the loss of the conversation and society that she had promised herself from such a mind. When suddenly she received a contrary report, followed by the happy arrival of [Montaigne] himself at court and in Paris, where she then, accompanying her mother, had come to spend some time, she sent to greet him and declare to him the esteem she felt for his person and his book. He came to see her and thank her on the very next day. . . .

All this gives us the following outline of the trip. By mid-January, 1588 or soon after, Montaigne was with Matignon in Moissac, preparing for a secret mission, with Matignon as his sponsor and his son, the distinguished commander Odet de Thorigny, as his escort, that would bypass the immediate entourages of both Henry of Na-

---

* The Spaniards, holding part of Navarre, refused to recognize Henry as king of Navarre and referred to him regularly as "el de Bearne" ("the man from Béarn").

† Again Corisande d'Andoins, comtesse de Guiche or de Guissen.

varre and Henry III in an attempt to draw the two kings into closer alliance against the League. Even Navarre's chief adviser, Duplessis-Mornay (like his military lieutenant Turenne), did not know what instructions Montaigne bore, though the mission made him hope for a respite from the fighting. Matignon, who like Montaigne was soon to give his full support to Navarre as King Henry IV, already paid him a sort of secondary allegiance; other reasons may explain his delay at Coutras, but hardly his sponsorship of Montaigne's trip. Thorigny's escorting role was probably an improvisation. He had just come to Moissac to break to his father the sad news, learned in Bordeaux, of the death of his younger brother Lancelot, recently named bishop of Coutances. His other concerns appear in his detour to offer condolences to the Joyeuse family at Montrésor; but his prompt return to the party shows Matignon's strong commitment to the mission.

Montaigne probably made the entire trip with Thorigny, as Stafford's first letter suggests. He may have spent a week or ten days at home in final preparations for an absence of nearly a year; he may have had affairs to wind up in Bordeaux as well; Thorigny may have had obligations of his own related to his brother's death. The party probably left Bordeaux (or possibly Montaigne) around February 3–6. The holdup took place, perhaps on the second day, in the forest of Villebois just southeast of Angoulême, apparently in reprisal for similar recent holdups by a Leaguer. The perpetrators were Protestants, ultimately responsible to "his Highness the Prince" de Condé, whose headquarters at Saint-Jean d'Angely were about sixty miles northwest of Villebois. Montaigne had few friends on this trip. Naturally the Leaguers and Spaniards bitterly opposed any such understanding as he sought; the Protestants feared abjuration and abandonment by their leader; and even the English ambassador was worried lest Henry of Navarre become too independent if he and Henry III drew very close without Queen Elizabeth's complicity.

The party reached Orléans on February 15 or perhaps earlier; it was there that Thorigny rejoined them after his visit to Montrésor. Montaigne's account of the holdup to Matignon was not the first; he presumably delayed writing until he could report Thorigny's safe return and the party's expectation of reaching court two days later.

The court meanwhile had been buzzing with the news that

Thorigny and Montaigne were coming on a mysterious mission. Over two weeks before, Stafford had been advised that they were to be "looked for every hour." Their delay helps explain how word of their misadventure grew into a report of Montaigne's death and even reached Marie de Gournay's ears in Picardy.

The Protestants in Paris were especially concerned. Many had attributed Navarre's actions after Coutras not to wise restraint but to frantic addiction to women. The choice of the Catholic Montaigne as emissary, his close ties with the Catholics Matignon and Corisande, seemed to mean that Henry III would have his way and persuade his royal cousin to abjure once more.

The similar features of Mendoza's and Stafford's reports need not surprise us; for Stafford was presumably Mendoza's informant. This seems wildly unlikely on the face of it. This was the year of the Armada, in which Mendoza played an important part. A brave army officer "kicked upstairs" because of his diplomatic skill, expelled from England for complicity in Throckmorton's plot against Queen Elizabeth on behalf of Mary Queen of Scots, he vowed to live for vengeance on the impudent English, and, becoming ambassador to France a year later, spent his money and his eyesight working for Spain and Catholicism against England and all Protestants and moderates. Not long after the loss of the Armada he was to lead the defense of Paris against Henry IV. Stafford, however, is a puzzling figure. He favored the conservatism of Lord Treasurer Burghley against the militant Protestantism of his own chief, Principal Secretary Walsingham, who mistrusted him; he was fond of gambling and often in debt; he sold information to Henri de Guise and repeatedly to Mendoza. Experts disagree, however, about whether he was a traitor or whether, perhaps quite honorably, he played a double game, getting information for himself and his queen by giving Mendoza intelligence that was sometimes false and sometimes too tardy to be useful. At times he was clearly not the willing tool that Mendoza —our most candid and outspoken witness—thought him; yet he did sell him news, and more than he appears to have got in the exchange.

At all events, he is clearly the "new confidant" of whom Mendoza writes on January 16, 1588 that he "turns himself inside out for me"; he reported Montaigne's trip more than three weeks before Mendoza did, and his arrival, more fully, five days before. Mendoza tells of interviews with the "new confidant" on the days of both his reports (February 25 and 28); and his accounts of Montaigne's arrival are almost a summary of Stafford's second letter. The only important difference is that he revises—one wonders on whose advice—Stafford's highly favorable estimate of Montaigne.

This trip of Montaigne's is important to our sense of his character. His constant preaching of disengagement, his frank acceptance of comfort and pleasure, and his failure to return into Bordeaux at the end of his mayoralty, have caused a good many readers to dismiss him as a selfish sybarite who admires heroism only from a very safe distance. As we have tried to show already, this picture is unfair. Like his staying with the dying La Boétie when warned that his illness might be contagious, like the effort that went into his *Essays,* like his vigilance as mayor of Bordeaux, his trip in 1588 offers a precious corrective. He was not well; it was almost certainly on this trip that Pierre de Brach reports he nearly died; two years later he was too ill to accept Henry IV's welcome invitation to come and join him; five years later he was dead. The trip was dangerous, with enemies on all sides; his holdup on the road was so like an earlier one that many critics consider them the same; he was a marked man, for later in Paris he was imprisoned by the League in reprisal for the arrest of a Leaguer by Henry III. Once again, as in the siege of Castillon, he was the moderate caught between unscrupulous extremists, a Guelf to the Ghibellines, a Ghibelline to the Guelfs. Like the mayoralty, which he had not wanted, he was asked to undertake the mission as the likeliest person to bring it off; it might be important to France; he accepted. "I do not want a man to refuse," he had written, "to the charges he takes on, attention, steps, words, and sweat and blood if need be." He was a man of more dedication than he claims and than he is often thought to have had.

For almost all the year 1588 Montaigne was in the north. We know nothing of his conferences with the king; nor how soon after the Day of the Barricades (May 12) he followed him from Paris to Chartres; nor whether he was still at Blois when Guise was assassinated. But occasional glimpses of him allow us to piece out a notion of his year.

Shortly after his arrival he received Marie de Gournay's note, no doubt both overemphatic and sincere; and the next day he went to call on her where she and her mother were staying. He met an intense young woman of twenty-two, highly emotional and intellectual, not ugly but not by any means beautiful, with a broad forehead, wide-set eyes, straight nose, small mouth, and an expression both wistful and imperious. Her account is the only one we have:

He came to see and thank her on the very next day, offering her affection and a father-to-daughter relationship; which she received with all the more applause because she marveled at the fated sympathy between his nature and hers; she having for her part promised herself in her heart such a relationship with him from her first inspection of his book, and this with regard to the proportion between their ages and the intention of their souls and characters. He stayed in the north for eight or nine months, continuing this noble and philosophical friendship.

Her devotion to him is unquestionable. A romantic, idealistic young bluestocking and apparently a born old maid, she had been so overwhelmed by her first reading of the *Essays* in 1585 or 1586 that it took Lipsius' praise of Montaigne to restore her prestige among her intimates. From the first she hailed him as a great author fully equal to the best of the ancients. She was amazed at her miraculous affinities with him, and aspired to the place left empty by La Boétie. She was to spend much of her life as his literary executrix, editor, and archdefender against all critics.

Exactly how he felt about her is harder to say. Three passages in the *Essays* allude to her, but each offers problems of interpretation. One of them reads as follows in the Bordeaux Copy:

I have seen a girl, to attest the ardor of her promises, and also her constancy, strike herself, with the bodkin she wore in her hair, four or five lusty stabs in the arm, which broke the skin and made her bleed in good earnest.

Marie de Gournay's editions, from 1595 on, replace the brief initial clause "I have seen a girl" by one that virtually identifies her as the subject: "When I came from those famous Estates of Blois, I had seen a girl in Picardy, a short while before. . . ." But its absence from the Bordeaux Copy raises the question whether it was Montaigne himself, or she, who wrote it.

The other passage that clearly deals with her is also lacking in the Bordeaux Copy and taken from the 1595 edition:

I have taken pleasure in making public in several places the hopes I have for Marie de Gournay le Jars, my *fille d'alliance*, whom I love indeed more than a daughter of my own, and cherish in my retirement and solitude as one of the best parts of my own being. She is the only person I still think about in the world. If youthful promise means anything, her soul will some day be capable of the finest things, among others of perfection in that most sacred kind of friendship which, so we read, her sex has not yet been able to attain. The sincerity and firmness of her character are already sufficient, her affection for me more than superabundant, and such, in short, that it leaves nothing to be desired, unless that her apprehension about my end, in view of my fifty-five years when I met her, would not torment her so cruelly. The judgment she made of the first *Essays*, she a woman, and in this age, and so young, and alone in her district, and the remarkable eagerness with which she loved me and wanted my friendship for a long time, simply through the esteem she formed for me before she had seen me, is a phenomenon very worthy of consideration.

Though it does not appear in the Bordeaux Copy, the place for it there is marked by the cross (apparently in Montaigne's hand) that he habitually used to show that an addition was to follow, and there are signs of paste on the margins of that page. This suggests that he pasted there, as he sometimes did elsewhere, a slip of paper that has since been lost.

However, many facts about the passage are disturbing. Its absence from the Bordeaux Copy is doubly so since the only identifying parts of the other passage (quoted above) do not appear there either. Though Marie was a scrupulous editor for her time, her standards were less rigorous than ours. In 1624, seeking to restore Ronsard's prestige against the ruthless denigration of Malherbe, she rewrote more than half the lines of his "Harangue of the Duke de Guise to the Soldiers at Metz" and published them—to be sure, with his final version on facing pages—as a still later version by Ronsard that she had discovered. She considered herself uniquely equipped to edit the *Essays* by her miraculous kinship with Montaigne, and herself revised his tribute to her for her 1635 edition. True, she acknowledged this boldness in her Preface, explaining that "in this way, I want to give the lie, now and for the future, to those who believe that if this book praised me less, I would cherish and serve it less also." But she was clearly not above revising her favorite authors and taking liberties, on personal grounds, with this very passage.

Most striking are the alterations she makes in the 1635 edition of this passage and the tone that results. In the first sentence she changes "more than a daughter" to "as a daughter," and deletes the entire ensuing clause ("and cherish . . . my own being"). Also deleted are sentence two ("She is the only person I still think about in the world"), the second half of sentence three ("among others of perfection . . . able to attain"), and sentence four ("The sincerity . . . so cruelly"). In sentence five, "the remarkable eagerness with which she loved me and wanted my friendship for a long time" is reduced to "the good will she devoted to me."

The revised form of the tribute cuts out precisely those parts that sound most like her and least like Montaigne: the effusive statements of their mutual love, of her unique place—like La Boétie earlier—in his life, of her torment over his approaching death—unlikely for him to write before it, likely for her to write after. I can well imagine Montaigne—like any other man—thinking "This young woman loves and admires me; it follows that she is a person of the highest character and intellect"; I cannot imagine him writing it, at least not without some touch of his characteristic self-mockery. Therefore I believe that the reduced 1635 version is roughly what Montaigne wrote, and that Marie embellished it in most of her editions with things he may have said, or even written elsewhere, or which she believed were true and thus might be justifiably published in his name.

A third allusion to Marie in the *Essays* was later cut out by Montaigne. In the 1588 edition, obviously speaking of La Boétie, he wrote:

And if I had not supported with all my strength a friend that I lost, they would have torn him into a thousand contrasting appearances. I know well that I will leave behind no sponsor anywhere near as affectionate and understanding about me as I was about him. There is no one to whom I would be willing to entrust myself fully for a portrait; he alone enjoyed my true image, and carried it away.

In the Bordeaux Copy, after 1588, he first added, after "portrait": "and if there should be any, I repudiate them, for I know them to be excessively prejudiced in my favor." Then he crossed out the entire passage except for the first sentence ("And if I had . . . contrasting appearances"). However, the fact that he did write it, and thus drew a sharp distinction between La Boétie and any other friend—including Marie—argues that he deleted it not for lack of conviction but out of consideration for his *fille d'alliance*.

In short, I cannot believe that Montaigne had anything like the feeling for Marie de Gournay that she had for him. An amiable man apparently unaccustomed to adulation, he was probably not immune to it. She was about the last type of friend he had dreamed the *Essays* might bring him; but her love of his book, however maladroit, was not undiscerning. Ailing and close to death, he basked in the warmth of her worshipful love. Her father having died ten years before, he proposed—or accepted her proposal—that she become his *fille d'alliance*, or daughter by a kind of friendly, unofficial, mutual adoption. He spent several months at her home, dictated some passages of the *Essays* to her, made her his literary executrix, and thought of her on his deathbed; his family received her later with open arms.

Yet he must often have shaken his head at her romantic enthusiasm: not only the stabs with the bodkin, but the attitudes that she was to publish in her Preface to the 1595 *Essays:* the hyperbolic praise, the attempt to claim La Boétie's place, the assumption that their kinship made for a kind of spiritual and intellectual equality. Though he did delete the statement rejecting all witnesses to his life, he left the famous warning just a few sentences earlier that applies to us all: "I would willingly come back from the other world to give the lie to any man who portrayed me other than I was, even if it were to honor me." And Marie herself reports one attempt of his to bring her down to earth: "My Father told me one day, wishing to give me pain, that in his estimation there were thirty people in our great city [Paris], where he then was, with as strong minds as he." To be sure, she resourcefully retorted that if there were, at least one would by then have come to welcome—if not worship—him; and Montaigne, who knew a stone wall when he saw one, appears—at least by her account—to have let it go at that.

As far as we know, Montaigne stayed mostly in Paris until after the Day of the Barricades (May 12) and the flight of the king, whom he followed to Chartres and to Rouen; though he may have paid a first brief visit to Gournay-sur-Aronde. The 1588 edition of the *Essays* was published in Paris in June, by Abel L'Angelier. Some have thought that Montaigne's good friend the Gascon poet Pierre de Brach saw it through the press; but since Montaigne was apparently in Paris most of the time until at least about mid-May, this may have been unnecessary. Montaigne's reasons for staying with the court until early July may be simple preference or loyalism; but he may have considered his mission not yet fully accomplished.

He had just returned to Paris from Rouen and was in bed with some sort of gout when he was haled off to prison by the League on July 10 in reprisal for the king's arrest of a Leaguer in Rouen. Within five hours the queen mother heard of it and prevailed on Guise to have him released. Since he recorded the event in his *Ephemeris* at first inadvertently as of July 20 and then cancelled this story and rewrote it as of July 10, we have two accounts. The first one he wrote is the more circumstantial:

July 20 [read July 10]
1588. Between three and four in the afternoon, being in Paris and in bed because of a pain that had seized me in the left foot three days before, which may be some sort of gout (and this was the first time I felt it), I was taken prisoner by the captains of the people [of Paris] at the time when Monsieur de Guise was in command there and had driven out the King (I had just come back from Rouen, where I had left his Majesty), and was taken by them on my horse to the Bastille. The Queen Mother, being at the council with the said sieur de Guise, with much insistence got him to have me let out. He gave a written order for this addressed to Le Clerc, who was then in command of the Bastille; which order was taken to the Provost of Merchants, needing his confirmation. At eight o'clock of the same day a steward of the Queen brought the said orders, and I was released by an unheard-of favor. Monsieur de Villeroy, among several others, had a big hand in this. It was the first prison I had seen. I was put there because the duke d'Elbeuf had me seized by right of reprisal for a gentleman of the League seized at Rouen.

The episode shows that Montaigne was still a marked man, whom the Leaguers singled out as a loyalist friendly to Henry of Navarre, whose imprisonment alarmed the *secrétaires d'Etat* and spurred the queen mother, "by an unheard-of favor," to make instant representations to Henri de Guise. What Guise thought of Montaigne we do not know, and despite Montaigne's firm opposition to his ambitions he may not have thought of him much; but as he promptly signed the order for his release, he may have remembered how Montaigne, no doubt a bit bluntly but with candor and good will, had once tried to draw him and Henry of Navarre off the collision course that was now going so well for Guise—but that, incredibly, was to end in his death less than six months later.

It was almost certainly during this year, and probably soon after this episode, that Montaigne suffered the grave illness which, soon after his death (February 4, 1593), his friend Pierre de Brach described in a letter to Justus Lipsius:

When we were together in Paris a few years ago, and the doctors despairing of his life and he hoping only for death, I saw him, when death stared him in the face from close up, push her well away by his disdain for the fear she brings. What fine arguments to content the ear, what fine teachings to make the soul wise, what resolute firmness of courage to make the most fearful secure, did that man then display! I never heard a man speak better, or better resolved to do what the philosophers have said on this point, without the weakness of his body having beaten down any of the vigor of his soul. He had cheated death by his assurance, and death cheated him by letting him get well.

Brach, who had lost his beloved wife Anne (the "Aimée" of his poems) just a year before, had come to Paris to solicit verses in her honor from men of letters such as Dorat, Baïf, and—possibly with Montaigne's help—Pasquier and Odet de Turnèbe. He was in Rouen on July 8, where (perhaps at Montaigne's urging) he wrote Lipsius to request verses from him. A devoted friend, he was probably with Montaigne for much of his stay in the north. Though his account may embellish Montaigne's courage, it accords too well with other tributes to leave any doubt that Montaigne confronted death in a manner fully worthy of La Boétie.

From midsummer to late fall and perhaps early winter Montaigne remained in the north, presumably in Paris and Rouen, certainly at Gournay and Blois, where the Estates General lasted from preliminaries in September and a royal opening in mid-October to the middle of January, 1589. We do not know just what part of that time Montaigne was there; but apparently he was at Gournay-sur-Aronde just before, and left there for Blois on November 23, 1588. An illness such as Brach describes was probably long, required a long convalescence, and left Montaigne in no hurry to visit the Estates but glad of the Gournays' loving solicitude. Marie tells how he and she strolled and talked in the gardens of the estate by the banks of the little Aronde. Her repeated stabs in the arm to prove her ardor and constancy suggest that he may have teased her at times by questioning her ostentatious but genuine devotion. On his last day there they read Plutarch's "Love Stories" together, and these prompted her to tell him a romance of her own devising—not wholly original but improved by her telling. Though he thought her better equipped for philosophy than fiction, he spoke kindly of it; and when he left she worked hard and late to set it down under the title *Le Proumenoir de Monsieur de Montaigne (Monsieur de Montaigne's*

Walk. Paris: L'Angelier, 1594). It was found among his papers after his death; she had sent it to him for comment and criticism; he may have put it aside and mislaid it, or simply thought it better unpublished.

In late November, 1588, he set out for Blois, where the situation was ominous. Henry of Navarre was of course not in the picture; the Guises and their supporters in the Third Estate were in control; the king, after a bold start, had been flouted again and again and was nearing the desperation that finally led him to have Guise killed.

Montaigne had long marveled at Guise's success, attributing it largely to his readiness for calculated risks. In a passage that he must have added to the *Essays* between June and late November, 1588, dictating it to Marie de Gournay (in whose hand it appears on the Bordeaux Copy) presumably during his last visit, he contrasts Navarre's excessive wariness (noted earlier in this chapter) with Guise's boldness: "I know another who has advanced his fortune beyond all expectations by following a wholly opposite plan."

In Blois Montaigne found many friends, of whom two left a record of their conversations. As we have seen, when Jacques-Auguste de Thou discussed the present troubles with him, Montaigne related his fruitless attempt to bring Guise and Navarre together at court between 1572 and 1576, the indifference of both men to religion, Guise's eagerness to win Navarre's friendship, and the latter's implacable resistance, understandable after the events of 1572.

Another friendly encounter was with the eminent lawyer and man of letters Estienne Pasquier (1529-1615), student of the French heritage in his *Researches on France*. Even as Montaigne liked his works, he admired Montaigne as "another Seneca in our language" and his book as "a real seedbed of fine and notable sayings." As a good friend, he took Montaigne aside to offer some constructive advice, which, to his surprise, went unheeded:

We were both together in the city of Blois at the time of that famous Assembly of the Three Estates of the year 1588 whose conclusion produced so many misfortunes for France. And as we were strolling in the courtyard of the château, I happened to say to him that he had made an oversight by not communicating his work to a few of his friends before publishing it, inasmuch as a reader could recognize in many places a certain Gascon wood-note . . . of which a friend of his could have warned him. And since he would not believe me, I took him to my room, where I had his book; and there I showed him many expressions familiar not to the French

but only to Gascons. . . . I thought that at the first later printing of his
book he would give orders to correct them. However . . . he did not.

Now Montaigne, by his own account, encouraged constructive criticism, even against his own best judgment. However, he had already
weighed and rejected, in the *Essays,* the kind of advice that Pasquier
now offered.

> When I have been told, or have told myself: "You are too thick in
> figures of speech. Here is a word of Gascon vintage. Here is a dangerous
> phrase." (I do not avoid any of those that are used in the streets of France;
> those who would combat usage with grammar make fools of themselves.)
> "This is ignorant reasoning. This is paradoxical reasoning. This one is too
> mad. You are often playful: people will think you are speaking in earnest
> when you are making believe." "Yes," I say, "but I correct the faults of
> inadvertence, not those of habit. Isn't this the way I speak everywhere?
> Don't I represent myself to the life? Enough, then. I have done what I
> wanted. Everyone recognizes me in my book, and my book in me."

We do not know how long Montaigne stayed at Blois. The fact
that he mentions the killing of Guise (December 23) in his *Ephemeris,* and without saying that it took place at Blois, inclines me to
believe he was still there at the time and left soon after, probably
with messages from the king to Matignon, who was still lieutenant
general in the southwest and mayor of Bordeaux. Marie de Gournay,
our only source, says that Montaigne went back to Guienne, "where
the League's war, which was consuming all France, attached him by
the command and in the service of the King." His close collaboration
with Matignon in these years appears from his two letters of 1590
to Henry IV. This doubtless took him often to Bordeaux, where he
probably went first on his way home, where Marie de Gournay addressed the *Proumenoir* to him in the second half of December, and
where he was late in the following spring (1589) when de Thou
and Schomberg passed through Montaigne in his absence and were
hospitably entertained by his wife.

Bordeaux had long been loyalist, and remained so; but the killing
of Guise inflamed League bitterness, and the accession of Henry IV
gave many Catholics divided loyalties. Matignon, generally with the
support of the Parlement, which repeatedly wrote urging Henry IV
to abjure, had to meet many threats in order to keep the city faithful
and at peace. For some time his task was made no easier by the plight

of the king's army, which was virtually on the run before the stronger forces of the new League leader, Mayenne. When the king moved north to the friendly port of Dieppe, closer to help from England, he came so near being captured that Montaigne writes of his triumph at Arques (September 21, 1589) as a "happy escape." Not until his crushing victory at Ivry six months later did he become truly master in the field; and the conquest of his kingdom was still several years and a second abjuration away.

Soon after learning of Henry IV's accession, Montaigne had written him, no doubt offering whatever services he might be pleased to use. Henry had his letter answered on November 30, 1589, summoning him to Tours, for a time the seat of his government. However, his reply reached the essayist only in mid-January; Montaigne's answering letter is dated January 18, 1590, from Montaigne. He congratulates the king on being able to stoop to the little people, but hopes that he owes his answer not to general vigor but to special good will. He has always regarded Navarre as his future king, and hoped for his successes "even when I had to confess it to my curate"; now he is free to "embrace them with my full affection." He looks forward in the coming summer to a trend in the king's favor which, once established, "will gather its own momentum and go all the way." He speaks as an active collaborator with Matignon when he writes:

We could not possibly draw from the justice of your cause such strong arguments to confirm or subdue your subjects as we do from the news of the prosperity of your campaigns. And I can assure Your Majesty that in producing the new changes to your advantage that you see in these parts, your happy escape from Dieppe has most opportunely seconded the frank zeal and marvelous sagacity of Marshal de Matignon, from whom I like to believe that you do not daily receive so many good and signal services without remembering my assurances and my hopes.

What Montaigne's assurances had been we do not know; but his hopes were to be a candid adviser to the king. He had written in the *Essays* that when people asked him what he thought he might have been good for if put to full use in his prime, his answer had always been "For nothing."

But I would have told my master home truths, and watched over his conduct, if he had been willing . . . piece by piece, simply and naturally, making him see how he stands in public opinion, and opposing his flatterers. . . .

I should have had enough fidelity, judgment, and independence for that. It would be a nameless office; otherwise it would lose its effect and its grace. And it is a part that cannot be played indiscriminately by all. For truth itself does not have the privilege to be employed at any time and in any way. . . . It often happens, as the world goes, that people blurt it out into a prince's ear not only fruitlessly, but harmfully, and even unjustly. . . .

For this occupation I should want a man who is content with his fortune . . . and born to a middle rank; because on the one hand he would not fear to touch his master's heart deeply and to the quick, at the risk of losing his preferment thereby; and on the other hand, being of middle station, he would have easier communication with all sorts of people.

After 1588 he added that one man alone should hold this office, lest this freedom lead to irreverence, and that he must have "above all, the fidelity of silence."

What we know of Montaigne's earlier relations with Henry of Navarre, both directly and through Corisande d'Andoins, clearly suggests that he may have played some such role earlier and that Navarre accepted it, perhaps welcomed it. Now, with due deference to the king of France, Montaigne allows himself to give the younger man frank advice on the ethics of conquest and rule.

I would have wished, to be sure, that the individual profit of the soldiers in your army and the need to content them had not robbed you, especially in that principal city,* of the fine recommendation of having treated your mutinous subjects, in the height of victory, with more solace than do their protectors; and that you had shown that they were yours, not by a passing and usurped claim, but by a paternal and truly royal protection.

To conduct such affairs as those you have in hand it is necessary to use uncommon ways. Moreover, it has always been observed that where conquests, because of their greatness and difficulty, could not be thoroughly completed by arms and by force, they have been completed by clemency and magnanimity, excellent lures to attract men, especially toward the just and legitimate side. If rigor and punishment occur, they must be put off until after the possession of mastery. A great conqueror of the past [Scipio the Elder] boasts that he has given his subjugated enemies as much occasion to love him as his friends. And here we already feel a somewhat promising effect from the impression received by the towns that have strayed from you when they compare their harsh treatment with that of the towns that are obedient to you. Wishing for Your Majesty, as I do, a more present and less hazardous felicity, and that you may be rather loved than feared

---

* Presumably Paris, the siege of which had not yet begun, but which Henry of Navarre had attacked briefly (November 1–3, 1589).

by your people,* and may consider your welfare as necessarily attached to theirs, I rejoice that this same progress that you are making toward victory is also a progress toward easier conditions of peace.

In conclusion, Montaigne explains that he has just received the king's letter (of November 30, 1589), too late to join him in Tours as directed. He is grateful that Henry "would take pleasure in seeing me, a person so useless, but yours even more by affection than by duty," and commends him for acting the part of a king without changing his inner ease and good nature. "You have been pleased to have consideration not only for my age but also for my wishes in summoning me to a place where you would be a little bit at rest from your labors and agitations. May it be soon in Paris, Sire; and there will be neither means nor health that I will not employ to come."

The other letter that we have from Montaigne to Henry IV was written late that summer, on September 2, 1590. Six weeks earlier the king had sent him instructions for conferring with Matignon and offered to pay his expenses. Montaigne, ill with a bad fever, had just received the letter. Wounded by the offer of money, he replied with the justified pride of a faithful and unselfish servant:

> Sire,
> The letter of July 20th that Your Majesty has been pleased to write me was delivered to me only this morning and found me caught up in a very violent tertian fever that has been popular in this region since last month.
> Sire, I take it as a very great honor to receive your commands, and I have not failed to write to Marshal de Matignon three times, very expressly, of my intention and obligation to go to see him, and I even marked out for him the route I would take to go to meet him in safety if he saw fit. Having had no answer to all this, I assume that he has considered, on my behalf, the length and hazard of the roads.
> Sire, may it please Your Majesty to do me the favor of believing that I will never begrudge my purse on the occasions for which I would not want to spare my life. I have never received any gift whatsoever from the liberality of kings, any more than I have asked it or deserved it; and I have received no payment for the steps I have taken in their service, of which Your Majesty has had partial knowledge. What I have done for your predecessors I will do still more willingly for you. I am, Sire, as rich as I

---

* Compare *Essays* II: 8 (S 285, OC 373): "Even if I could make myself feared, I would much rather make myself loved." The impact of Machiavelli's *Prince* made this a very live question.

wish to be. When I have exhausted my purse with Your Majesty in Paris, I will make bold to tell you so; and then, if you consider me worth keeping any longer in your retinue, I will cost you less than the least of your officers.

Sire, I pray God for your prosperity and health.

Your very humble and very obedient servant and subject,

Montaigne

War, illness, and death combined to prevent Montaigne from ever joining Henry IV; but he remained a devoted loyalist to the very end.

Chapter 16: The Final Additions [1588–1592]

N THE LAST FOUR YEARS of his life Montaigne continued to work over his *Essays*. He added no new
books or chapters, but about a thousand passages, ranging in length from a word or two to several pages and
making up about one quarter of the entire work, on
the unbound pages of a copy of his 1588 edition, in the spacious
margins; or, when he ran out of room there, on separate slips of paper.
These pages, now rebound, we call the "Bordeaux Copy," the basic
text of the final *Essays*. Because their margins were later cut by a
thoughtless binder, they must be supplemented by the 1595 edition,
prepared by Marie de Gournay and Pierre de Brach from a copy of
the "Bordeaux Copy." On the frontispiece Montaigne changed "fifth
edition" to "sixth" and placed a confident new epigraph, "*Viresque
acquirit eundo*—He gains strength as he goes"; on the flyleaf he
wrote careful instructions to the printer. Long before, he had said
that we must always be booted and ready to go. Although death
kept him from adding still more to his book, it did not find the
book unready.*

* Some notion of the work of Montaigne's final years may be gained from a sample

He was not the casual writer he claims to be; the manuscript often shows several successive versions, normally aiming to strengthen and clarify the thought and expression. We find no important changes within the new material or from that of 1588; and the fact that Montaigne now writes no new essays suggests his awareness of this. We do observe more boldness and readiness to contradict his early views. He has delivered the substance of his message; what remains is to complete and sharpen it.

The greater boldness is evident chiefly in five areas: self-revelation, obscenity, his book and his plan, the evils of religion in his time, and his own independent morality.

Since his final remarks reveal him most fully, many have already been noted. Some, like the description of his library, simply add information; most of them take us further into his confidence. He tells us more about his defects and those imputed to him: coolness, reluctance to take advice, equanimity over the loss of his children and the plight of France. Here are the complaints he hears: " 'Idle. Cool in the duties of friendship and kinship, and in public duties. Too self-centered.' The most insulting do not say, 'Why did he take what he did? Why didn't he pay for it?' but 'Why doesn't he cancel what is owed him? Why doesn't he give more?' " Such complainants, he says, demand of him what he does not owe but not of themselves what they owe; he could be tempted to return their reproaches.

Often he shows himself in a comic light. Though his errors, he says, are now incorrigible, they may be object lessons if published. He is franker in confessing to an avaricious stage when "I . . . spoke of my money only to lie." He comments wryly on his decrepit old age—"Guide me no more, I can go no more. . . . My world is done for, my form is emptied"—and the ripe wisdom it is supposed to bring: "Myself now and myself a while ago are indeed two; but when better, I simply cannot say." For aging is no progression, but "a drunkard's motion, staggering, dizzy, wobbling." He illustrates a serious point with a droll glimpse of himself: "When I call him [my valet] a clown or a calf, I do not undertake to sew those labels on him forever; nor do I think I contradict myself when I presently call him a fine fellow. No quality embraces us purely and universally.

---

passage in translation in all its successive published versions (Appendix B) and a photographic reproduction (between pp. 264–265) of one of the pages of the Bordeaux Copy.

If it did not seem crazy to talk to oneself, there is not a day when I would not be heard growling to myself: 'Confounded fool!' And yet I do not intend that to be my definition."

Montaigne's obscenity continues to grow as a comic reminder of our "peacock's feet." To a list of involuntary movements he now adds that the stomach rises at one object, "at another, a certain part lower down." He is more explicit about "the unruly liberty of this member, obtruding so importunately when we have no use for it, and failing so importunately when we have the most use for it, and struggling for mastery so imperiously with our will, refusing with so much pride and obstinacy our solicitations, both mental and manual," and defends it comically against our other parts. His most immodest chapter, "On Some Verses of Virgil" (III: 5), grows more so. Love, he had said, is merely a thirst for sexual enjoyment; now he adds: "and Venus nothing else but the pleasure of discharging our vessels." "Each one of my parts," he writes of his penis, "makes me myself just as much as every other one. And no other makes me more properly a man than this one." Now he offers his most piquant reminders of the blinkers we wear: "We imagine much more appropriately an artisan on the toilet seat or on his wife than a great president, venerable by his demeanor and his ability." His comments become ever more pungent. For those who marry their mistresses he quotes the saying: "Shit in the basket and then put it on your head." About philosophizers who disdain anything nonintellectual he asks: "Won't they try to square the circle while perched on their wives?" His final pages abound in examples; the next-last paragraph (his last chance for irony before the triumphant finale) now ends thus: "On the loftiest throne in the world we are still sitting only on our own rump."

As it grows, his obscenity becomes more explicitly didactic. To the ancient philosophers, he points out, our notion of decency—"not to dare to do openly what it is decent for us to do in private"— seemed stupid. His own aim likewise is the whole truth:

I owe a complete portrait of myself to the public. The wisdom of my lesson is wholly in truth, in freedom, in reality . . . of which propriety and ceremony are daughters, but bastard daughters.

. . . Whoever would wean man of the folly of such a scrupulous verbal superstition would do the world no great harm. Our life is part folly, part wisdom. Whoever writes about it only reverently and according to the rules leaves out more than half of it.

Montaigne is clearer now about his plan. Now he dares "not only to speak of myself, but to speak only of myself"; any other subject is a digression. However, he can view himself with detachment, like "a neighbor or a tree." He draws important conclusions which before had been merely implicit: on the relation of the "Apology" to self-study—"And he who understands nothing about himself, what can he understand?"—and on the total range of his own inquiry: "man in general, the knowledge of whom I seek." As a dispassionate man who has had access to the great, he has often been urged to write a history of his time; but he lacks composition, application, and incentive. A stronger reason is his sense—like Aristotle's when he calls poetry more philosophical than history—that history is limited to the random event that has actually happened. Montaigne makes his domain the possible, and uses even fabulous testimonies. "Whether they have happened or no . . . they exemplify . . . some human potentiality. . . . There are authors whose end is to tell what has happened. Mine, if I could attain it, would be to talk about what can happen." His sense of innovation in following not books but nature leads him to use new words (now long familiar) for his activity: "We *naturalists*" value invention far more than quotation. "If I were of the trade, I would *naturalize* art" as much as the bookish theorists "artify nature."

He has noted that authors' criticisms of their books are really maternal love taps; but he needs more freedom in this, because his writings are part of his behavior and must be portrayed. His confidences grow more frequent and candid, partly because he is not writing new essays but studying the old, partly because he is franker and has lived longer with his plan.

He calls his book a memory of paper, a record of his illness that sometimes gives him hope when things look bad. His gifts to it are irrevocable; it is his child: "It may know a good many things that I no longer know. . . . If I am wiser than it, it is richer than I." Those who praise him for his style are really damning the sense. He is proud of his rich material; no man has ever penetrated his own more deeply or plucked it cleaner. "I am much mistaken . . . if any writer has sown his materials more substantially or at least more thickly on his paper. In order to get more in, I pile up only the headings of subjects. . . . My stories and quotations . . . often bear, outside of my subject, the seeds of a richer and bolder material, and sound obliquely a subtler note, both for myself, who do not wish to express anything more, and for those who get my drift."

Order is less important than weight and utility: "Fine materials are always in place, wherever you sow them." His book is always one; but in each new edition, to give the reader his money's worth, "I allow myself to add, since it is only an ill-fitted patchwork, some extra ornaments. These are only overweights, which do not condemn the original form, but give some special value to each of the subsequent ones, by a bit of ambitious subtlety."

Two chapters in particular show how much more Montaigne now sees and reveals about his plan. He had ended "Of Practice" (II: 6), even in 1588, by saying that his writing is his study, not his teaching, a lesson not for others but for himself. Now he goes on to discuss his plan at length: "It is a thorny undertaking, and more so than it seems, to follow a movement so wandering as that of our mind, to penetrate the opaque depths of its innermost folds, to pick out and immobilize the innumerable flutterings that agitate it. . . . There is no description equal in difficulty, or certainly in usefulness, to the description of oneself." Superficial self-study fosters conceit; the serious kind is humbling. Candor must be the rule: "If I seemed to myself good and wise or nearly so, I would shout it out at the top of my voice." His trade and his art is living; he must be free to tell what he has learned of it. "What I chiefly portray is my cogitations, a shapeless subject that does not lend itself to expression in actions. It is all I can do to couch my thoughts in this airy medium of words. . . . I expose myself entire: my portrait is a cadaver. . . . It is not my deeds that I write down; it is myself, it is my essence." Self-portrayal makes a man arrange himself to appear in public; thus since Montaigne is constantly describing himself, he is constantly adorning himself.

The formative aspect of self-portrayal becomes even clearer in "Giving the Lie" (II: 18). In the 1580 version, to which he added little in 1588, Montaigne had said that his portrait was meant only for a library nook, to amuse a friend. In his final additions he defends his project: "Have I wasted my time by taking stock of myself so continually, so carefully? For those who go over themselves only in

their minds and occasionally in speech do not penetrate to essentials
in their examination as does a man who makes that his study, his
work, and his trade, who binds himself to keep an enduring account, with all his faith, with all his strength." It has diverted him
from annoying thoughts, given him purpose and discipline—he
listens to his reveries because he has to record them—and led him to
study not to make a book, but because he has made one, not to form
his opinions, but to confirm those already formed. The main effect
has been this: "In modeling this figure upon myself, I have had to
fashion and compose myself so often to bring myself out, that the
model itself has to some extent grown firm and taken shape. Painting
myself for others, I have painted my inward self with colors clearer
than my original ones. I have no more made my book than my book
has made me—a book consubstantial with its author, concerned
with my own self, an integral part of my life."

In religious matters Montaigne is still deferential but a little
freer now. He never did make the changes that the papal censors
suggested, but added two notes in his own defense and enlarged his
introductory disclaimer in "Prayers" (I: 56) to welcome official condemnation or approval and disown as execrable anything he may have
said, "ignorantly or inadvertently, against the holy prescriptions of
the Catholic, Apostolic, and Roman Church, in which I die and in
which I was born."

Now his criticism of Protestant motives becomes devastating.
He doubts that there has been a man so unintelligent as to believe
"that he was moving toward reformation by the worst of deforma-
tions; that he was heading for his salvation by the most express
ways that we have of very certain damnation; that by overthrowing
the government, the authorities, and the laws under whose tutelage
God has placed him, by dismembering his mother and giving the
pieces to her ancient enemies to gnaw on, by filling the hearts of
brothers with parricidal hatreds, by calling the devils and the furies
to his aid, he could bring help to the sacrosanct sweetness and justice
of the divine word." But if they are most to blame, their opponents
are little better. Both sides twist religion so cynically to suit their
passions that any real doctrinal difference between them seems incredible. He has seen them exchange places over the right to revolt
against their king, the Protestants claiming it under Henry III and

the Catholics under Henry IV: "See the horrible impudence with which we bandy divine reasons about, and how irreligiously we have both rejected them and taken them again, according as fortune has changed our place in these public storms." Men use the religion of love and mercy as a pretext for wickedness: "We willingly accord to piety only the services that flatter our passions. There is no hostility that excels Christian hostility. Our zeal does wonders when it is seconding our leaning toward hatred, cruelty, ambition, avarice, detraction, rebellion. Against the grain, toward goodness, benignity, moderation, unless as by a miracle some rare nature bears it, it will neither walk nor fly. Our religion is made to extirpate vices; it covers them, fosters them, incites them."

Lastly, Montaigne's final additions clearly bring out his independent, practical morality. "Since philosophy," he writes, "has not been able to find a way to tranquillity that is suitable to all, let everyone seek it individually."

His emphasis on our duty to ourselves is stronger than ever. We worry over cosmic generalities, he finds, which get along nicely without us, and we leave behind "our own affairs and Michel, who concerns us even more closely than man in general." Old people especially should turn the offices of friendship inward. Anyone who knows himself—as he must if he is to do his job as a man—puts aside extraneous business and "loves and cultivates himself before anything else."

Montaigne intensifies his praise of pleasure as a form of profit which we should treasure and extend in every way possible. He loves to remind men that the goal even of virtue is "voluptuousness," and to "beat their ears" with that word. Here too he uses correctives to aim for balance. He seeks equanimity in the face of both pain and pleasure. To an old man like himself, even as he preaches self-indulgence he is preaching self-control: "Let him indulge and care for himself, and especially govern himself, respecting and fearing his reason and his conscience, so that he cannot make a false step in their presence without shame."

When he speaks of pleasure as the object of virtue, it is in a special sense, since to him virtue is itself the highest of pleasures. That "other baser sort of voluptuousness" should have no monopoly on the name; its enjoyment is watery and weak, its hardships great, and the ensuing satiety equivalent to penance. True virtue is gay and joyous:

Virtue . . . is not, as the schoolmen say, set on the top of a steep, rugged, inaccessible mountain. . . . On the contrary . . . she is established in a beautiful plain, fertile and flowering, from where, to be sure, she sees all things beneath her; but you can get there, if you know the way, by shady, grassy, sweetly flowering roads, pleasantly, by an easy smooth slope, like that of the celestial vaults. It is because they have not associated with this virtue—this supreme, beautiful, triumphant, loving virtue, as delightful as she is courageous, a professed and implacable enemy of sourness, displeasure, fear, and constraint, having nature for her guide, fortune and pleasure for companions—that some men in their weakness have made up this stupid, sad, quarrelsome, sullen, threatening, scowling image and set it on a rock, in a solitary place, among the brambles: a phantom to frighten people.
      . . . She is the nursing mother of human pleasures. By making them just, she makes them sure and pure. By moderating them, she keeps them in breath and appetite. By withdrawing the ones she refuses, she makes us keener for the ones she allows us; and she allows us abundantly all those that nature wills. . . . She knows how to be rich and powerful and learned, and lie on perfumed mattresses. She loves life, she loves beauty and glory and health. But her own particular task is to know how to enjoy those blessings with temperance, and to lose them with fortitude: a task far more noble than harsh, without which the course of any life is denatured, turbulent, and deformed, and fit to be associated with those dangers, those brambles, and those monsters.

For all Montaigne's love of paradox and self-depreciation, his strong moral convictions are clear. A central commitment is to integrity. He refuses to break a promise even if extracted by fear. He believes that even a weak man can achieve anything whatever except "order, moderation, and constancy." Since inconsistency is one form that hypocrisy may take, he hopes to keep his death from "saying anything that my life has not already said."

Integrity also implies truth. This, Montaigne says, is the wisdom of his lesson. His soul hates "even to think a lie." He rejects false values and views because he considers falsity a great evil. "Truth is the first and fundamental part of virtue. We must love it for itself."

Montaigne's other great and ever-growing complex of values centers in naturalness and humanness. For him nature is the benign agent of God in his creation: "In this universe . . . the goodness and capacity of the governor should free us absolutely and fully from worrying about his government. . . . As she [Nature] has furnished us with feet to walk with, so has she given us wisdom to guide us in life. . . . The more simply we trust to Nature, the more wisely we trust to her."

The test of man is his humanness. The fools who regard our being as vice illustrate the singular accord between "supercelestial thoughts and subterranean conduct." Montaigne's faith is in the highroad of humanity; the ecstasies and daemon even of a Socrates alarm him. Belief is of little moment; our conduct is why we are here; and for conduct Montaigne now criticizes the motivation of law and even of religion as a kind of slave morality. He wants a virtue born of reason, all our own.

Shall I say this in passing: that I see held in greater price than it is worth a certain idea of scholastic probity, almost the only one practiced among us, a slave to precepts, held down beneath fear and hope? What I like is the virtue that laws and religions do not make but perfect and authorize, that feels in itself enough to sustain itself without help, born in us from its own roots, from the seed of universal reason that is implanted in every man who is not denatured. This reason, which straightens Socrates from his inclination to vice, makes him obedient to the men and gods who command in his city, courageous in death not because his soul is immortal but because he is mortal. It is a ruinous teaching for any society, and much more harmful than ingenious and subtle, which persuades the people that religious belief is enough, by itself and without morals, to satisfy divine justice. Practice makes us see an enormous distinction between devoutness and conscience.

His pride in humanness fills his chapter on repentance, where he now says that his conscience is content with itself, "not as the conscience of an angel or a horse, but as the conscience of a man," and rejects the gouty morality of age:

Miserable sort of remedy, to owe our health to disease! . . .

. . . It is living happily, not . . . dying happily, that constitutes human felicity. I have made no effort to attach, monstrously, the tail of a philosopher to the head and body of a dissipated man; or that this sickly remainder of my life should disavow and belie its fairest, longest, and most complete part. I want to present and show myself uniformly throughout. If I had to live over again, I would live as I have lived. I have neither tears for the past nor fears for the future. . . . I have seen the grass, the flower, and the fruit; now I see the dryness—happily, since it is naturally.

For the great thing in life is living—simply, gratefully, as human beings. To do so is the key to happiness and our noblest task:

We are great fools. "He has spent his life in idleness," we say; "I have done nothing today." What, have you not lived? That is not only the fundamental but the most illustrious of your occupations. "If I had been placed in a position to manage great affairs, I would have shown what I could do." Have you been able to think out and manage your own life? You have done the greatest task of all. To show and exploit her resources Nature has no need of fortune; she shows herself equally on all levels and behind a curtain as well as without one. To compose our character is our duty, not to compose books, and to win, not battles and provinces, but order and tranquillity in our conduct. Our great and glorious masterpiece is to live appropriately. All other things, ruling, hoarding, building, are only little appendages and props, at most.

Montaigne's resolve to express himself wholly makes him readier now to modify or contradict some of his early views. His criticism of asceticism is keener: he condemns Spurina's self-mutilation because his beauty aroused carnal desire as "in a sense dying to escape the trouble of living well." His anti-Stoical sallies become sharper: "The true image of Stoic virtue" (Cato the Elder) becomes "That censor and corrector of others." The extreme withdrawal expressed in his early remark "The greatest thing in the world is to know how to belong to oneself," though not contradicted, is not reaffirmed; and one of the final additions tends to modify it: "He who lives not at all unto others, hardly lives unto himself." He no longer blames our unhappiness on our mind itself. His illness had led him to write in 1579 that "most of the faculties of our soul trouble the repose of our life more than they serve it." Now, after "our soul," he adds: "as we employ them."

We noted earlier how Montaigne's conviction of the arbitrariness of the soul, at first a proof that we cannot have perfect knowledge, after 1588 becomes a guarantee of our power to be happy. His final statement virtually contradicts the original version of I: 14, "That the Taste of Good and Evil Depends in Large Part on the Opinion We Have of Them." At first he had found this statement often true of death, but not of pain, which we can only tense ourselves against and resist. Now when he returns to this essay he has found the solution. He does not change his statement that our contentment lies in the soul; but since opinion gives value to things, his earlier reasons are reversed. Whatever the soul might accomplish by resistance, he now sees its power in its caprice, which we can mold:

The soul is the one and sovereign mistress of our condition and conduct. . . . It may be shaped into all varieties of forms, and molds to itself and to its every condition the feelings of the body and all other accidents. Therefore we must study it and look into it, and awaken in it its all-powerful springs. There is no reason, prescription, or might that has power against its inclination and its choice. Out of the many thousands of attitudes at its disposal, let us give it one conducive to our repose and preservation, and we shall be not only sheltered from all harm, but even gratified and flattered, if it please, by ills and pains. The soul profits from everything without distinction. Error and dreams serve it usefully, being suitable stuff for giving us security and contentment.

Each man is as well or as badly off as he thinks. "Fortune does us neither good nor harm; she only offers us the material and the seed of them, which our soul, more powerful than she, turns and applies as it pleases, sole cause and mistress of its happy or unhappy condition."

He returns to this happy paradox in "Democritus and Heraclitus" (I: 50), where it fits less well, though related by the theme of our inanity.

Things in themselves may have their own weights and measures and qualities; but once inside, within us, she [the soul] allots them their qualities as she sees fit. Death is frightful to Cicero, desirable to Cato, a matter of indifference to Socrates. Health, conscience, authority, knowledge, riches, beauty, and their opposites—all are stripped on entry and receive from the soul new clothing, and the coloring that she chooses—brown, green, bright, dark, bitter, sweet, deep, superficial—and which each individual soul chooses; for they have not agreed together on their styles, rules, and forms; each one is queen in her realm. Wherefore let us no longer make the external qualities of things our excuse; it is up to us to reckon them as we will. Our good and our ill depend on ourselves alone.

We have noted Montaigne's early insistence that "The goal of our career is death. It is the necessary object of our aim." By 1588, after seeing the peasants in the plague, he urged us to stop worrying and let nature take charge. In the final additions he flatly contradicts his early view. Now learning to die is only a minor concern.

If we have not known how to live, it is wrong to teach us how to die, and make the end inconsistent with the whole. If we have known how to live steadfastly and tranquilly, we shall know how to die in the same way. . . . It seems to me that death is indeed the end, but not therefore the goal, of life; it is its finish, its extremity, but not therefore its object. Life should be an aim unto itself. . . . Among the many other duties comprised in this general and principal chapter on knowing how to live is this article on knowing how to die; and it is one of the lightest, if our fear did not give it weight.

Montaigne now contradicts his early view that pain is always to be avoided. In 1588 he emphasized its interdependence with pleasure and urged men to blend the two harmoniously. His final additions go much further. To reject pain is now to reject life and man's estate. Once he had written in the "Apology": "The wretchedness of our condition . . . makes the extremest pleasure not touch us so much as a slight pain. . . . To have no ill is to have the most good that man can hope for." He never changed this passage; but as he read it over after 1588 his sense of the goodness of life made him add this rebuttal: "I am glad not to be sick; but if I am, I want to know I am; and if they cauterize or incise me, I want to feel it. In truth, he who would eradicate the knowledge of evil would at the same time extirpate the knowledge of pleasure, and in fine would annihilate man. . . . Evil is in its turn a good to man. Neither is pain always something for him to flee, nor pleasure always for him to pursue."

One of Montaigne's final additions is, if I read it rightly, more properly a substitution; not a contradiction, but a corrective that has the force of one. Twice in the "Apology" he speaks of *"le vulgaire"* (the vulgar, the common herd), apropos of their credulity. Here is the original version of both passages:

[1.] For the vulgar (and almost everyone is of this sort), not having the faculty of judging things in themselves and by reason, let themselves be carried away by chance and by appearances, when once they have been given the temerity to despise and judge the opinions that they had held in extreme reverence, such as are those in which their salvation is concerned.

[2.] To believe all likelihoods that we cannot shake off is a great simplicity. The result of that would be that all the vulgar and the common people would have their belief as easy to turn as a weathercock; for their soul, being soft and without resistance, would be forced to receive incessantly more and more different impressions, the last one always effacing the traces of the preceding one.

In his last years Montaigne crossed out, in passage 1, "(and almost everyone is of this sort)." In passage 2, after "the vulgar," he deleted "and the common people" and added "—and we are all of the vulgar—." He probably made the two changes at different times; they are over a hundred pages apart, and the ink seems different;

but their similar context and content suggests a substitution. To the obvious question, "Why didn't he simply change his statement in passage 1?" the answer is equally obvious: to change it there would imply that he was a Protestant on his way to atheism; and he was anything but that.

He was trained as a humanist in the sixteenth-century sense: as a lover of Greek and Roman antiquity and humane letters, eager to learn the wisdom of the ancient masters. Humanistic in this sense are his friendship with La Boétie, his inscription on retiring, his bookish early essays, and the Stoical coloration of his early thought. Now the typical humanist's view of the vulgar was dim; the ancients had taught him that they were to be hated and thrust aside. Montaigne's vulgar are not a social class; he finds democratic rule the most natural and equitable and goodness commonest among the humble. Primarily his vulgar are the unthinking opposites of the philosophic sage.

His remarks about them before 1580 are almost always disdainful. He marvels to find occasional bravery and goodness in the crude herd, the soft and effeminate mob. They are as gullible as children, a prey to frivolous delusions and to the insane imaginings of fear; their opinions and complaints are to be shunned; they are slaves to custom; their refusal to think of death is a "brutish stupidity." The cruelty of the beastly rabble in victory is an ugly product of cowardice. Their conduct is base and vile. In the "Apology" he refuses to consider "the people . . . who are not conscious of themselves, who do not judge themselves, who leave most of their natural faculties idle." He finds "more distance . . . than between heaven and earth" separating the sage from "the mob of our men, ignorant, stupid, and asleep, base, servile, full of fever and fright, unstable and continually floating in the tempest of the diverse passions that push and drive them; depending entirely on others."

After 1580 Montaigne has less criticism, and much praise, of the *vulgaire*. He recognizes a difference between his kind and theirs, but only to insist on the need to talk their language. If we scorn to adapt ourselves to "humble and vulgar souls" we should keep out of all affairs, since all are worked out with such souls—"and the humble and vulgar ones are often as well-regulated as the subtler ones." More and more he places them on the side of nature. From the most vulgar and natural motives Socrates built the finest life ever. Nature's traces may still be seen in "that rustic mob of unpolished men." If it is stupidity that makes them brave, we had better hold a school of it.

There is irony in all this, of course, and also semantic change, since now Montaigne's favorite *vulgaire* is the peasants, obedient to nature and thus true philosophers. But the real change is this: now it is with the common people that he proudly identifies himself. He is "of the common sort," he writes twice—once to add "except in that I consider myself so." His life is "common and private," his soul "low and common," his opinions and conduct "low and humble." Now he urges anyone incapable of Stoical impassibility to "take refuge in the bosom of this plebeian [*populaire*] stupidity of mine." Now the term *vulgaire* is often virtually synonymous with *human*. And this, as we have seen, is Montaigne's highest praise.

The most striking example of his final attitude is the change he made in the "Apology" from "almost everyone is of this sort" to "we are all of the vulgar." The new statement is a sally, to be sure. But now it is *we*, not *they*, who belong to the vulgar; now Montaigne includes in it all mankind—and he is proud of mankind. The human values that he most admires lead him to equate the vulgar with humanity. This is the final step in the growth of his confidence, in the humanization of the humanist.

N THE LAST TWO YEARS of his life (1591–92) age and illness confined Montaigne increasingly to his château. His mind had never been more vigorous and incisive, as the final additions to the *Essays* prove; but his body was crumbling. Both his letters of 1590 to his new king show him at home; the second shows him ill. His old dream of Venice was fading. He still enjoyed his favorite associations, with attractive men, women, and books. His visitors seem to have included old friends—Florimond de Raemond, Pierre de Brach—and two more recent ones, the preacher Pierre Charron and the Englishman Anthony Bacon, older brother of the future essayist and chancellor; his correspondents, Marie de Gournay, Justus Lipsius, and Arnauld d'Ossat, the future cardinal and agent of Henry IV's abjuration.

He lived to be a grandfather. One spring Sunday (May 27) in 1590 his only child, now eighteen, the slender, retiring Léonor, was married at the château, in the presence of her parents and the groom's father, to a thirty-year-old nobleman, François de la Tour. After spending almost four weeks more at the château they set out one Saturday at daybreak (because of the extreme heat) for her

new home in Saintonge. Their first child, soon conceived, was born
at La Tour on March 31, 1591, and baptized by François's uncle
and Léonor's mother, who named the baby Françoise after herself.
Montaigne's account reads as though he was not there; he had just
finished work on Trans's will, and he may not have been well. Young
Françoise was to marry and die in childbirth; Montaigne's other
grandchild, Marie de Gamaches, was to continue the line of descent,
which is still unbroken.

Montaigne was prepared to live with illness. He had watched
"colds, gouty discharges, looseness, palpitations of the heart, mi-
graines, and other ailments . . . grow old and die a natural death"
within him. Other diseases, like the stone, were still vigorous. His
policy was to live and let live, since we die not of illness but of
being alive, and the stone may be as fond of life as we are. "Let us
give Nature a chance," he writes; "she knows her business better
than we do. 'But so-and-so died of it.' So will you, if not of that
disease, of some other. And how many have not failed to die of it,
with three doctors at their backsides?" Illness is nature's gentle way
of weaning men from life; when you shake hands with death every
month, you may well hope that "being so often led to the port,
confident that you are still within the accustomed limits, some morning you and your confidence will have crossed the water unawares."
The kidney stone, Montaigne's companion for fourteen years until his
death, allows us complete freedom; at its worst he has held out ten
hours on horseback: "Just bear it, you need no other regimen. Play,
dine, run, do this and do that too, if you can; your dissipation will
do more good than harm." The euphoria after voiding a stone so
far outweighs the preceding pain as to make Montaigne claim that
"Nature has lent us pain for the honor and service of pleasure and
painlessness." In his final years he finds pain and pleasure fully inter-
dependent and equally necessary, and watches his life fade away
without regret or fear: "I have seen the grass, the flower, and the
fruit; now I see the dryness—happily, since it is naturally."

Montaigne died at his château on September 13, 1592. We have
no eyewitness account, and must depend mainly on Estienne Pasquier,
who was then in Tours and may have learned the details from Montaigne's widow:

He died in his house of Montaigne, where a quinsy attacked his tongue in such a way that he remained three whole days full of understanding but unable to speak. As a result he was forced to have recourse to his pen to make his wishes known. And as he felt his end approaching, he wrote a little note asking his wife to summon a few gentlemen neighbors of his, so as to take leave of them. When they had arrived, he had Mass said in his room; and when the priest came to the elevation of the *Corpus Domini,* this poor gentleman rose up as best he could in his bed, with a desperate effort, hands clasped; and in this last action gave up his spirit to God. Which was a fine mirror of his inmost soul.

A student of local customs, Bernard Automne, adds a piquant item:

The late Montaigne, author of the *Essays,* feeling the end of his days draw near, got up out of bed in his nightshirt; taking his dressing gown, opened his study, had all his valets and other legatees called in, and paid them the legacies he had left them in his will, foreseeing the difficulties his heirs would make over paying the legacies.

Our earliest dated reports are two letters from Montaigne's devoted friend Pierre de Brach, to Anthony Bacon (October 10, 1592) and to Justus Lipsius (February 4, 1593). These are not accounts, however, but tributes and laments. Brach has lost the best of his friends, France "the most whole and vigorous mind it ever had," and the world "the true pattern and mirror of pure philosophy." Thus to Bacon; and to Lipsius: the loss and the bitterness are ours alone, for Montaigne "tasted and took death with sweetness," bringing a happy life to a happy close. Brach is sure of this, having seen Montaigne on the brink of death in Paris a few years earlier. Besides the stone, a hopeless case of gout would have made any further life a life of pain. Two factual details emerge: the last letter Montaigne received was Bacon's, which Brach sent him but death kept him from answering; and Montaigne mentioned Brach in his very last words, "which makes me regret all the more not having been there, since he said he was sorry not to have anyone with him to whom he could disclose the last notions of his soul."

Lipsius, breaking the news to Marie de Gournay nine months after the event (June, 1593), echoes Brach's theme of "Montaigne's gain, our loss," but gives no further information. Marie adds that Montaigne had sent her a tender farewell, which, entrusted to his brother Pierre de la Brousse, had been lost on the road. Her grief was of course extreme, as Raemond and Pasquier also testify, and her eagerness for details so great that she went to Chartres just to learn them from his cousin Bussaguet, only to find that he had not been present. No further facts emerge from the tributes of de Thou, Malvin de Cessac, and Florimond de Raemond. Raemond would like to praise Montaigne in verse but modestly leaves that honor to the abler Pierre de Brach. He laments the loss of a "vivid and incomparable light of learning, eloquence, and capacity for the affairs of the world," and singles out for special praise Montaigne's courage in great pain, his "exquisite and prompt judgment, and his delightful conversation."

We have no reason to question Pasquier's account or the details added by Brach and Marie de Gournay. Automne's item about the legacies sounds like gossip but may well contain at least a kernel of truth. It is striking how unanimous Montaigne's friends are in praising his cheerful courage in the face of acute pain and death. Much as he loved life, death must have been in some measure a release. That he died as a good Catholic is exactly what we would expect.

The funeral arrangements are noted in the *Ephemeris*. "His heart was placed in the church of Saint-Michel [de Montaigne], and Françoise de La Chassaigne, his widow, had his body taken to Bordeaux and buried in the church of the Feuillants, where she had a raised tomb built for him, and bought the rights for this from the church." The choice of the Feuillants is surprising on the face of it; for on December 15, 1592, the canons of the Bordeaux cathedral of Saint-André had authorized the family to bury Montaigne there. However, their approval was tentative and likely to be overruled by the archbishop. Since the order of the Feuillants was new and still somewhat insecure, they were probably readier to accept a tomb on the conditions that the family wanted. Most important, the order was noted for its loyalism. Further details, negotiated by the ever-faithful brother Pierre, provide for the construction, in front of the main altar, of a cave to hold not only Montaigne's body but later those of his wife and descendants; the erection of a sepulchral monument above it; the display of Montaigne's coat of arms; and regular Masses on his behalf. His body was laid to rest there on May 1, 1593. About ten years later, however, work began on an enlargement of the church that left the tomb remote from the main altar. Montaigne's widow had to bring suit to gain a satisfactory place in exchange, in and under the new Saint-Bernard chapel, nearest to the main altar on the left. In 1614 Montaigne's tomb and remains were moved there; and there his widow and daughter were buried later.

The Revolution brought a comic contretemps. In 1800 the authorities decided that Montaigne was too good a *philosophe* to remain buried in a church among the *ci-devant* enemies of enlightenment. Citizen Thibaudeau, Prefect of the Gironde, ordained a fresh burial in the hall of monuments of the *ci-devant* Academy (the Bordeaux Society of Sciences, Letters, and Arts) after a ceremonious procession involving eighteen groups in all, from cavalry with trumpets to a platoon of Basques and cavalry. Two and a half years later, however, Joseph Montaigne, a descendant of Michel, reported to the new Prefect, Delacroix, that the baron de Caila of the Bordeaux Academy had given his colleagues conclusive proof that a mistake had been made. The ashes moved were positively not those of Montaigne but presumably those of a niece of his by marriage, Marie de Brian, widow of his nephew Guy de Lestonnac. At Joseph Montaigne's request, permission was granted to return the niece's ashes and reconstruct a mausoleum over those of Montaigne.

The tomb, already in disrepair when a big fire in May, 1871 destroyed the church, lay bare for almost ten years thereafter. Then in December, 1880, it was officially opened; the lead shell holding Montaigne's remains was found to be so eroded that the bones were exposed; it was placed inside a marked oak coffin. After five years in temporary quarters in the Depository of the Charterhouse, it was installed (March 11, 1886) in the entrance hall of the new building of the Faculties of Theology, Science, and Letters of the University of Bordeaux, where it still stands, only a few yards from its original site. A rectangular sarcophagus, resting on a pedestal, bears the recumbent statue of Montaigne in full armor, hands joined in prayer, helmet behind his head, gauntlets at his sides, a lion couchant at his feet. On either side above his coat of arms are epitaphs, probably by the Bordeaux lawyer Jean de Saint-Martin, one in Greek verse, the other in Latin prose. In the one in Greek Montaigne addresses the passer-by in a pompous vein that he would have deplored, stressing his alliance of Pyrrho's skepticism with the dogma of Christ. More to the point, the Latin notes his "gentle ways, keen mind, ever-ready eloquence, and incomparable judgment"; credits him with unswerving attachment to the religion of his ancestors and the laws of his country, but still with being a friend not only to "the greatest kings, the leading personages of France," but also to "the leaders of the parties of error"; and concludes:

Having never injured anyone, incapable of flattery or insult, he remains dear to all alike; and since all his life he had professed a wisdom proof against all the threats of pain, so, having come to the supreme combat, after struggling long and courageously against a pain that tormented him without respite, setting his actions in accord with his precepts, he concluded, with God's help, a fine life by a fine end.

Françoise de La Chassaigne, left a prey, alas, to perpetual mourning, has erected this monument to the memory of this husband whom rightly she regrets. He had no other wife; she will have had no other husband.

As Marie de Gournay emphatically attests, Madame de Montaigne showed the same devotion to her husband's book as to his ashes. He had left not only the thousand-odd pages that now compose the Bordeaux Copy, with their thousand-odd additions and myriad other revisions, but also all the extra slips of paper. A careful examination convinced the widow and their daughter, Léonor (herself widowed in 1594), that they needed the hand of someone versed in letters like Pierre de Brach, who consented to help. He proved his devotion and won Marie's gratitude by "always carefully assisting Mme de Montaigne in the first concern for its [the book's] fortune, interrupting for that activity the poetry with which he honors his Gascony." The result was this: "A year and a half after the death of Montaigne, the widow and only daughter of this great man sent the *Essays* to Mlle de Gournay, then retired in Paris, to have them printed, asking her to come to see them afterward, so as to take full and mutual possession of the friendship by which the deceased had bound the three of them together; which she did, and stayed fifteen months with them."

We do not know just what version of the *Essays* Marie de Gournay received in Paris early in 1594 and carefully saw through the presses of Abel L'Angelier by the end of that year; it has evidently been lost. It was not the Bordeaux Copy; that is too different from her edition, and is probably the "other copy" she speaks of "that remains in his house" and that she claims would attest the fidelity of her edition. Strowski thought it must be a copy of the Bordeaux Copy, made by Pierre de Brach or under his direction; but Zeitlin, whose analysis of the variants is the most thorough we have in print, rejects this hypothesis mainly because many readings of the 1595 edition appeared at first on the Bordeaux Copy but were later changed there. On his theory, Montaigne had two working versions of the *Essays*, the Bordeaux Copy and another, which he kept fairly near identical; where they differ, the Bordeaux Copy shows his final intent. Pierre de Brach recognized the latter as the more authentic of the two, decided to keep it and send the other, and therefore corrected the other from it, but often not thoroughly enough. It was this "other copy" that Marie de Gournay used for her 1595 edition; she never saw the Bordeaux Copy until later, when she made the long-awaited, hazardous trip across France to the home of her dead "father" and spent a year and a quarter with the widow and daughter.

Although Marie, in deference to the taste of the age of Richelieu, made a few minor changes in the last (1635) of her many editions, it still was basically her 1595 edition that *was* the *Essays* for almost three centuries. For two of these the Bordeaux Copy, left by Montaigne's widow to the Feuillants of Bordeaux, lay virtually unnoticed in their library, mentioned in print in 1773 and 1777 but little used. Early in the Revolution it was transferred to the Bordeaux Municipal Library, where it has remained to this day. Diderot's friend Naigeon was the first to use it for an edition (in 1802); but he did a poor job and made things worse by the violence of his introduction. Scholars began to take note of the Bordeaux Copy, but only to reject it, partly because of Naigeon and partly through a bewildering blindness to Montaigne's humor. In his chapter on education (I: 26) he had written that if his pupil should prefer dancing or ball-playing to jousting, "I see no other remedy than for his tutor to strangle him early, if there are no witnesses, or apprentice him to a pastry cook in some good town, even though he were the son of a duke." In the 1595 edition, for reasons unknown, the passage "to strangle him, if there are no witnesses, or" is omitted; so it naturally became a touchstone. Even Naigeon took it in earnest as "one of those acts of rigor which the public interest and reasons of state sometimes demand and always justify," since sometimes it would have forestalled bloodshed and disaster. Another editor, de l'Aulnaye, cited it as a variant "no doubt torn from Montaigne by an impulse rather of indignation than of philosophical reflection." Johanneau quoted it in his edition as a variant with Naigeon's comment; after which his publisher Lefèvre summed up the views of French Montaigne scholars a century and a half ago:

If this passage, which is indeed very remarkable, is not found in the other editions, the reason is no doubt that it was not preserved by Montaigne, whose mind was too enlightened not to recognize, after some reflection, the horrible abuses that the use of such a *remedy* would produce. Its suppression is another proof that the manuscript published by Mademoiselle de Gournay is later than the annotations written by Montaigne on the copy of the 1588 edition that M. Naigeon followed.

It took almost another century before the Bordeaux Copy, thanks to the studies of Reinhold Dezeimeris and others, was fully recognized as the best text and reproduced in the magnificent Bordeaux Municipal Edition to serve as the basis for editions ever since.

The Montaigne that survives in the book has appeared to evolve like the Montaigne who wrote it: from the stoical, sententious "French Seneca" that his contemporaries most admired to the spokesman, in the seventeenth century, of the *honnête homme* and of Pyrrhonistic skepticism, to the self-portrayer that Rousseau both liked and resented, and to the exponent of an independent natural morality that a century of readers, from Sainte-Beuve to Gide, have found in him.

To Montaigne, the reception of the *Essays* was gratifying; to Marie de Gournay, disappointing. The reason is not merely that the author was satisfied with much less than his worshipful editor; it was partly that Montaigne was referring mainly to the *Essays* of 1580, Marie to those of 1588. What to us is the derivative Stoicality of the earliest *Essays* is what delighted his first readers; what to us is the originality of Book III and the additions seemed to them just short of dotage. Estienne Pasquier is our best witness to his friend's impact on his contemporaries:

He was a bold person who followed his own advice, and as such he easily let himself be carried away by the beauty of his mind; so much so that in his writings he took pleasure in being pleasantly displeasing. Whence it happens that you will find in him several chapters whose heading bears no relation at all to the rest of the body, except the feet. . . . In just the same way he often allowed himself to use unfamiliar words, which, unless I am mistaken, he will not easily bring into fashion. . . . I have never been able to understand what he meant by that word *diversion*, on the model of

which however he offered us a very long chapter [III: 4]. But then what?
I will reply to all the above for him (for I want to be his advocate; and I
feel sure that if he were alive, he would not disavow me). Take of him
what is good . . . don't pay attention to the title, but to his treatment;
he brings you enough matter to content you. In this matter he meant de-
liberately to make sport of us, and perhaps of himself, by a particular freedom that was born with him.

. . . While he gives the appearance of disdaining himself, I never read
an author who esteemed himself as much as he. For if anyone had scratched
out all the passages he used to talk about himself and his family, his work
would be shortened by a good quarter, especially in his third book, which
seems to be a story of his ways and actions; a thing which I attribute rather
to the freedom of his old age when he composed it.

You will judge from all I have set forth to you above that since his
death the sieur de Montaigne has a professed enemy in me, who during his
lifetime considered myself very happy to be honored by his friendship. God
forbid. I love, respect, and honor his memory, as much as any other man
and more. And as for his *Essays* (which I call masterpieces), I have no book
in my hands that I have so fondled as that one. I always find something
in it to content me. He is another Seneca in our language. To all these
Gascon expressions and other unused words . . . I oppose an infinity of
fine bold French traits; an infinity of fine witty phrases, which are all his
own, according to the abundance of his content. And I still cannot be
offended when he lets himself go and talks about himself. It is said in such
a manner that I take as much pleasure in it as if he were speaking of another.
But above all, his book is a real seed-bed of fine and notable sayings. . . .*

What? Were there ever finer sayings in all antiquity than these? . . .
His whole book is not really a flower bed, arranged in various plots and
borders, but a sort of diversified prairie of many flowers, pell-mell and
without art.

The six criticisms that Marie de Gournay lists in her 1595
Preface as most prevalent are these: 1) "some usurpation of Latin,
and the fabrication of new words"; 2) "the licentiousness of his
remarks about ceremony"—meaning, apparently, about sex; 3) ob-
scurity; 4) "choppy, rambling developments, with no obligation to
treat one point fully"; 5) listing a heretic among the leading poets
of the time, or (adds Marie) "some other similarly trivial detail"; and
6), the "most general censure": "that, by a plan that is all his
own, the author portrays himself . . . even to the slightest details
of his education." Criticism 5 goes back to 1580–81 and the Master
of the Sacred Palace; the others are all in Pasquier, and all but one
in the passage just quoted. The main stumbling block is the self-

---

* Here Pasquier quotes eighteen sayings, more or less from memory.

portrait, which Pasquier attributes to the weakness of age and such readers as Du Puy, Baudier, and Scaliger greet with impatience. All the details of Montaigne's tastes and habits, as well as his lack of systematic order and of reverence for sheer learning, stung the rather heavy-handed erudites of his time, and neither they nor their descendants were soon ready to forgive.

In general, then, the first reception of the *Essays* was fairly good, though probably better in 1580 than in 1588, the plaudits varying in inverse proportion to the originality of the book. The only reader who wholeheartedly praises his self-portrait is Marie de Gournay. Though there is widespread admiration for his judgment and the charm of his style, his main appeal lies in his stoical maxims.

From the first, however, many readers were even more struck by Montaigne's challenge, especially in the "Apology for Raymond Sebond," to generally accepted views of man's powers and place in the universe. It was this, as well as the insights into human nature, that struck the English imagination and led to the borrowings (which Ben Jonson derides) by Bacon, Marston, Webster, Burton, many lesser writers, and even Shakespeare.

In France the center of attention was soon Montaigne's skepticism, both in general and in combination with Catholic faith. This is of course not new with Montaigne; but it was he more than anyone who brought it out of the schoolroom into the main stream of literature and thought. In its extreme form he himself warned against it, and it never became an official Catholic position; but for three quarters of a century it was a popular argument of the Counter Reformation against the Protestant appeal to individual reason and conscience; for if both sides were disarmed of the weapon of reason, a strong presumption remained on the side of the Church's long-established authority. As we have noted, the papal censors in 1580–81 made no criticism of Montaigne's fideism; and for years after his death it was drawn on freely by such Catholic apologists as Florimond de Raemond, Jean-Pierre Camus, and Pierre Charron.

Charron (1541–1603) deserves our special attention. A fiery and successful preacher, drawn to the League for a time after the killing of Guise, he had lived in Bordeaux in the 1580's and made friends with Montaigne, who, having no male child, authorized him to bear his coat of arms after his death; much later Charron left most of his

large estate to Montaigne's sister Léonor de Camain. Our one glimpse
of the two men together is curious. Just before the siege of Castillon,
on July 2, 1586, Charron was a guest in Montaigne's château, where
his host gave him a copy of a book which he had noted as being on
the Index, the *Cathechism* of the Italian Reformist Bernardino
Ochino.

Charron is remembered mainly for two books. In the year of
Henry IV's abjuration (1593) he answered Mornay's influential
Protestant *Truth of the Christian Religion* (1581) with *The Three
Truths,* which sought to prove the existence of God, man's need of
religion, and—in the main part, with a heavy debt to Montaigne's
Christian skepticism—the truth of Catholicism against Protestantism.
But his borrowing was far greater still in his major work, *Of Wisdom*
(1601), which more than one reader has called an analytical table of
contents of the *Essays.* Book One of this work, on the knowledge of
man, is an arrangement of Montaigne's remarks on the need for self-
knowledge, the inequality of men and their near equality with the
animals, and man's vanity, weakness, inconstancy, misery, and presumption. Book Two, on the general rules of wisdom, is still largely
Montaigne methodized; Book Three, on special rules of wisdom, is
less derivative but still increases Charron's debt.

Charron probably considered Montaigne's brilliant insights
wasted in the disorder of the *Essays* and hoped that the regular plan
of his own *Wisdom* would preserve them. Many readers felt this
way; and for two thirds of a century the two works were equally
popular, with new editions appearing at the same good pace. Though
his popularity may have cut down Montaigne's readership, it con-
tributed considerably to the diffusion of his thought. But in so doing
it altered its implications and context, making earnest conclusions
out of Montaigne's paradoxes and conjectures. Gone is the grace and
charm, the freedom of the self-portrait, the play with ideas. The
result is abstract and didactic; even the thought, reduced and de-
formed, often loses its subtlety; "What do I know?" becomes "I know
not." Montaigne's distinction between religious belief and morality
becomes a gulf in Charron. Meanwhile this common stress of theirs,
suited to an age of religious atrocities, came to seem, in more peaceful
times, a scandalous indifference. Even while Christian apologists were
still using Montaigne's fideistic arguments, Charron's *Wisdom,* four

years after it appeared, was placed on the Index (1605). Soon its enemies extended their attacks to the *Essays*, and in 1676 they were on
the Index too.

The challenge of Montaigne's skepticism to the seventeenth
century is best seen in two of his greatest readers, Descartes and
Pascal, who both start from it in their quest of certitude and of
faith. Descartes begins his *Discourse on Method* by applying seriously
Montaigne's paradox that good sense is evenly distributed, since all
men are satisfied with their share. He tells of turning from fallible
books to seek truth within himself; adopts a provisional morality
reminiscent of Montaigne's; uses his technique of moving from
modest autobiography ("this is a method I have found to work for
me") to assertive conclusiveness ("this method is valid for all"); and
bases the keystone of his system, "I think, therefore I am," on an act
of doubt; for this is indubitably an act of thought and thus a proof
of existence. Even where these resemblances cover important differences, they reveal Descartes's view of Montaigne as the man he had to
reckon with and whose skepticism he had to refute.

Pascal is even more steeped in Montaigne. Interviewed by M. de
Sacy for acceptance among the austere solitaries of Port-Royal, he
appears as the man of two authors, Epictetus and Montaigne. The
former knew man's greatness, the latter man's misery; but they contradict and do not complete each other. In the unfinished Apology
that we know as his *Pensées,* Pascal's debt to Montaigne is enormous
as he demonstrates man's frailty, fallibility, vanity, boredom, and
ignorance, and argues that in the realm of religion, where reason falls
short, our misery is such as to justify the wager of faith. Christianity
alone explains man's dual nature: his greatness as a child of God, his
misery since the fall.

However, in Sainte-Beuve's phrase, Montaigne remains the fox in
Pascal's bosom; for Pascal's "misery of man" is Montaigne's "human
condition," and no one can prove that we should not accept it gratefully instead of regarding it with horror. Pascal makes a powerful
case, especially in locating boredom at the center of the soul; but
within a century Voltaire takes Montaigne's side, and the debate still
goes on.

In seventeenth-century France Montaigne is not only the skeptic
but also the educator of the *honnête homme*. The French humanist
of the sixteenth century had been an erudite, solidly versed in Latin,

often in Greek, sometimes in Hebrew, and venerating the thought
and literature of Greco-Roman antiquity. It was not at all this reader
that Montaigne sought, but rather his *"honneste et habile homme,"*
the rounded, preferably wellborn man of experience and judgment.
Castiglione's influential *Courtier* and manuals like Guazzo's *Civil
Conversation* helped fashion this ideal in France; but as Thibaudet
wrote, "Montaigne, more than anyone else, created that public of
honnêtes gens capable of judging and tasting, constituted outside of
the learned, and against them. (17th century, Descartes, Pascal.)
Souls regulated and created by themselves, not from without. One
of the main effects, on the 17th century, of reading Montaigne will
consist precisely in emphasizing these human personal values, in sub-
stituting authentic humanism for the humanism of erudition."

Finally, Montaigne put such a spotlight on the human psyche as
it never had before and was never to lose again. It is striking that both
Descartes and Pascal based their arguments for knowledge and faith
on their analysis of the human soul. Followers of Montaigne in this
regard include La Fontaine, Mme de Sévigné, La Rochefoucauld, La
Bruyère, and Molière. More than anyone else, Montaigne set a whole
great literature on the trail of his favorite quarry, human behavior.

However, after almost a century of frequent publication, the
1669 edition of the *Essays* was the last to appear for fifty-five years;
and seven years later the book was put on the Index, where it still
remains. The condemnation probably reflected Montaigne's increasing
use by freethinkers, a growing mistrust of fideism, and the mounting
attacks on him by all kinds of theologians: not only Pascal but
Arnauld, Nicole, Bossuet, and Malebranche. Their censure, however,
may have had less to do with the eclipse of the *Essays* than the
growing insistence on regularity and decorum.

In the eighteenth century Montaigne came to seem less immediate and pertinent, more curious and quaint. Many who liked him
held that he could find a public only in selections in modern French.
The first regular edition, by Pierre Coste, was published in England
in 1724; it had only one successor, that of Bastien, though both were
often reprinted. His place on the Index and use by freethinkers led
to a stereotype popularized by Voltaire, which was to survive well
beyond the Revolution. A victim of the primitive age he lived in,
Montaigne is barred from the Temple of Taste by the naïve crudity
of his style. However, in a time of brutal fanaticism he had the

courage and wisdom to doubt; he was basically anti-Christian, a *philosophe* before the fact. For many who claim to know him, this cliché substitutes for a reading—at least of anything more than excerpts. When Voltaire defends his self-portrayal he is less concerned to praise Montaigne than to discredit Pascal.

He still has distinguished readers, however, some of whom show a new response. There are two pithy remarks by Montesquieu: "In most authors I see man writing; in Montaigne, man thinking"; and "The four great poets, Plato, Malebranche, Shaftesbury, Montaigne." Marivaux envied the freedom of his style. Diderot knew him well and borrowed from him with zest. The encyclopedist in him deplored Montaigne's skepticism, which made him lag in the pursuit of empirical knowledge; but he loved the pith and naturalness of Montaigne's organic, associative style; and in morality and esthetics, where truth was rarely demonstrable, he showed a comparable open-mindedness in the way he used the dialogue form.

Rousseau speaks of Montaigne seldom but uses him much, as an imperfect but often admirable ancestor. His impassioned attack on civilization in the name of nature often draws on Montaigne's ironic critique. In education he often looks back to Montaigne as he demands that it be rounded, enjoyable, liberating, a matter not merely of memorizing but of judging and doing. And despite their great differences in temperament and aim—Montaigne's dispassionate curiosity and sense of both individuality and typicality, Rousseau's painful confession, proud self-defense, and insistence on his own absolute uniqueness—Rousseau is keenly aware of Montaigne's self-portrait as he writes his own *Confessions,* which set off a tidal wave of self-portrayal and in the process legitimized that of Montaigne.

This did not, however, insure its popularity in the nineteenth century. The romantic sensibility fed on Montaigne's chapter on friendship; among countless others, George Sand loved it, and so, for a while, did Lamartine; but many readers found his constant appeal not to the heart but to the judgment rather cold. What renewed his popularity was the new esthetic. The quest for preneoclassical ancestors made it no longer disastrous to have written in French before 1636. Montaigne's organic, unsystematic order, his love of nature rather than art, his nonchalance, vigor, and concreteness, changed rapidly from regrettable weaknesses to rich beauties. Even as English criticism of Shakespeare was discarding the "diamond-in-the-rough" view, French readers of Montaigne came to see him less as capriciously naïve, more and more as profoundly consistent. The aura of quaintness once dispelled, he becomes again a mind to reckon with. Admirers of his style, now legion, include Sénancour, Mme de Staël, Chateaubriand, Nodier, Stendhal, George Sand, Michelet (who dislikes the man), Mérimée, Veuillot. Flaubert loves the masculine vigor of his sentences and compares him to an exquisite, unbearably succulent fruit whose juice goes straight to the heart.

What is more, Flaubert, like many others, goes beyond the style to the man. He keeps the *Essays* by his bedside, often reads them from cover to cover, and prescribes them as a source of strength and serenity. He calls Montaigne his "foster father" and identifies himself with him: "I am rereading Montaigne; it is singular how full I am of that fellow! We have the same tastes, the same opinions, the same way of life, the same manias. There are people I admire more than him, but there are none I would call back more gladly and have a better chat with."

In England and America, where Montaigne's personality and essay style attract such friends as Sterne, Byron, Hazlitt, Landor, Thackeray, Fitzgerald, Stevenson, and Pater, Emerson is one of his warmest admirers, and on many of the same grounds as Flaubert. Although, like his friend Carlyle, he deplores Montaigne's "gross, semisavage indecency," he finds his downright truthfulness as "wild and savoury as sweet fern" and recognizes himself in his pages. Of his first reading he writes: "It seemed to me as if I myself had written the book, in some former life, so sincerely it spoke to my thought and experience." In making "Montaigne; or, the Skeptic" one of his six *Representative Men,* he speaks out strongly for the sturdy honesty of thought that extends to his style: "The sincerity and marrow of the man reaches to his sentences. I know not anywhere the book that seems less written. . . . Cut these words, and they would bleed; they are vascular and alive."

The most influential nineteenth-century reader of Montaigne— and one of the most influenced—was Sainte-Beuve. He always delighted in Montaigne's style, that "perpetual figure, renewed at every step" by which "you receive ideas only in images." When in his early thirties, still wistful for religion, he undertook his searching study of Port-Royal, he met Montaigne head on in the context of Jansenism, examined him through Pascal's eyes—or, rather, through the eyes

which his own malaise lent to Pascal—and proclaimed him the great
tempter: a perfidious enemy of religion posing as its defender; the
first great spokesman for the unrepentant ego; the embodiment of
man's forgetfulness of God: "Nature complete without Grace."

In the last quarter century of his life, resigned to sharing Montaigne's supposed unbelief, Sainte-Beuve never repeated his charge of
perfidy. Montaigne remained a disillusioned sage whose wisdom, one
of the four forms of moral happiness and truth, was "the skepticism
that understands all things, that changes itself into each thing in
turn, and that conceives human thought as the dream of all things
and as creating the object of its dream." At sixty he wrote: "I have
reached the age at which death came to Horace, Montaigne, and
Bayle, my masters; I can die." He loved Montaigne's zest for life,
which elicited his highest praise:

> It is never a waste of time to accost him. . . . What a happy nature,
> curious, open to everything, detached from himself and the parochial, freed
> from illusion, cured of all stupidity, purged of all prejudice. And what
> serenity, indeed what blitheness, even in suffering and pains! What affability
> to all comers! What good sense in all matters! What vigor of mind! What
> a feeling for greatness, when appropriate! What boldness in him, and skill
> as well! I call Montaigne "the wisest Frenchman that ever lived."

The nineteenth century witnessed Montaigne's full acceptance
—personality, self-portrait, ideas, and style—as a great French classic.
And the heightened concern with history led to an extraordinary
period of Montaigne scholarship from the 1840's to World War I,
from Brunet and Payen to Dezeimeris, Malvezin, Bonnefon, and to
Armaingaud, Strowski, and Villey. Out of their painstaking findings
came a sharper, truer sense of the man, the time, and the book. Villey
and Strowski, with their view of an evolving Montaigne, showed that
his thought was responsible and consistent. Against the background
of religious strife, his fideism proved itself manifestly and simply
Catholic. New documents revealed a more vigilant mayor and active
negotiator than the *Essays* suggest. Our picture of him today, though
sketchy in many places, is firm and clear.

In the twentieth century Montaigne's presence seems more per-
vasive than ever. Where before, his foreign admirers had been mainly
Anglo-Saxons, now they abound in Holland, Germany, and Scandinavia; the earliest good edition of the *Travel Journal* was in Italian,
one of the best books on Montaigne is in German; he is read now in

Polish, in Russian, in Turkish, in Japanese, and many good Japanese scholars are at work on him. Such figures as André Gide and (with illustrations) Salvador Dali have published selections from his work. French admirers—to name but a few—have included such diverse authors as Alain and Anatole France, Duhamel and Malraux, Maurois and Montherlant. He was one of the two great literary heroes of Albert Thibaudet, who considered him the ancestor of his other hero, Bergson, edited him, and wrote on him extensively and with insight. Stefan Zweig considered him the patron saint of every free man on earth and started a book on him that he did not remain alive to finish. Justice Holmes was just one of his many American admirers. T. S. Eliot considered him "a very great figure" in that "he succeeded, God knows how . . . in giving expression to the skepticism of *every* human being." Aldous Huxley writes with loving insight on his mastery of the essay form:

By the time he had written his way into the Third Book he had reached the limits of his newly discovered art. . . . Free association artistically controlled—this is the paradoxical secret of Montaigne's best essays. One damned thing after another—but in a sequence that in some almost miraculous way develops a central theme and relates it to the rest of human experience. And how beautifully Montaigne combines the generalization with the anecdote, the homily with the autobiographical reminiscence! How skilfully he makes use of the concrete particular, the *chose vue,* to express some universal truth, and to express it more powerfully and penetratingly than it can be expressed by even the most oracular of the dealers in generalities!

Most readers are drawn by Montaigne's art of living and the breadth and depth of his self-portrait. "As the centuries go by," wrote Virginia Woolf, "there is always a crowd before that picture, gazing into its depths, seeing their own faces reflected in it, seeing more the more they look." And what they see, she goes on, is a source of serenity and cheer. "This great master of the art of life . . . achieved at last a miraculous adjustment of all these wayward parts that constitute the human soul. He laid hold of the beauty of the world with all his fingers. He achieved happiness."

André Gide was one of Montaigne's greatest modern admirers. He identified himself with him, as he knew others did: "To what a point I make him my own . . . it seems to me that he is myself. . . . In him each reader of the *Essays* recognizes himself." He cherished the sturdy integrity that made Montaigne, as he puts it, meet Pilate's atrocious question with a purely human version of Christ's answer "*I* am the truth." The main teaching he derived and took for his own is that "to be truthful is the beginning of a great virtue." He also relished his style, resolved never to travel without him, and once on a dull boat trip wrote of him: "Derived a little pleasure from life only with Montaigne, whom I am rereading rapidly with a view to an anthology . . . but at times rapture stops me, and I wonder if ever human writing has given me more amusement, satisfaction, and joy."

Montaigne's apparently complete acceptance today seems a little surprising. He scoffs at our faith in medicine, in science, in progress, in the perfectibility of human knowledge; doubts the efficacy of social and governmental change; questions the equality of man; and resists both involvement and our conviction that any involvement is a virtue. Yet the doctors, scholars, Protestants, reformers, and dogmatists whom he derided shrug off his criticisms as those of an erratic friend—or perhaps as applying only to the other fellow—and still cherish him. He has so few enemies that it is almost alarming. But he saw no value in enmity, and there are good reasons for his congeniality today.

Modern "mobilism" (in Thibaudet's phrase), the sense of life and existence as process, the only reality, comes down of course from the ancient concept of flux; but it goes further beyond paradox to deal with a lived reality. Montaigne's sense of it was acute; as Thibaudet has noted, he lived and saw himself mainly in the present, in a fluid succession of independent moments of duration. "The central element, the hearth, of Montaigne's philosophy, as of any philosophy, is a feeling of the life of the moment, intense, all in the instant that enjoys it, in the present." In portraying not being but passing, Montaigne anticipates not only philosophers like Bergson but novelists like Proust and Joyce.

Long before Freud, Jung, Adler, and their followers, Montaigne had a strong sense of the conflicts within the psyche, of the myriad parts that may rebel, openly or covertly, against our will, and of the need for a kind of whole-souledness. Like a modern psychiatrist, he is realistic, concerned with the art of the possible, not overindulgent but careful not to demand too much of the limited creatures that we are, and aware that hatred of self is a mortal enemy to love of others. When he writes that thanks to his reason and judgment "I customarily do wholeheartedly whatever I do, and go my way all in one piece," and that "I do not know how to foster quarrels and conflict within me," he recognizes what the last hundred years have made a commonplace: that what we cannot do with a fairly whole soul we do at our own risk and often at that of others; that to live truly at peace with others we must be at peace with ourselves.

The absurd is almost a creed today, in life, in man, in the human condition. Few men before our time have been more aware of what Montaigne, with a bit more modesty and humor but with much the same thing in mind, prefers to call our absurdity. We are not, he reminds us, "so full of evil as of inanity," nor more able to laugh than fit to be laughed at. Man, who embraces the universe, is "the investigator without knowledge, the magistrate without jurisdiction, and all in all, the fool of the farce." However, Montaigne sees just as clearly in man a genuine dignity, which indeed depends on our accepting our absurdity. One passage from his final chapter, almost the very conclusion of the *Essays*, shows how he relates and harmonizes these two main aspects of man:

It is an absolute perfection and virtually divine to know how to enjoy our being rightfully. We seek other conditions because we do not understand the use of our own, and go outside of ourselves because we do not know what it is like inside. Yet there is no use our mounting on stilts, for on stilts we must still walk on our own legs. And on the loftiest throne in the world we are still sitting only on our own rump.

Few ages—not even those of Herodotus and of Plutarch—have been as obsessed with relativism, perspective, and cultural pluralism as our own. In this day of "one world," whether or not we understand other values better, we know it is good to do so. Montaigne is always on this side: often paradoxically, as a corrective, to shame the civilized with examples of cannibal dignity or animal ingenuity, but often in full earnest, as when he praises the heroism of his peasant neighbors. He seeks perspective in place through travel, in time through history and biography, everywhere through imaginative empathy. Wherever he travels, he seeks to break down barriers. He puts himself in the place of the beggar at his door, even of his cat— is he playing with her, as he supposes, or she with him? He delights in trying to place himself inside the skin of others.

As cultural relativists, we reject set rules of esthetics, so much so

that today only the specialist can recognize and enjoy a masterpiece
of poetry, music, or painting. For two centuries Montaigne was
blamed for not following schoolroom rules of order; today we admire
him for creating his own form of discourse. An appreciation like
Huxley's above would have been unlikely a century ago, incon-
ceivable earlier. To fill the place of rules we have learned our love of
complex patterns and problems, which finds much to feed on in
Montaigne's order.

It is part of our relativism that, perhaps as never before, we take
it for granted that ready-made absolutes will not do, that each of us
must find his own answers, and that maturing is precisely this quest.
As ethical individualists we are all descendants of Montaigne about
as much as of any other man; even his master Socrates—at least as
portrayed in Plato—believed in absolutes as the only reality. Now to
be sure Montaigne favors his own type of person—a reasonable,
truthful, reflective, self-possessed man of good will, loyal to his state
and his religion, loving life, convinced of the importance of the
body, the legitimacy of pleasure, and the goodness of happiness. But
as long as a man is honest, law-abiding, and well disposed toward his
fellows, Montaigne's advice for him is to discover himself and his
human condition, learn from that what his conduct should be, and
become himself. When he tells of having his own laws and court to
judge himself, it is to urge others to follow not his but their own.
"Others do not see you, they guess at you. . . . Therefore do not
cling to their judgment; cling to your own."

Thus his plan of education is primarily the training necessary for
independent moral living. Other key ideas of his on this subject have
a congenial ring of modernity—the stress on thinking, not memori-
zation, on discussion, on learning by doing, on enjoyment, on de-
veloping a whole man—but none is more important to us or central
to him. The judgment, which he seeks to develop above all, dis-
tinguishes not only true from false but good from bad and better
from worse. Thus its training provides moral as well as intellectual
education. Montaigne's ideal pupil must pass everything through a
sieve, accept no principles on authority but only on the approval of
his judgment, and "not so much say his lesson as do it." Montaigne
wants nothing less than to educate him for life, to make him better
and wiser, to set him free to be his own master: "Among the liberal
arts, let us begin with the art that liberates us." Only thus, as a

mature moral being, will he be prepared to follow Montaigne's ultimate precept: "Let him be able to do all things, and love to do only
the good." *

   In times when moral values are questioned, the one that remains
is often honesty. The less we can assume about other standards, the
more we need to know what they truly are. Without honesty there
is no communication. Montaigne felt this keenly and spoke of it
often: "Truth is the first and fundamental part of virtue. . . . We
are men, and hold together, only by our word. . . . He who breaks
his word betrays human society. . . . It is the interpreter of our soul.
If it fails us, we have no more hold on each other, no more knowledge of each other." Here, as so often, his tastes and his ethics meet;
for he craves full communication. He tries to be whole-souledly
truthful; where he finds himself mixed and variable, he is careful to
say so. His portrait may not always be completely candid, for modesty, wit, and paradox have their place; but it must be completely
faithful, and Montaigne is at pains to make it so.

   I believe it is above all his sturdy, honest independence, his
cheerful self-acceptance, that draws the crowd of readers to his book
today. Our love of moral independence is ambivalent; our anxiety
and sense of guilt make us often hanker rather for an "escape from
freedom." And here we have a man, not the best that ever lived no
doubt but assuredly far from the worst and better than most of us,
who with scandalous serenity lays himself on the line and says in
effect, quite simply, Here I am. "If I had to live over again," he
writes, "I would live as I have lived. I have neither tears for the
past nor fears for the future." In sounding the human soul others
may have gone deeper; but few if any have probed so well with such
detachment, honesty, and good humor. His serenity is the more com-
pelling because for him it is simply natural.

A generous heart should not belie its thoughts; it wants to reveal itself even
to its inmost depths. There everything is good, or at least everything is
human.

   * I am not for a moment suggesting that these are all achievements of modern education; but they are commonly held aims.

Appendix A: Table of Contents of

Montaigne's Essays

With their length and approximate dates of composition *

To the Reader (1580)   2

BOOK I
1. By Diverse Means We Arrive at the Same End (1578–80)   3
2. Of Sadness (1572–4)   6
3. Our Feelings Reach Out beyond Us (1572–4)   8
4. How the Soul Discharges Its Passions on False Objects When the
   True Are Wanting (1572–4)   14
5. Whether the Governor of a Besieged Place Should Go Out to Parley
   (1572–4)   16
6. Parley Time Is Dangerous (1572–4)   18
7. That Intention Is Judge of Our Actions (1572–4)   19
8. Of Idleness (1572–4)   20
9. Of Liars (1572–4)   21
10. Of Prompt or Slow Speech (1572–4)   25
11. Of Prognostications (1572–4)   27
12. Of Constancy (1572–4)   30
13. Ceremony of Interviews between Kings (1572–4)   32
14. That the Taste of Good and Evil Depends in Large Part on the
    Opinion We Have of Them (1572–4)   33
15. One Is Punished for Defending a Place Obstinately without Reason
    (1572–4)   47
16. Of the Punishment of Cowardice (1572–4)   48
17. A Trait of Certain Ambassadors (1572–4)   49
18. Of Fear (1572–4)   52
19. That Our Happiness Must Not Be Judged until after Our Death
    (1572–4)   54
20. That to Philosophize Is to Learn to Die (1572–4)   56
21. Of the Power of the Imagination (1572–4)   68
22. One Man's Profit Is Another Man's Harm (1572–80)   76
23. Of Custom, and Not Easily Changing an Accepted Law (1572–4)   77
24. Various Outcomes of the Same Plan (1572–80)   90

* The length is based on the pages in the Stanford University Press translated editions of *The Complete Works* (1957) and *The Complete Essays* (1958); the dates, on Villey's theories in *Les Sources et l'évolution des Essais de Montaigne* (Paris: Hachette, 1908, 2 vols.).

25. Of Pedantry (*1572–8*) 97
26. Of the Education of Children (*1579–80*) 106
27. It Is Folly to Measure the True and False by Our Own Capacity (*1572–4*) 132
28. Of Friendship (*1572–6, 1578–80*) 135
29. Twenty-nine Sonnets of Etienne de La Boétie (*1578–80*) 145
30. Of Moderation (*1572–80*) 146
31. Of Cannibals (*1578–80*) 150
32. We Should Meddle Soberly with Judging Divine Ordinances (*1572–4*) 159
33. To Flee from Sensual Pleasures at the Price of Life (*1572–4*) 161
34. Fortune Is Often Met in the Path of Reason (*1572–4*) 163
35. Of a Lack in Our Administrations (*1572–4*) 165
36. Of the Custom of Wearing Clothes (*1572–4*) 166
37. Of Cato the Younger (*1572–4*) 169
38. How We Cry and Laugh for the Same Thing (*1572–4*) 172
39. Of Solitude (*1572–4*) 174
40. A Consideration upon Cicero (*1572–4*) 183
41. Of Not Communicating One's Glory (*1572–4*) 187
42. Of the Inequality That Is between Us (*1572–4*) 189
43. Of Sumptuary Laws (*1572–4*) 196
44. Of Sleep (*1572–4*) 198
45. Of the Battle of Dreux (*1572–4*) 200
46. Of Names (*1572–4*) 201
47. Of the Uncertainty of Our Judgment (*1572–4*) 205
48. Of War Horses (*1572–4*) 209
49. Of Ancient Customs (*1572–80*) 215
50. Of Democritus and Heraclitus (*1572–80*) 219
51. Of the Vanity of Words (*1572–80*) 221
52. Of the Parsimony of the Ancients (*1572–80*) 224
53. Of a Saying of Caesar's (*1572–80*) 224
54. Of Vain Subtleties (*1572–80*) 225
55. Of Smells (*1572–80*) 228
56. Of Prayers (*1572–80*) 229
57. Of Age (*1572–80*) 236

BOOK II

1. Of the Inconsistency of Our Actions (*1572–4*) 239
2. Of Drunkenness (*1573–4*) 244
3. A Custom of the Island of Cea (*1573–4*) 251
4. Let Business Wait till Tomorrow (*1573–4*) 262
5. Of Conscience (*1573–4*) 264
6. Of Practice (*1573–4*) 267
7. Of Honorary Awards (*1578–80*) 275
8. Of the Affection of Fathers for Their Children (*1578–80*) 278
9. Of the Arms of the Parthians (*1578–80*) 293

10. Of Books (*1578–80*)   296
11. Of Cruelty (*1578–80*)   306
12. Apology for Raymond Sebond (*1573–6, 1578–80*)   318
13. Of Judging of the Death of Others (*1572–80*)   458
14. How Our Mind Hinders Itself (*1575–6*)   462
15. That Our Desire Is Increased by Difficulty (*1575–6*)   463
16. Of Glory (*1578–80*)   468
17. Of Presumption (*1578–80*)   478
18. Of Giving the Lie (*1578–80*)   503
19. Of Freedom of Conscience (*1578–80*)   506
20. We Taste Nothing Pure (*1578–80*)   510
21. Against Do-nothingness (*1578–80*)   512
22. Of Riding Post (*1578–80*)   515
23. Of Evil Means Employed to a Good End (*1578–80*)   516
24. Of the Greatness of Rome (*1578–80*)   519
25. Not to Counterfeit Being Sick (*1578–80*)   521
26. Of Thumbs (*1578–80*)   522
27. Cowardice, Mother of Cruelty (*1578–80*)   523
28. All Things Have Their Season (*1578–80*)   531
29. Of Virtue (*1578–80*)   532
30. Of a Monstrous Child (*1578–80*)   538
31. Of Anger (*1578–80*)   539
32. Defense of Seneca and Plutarch (*1578–80*)   545
33. The Story of Spurina (*1578–80*)   550
34. Observations on Julius Caesar's Methods of Making War (*1578–80*) 556
35. Of Three Good Wives (*1578–80*)   563
36. Of the Most Outstanding Men (*1578–80*)   569
37. Of the Resemblance of Children to Fathers (*1579–80*)   574

BOOK III

 1. Of the Useful and the Honorable (*1585–8*)   599
 2. Of Repentance (*1585–8*)   610
 3. Of Three Kinds of Association (*1585–8*)   621
 4. Of Diversion (*1585–8*)   630
 5. On Some Verses of Virgil (*1585–8*)   638
 6. Of Coaches (*1585–8*)   685
 7. Of the Disadvantage of Greatness (*1585–8*)   699
 8. Of the Art of Discussion (*1585–8*)   703
 9. Of Vanity (*1585–8*)   721
10. Of Husbanding Your Will (*1585–8*)   766
11. Of Cripples (*1585–8*)   784
12. Of Physiognomy (*1585–8*)   792
13. Of Experience (*1587–8*)   815 (–857)

Appendix B: A Sample Page Illustrating the Changes in Montaigne's Text in Successive Editions

From Book II, chapter 18, "Of Giving the Lie" (S 503, OC 646–7; Edition Phototypique, plate 597).

Words or passages added since the previous edition are italicized; those deleted in the next edition are bracketed; one MS addition on the Bordeaux Copy which Montaigne later deleted is shown here in boldface.

1580 EDITION

I am not building here a statue to erect at the town crossroads, or in a church or a public square; this is to hide in a nook in a library, and to amuse someone who may have a particular interest in knowing me: a neighbor, a relative, a friend who will take pleasure in associating and conversing with me in this image. Others have taken courage to speak of themselves because they found the subject worthy and rich; I, on the contrary, because I have found mine so vain and so meager that no suspicion of ostentation can fall upon my plan.

1588 EDITION

I am not building here a statue to erect at the town crossroads, or in a church or a public square:

> *I do not aim to swell my page full-blown*
> *With windy trifles [fit to give weight to smoke.]*
> *We two talk alone.**

This is [to hide in] a nook in a library, and to amuse [someone who may have a particular interest in knowing me:] a neighbor, a relative, a friend who will take pleasure in associating and conversing with me in this image. Others have taken courage to speak of themselves because they found the subject worthy and rich; I, on the contrary, because I have found mine so [vain] and so meager that no suspicion of ostentation can fall upon my plan. *I do not find so much good in myself that I cannot tell it without blushing.*

* Montaigne's quotation, here and in the later version, is in the original Latin, with no indication of the source (Persius, *Satires*, V, 19 ff.).

BORDEAUX COPY AND 1595 EDITION

I am not building here a statue to erect at the town crossroads, or in a church or a public square:

> I do not aim to swell my page full-blown
> With windy trifles . . .
> We two talk alone.

This is *for* a nook in a library, and—as it appears from the useless subject I have taken—only to amuse a neighbor, a relative, a friend, who will take pleasure in associating and conversing with me in this image. Others have taken courage to speak of themselves because they found the subject worthy and rich; I, on the contrary, because I have found mine so *barren* and so meager that no suspicion of ostentation can fall upon my plan.

I willingly judge the actions of others; I give little chance to judge mine * *because of their nullity.* I do not find so much good in myself that I cannot tell it without blushing.

* Montaigne's original MS version was: "I give nothing to judge of mine. . . ."

Notes

ABBREVIATIONS AND CONVENTIONS

AHG *Archives Historiques du Département de la Gironde* (normally annual), Paris (Aubry, Picard, Champion) and Bordeaux (Gounouilhou, Lefebvre, Feret), 1859–1936, 59 volumes.

BHR *Bibliothèque d'Humanisme et Renaissance* (annual after the first few years), Geneva: Droz, 1941– ———.

BSAM *Bulletin de la Société des Amis de Montaigne*, 1913– ———. (Series II, #1–14 are entitled *Bulletin des Amis de Montaigne*.) Series I, 1913–21, 4 numbers. Series II, 1937–56, 19 numbers. Series III, 1957–64, and Series IV, 1965– ———, quarterly. References will appear as follows: *BSAM* II: 16 (1953–4), 17–20; meaning Series II, no. 16 (1953–4), pp. 17–20.

c. Copyright. (This date is used when publication date is not given.)

DB Montaigne: *Essais,* ed. Dezeimeris and Barckhausen (re-edition of the 1580 edition), Bordeaux: Gounouilhou, 1870–3, 2 vols.

Ed. Munic. Montaigne: *Essais,* Edition Municipale de Bordeaux, by Strowski *et al.,* Bordeaux: Pech, 1906–33, 5 vols. (Gives all variants of the six basic editions.)

Ephemeris *Le Livre de raison de Montaigne sur l'Ephemeris historica de Beuther,* ed. Jean Marchand, Compagnie Française des Arts Graphiques, 1948. (The text is not paginated; most references are to be located by the day of the year: *e.g.,* July 10.)

Historiarum . . . Jacques-Auguste de Thou, *Historiarum sui temporis libri CXXXVIII,* London: Buckley, 1733 ed., 7 vols.

OC Montaigne: *Œuvres complètes* (Bibliothèque de la Pléiade), Gallimard, c. 1962, xxiv + 1791 pp. (Textes établis par Albert Thibaudet et Maurice Rat; Introduction et Notes par Maurice Rat.) This is the French edition of reference for Montaigne's *Essays,* letters, and *Travel Journal.*

"Problèmes . . ." Roger Trinquet: "Problèmes posés par la révision de la biographie de Montaigne," *Cahiers de l'Association Internationale des Etudes Françaises,* no. 14 (March 1962), pp. 285–99; reprinted in *BSAM* III: 23–24 (July–Dec. 1962), 12–21.

RHB *Revue Historique de Bordeaux et du Département de la Gironde* (normally annual), Bordeaux: Feret *et al.,* 1908– ———.

RHLF *Revue d'Histoire Littéraire de la France* (annual except not published 1940–6), Colin, 1894– ———.

S   Montaigne: *The Complete Works* (1957) and *The Complete Essays* (1958), Frame tr., Stanford, Cal.: Stanford University Press. The pagination of the *Essays* is the same in both. These are the English editions of reference for Montaigne.

TJ   Montaigne: *Travel Journal* (*Journal de Voyage*).

All works not otherwise listed were published in Paris.

Notes are listed by page numbers, usually followed by a paraphrase or summary of the passage or subject to which the note refers; or where this seemed pointlessly cumbersome, by a direct quotation from the text, normally identifiable by three dots (. . .) before, after, or within the passage quoted.

All references to Montaigne's writings are to two editions listed above: 1) the Stanford University Press *Complete Works* (and, for the *Essays,* their *Complete Essays*) (S); and 2) the 1962 Pléiade edition of the *Œuvres complètes* (OC). Page references to these are preceded by the identifying letters S and OC. References to the *Essays* begin with the book number (in Roman capitals) and, after a colon, the chapter number in Arabic numerals. References to letters normally begin with the date; to the *Travel Journal,* with the letters *TJ* followed by the place and the date.

For the 1580 text of the *Essays* (Books I and II in their original form), the basic edition of reference is that of Dezeimeris and Barckhausen (DB).

EXAMPLES:

   6 Montaigne's letter to Paul de Foix.   Sept. 1, 1570; S 1062–5, OC 1367–70. (Meaning: the material on p. 6 quoted from or alluded to in that letter, which is dated Sept. 1, 1570, is found in the Stanford *Complete Works* on pp. 1062–5, and in the Pléiade *Œuvres complètes* on pp. 1367–70.)

  10 "I remembered . . . public-spirited soul."   III: 10, S 769, OC 983. (Meaning: the quotation on p. 10 beginning and ending as shown is from the *Essays,* Book III, ch. 10, and is found in the Stanford *Complete Works* and *Complete Essays* on p. 769, in the Pléiade *Œuvres complètes* on p. 983.)

  17 Montaigne rebuked by the papal censors.   *TJ*, Rome, March 20, 1581; S 955–6, OC 1228–9. (Meaning: the rebuke is related in the *Travel Journal* as occurring on March 20, 1581, in Rome; it is found in the Stanford *Complete Works* on pp. 955–6, in the Pléiade *Œuvres complètes* on pp. 1228–9.)

GENERAL

All Montaigne scholars are eagerly awaiting M. Roger Trinquet's two theses for the French state doctorate, his edition of Montaigne's letters and especially his historical and psychological biography of Montaigne from birth to retirement (1533–71), which promises to make all earlier studies outdated. His already published findings have us all in his debt, notably his article listed above (hereafter "Problèmes . . ."), "Problèmes posés par la révision de la biographie de Montaigne."

Among the least outdated are four works of the 1930's: Jacob Zeitlin's scholarly and judicious Introduction (I, xvii–xlvi) and Notes to his translation of the *Essays* (New York: Knopf, 1934–6, 3 vols.); Maturin Dreano's *La Pensée religieuse de Montaigne* (Beauchesne, 1936), which sheds much light on Montaigne's life; Jean Plattard's sound *Montaigne et son temps* (Boivin, 1933); and Fortunat Strowski's vivid though sometimes venturesome *Montaigne, sa vie publique et privée* (Nouvelle Revue Critique, 1938). For certain chapters of the present book (especially 5, 7, 9–11, 14, 16) I have drawn on my own *Montaigne's Discovery of Man: The Humanization of a Humanist* (New York: Columbia University Press, 1955).

Still useful in its own area and especially for its wealth of legal documents is Théophile Malvezin's *Michel de Montaigne, son origine, sa famille* (Bordeaux: Lefebvre, 1875). Also valuable for documents are the *Archives Historiques de la Gironde* (*AHG*) and the publications of Dr. J.-F. Payen (*Documents inédits ou peu connus sur Montaigne*, etc., Jannet and Techener, 1847–56, 4 vols. of about 200 pp. in all; some are reproduced in early numbers of the *BSAM*). The standard substantial biography is still Paul Bonnefon's *Montaigne, l'homme et l'oeuvre* (Bordeaux: Gounouilhou, Rouam, 1893) or its slightly enlarged later version, *Montaigne et ses amis* (Colin, 1898, 2 vols.).

Three other writers are recommended with caution. Alphonse Grün, using Dr. Payen's materials, wrote a readable but often highly unreliable *La Vie publique de Michel Montaigne* (Amyot, 1855). André Lamandé's charming biographical novel *La Vie gaillarde et sage de Montaigne* (Plon, 1927) is available in English as *Montaigne Grave and Gay* (New York: Holt, 1928). Alexandre Nicolaï's *Les*

Belles Amies de Montaigne (Dumas, c. 1950) and *Montaigne intime* (Aubier, c. 1947) are based on solid research but often fail to distinguish fact from conjecture.

For the general historical background I have relied mainly on the histories of Ernest Lavisse, James Westfall Thompson, and Henri Hauser.

Both text and notes contain many translated titles and quotations. Except as otherwise indicated, the translations are my own.

Chapter 1: *The Eyquems of Bordeaux*

Most useful here is Malvezin; then Bonnefon, Dreano, Plattard, and Strowski. Malvezin and the *AHG* are rich in documents.

Page

3–6, 10 Medieval and Renaissance Bordeaux and Gascony.   See especially Dom Devienne, *Histoire de la ville de Bordeaux* (Bordeaux: Court *et al.*; Paris: Desaint *et al.*, 1771, 2 vols.); Francisque Michel, *Histoire du commerce et de la navigation à Bordeaux* (Bordeaux: Delmas, 1867–70, 2 vols.); Paul Courteault, *Histoire de Gascogne et de Béarn* (Boivin, c. 1938); Leo Drouyn, *Bordeaux vers 1450: description typographique* (Bordeaux: Gounouilhou, 1874); and Camille Jullian, "Bordeaux au temps de la mairie de Montaigne," *RHB*, XXVI (1933), 5–18.

6 Brantôme furious at Henry III.   Brantôme, *Œuvres complètes,* ed. Lalanne (Renouard, 1864–82, 11 vols.), V, 205–11.

6 Montaigne's letter to Paul de Foix.   Sept. 1, 1570; S 1062–5, OC 1367–70.

6–7, 10 The name Eyquem around Bordeaux.   See *AHG*, XIII, 370; XXVI, 74, 153; and *passim*; and especially Alexandre Nicolaï, "A propos des ascendances de Montaigne" and "Les Véritables Ascendances de Montaigne," in *Revue Bleue*, LXXV (1938), 342–4, 444–9.

7–8 Ramon Ayquem becomes lord of Montaigne.   *AHG*, VIII (1866), 547–51.

7–10 Montaigne's ancestors.   Besides the books listed above, see *AHG*, VIII, 547–51; X, 508–10; and *passim*; and Montaigne: *Essays*, II: 37, S 579–80, OC 742.

9 Pierre de Gaujac and the Cour des Aides of Périgueux.   Trinquet, "Problèmes . . ."

9 Gaujac and his death at sixty-six.   Montaigne says sixty-seven, but probably means "in his sixty-seventh year."   II: 37, S 579, OC 743.

9–10 His son tells us . . .   II: 2, S 248, OC 325–6; cf. I: 35, S 166, OC 220. Between 1588 and 1592 Montaigne added Lautrec's name, then crossed it out; see Edition Phototypique (Hachette, 1912), plate 285; Ed. Munic., II, 16.

10 "I remembered . . . public-spirited soul."   III: 10, S 769, OC 983.

11 His son was to envy . . . as he found it.   III: 9, S 726, 764, OC 928, 977.

11 "that good man . . . with custom,"   I: 26, S 129, OC 174.

11 "a man of very clear . . . and nature."   I: 35, S 165, OC 220.

11 My house has . . . worship them.   II: 12, S 319, OC 415.

12 Pierre de Montaigne's speech as mayor.   *AHG*, VI, 224 (Nov. 10, 1554).

12 "the best father there ever was,"   II: 12, S 320, OC 416.

12 "the good father . . . my own fortune."   III: 13, S 844, OC 1079.

12 "to keep his desires . . . so good a father."   III: 9, S 726–7, OC 928–9.

12 "straight and . . . to brown."   II: 2, S 248, OC 326.

12 "He scarcely ever . . . bodily exercise.   II: 17, S 486, OC 625.

12–13 I have even seen . . . back to our bottles.   II: 2, S 247–8, OC 325–6.

13 One of the great . . . in a faint."   III: 2, S 615, OC 788.

13 A little later . . . military service.   Malvezin, p. 283; cf. p. 96. The declaration is dated Feb. 24, 1558.

13 For his last seven . . . in his bladder."   II: 37, S 578, OC 742. The last sentence quoted comes first in the text.

13–14 The fatal day . . . very happy life."   S 1056, OC 1361.

14 following his preference in dress . . .   I: 36, S 168, OC 223.

14 "I have not banished . . . in his hand."   II: 18, S 503, OC 647.

14 "They are dead . . . very much alive."   III: 9, S 762, OC 975.

14–15 Pierre de Montaigne's second and final will.   Published by Auguste Salles in *BSAM* II: 4 (Nov. 1, 1938), 5–11, and 5 (Feb. 1, 1939), 6.

15 "were formerly surnamed Eyquem,"   II: 16, S 475, OC 610.

15 "Truly it would . . . I would be!"   II: 18, S 503, OC 647. The first sentence quoted follows the others in the text.

15 But I do . . . avoid these extremes.   Published 1570; S 1053, OC 1356.

15 "Not that I have . . . brotherly concord."   I: 28, S 137, OC 184.

Chapter 2: The Lopez de Villanueva

The leading authority on the family is Cecil Roth; see "L'Ascendance juive de Michel de Montaigne," *Revue des Cours et Conférences*, XXXIX(1) (Dec. 1937–March 1938), 176–87; "The Montaigne

Family Tree" in *Personalities and Events in Jewish History* (Philadelphia: The Jewish Publication Society of America, 1953), p. 324; and for general background, *A History of the Marranos* (Philadelphia: The Jewish Publication Society of America, 1941). For the Jews in Bordeaux, Théophile Malvezin, *Histoire des Juifs à Bordeaux* (Bordeaux: Lefebvre, 1875), esp. pp. 26–121. For Montaigne's mother, Paul Courteault, "La Mère de Montaigne," in *Mélanges offerts à Paul Laumonier* (Droz, 1935), pp. 305–27.

Page

16 Montaigne's two mentions of his mother. II: 37, S 579, OC 742; and I: 26, S 128, OC 173.

17 "As for me . . . unbearable tortures." II: 11, S 314, OC 410.

17 "I think there . . . after he is dead." I: 31, S 155, OC 207–8.

17 Montaigne rebuked by the papal censors. *TJ*, Rome, March 20, 1581; S 955–6, OC 1228–9.

17 Montaigne godfather to a marrano. Cardozo de Bethencourt, "Montaigne parrain d'un marrane portugais," *RHB*, XXXI (1938), 31.

17 Montaigne's references to the Jews are sympathetic. I: 48, S 211, OC 278; I: 56, S 232, OC 306; II: 3, S 256–7, OC 336–7; II: 12, S 433, OC 558; II: 27, S 530, OC 679.

17–18 Jews made to race in Rome. *TJ*, Feb. 7, 1581; S 946, OC 1216–7.

17–18 Other accounts of these races. See Armand Lunel, "Montaigne et les Juifs," *BSAM* III: 19 (July–Dec., 1956), 40–9.

18 Montaigne blamed for failing to protest. Lunel article, p. 46; Emmanuel Rodocanachi, *Le Saint Siège et les Juifs* (Didot, 1891), pp. 192–3.

18 The renegade rabbi. *TJ*, Rome, Lent, 1581; S 956–7, OC 1230.

18 Synagogue in Verona. *TJ*, Verona, Nov. 1, 1580; S 918, OC 1180.

18 Visits a synagogue, sees a circumcision in Rome. *TJ*, Jan. 30, 1581; S 944–6, OC 1214–6.

18–19 Osorius and the Jews in Portugal. I: 14, S 35–6, OC 53–4. Hieronymus Osorius, *De rebus Emmanuelis Lusitaniae Regis*, Book I. Maurice Riveline, "Montaigne et les Juifs," *BSAM* III: 16 (1953–4), 17–20.

20 Jews conforming in public, Judaizing in private. Lunel article, p. 42.

21 His first charge . . . Lopès family. Malvezin, *Histoire des Juifs à Bordeaux*, pp. 179–83. Report by M. de Puddefer, Dec. 8, 1733.

21–23 Montaigne's maternal ancestry. See Roth titles, above.

23–24 Marriage contract of Montaigne's parents. Published in *AHG*, New Series I (1933–6), 323–31.

24 Pierre de Montaigne's wills.   The first is published in *AHG*, XXIII, 87–93; the second in *BSAM* II: 4 (Nov. 1, 1938), 5–11, and 5 (Feb. 1, 1939), 6.

24 Father predicted he would ruin the estate.   III: 9, S 764, OC 977.

24–25 Act of agreement between Montaigne and his mother.   Published in Malvezin, pp. 297–300.

25–26 The gold chain.   Pertinent excerpts of the act are in Malvezin, p. 300.

26–27 Montaigne's mother's will.   Published in Courteault article, pp. 319–22.

26 Mother lived elsewhere for ten years.   Jacques-Auguste de Thou reports that when he and Schomberg visited the château in 1589 in Montaigne's absence they were entertained by his wife; he does not mention his mother (*Historiarum* . . . , VII, *De vita sua*, p. 97; and *Mémoires*, in Buchon, *Choix de chroniques* . . . , Panthéon Littéraire, 1854 ed., p. 637). Antoinette de Louppes was absent from the signing of the marriage contract, and from the first marriage, of her son's only surviving child, Léonor, in 1590. In 1595–6 Marie de Gournay stayed at Montaigne with Michel's widow and daughter, but apparently not his mother. (Her quatrain to the mother, incidentally, tells us nothing.) See also the following note.

26 . . . in the period of twelve years or more . . .   Since we do not know of Jeanne de Camain's living at Montaigne, this might mean that Antoinette de Louppes had been living elsewhere that long.

27 Third-generation nobles regarded as genuine.   Gaston Zeller, *Les Institutions de la France au XVIe siècle* (Presses Universitaires de France, 1948), p. 17.

27–28 Montaigne's views on family authority.   II: 8, S 288, OC 377. For women's natural unfairness, cf. S 290, OC 379.

28 Montaigne's chapter on paternal affection.   II: 8.

Chapter 3: The Early Years

Generally Trinquet's "Problèmes . . ."; Bonnefon, Dreano, Malvezin, Plattard, Strowski; and the *Ephemeris*. Documents in Malvezin and *AHG*.

Page

29 Montaigne born in February, 1533.   I: 20, S 58, OC 82.

29 His parents' third child.   II: 37, S 579, OC 742.

29–30 Beauregard at La Boétie's deathbed.   Montaigne's letter, published in 1570; S 1052–3, OC 1356. The fact that La Boétie died in Lestonnac's house is shown by his will. See *AHG*, XVII, 161; and Bonnefon's ed. of La Boétie's *Œuvres complètes* (Bordeaux: Gounouilhou, and Paris: Rouam, 1892), pp. 427–8.

30 Pierre de Montaigne's wills.   See note on p. 24, above.

30 Bussaguet died in 1563.   *AHG*, XLIV, 277.

30 Beauregard's suit in 1607.   Malvezin, pp. 140–1.

30 Montaigne and brothers settle father's will.   *AHG*, X, 252–6.

30 Montaigne's only reference to Thomas.   I: 31, S 151, OC 202.

30–31 Marie de Gournay's quatrains.   Quoted by Nicolaï, *Les Belles*
35 *Amies de Montaigne*, pp. 196–7, from Marie's *Le Proumenoir de Monsieur de Montaigne* (L'Angelier, 1594), pp. 105 verso–106 verso.

31 La Brousse's suit of armor.   *AHG*, XV, 278.

31 Montaigne's only reference to La Brousse.   II: 5, S 264, OC 346.

32 La Brousse died Nov. 27, 1595.   *Ephemeris.*

31 Jeanne de Lestonnac's knowledge of Greek.   Jean de Gaufreteau, *Chronique bordeloise* (Bordeaux: Lefebvre, 1877–8 ed., 2 vols.), I, 238.

32 Saint Jeanne de Lestonnac.   See Pierre Hélyot, *Histoire des ordres religieux et militaires* (Louis, new ed., 1792, 8 vols.), VI, 343–59; Dreano, pp. 45–9; Jean Stiénon du Pré, *Sainte Jeanne de Lestonnac* (La Colombe, c. 1955); and especially L. Entraygues, *La Bienheureuse Jeanne de Lestonnac* (Périgueux: Roux, 2nd ed., 1940).

32 Beauregard's second wife tries to convert young Jeanne de Lestonnac.   Dreano (p. 46) and Strowski (p. 19), among others, say that a second sister of Montaigne joined the mother in trying to make the girl a Protestant; Malvezin (p. 125) traces the report through Father Julia to Abbé Sabathier in 1843. But in 1568 Léonor was sixteen, Marie only thirteen; in 1577 Marie helped baptize Montaigne's fifth child; nothing suggests that either was ever a Protestant. Presumably since an aunt of young Jeanne's (Beauregard's wife) did work for this, someone assumed that that aunt must be a sister of Montaigne.

32 The canonization of St. Jeanne de Lestonnac.   *BSAM* II: 15 (1949–52), 47; III: 9 (Jan.–March, 1959), 4–5.

32 Saint-Martin at the Collège de Guyenne.   His uncle Pierre de Gaujac made him a gift on Sept. 17, 1557 (Malvezin, pp. 68–9).

33 Montaigne on Saint-Martin's death.   I: 20, S 59, OC 84.

33 Charron and Léonor de Camain.   *AHG*, XVIII, 463–7; XXIV, 229–34.

33 Bernard de Cazalis in Padua.   *TJ*, Nov. 12, 1580; S 921, OC 1184.

33–34 Mattecoulon traveling with Michel.   *TJ*, Sept. 5, 1580, S 867, OC 1115; Oct. 30, 1580, S 915, OC 1177; Nov. 27, 1580, S 934, OC 1200–1; Dec. 29, 1580, S 938–9, OC 1206–7.

34 Mattecoulon remains in Rome.   *TJ*, Oct. 15, 1581; S 1029, OC 1326.

34 Montaigne on Mattecoulon's duel.   II: 27, S 526–7, OC 675.

34 Brantôme on Mattecoulon's duel.   "Discours sur les duels" in *Œuvres complètes* (Renouard, 1864–82, 11 vols.), VI, 322–3.

34–35 Mattecoulon's later life.   Nicolaï, *Les Belles Amies de Montaigne*, p. 197; Dreano, p. 42. Dreano draws on Charles de Gamaches, *Le Sensé raisonnant sur les passages de l'Escriture Saincte, contre les pretendus Reformez* (1623), ch. "Des prières."

35 Mattecoulon and the *Ephemeris*.   Roger Trinquet, "Bertrand de Mattecoulon et l'Ephéméride de Beuther," in *BSAM* II: 15 (1949–52), 54–57, and in *BHR*, XV (1953), 226–9; and Mme Léonie Gardeau, "Bertrand de Montaigne, Seigneur de Matecoulon, et le 'Livre de Raison' de Montaigne," in Georges Palassie, ed., *Mémorial du Ier Congrès International des Etudes Montaignistes* (Bordeaux: Taffard, 1964), pp. 129–35.

35 Pierre Bunel and Sebond's book.   II: 12, S 319–20, OC 415–6.

37–38 Montaigne's château.   See the account, with a plan, of the château in 1778, by François-de-Paule Latapie, inspecteur des manufactures, in his *Notice de la généralité de Bordeaux*, in *AHG*, XXXIV, 283–6; and his notes for this account, XXXVIII, 482–8.

38 "perched on . . . to the winds."   III: 3, S 629, OC 807.

38 Montaigne carried eleven months.   II: 12, S 418, OC 539.

38–39 His grateful . . . power over me.   III: 13, S 844, OC 1079. We do not know how long Montaigne was put out to nurse or just how early he began to be taught Latin.

39 Back home . . . that very softly."   II: 8, S 281, OC 368–9.

39 Since his father . . . and constraint."   I: 26, S 129, OC 174.

39 Du Bellay on learning Greek and Latin.   *Deffence et Illustration de la langue françoyse*, Book I, chapter x.

39–40 Montaigne learning Latin.   I: 26, S 128–9, OC 173.

40–41 Erasmianism at the Collège de Guyenne.   Trinquet, "Nouveaux Aperçus sur les débuts du Collège de Guyenne. De Jean de Tartas à André de Gouvéa (1533–1535)," *BHR*, XXVI (1964), 510–58, and *BSAM* IV: 2 (April–June, 1965), 3–28; Zeitlin, I, xxii.

40–42 Montaigne on his own schooling.   I: 26, S 128–31, OC 173–6.

40 Twelve-year course in the Collège de Guyenne.   Principal Elie Vinet stated in 1583 that this was the length of the course in the years when Montaigne was there; see Louis Massebieau, *Schola Aquitanica* (Delagrave, 1886), p. 4.

40 Montaigne's private tutors Grouchy, Guerente, and Buchanan.   Montaigne also mentions (I: 26, S 129, OC 173) "Marc-Antoine Muret, whom France and Italy recognize as the best orator of his time"; but Muret seems not to have been there when Montaigne was.

40–41 Montaigne at the Collège de Guyenne.   Alexandre Nicolaï twice

states (*Les Belles Amies de Montaigne*, p. 31; *BSAM* II: 19, July–
Dec., 1956, p. 7) that he had the three sons of the Marquis de
Trans as his schoolmates there; but they seem to have been too
young for this. Jean Marchand says (*Ephemeris*, pp. 275, 296)
that they were all sons by Trans's second wife, Marguerite, whom
he married only in 1555.

40 (probably the *Baptistes* . . . *Caesar* of Muret)   Zeitlin, I, 364.

41 Curriculum of the Collège de Guyenne.   Vinet in Massebieau,
Schola Aquitanica, p. 6. See also Zeitlin, I, xxi, 363; and W. H.
Woodward, *Studies in Education during the Age of the Renaissance, 1400–1600* (Cambridge: University Press, 1906), pp.
144–9.

41 Montaigne's understanding tutor.   Joseph Saint-Martin,
" 'L'Homme d'entendement de précepteur' de Montaigne," in
BSAM III: 11–12 (July–Dec., 1959), 7–15.

41–42 They are a real . . . him to them."   I: 26, S 122–3, OC 165.

42 There is nothing . . . espouse it.   I: 26, S 131, OC 177.

42 Though my health . . . from all this.   I: 26, S 129, OC 174.
The original version of this was harsher and probably less true; it
speaks of his "sleepy appearance," "soft mind," and "stupid imagination." See DB I, 127.

42 "No one predicted . . . I should do nothing."   I: 26, S 130,
OC 175. The last sentence quoted here comes first in the text.

42 Moneins and the salt-tax revolt.   Montaigne says that he saw
this (I: 24, S 95–6, OC 129–30); but he often uses *"je vis"* ("I
saw") to mean merely "I learned about."

42–43 Montaigne may have had . . . duels, or war.   Strowski, p. 37.

43 He may have been . . . Collège de France.   Trinquet in *BSAM*
III: 4 (Oct.–Dec., 1957), 3. Montaigne refers to one *lecteur royal*,
Sylvius (Jacques Dubois), who died in 1555, as someone he has
heard (II: 2, S 246–7, OC 324).

43 Paris had his heart since his childhood.   III: 9, S 743, OC 950.

43 He may have studied further in Bordeaux.   Bonnefon, pp. 50–6.

43–44 He may have studied law at Toulouse.   Georges Hubrecht,
"Montaigne juriste," in *IVe Centenaire de la naissance de Montaigne* (Bordeaux: Delmas, 1933), pp. 239–97.

43 Montaigne's uncle a law student at Toulouse.   Raymond Cor-
raze, in "Le Père de Michel Montaigne à l'Université de Toulouse"
(*Bulletin Philologique et Historique*, 1938–9, pp. 191–6), published a deed of gift dated Oct. 18, 1526, from one Grimon de
Lansac to one Petrus Eyquem of Bordeaux; but the recipient could
hardly have been Montaigne's father and must almost certainly
have been his uncle Pierre Eyquem de Gaujac.

43–44 The Faculty of Law at Toulouse.   Antonin Deloume, *Histoire
sommaire de la Faculté de Droit de Toulouse* (Toulouse: Privat,

1905)); René Gadave, *Les Documents sur l'histoire de l'Université de Toulouse* (Toulouse: Privat, 1910).

43 It may have . . . without sin!" II: 3, S 257, OC 338.

43 Corras and the Martin Guerre case. III: 11, S 788, OC 1008. Cf. Corras: *Arrest memorable du Parlement de Tolose, contenant une histoire prodigieuse, de nostre temps* (1561).

43–44 Simon Thomas. I: 21, S 68, OC 95.

44 Pasquier at Toulouse. In her ed. of Pasquier, *Choix de lettres* (Geneva: Droz, 1956, p. vii), D. Thickett says he was there in 1547. For Pasquier as a friend of Montaigne, see p. 43.

44 Montaigne's friends who studied law at Toulouse. Bunel: II: 12, S 319, OC 415–6. Turnebus: I: 25, S 102, OC 138–9; II: 12, S 320–1, OC 417; II: 12, S 436, OC 562; II: 17, S 502, OC 645. Du Ferrier: *TJ*, Venice, Nov. 6, 1580, S 920, OC 1183; and letters of Jan. 26–Feb. 13, 1585, S 1078–82, OC 1384–5, 1387–9. Mesmes: Letter of April 30, 1570; S 1057–8, OC 1361–2. Foix: Letter of Sept. 1, 1570, S 1062–5, OC 1367–70; *TJ*, Rome, March 22, 1581, S 956, OC 1229; Oct. 10, 1581, S 1028, OC 1325.

44 Montaigne's tribute to Foix and Pibrac. III: 9, S 731, OC 935.

44 Rabelais on the University of Toulouse. *Pantagruel* (II), ch. v.

44–45 Mesmes on student life in Toulouse. Mesmes, *Mémoires inédits*, ed. Fremy (Leroux, undated), pp. 139–45.

45 Pierre de Brach on student life at Toulouse. Brach, *Œuvres poétiques*, ed. Dezeimeris (Aubry, 1861–2, 2 vols.), II, 194.

Chapter 4: The Magistrate

Generally, Bonnefon, Dreano, Plattard, Strowski; Trinquet, "Problèmes . . ."; Georges Hubrecht, "Montaigne juriste," in *IVe Centenaire de la naissance de Montaigne* (Bordeaux: Delmas, 1933), pp. 239–98; and Nussy Saint-Saens, "Montaigne au Parlement de Bordeaux," *RHB*, New Series II (1953), 119–35.

For the Bordeaux Parlement in general, C.-B.-F. Boscheron des Portes, *Histoire du Parlement de Bordeaux* (Bordeaux: Lefebvre, 1877, 2 vols.), and Gaston Zeller, *Les Institutions de la France au XVIe siècle* (Presses Universitaires de France, 1948); for details, *AHG, passim,* and the MS *Registres secrets du Parlement de Bordeaux,* especially the *Registre commencé depuis le xiii jour de Novembre 1531 jusques au xvii May 1564,* Bibliothèque Nationale, Paris, MS Fonds français 22.372. For the Bordeaux Parlement and the Cour des Aides, Boscheron des Portes and especially Simone Quet, "La Cour

des Aides de Guyenne. Ses Rapports avec le Parlement de Bordeaux,"
RHB, XXXII (1939), 97–111.

Page

46 Pierre de Gaujac and the Cour des Aides.   See Trinquet, "Problèmes . . ."

46 . . . doubt that he served long—   Trinquet in *BSAM* III: 4 (Oct.–Dec., 1957), 3.

46 —if at all—   Pierre Barrière, "Montaigne et l'expérience parlementaire," in *BSAM* III: 2 (April–June, 1957), 7.

46 The letters patent of 1557.   Published by Malvezin, pp. 282–3.

46–51 The Cour des Aides and the Bordeaux Parlement.   See mainly Boscheron des Portes, Zeller, *Registres secrets*, Quet, Saint-Saens.

47 The long robe against the short.   Cf. *Essays*, I: 23, S 85, OC 116–7.

48 Members of the Cour des Aides.   Boscheron des Portes, pp. 108–9; also Malvezin, pp. 282–3.

49–50 Relatives in the Bordeaux Parlement.   Dr. Payen (*Nouveaux Documents inédits ou peu connus sur Montaigne,* Jannet, 1850, p. 63 and facsimile at end) thought that another uncle, Thomas de Saint-Michel, was still alive in 1567; but his will is dated Aug. 5, 1541, and by 1546–7 his brother Gaujac had inherited his ecclesiastical appointments (Malvezin, pp. 267–73).

51–52 Montaigne's speech of Nov. 13, 1561.   *AHG*, VI, 7–8.

52–54 Lagebaston, Candale, Trans, d'Escars, *et al.*   Strowski, Boscheron des Portes, Dom Devienne (*Histoire de Bordeaux*), and Nicolaï, "Germain-Gaston de Foix, marquis de Trans," in *BSAM* II: 19 (July–Dec., 1956), 7–26.

53 Montaigne's oath in Paris in 1562.   Dreano, p. 139; Strowski, pp. 62–3; etc.

54 Malvin de Cessac.   See his letter to Montaigne's widow about Montaigne's death, in *AHG*, XXXIV, 323.

54–55 Montaigne's counterprotest against Lagebaston.   Quoted by J.-F. Payen, *Recherches sur Montaigne. Documents inédits. N° 4* (Techener, 1856), p. 20.

55 Montaigne defending Lagebaston.   Saint-Saens article, pp. 130–1.

55 Montaigne's suggestions for Charles IX.   F. Hauchecorne, "Une Intervention ignorée de Montaigne au Parlement de Bordeaux," *BHR*, IX (1947), 164–8.

55–56 Charles IX's reception in Bordeaux.   J. M. Chartrou, "Les Entrées solennelles à Bordeaux au XVIe siècle," *RHB*, XXIII (1930), 99–102.

56 The case reported by Montaigne.   *AHG*, XXVIII, 143 (April 6, 1562); cf. pp. 144–7. The other cases reported by him that we possess are dated May 15, July 24, and Dec. 24, 1563, and April 18, 1564.

57 Montaigne's trips to court.   Bonnefon, Strowski, Saint-Saens, Hubrecht; *Registres secrets;* Nicolaï, "Les Grandes Dates de la vie de Montaigne," *BSAM* II: 13–14 (Oct. 1948–Jan. 1949), 28–30. Also Montaigne, *Essays,* I: 43, S 197, OC 260; I: 46, S 201, OC 266; I: 48, S 215, OC 284; II: 17, S 496, OC 637; III: 8, S 717, OC 918. Letters of Aug. 10 (Paris), Sept. 1 (Montaigne), and Sept. 10 (Paris), 1570; S 1061, 1065–6; OC 1370–1, 1719.

57 Montaigne as member of the Chambre des Enquêtes.   Authorities differ on his exact place; on what evidence, I cannot determine. Dreano (p. 141) locates him in the first Chambre des Enquêtes, Saint-Saens (p. 124) in the new one that replaced the Chambre des Requêtes; Strowski (p. 112) makes him tenth councillor in the Enquêtes, Hubrecht (p. 272) in the Requêtes. Bonnefon (*Montaigne et ses amis,* I, 60) places him in one of the Chambres des Enquêtes, but does not know which. Nor do I.

58 De Thou on Montaigne.   *Historiarum . . . ,* V, 180.

58 Pasquier.   "Lettre à Monsieur de Pelgé" (*Lettres,* XVIII, i) quoted from *Choix de lettres* (Geneva: Droz, 1956), p. 44.

58 "mortgaging" his will,   III: 9, S 736, OC 941; III: 10, S 767, OC 980–1.

58 "gains ceasing . . . ensuing,"   III: 9, S 737, OC 943.

58 "Item."   I: 46, S 201–2, OC 265–7.

58 "not lawyer-like, but rather soldierly."   I: 26, S 127, OC 171.

58–59 Montaigne's defense of the male member.   I: 21, S 73, OC 101; cf. S 72, OC 100.

59 Bordeaux Parlement examines candidates on judgment.   See the records of receptions of La Boétie and Florimond de Raemond (*AHG,* XXV, 336–7, 410–1). Cf. *Essays,* I: 25, S 103, OC 139.

59 Magistrate using 200 quotations.   III: 12, S 808–9, OC 1033–4.

59 Councillor praying *Non nobis.*   III: 10, S 782, OC 1000. Florimond de Raemond identifies him as the Huguenot Bernard Arnoul; see Alan M. Boase, "Montaigne annoté par Florimond de Raemond," *Revue du Seizième Siècle,* XV (1928), p. 274.

59 Judge sentencing adulterer.   III: 9, S 756, OC 967.

59–61 Montaigne's remarks about laws (except as otherwise noted). III: 13, S 815–7, 819–21, OC 1042–4, 1047–9.

60 For it is certain . . . the scales.   II: 12, S 424–5, OC 547–8.

60 'Question for my friend'   II: 12, S 439, OC 566.

61 Judges obtaining confession by fraud.   III: 1, S 600, OC 768.

61 Cruelty of penalties.   II: 11, S 314–5, OC 410–11; cf. II: 27, S 530, OC 679.

61 Montaigne too lenient a judge.   III: 12, S 814, OC 1040.

61 "Justice in itself . . . of our governments."   III: 1, S 604, OC 773.

61 fn. "more often by wicked men . . ."   *Essais,* III: 13. In Ed.

Munic., III, 370 fn.; in Edition Phototypique (Hachette, 1912), plate 975.

62 Montaigne on Navarre's plan for judiciary reform.   Bonnefon, pp. 358–9 fn.; Hubrecht, pp. 292–3.

62 fn. Montaigne complimented by Loisel.   Paul Courteault, "Montaigne maire de Bordeaux," in *IVe Centenaire* . . . , pp. 86–88.

Chapter 5: La Boétie

Generally, *Essays, passim;* Bonnefon, Strowski.

On La Boétie and the friendship: Montaigne: *Essays,* I: 28, and letter in S 1046–56, OC 1347–60. Bonnefon: Introduction to La Boétie: *Œuvres complètes* (Bordeaux: Gounouilhou, and Paris: Rouam, 1892). *BSAM* III: 2 (April–June, 1957), a number devoted to celebrating the four hundredth anniversary of their meeting. Harry Kurz, "Montaigne and La Boétie in the Chapter on Friendship," *Publications of the Modern Language Association of America,* LXV (June, 1950), 483–530. Maurice Riveline, *Montaigne et l'amitié* (Alcan, 1939). Trinquet, "Montaigne et la divulgation du 'Contr'un'," *RHLF,* LXIV (1964), 1–12.

Page

63–64 Montaigne's build.   II: 17, S 485–6, OC 623–5; cf. II: 22, S 515, OC 661. Montaigne also liked walking, but not on city streets, where he got jostled and muddy: III: 13, S 841, OC 1075.

64 Signs of pride in Montaigne's carriage.   II: 17, S 479, OC 615.

64 Montaigne wears black and white.   I: 36, S 168, OC 223.

64 Montaigne likes adornment.   III: 6, S 688, OC 880.

64 "a cloak . . . stocking. . . .   I: 26, S 127, OC 171.

64 . . . If I have . . . reform halfway."   III: 9, S 722, OC 924.

64 Carrying a rod.   II: 25, S 521, OC 669. A later variant shows him as rarely without a rod: Ed. Munic., III: 13, 415 fn.

64 Montaigne is affable.   II: 17, S 479, OC 616.

64 "vigorous, full, lazy . . ." "kindles . . . enthusiasms."   III: 5, S 641, OC 821.

64 . . . not merely . . . verdure and cheer,"   II: 6, S 268, OC 352.

64 He eats greedily . . . restless . . . My walk is quick . . . I place them.   III: 13, S 848, OC 1085.

64 A loud talker.   III: 13, S 834, OC 1065–6.

64 Quick to anger.   I: 38, S 173, OC 230; II: 31, S 543–4, OC 697–8; cf. III: 13, S 822, OC 1051.

64 He cannot . . . on horseback.   III: 3, S 629, OC 806; III: 5, S 668, OC 854.

64–65 I have scarcely . . . birds, or horses.   II: 17, S 486–7, OC 625.

65 "I have a distaste . . . passive."   III: 7, S 700, OC 896.

65 Thoughts all his own.   I: 26, S 129, OC 174.

65 . . . elbowroom in all directions."   III: 9, S 740, OC 947.

65 He hates involvement.   III: 10, S 766–7, OC 980–1.

65 . . . his blood as readily as his care.   II: 17, S 487, OC 626.

65 He is happier . . . paying debts.   I: 14, S 43–4, OC 63–4; cf. S 45–6, OC 65–6.

65 "a little natural . . . freedom."   III: 9, S 740–1, OC 947.

65 Seldom gives or takes advice.   III: 2, S 618, OC 792–3.

65 Combats habit.   III: 13, S 830, OC 1061.

65 Learns from good fortune.   III: 2, S 619, OC 794.

65 Learns from contrast.   III: 8, S 703, OC 899.

65 "the first and fundamental part of virtue"   II: 17, S 491, OC 631.

65 "we are men . . . by our word."   I: 9, S 23, OC 37; cf. II: 18, S 505, OC 649–50.

65 Cannot bear to be misunderstood.   III: 9, S 751, OC 961.

65 Changes tone, not meaning.   III: 1, S 602, OC 771.

65 Blunt in amorous approaches.   III: 5, S 679, OC 868.

65 He would rather . . . dissimulating flatterer.   II: 17, S 492, OC 632.

65 . . . men would not compete . . .   III: 7, S 701, OC 897.

65 Too much . . . public office.   I: 57, S 237–8, OC 312–4.

65 Conservative convictions.   II: 12, S 428, OC 553.

65 Hard to choose an opinion.   II: 17, S 496, OC 637.

66 once overready to make light . . .   I: 27, *passim.*

66 Tempting hazards of Reform.   I: 56, S 232, OC 305.

66 Protestantism leads to atheism.   II: 12, S 320, OC 416.

66 . . . the laws have given him a master . . .   III: 1, S 603, OC 772.

66 "on the . . . holy word."   II: 12, S 437, OC 563.

66 For whatever . . . has produced.   II: 12, S 428, OC 553.

66 Order of Saint Michael.   II: 12, S 434, OC 560–1.

66 Ostentation in studies and books.   III: 3, S 629–30, OC 807.

66 Degree of Montaigne's ambition.   II: 17, S 489, OC 628; III: 9, S 759, OC 970–1.

66 Neither gregarious . . . communication.   III: 3, S 621–3, 625, OC 796–9, 801.

66 Sweets, wines, and sauces.   III: 5, S 640, OC 820; III: 13, S 843, OC 1078.

66 Women unfit for theology.   I: 56, S 235, OC 310.

66 Montaigne's love of poetry.   I: 37, S 171, OC 228.

66 "an amusement . . . his favorites;   III: 3, S 624, OC 801, and *passim.*

66 Essays dedicated to women.   I: 26 to Diane de Foix, countess

of Gurson; I: 29 to Diane de Gramont, countess of Guissen; II: 8 to Madame Louise d'Estissac; II: 37 to Madame de Duras. II: 12 is not dedicated but addressed to a princess, almost certainly Margaret of Valois.

66 . . . salon into the boudoir.   III: 5, S 644, OC 825.

67 His first amorous . . . up to six.   III: 13, S 833, OC 1064. W. H. Auden ("Montaigne," in *Collected Poetry*, 1945, p. 98) once described Montaigne as "undersexed," presumably on the theory that he protests too much. But if Montaigne's own testimony is not conclusive, La Boétie's (noted later in this chapter) seems indisputable.

67 He once let . . . reckless passion."   III: 3, S 626, OC 803.

67 Montaigne's love letters.   I: 40, S 186, OC 247.

67 "the close kisses of youth,   I: 55, S 228, OC 301.

67 Montaigne's poor timing.   III: 5, S 659, OC 843.

67 I swore to them . . . them of it. . . .   III: 5, S 678–9, OC 867–8.

67–68 Little traffic with prostitutes.   III: 3, S 627, OC 804.

68 It is a vain . . . toward his ruin.   III: 5, S 680–2, OC 870–2.

68 "I gave them up . . . them within."   III: 10, S 776, OC 992.

68 Montaigne skipping a meal.   III: 13, S 846, OC 1082.

68 "gain a glimpse of it."   III: 13, S 854, OC 1092.

68 Seeking to control . . . possess me,"   II: 12, S 428, OC 552.

68 but has found . . . chaster men claim.   II: 11, S 313, OC 409.

68 "In this business . . . but no folly."   III: 5, S 680, OC 869.

68 "When I consider . . . can accomplish."   III: 2, S 617, OC 791.

69 Since my earliest . . . his duration.   I: 20, S 60–1, OC 85–6.

69 They probably met in 1559,   The earliest statement we have on the duration of their friendship is Montaigne's, in the "Notice to the Reader of La Boétie's Translations" (August 10, 1570; S 1060, OC 1719), that "our acquaintance began only six years before his death." (La Boétie died on August 18, 1563.) In his chapter "Of Friendship" Montaigne first wrote that he knew his friend for "four or five years" (I: 28; DB I, 145), then changed this to "four years" (S 143, OC 192). The quadricentenary of their meeting was celebrated on June 10, 1557, by the Société des Amis de Montaigne (see *BSAM* III: 2, April–June 1957, *passim*); but apart from one unsupported statement (by P. Barrière, p. 9) that Montaigne met La Boétie on first arriving in the Bordeaux Parlement, no reason is given for choosing that year. Though Montaigne is erratic with dates, I lean to 1559 because it seems to me likeliest 1) that he successively corrected himself; and 2) that he was tempted to exaggerate the length of the friendship, so that the shortest span he mentions is the most reliable.

69 We sought . . . as each other.   I: 28, S 139, OC 187.

69–70 Montaigne on beauty and on La Boétie's ugliness.   III: 12, S 809–10, OC 1035. For interesting variants showing Montaigne's hesitations in writing this account, see Ed. Munic., III, 351 fn.

70 Everything a very . . . true father.   Montaigne's letter on La Boétie's death, S 1049, OC 1351–2.

70–73 La Boétie.   Bonnefon, Introduction to La Boétie, *Œuvres complètes,* and *Montaigne et ses amis,* I, 103–224; Kurz article; and (especially for the *Voluntary Servitude* and Montaigne's relation to it), Trinquet, "Montaigne et la divulgation du 'Contr'un'," *RHLF,* LXIV (Jan.–March, 1964), 1–12.

71 . . . Ronsard personally.   La Boétie was brother-in-law to Lancelot de Carle, a close friend of Jean de Belot, and known to Michel de L'Hôpital—all three friends and supporters of Ronsard.

71 "so unpleasant a season,"   So Montaigne had called it in this connection in a dedicatory letter of August 10, 1570; S 1061, OC 1719.

71 "He wrote it," . . . to "sixteen."   I: 28, DB I, 135–6, 146; S 135, 144; OC 182, 193.

71 La Boétie on the Pléiade.   In Bonnefon's 1922 edition of the *Servitude volontaire* and the *Mémoire touchant l'Edit de Janvier, 1562* (Bossard), p. 88; in Maurice Rat's edition of the *Servitude volontaire,* Colin (Bibliothèque de Cluny), c. 1963, pp. 81–2. Du Bellay's first published volume of poems appeared in 1549, Ronsard's in 1550, Baïf's in 1552.

71 "if I had not . . . appearances,"   III: 9, S 752, OC 961.

71–72 Because I have . . . ages than this.   I: 28, S 144, OC 193.

72 "the primary reason . . . is habit."   Bonnefon ed., p. 74; Rat ed., p. 69.

72 Anti-Dictator.   Subtitled: The *Discours sur la servitude volontaire* of Etienne de La Boétie, Rendered into English by Harry Kurz. New York: Columbia University Press, 1942.

73 "long before . . . three centuries."   I: 28, S 136, OC 182.

73–74 Most human relationships . . . of this union.   I: 28, S 139, OC 186–7; cf. S 136–8, OC 182–5.

74 He wrote . . . his or mine.   I: 28, S 139, OC 187.

74 For in truth . . . of friendship.   I: 28, S 143, OC 192.

74–75 La Boétie's account of the friendship.   In *Œuvres complètes,* p. 225, lines 4–11, 23–27.

75 Montaigne's remarks about La Boétie.   Dedicatory letters of 1570 in S 1057–65, especially pp. 1057, 1059, 1062–4; OC 1361–70, 1719, especially 1362–3, 1366–9.

75 "a soldierly vigor."   Ed. Munic., II, 446 fn. (a MS variant later deleted).

75 To be sure . . . learning and study.   II: 17, S 500, OC 643.

75–76 La Boétie's Latin poems.   "Ad Belotium et Montanum," "Ad Michaelem Montanum," "Ad Michaëlem Montanum," in *Œuvres complètes,* pp. 207–9, 210–3, 225–35. There is a good French translation by Louis Cestre in *BSAM* I: 4 (1921), 351–67.

76 "Shall I bend . . . a gray head." Lines 65–70; *Œuvres complètes,* p. 227; Cestre, p. 357.

76 "with winged foot . . . the crowns." Lines 5–7 of the second poem; *Œuvres complètes,* p. 211; Cestre, p. 353.

76 "against the . . . La Boétie," II: 6, S 270, OC 354.

76–79 Montaigne's letter on La Boétie's death. S 1046–56, OC 1347–60.

77 . . . stay with the Lestonnacs, La Boétie's will shows that he stayed there; see his *Œuvres complètes,* p. 427.

78 In the evening the notary . . . From Montaigne's account this seems to be Sunday evening, August 15; but La Boétie's will is dated August 14.

79–80 Did Montaigne embellish the friendship? Floyd Gray ("Montaigne's Friends" in *French Studies,* XV, July, 1961, 203–12) argues that he did, stressing the references, on the title page and in the privilege, to Montaigne's "letter" on La Boétie's death as a "discourse." He makes a pretty good case, but in my judgment fails to do justice to the negative evidence. For example, he stretches matters when he writes (p. 205) "that our idea of their relationship as it is usually described depends almost completely on the essay that Montaigne dedicated to it." In arguing that Montaigne's "letter" was written in 1570, not 1563, he assumes (p. 208) that Montaigne "probably saw" his father "every day" in 1563, whereas it seems likelier to me that while Montaigne was in and near Bordeaux when La Boétie died, his father was at Montaigne; and he seems to ignore the strong unlikelihood of Montaigne's relating his friend's death to his father in the form of a letter *after* his father's death.

80 "absence, . . . their part"; Gray article, p. 211.

80 [To the shades . . . for the mind. This inscription, discovered and published by Prunis in 1774 and later destroyed, was probably made when Montaigne solemnized his retirement in Feb., 1571. See Bonnefon, *Montaigne et ses amis,* I, 245, and Riveline, pp. 95–6 for good tentative reconstructions.

80 He knows by experience . . . our wills richer. III: 9, S 745–7, OC 953–5.

80–81 Once, after . . . this privation? II: 8, S 286–7 and fn., OC 375. Cf. Ed. Munic., II, 83 and fn.

81 This same morning . . . much harm. *TJ,* La Villa, May 11, 1581; S 989, OC 1270.

81 The *Essays* a compensation. Thibaudet, *Montaigne* (Gallimard, c. 1963), pp. 143, 149, 151, 153.

81 "sociable to excess," III: 9, S 750, OC 960.

81 "hungry to make myself known," III: 5, S 643, OC 824.

81 "all in . . . and friendship."   III: 3, S 625, OC 801.
81 "somewhat barren . . . proof of this."   III: 3, S 623, OC 798.
81 It is rare . . . of a companion.   III: 9, S 754, OC 965.
82 If there are . . . flesh and bone.   III: 5, S 640, OC 821.
82 Besides this profit . . . water and fire!   III: 9, S 749–50, OC 959.
82 "It was a melancholy . . . with writing."   II: 8, S 278, OC 364.
82–83 I know well . . . so painstakingly.   This passage was crossed out, probably in consideration for Marie de Gournay. III: 9, S 752 fn., OC 1652–3. Cf. Ed. Munic., III, 255 fn.
83 Letter writing . . . more successful.   I: 40, S 185–6, OC 246.
83–84 Intensity and importance of friendship.   This may raise the question of homosexuality in the modern reader's mind; but there is no evidence for, and much against, any such interpretation.

Chapter 6: Marriage

The main source here is the *Essays*, especially III: 9. There is a very good study by Paul Laumonier, "Madame de Montaigne, d'après les *Essais*," in *Mélanges offerts à M. Abel Lefranc* (Droz, 1936), pp. 393–407. Other sources appear below in individual notes.

Page

85–86 Montaigne's wife and her family.   See *Ephemeris,* and Boscheron des Portes, *Histoire du Parlement de Bordeaux.*
86 *Cléandre.*   Villey, *Montaigne devant la postérité* (Boivin, 1935), pp. 23, 343–4. Elsewhere Villey points out that Montaigne may also have incurred a very slight debt to Pressac: Ed. Munic., IV, lxvii, and "Note sur la bibliothèque de Montaigne," *RHLF,* XVII (1910), 345–6.
86 Montaigne's marriage contract.   Dated Sept. 22, 1565, it is published in *AHG,* X, 163–7, and in Malvezin, pp. 294–5.
86 Montaigne's children.   *Ephemeris, passim.*
86 De Thou's visit.   De Thou, *Historiarum . . . ,* VII, *De vita sua,* p. 97; *Mémoires,* Buchon ed., p. 637.
86 Marie de Gournay.   Marjorie H. Ilsley, *A Daughter of the Renaissance. Marie Le Jars de Gournay* (The Hague: Mouton, 1963), ch. 2–5; Nicolaï, *Les Belles Amies de Montaigne,* pp. 193–5, 213, 216; Villey, *Montaigne devant la postérité,* p. 47; J.-F. Payen, "Recherches sur Michel Montaigne. Correspondance relative à sa mort," in *Bulletin du Bibliophile,* 1862, pp. 1303, 1306. Marie de Gournay, *Le Proumenoir de Monsieur de Montaigne* (L'Angelier, 1594), p. 105 verso; Preface to 1595 ed. of Montaigne's *Essays,* p. ã ii verso; and "Copie de la vie de la demoiselle de Gournay" in *Les Advis ou les presens de la demoiselle de Gournay,* 1641 ed.

86–87 Malvin de Cessac's letter.   *AHG*, XXXIV, 323.

87 Charles de Gamaches.   *Le Sensé raisonnant sur les passages de l'Escriture Saincte, contre les pretendus Reformez* (1623), pp. 37, 232–3. See Dreano, pp. 37–8.

87–89 Françoise de La Chassaigne's letters.   In Gabriel Richou, *Inventaire de la collection des ouvrages et documents réunis par J.-F. Payen et J.-B. Bastide sur Michel de Montaigne* (Techener, 1878), pp. 275–324.

87 Marmelade, lemons, oranges.   Richou, pp. 290–1, 302.

87 Feeding-cup, coral spoons.   Pp. 287, 297, 304.

87 Muslin, taffeta, hay, butter.   Pp. 309, 311–2, 315.

87 Legal and financial matters.   Pp. 290, 297–8, 317.

88 Wants her charity voluntary. "So many . . . to me so!"   P. 298.

88 Money matters.   Pp. 292, 297, 302–3, 316–7, 319.

88 Devotion to spiritual director.   Pp. 284–6, 306–7, 312–3, 317–9.

88 Her first letter.   Pp. 284–6.

88 "I would . . . miserable weather."   P. 302; cf. pp. 297, 306.

88 Concern with infirmities and death.   Pp. 299–302, 306, 308, 313, 318–9.

88–89 "My health . . . holy will. . . ."   Pp. 313, 319.

88 fn. Charles de Lur-Saluces, Marie de Gamaches.   Richou seems right that these are the children in question though his date for the birth of Lur-Saluces is corrected by Marchand in the *Ephemeris.*

89 The document concerning the gold chain.   Malvezin, p. 300.

89 Malvezin's speculation.   Malvezin, p. 148.

89–90 The theory of adultery.   Nicolaï, *Montaigne intime*, pp. 75–8. Maurice Rat, "Le Ménage de Montaigne," *BSAM* II: 15 (1949–52), 14–23; cf. II: 18 (Jan.–June, 1956), 26–7.

90–91 Ruth Kelso's summary.   *Doctrine for the Lady of the Renaissance* (Urbana: University of Illinois Press, 1956), pp. 87–9. Her authorities in this section are Bouchet, Gouge, Lesnauderie, Tasso, Tillier, Vives. Cf. Pierre Barrière, *Montaigne, gentilhomme français* (Bordeaux: Delmas, 2nd ed., 1948, pp. 65–6); René de Maulde La Clavière, *Les Femmes de la Renaissance* (Perrin, 1898); W. L. Wiley, *The Gentleman of the French Renaissance* (Cambridge, Mass.: Harvard University Press, 1954); and Maurice Valency, *In Praise of Love* (New York: Macmillan Paperbacks, 1961 ed.), p. 66 and *passim.*

91 Montaigne's mother and the rest of the household.   See above, ch. 2.

91 Montaigne deplored scandal in marriage.   III: 5, S 648, OC 830.

91 Grief and diversion by love.   III: 4, S 634, OC 813.

91 Of my own choice . . . or expected.   III: 5, S 648, OC 830.

91 Married at a good age.   II: 8, S 282, OC 369.

91–92 Connections and . . . be the model.   III: 5, S 645–7, OC 827–9.

92 To be sure . . . fitful flame.   I: 28, S 137–8, OC 183–4.

92 Least successful . . . sacred alliance,"   III: 5, S 646, OC 827.

92 this "religious . . . of nature."   I: 30, S 147, OC 196.

92 Make love infrequently . . . take their time   I: 21, S 72, OC 99–100; III: 5, S 646, OC 827.

92 Sleeps without a woman.   III: 13, S 840, OC 1075.

92 "I cannot . . . standing up."   III: 13, S 830, OC 1061.

92–93 We have not . . . if need be.   III: 9, S 746, OC 954.

93 "the members . . . to cover up."   I: 3, S 11, OC 22.

93 Florimond de Raemond's report.   His note is opposite Montaigne's advice to husbands (I: 30), part of which is quoted above, "Those shameless excesses . . . for our need." See Alan M. Boase, "Montaigne annoté par Florimond de Raemond," *Revue du Seizième Siècle*, XV (1928), 239.

93–94 Montaigne's letter to his wife.   Dedicatory Epistle dated Sept. 10, 1570; S 1065–6, OC 1371.

94 Unconcern about having children.   I: 14, S 42, OC 61–2: "And I have lost two or three (but while they were still nursing), if not without grief, at least without repining." He has been much reproached for this callousness; but it should be noted that he considers "repining" (*fascherie*) as an unworthy excess. He and his wife may well have clashed over the degree of grief that each felt appropriate for the death of their infants.

94 Though he seems . . . with my wife."   II: 8, S 284–5, 293, OC 371–3, 383.

94–95 Births and deaths of children.   See *Ephemeris;* OC 1407–9.

95 An amiable household.   Most editors of the *TJ* (Rat, Dédéyan, *et al.*) see a reference to his wife in Montaigne's remark about the mineral water of La Villa (May 10, 1581; S 987, OC 1268): "They take it to cool the liver and get rid of red pimples on the face, a fact that I carefully note as a service I owe to a very virtuous lady in France."

95 "We have just . . . in between."   I: 54, S 226, OC 298.

95 "I handle the cards . . . for keeps."   I: 23, S 79, OC 108.

95 Montaigne carried home from accident.   II: 6, S 271, OC 356. See below, ch. 8.

95 Daughter brought up gently.   II: 8, S 281–2, OC 368–9.

95–96 My daughter . . . reprimand and interdict. . . .   III: 5, S 651, OC 834.

96 Montaigne considers . . . up near me."   II: 8, S 280, 290, OC 366, 379.

96 Infants not to be reared by parents.   III: 13, S 844, OC 1079.

96 A widow . . . weakness of the sex."   II: 8, S 288, OC 377.

96 "We must reserve . . . do without them."   I: 39, S 177, OC 235.

96–97 There is my . . . to be alone.   III: 3, S 629, OC 807.

97 Although the task . . . of my friends.   III: 9, S 724, 728, OC 926, 931–2.

97 Don't tell me! . . . the form.   III: 9, S 745, OC 952–3.

97–98 Since his wife . . . drippings wear me down.   III: 9, S 724–5, 727, OC 926–8, 930.

98 Montaigne on anger.   II: 31, S 540, 543–4, OC 692, 697–8. Montaigne once had some uneasy moments in Italy after giving a local driver a box on the ear. *TJ*, La Muccia, April 22, 1581; S 969, OC 1246.

98 he is as candid . . . he can be: II: 8, S 288, OC 376.

98 Montaigne on the well-shaped shoe.   III: 9, S 723–4, OC 925.

98–99 Plutarch on the well-shaped shoe.   *Lives* (Loeb Classical Library; London: Heinemann, and New York: Putnam, 1914–26, 11 vols.), VI, 364–7; *Moralia* (Loeb, 1927–59, 14 vols.), II, 312–5. For La Boétie's translation see his *Œuvres complètes*, pp. 169–70 and *passim*, pp. 161–84.

99 The bitternesses . . . about it.   III: 5, S 662, OC 848. This passage may imply that Montaigne finds marriage less irksome than his book suggests; for the book, being his only outlet, may give an exaggeratedly bad impression.

99 "A good marriage . . . getting wedded."   III: 5, S 646–8, OC 827–30.

99–100 "What do you lack? . . . find it?"   III: 9, S 755, OC 965–6.

100 "Marital love . . . of my home."   III: 9, S 745, OC 953.

100 Whoever supposes . . . is a fool.   I: 38, S 173, OC 230.

100 "They don't come by the dozen,   II: 35, S 563, OC 722.

100 Wives always . . . grace and authority.   II: 8, S 286, OC 374.

100 keep up . . . a gardener,   III: 3, S 623, OC 799.

100 "mean and sickly . . . worth per yard."   III: 8, S 704, OC 900–1.

100 Unreasonable women.   II: 8, S 288, OC 377.

100–101 Headstrong women.   II: 31, S 542, OC 695–6. When Montaigne writes elsewhere (II: 32, S 548, OC 702–3) that "we see every day" examples of frenzied stubbornness in women, one might think he had his wife in mind; but he had written just before this that he had known "hundreds of women" of this sort.

101 A shrewish wife . . . naked blade."   II: 11, S 307, OC 401.

101 Jealousy in a wife . . . we small fry to do?   III: 5, S 657, 663, OC 841, 848.

101 In our age . . . exist no longer?   II: 35, S 563, OC 722; cf. III: 4, S 630, OC 808.

101 "I know a hundred . . . discreditably."   III: 5, S 662, OC 847; cf. S 660–4, OC 845–50.

102 Did Madame de Montaigne read the *Essays?* Roger Trinquet has shown the relation between a passage in the *Essays* (I: 26, S 130, OC 176) and the wish she expresses in her seventies (noted earlier in this chapter) to keep her giving voluntary; but he implies that she remembers Montaigne's spoken, not his written, words. "Sur un texte obscur des *Essais* éclairé par une lettre de Mme de Montaigne," *BSAM* II: 17 (1955), 45–8; however, cf. p. 7 of the same issue.

Chapter 7: Translation, Inheritance, Retirement

For Montaigne's translation, see Joseph Coppin's excellent study, *Montaigne traducteur de Raymond Sebon* (Lille: Morel, 1925), to which we are all indebted. Zeitlin offers a very good summary in his Introduction (I, xxxiii–xxxiv).

For Sebond's text I have used the editions of 1496 (Strasbourg: Martin Flach) and 1526 (Lyons: Jacques Myt), modernizing the punctuation to avoid useless obstacles to clarity; for Montaigne's translation, the 2nd ed. (Gourbin, Sonnius, Chaudiere, 1581) and Armaingaud's modern text in vols. IX–X (1932–5) of his ed. of Montaigne's *Œuvres complètes*. Since Sebond's chapters are short, I have given their numbers alone for reference to his work and dispensed with page numbers as unnecessary.

Page
103 Sebond's life, his book, its fortunes. Coppin, pp. 11, 13, 17–18.
103 Sebond's main purpose. Augustin Renaudet, *Préréforme et humanisme à Paris pendant les premières guerres d'Italie (1494–1517)* (2nd ed., Librairie d'Argence, 1953), pp. 520–1.
105 Since, as I . . . worthy of him. Chapter 322, beginning. I have translated this passage from Montaigne's French, which stays pretty close to Sebond's Latin but is less crabbed.
105 Sir, in carrying . . . he is worth. Dedication, June 18, 1568; S 1056, OC 1360–1.
106 Montaigne's account in the "Apology." II: 12, S 319–21, OC 415–7.
107–108 Montaigne's changes in translating Sebond's Prologue. Coppin (pp. 67–70) was the first to point these out.
107 There follows . . . *any other* [necessary]. The Latin and the French of the italicized (altered) passages are the following: 1) "quae est necessaria omni homini, et ei naturalis, et conveniens" —"convenable, naturelle et utile à tout homme . . ." 2) "omne" —"presque tout . . ." 3) "omnem veritatem homini necessariam"—"la verité, autant qu'il est possible à la raison natu-

relle . . ." 4) "Et per istam scientiam homo cognoscit, sine difficultate et realiter, quicquid in sacra scriptura continetur; et
quicquid in sacra scriptura dicitur et praecipitur, per istam scientiam cognoscitur infallibiliter, cum magna certitudine"—"luy
donne grand accez à l'intelligence de ce qui est prescrit et com-
mandé aux sainctes escritures . . ." 5) "omni dubitatione post-
posita"—"deslivré de plusieurs doubtes . . ." 6) "toti sacrae
scripturae assentiat, et certificatur, ut non possit dubitare quaes-
tionem in ista scientia. Et per istam scientiam potest solvi omnis
quaestio quae debet sciri tam de deo quam de seipso, et hoc sine
difficultate"—"consent hardiment à ce qu'elles contiennent con-
cernant la cognoissance de Dieu, ou de soy-mesme." 7) "omnes"—
"les . . ." 8) "tota fides catholica infallibiliter"—"la foy Catho-
lique . . ." 9) "necessariam"—"necessaire avant tout autre."

108 Sebond's Prologue and book on the Index.   Coppin, pp. 65–6.

108 Common major themes.   Sebond, ch. 1, 210. Montaigne, II: 12,
S 418, OC 539; III: 13, S 815, 819, 821–2, OC 1041, 1047,
1050–1.

108 Minor affinities.   Sebond, ch. 188, 191–2, 194, 253. Montaigne:
I: 21, 46; II: 16.

109 Pierre Bunel . . . than 1565.   Coppin, pp. 25–55; Zeitlin, I,
xxxiii–xxxiv.

109 "with the nonchalance . . . of this."   II: 12, DB II, 19.

110 One earlier translator.   Coppin, p. 34.

110–111 Montaigne's amplification of a passage in Sebond.   Coppin, who
points out this comparison (pp. 53–4), limits it to the first parts
of each text ("From all these . . . against the believers."—"All
this teaches . . . in a thousand ways . . ."). The translation here
is so free that it is hard even to say precisely what renders what;
but I think the amplification is more fully and accurately shown
by the longer passages quoted here.

110–111 Montaigne's version.   For the unbeliever tossed on a sea of doubt,
cf. *Essays* II: 12, S 386–7, OC 500–1. For the burden of proof
he bears, I: 23, S 86–7, OC 118; II: 17, S 489–90, OC 628–9;
III: 12, S 798, OC 1020; etc.

111–112 Literary qualities of Sebond's text and of Montaigne's translation.
Excellent treatment in Coppin, pp. 81–100. See especially p. 84
for Montaigne letting in light and air; p. 93 for the passage from
Sebond, ch. 108.

112 "I would have . . . less my own. . . .   III: 5, S 667, OC 853.

112 My language has . . . not attain it."   II: 17, S 483–4, OC 621.

112 Montaigne's father in old age.   See above, ch. 1.

112 His son twice . . . years of his life."   II: 37, S 578, OC 742;
Ephemeris, June 18, OC 1406.

113 Agreement between Montaigne and three brothers.   AHG, X,
252–6; published in part in Malvezin, pp. 295–7.

113 Settlement between Montaigne and his mother.   See above, ch. 2.

114 Collision on horseback.   II: 6; see below, ch. 8.

114 The king's letters patent.   *AHG,* XXV, 410–1.

114 Dedications of La Boétie's works.   S 1057–66, OC 1361–71, 1719.

114 . . . either twice or for one long stay . . .   Montaigne dates a "Notice" from Paris, Aug. 10, 1570, a dedication from Montaigne, Sept. 1, and another from Paris, Sept. 10 (S 1060–6, OC 1370–1, 1719); which speaks for two separate trips. However, as Bonnefon pointed out (La Boétie, *Œuvres complètes,* p. 365), the slowness of travel in Montaigne's day makes the two September dates and places virtually irreconcilable.

114 —as he had . . . friend's death—   "Notice" of Aug. 10, 1570; S 1061, OC 1719.

115 The Latin inscription.   The Latin text is given in Plattard, *Montaigne et son temps* (Boivin, 1933), p. 107 fn., and, with a French translation, in Villey's 1930–1 ed. of the *Essais* (Alcan, 3 vols.), I, xxvii–xxviii, lxi–lxii; Zeitlin gives an English translation in his ed. of the *Essays,* I, xxxiv.

The Latin text reads as follows:

An.[no] Christi [1571] aet.[ate] 38, pridie cal.[endas] Mart.[ias], die suo natali, Mich.[aelis] Montanus, servitii aulici et munerum publicorum jamdudum pertaesus, dum se integer in doctarum Virginum recessit sinus, ubi quietus et omnium securus [quant]illum id tandem superabit decursi multa jam plus parte spatii, si modo fata duint, exigat istas sedes et dulces latebras avitasque libertati suae tranquillitatique et otio consecravit.

(The bracketed bits are completions of abbreviations or parts missing when the inscription was first copied.)

Chapter 8: At Home

The main source here is the *Essays.* Colorful and readable though often romanced are two accounts which I have used only very sparingly: Alexandre Nicolaï's *Montaigne intime* (Aubier, c. 1941) and André Lamandé's *La Vie gaillarde et sage de Montaigne* (Plon, c. 1927), available in English as *Montaigne, Grave and Gay* (New York: Holt, c. 1928).

Page

116–117 The French country gentleman.   See Pierre de Vaissière, *Gentilshommes campagnards de l'ancienne France* (Perrin, 1904, 4th ed.), especially ch. 1, pp. 1–174; Lucien Romier, *Le Royaume de Catherine de Médicis* (Perrin, 1922, 2 vols.), I, especially pp. 188–208; W. L. Wiley, *The Gentleman of Renaissance France* (Cambridge, Mass.: Harvard University Press, 1954); Abel Lefranc, *La Vie quotidienne au temps de la Renaissance* (Hachette, 1938), pp. 107–28; Philippe Erlanger, *La Vie quotidienne sous Henri IV* (Hachette, 1958), pp. 96–119.

117 "virgin of lawsuits,"   III: 10, S 779, OC 995.

118 Brantôme.   On Mattecoulon: *Œuvres complètes* (Lalanne ed.; Renouard, 1864–82, 11 vols.), VI, 322–3. (All references are to this edition.) On the duke of Milan and Montaigne, VI, 499 (*Discours sur les duels*). On the order of Saint Michael, V, 92–3 (*Grands Capitaines françois:* Tavannes). On La Noue, V, 381 (*Discours sur les couronnels de l'infanterie de France*).

118 May have had an older brother.   We do not know the sex of the two older children (II: 37, S 579, OC 742), who evidently died very young. Thibaudet (*Montaigne*, Gallimard, 1963, p. 2) argues that they were probably both boys and destined to bear arms, whereas Michel, as the third, was destined for the law.

118 The Pléiade poets.   Du Bellay, *Deffence et Illustration de la langue françoyse*, Book I, ch. 7 (2nd Chamard ed., Didier, 1948), p. 42.

118 Montaigne on education.   I: 26, S 112, OC 151.

118–119 Montaigne's mistrust of learning.   I: 26, S 121, OC 163; II: 17, S 501, OC 644; III: 13, S 818, OC 1046; and *passim.*

119 Learning . . . a mass of pills."   I: 26, S 109–10, OC 148.

119 The test of quality . . .   I: 14, S 38, OC 56.

119 Horseman rather than logician.   III: 9, S 726, OC 929.

119 "less a maker . . . all respects"   II: 37, S 596, OC 764. Cf. I: 20, S 62, OC 88; I: 40, S 183–4, OC 243–4.

119 Ancestors born at château.   III: 9, S 741, OC 948.

119 "formerly surnamed Eyquem";   II: 16, S 475, OC 610.

119 Refers to himself as a soldier.   I: 3, S 11, OC 22; III: 13, S 831, OC 1063.

119 Joys of military life.   III: 13, S 831, 841, OC 1063, 1075–6.

119 For although he . . . in a woman.   II: 7, S 277–8, OC 363–4. On chastity, see also III: 5, S 655, OC 838.

119 "who have . . . than valor."   II: 17, S 500, OC 642.

119–120 The long robe and the short.   I: 23, S 85, OC 117.

120 The man you see . . . in the attempt.   I: 39, S 177–8, OC 235–6.

120 Bell that rings the *Ave Maria*.   I: 23, S 78, OC 107.

120 He calls it . . . thousand volumes: II: 17, S 493, OC 634; III: 12, S 808, OC 1033.

120–121 When at home . . . There is my throne.   III: 3, S 628–9, OC 806–7.

121 Best ideas on horseback.   III: 5, S 668, OC 854.

121 Books are a diversion . . . always there.   III: 3, S 621, 628–9, OC 797, 805–7.

121 Emerson on Montaigne. *Journal* (Boston and New York: Houghton Mifflin, 1909–14, 10 vols.), IX, 152 (1858).

121 Prefers horse to litter or walking. III: 6, S 687, OC 878; III: 13, S 841, OC 1075.

121 Once good at riding post. II: 22, S 515, OC 661.

121 —a lawyer or a Venetian. III: 8, S 703, OC 900.

121 and when he . . . insolent ardor." III: 13, S 839–40, OC 1073–4.

121 . . . my rear in the saddle." III: 9, S 755, OC 965.

121–123 Montaigne's collision on horseback. II: 6, S 268–72, OC 352–7.

123 "under the aspect . . . same nature." II: 12, S 336, OC 436.

123 "I have not . . . proper time, II: 11, S 316, 318, OC 412, 414.

123 "When I play with my cat, II: 12, S 331, OC 430, 1546. The last two sentences are not in the Bordeaux Copy but in the 1595 edition.

123 Father, cat, and bird. I: 21, S 75, OC 103. For Montaigne's father's role in this, DB I, 72.

123 Children nursed by goats. II: 8, S 290–1, OC 380.

123 Creatures that hens fear. II: 12, S 445–6, OC 574.

123 Horse out to stud. II: 15, S 464–5, OC 597.

123 Beauty and intelligence of animals. II: 12, S 356–7, OC 462–3. Cf. II: 12, S 331–55, OC 430–61, *passim.*

124 Lackey unchaste, cook profane. I: 28, S 142, OC 191.

124 "accidental privilege of fortune," III: 3, S 623, OC 799.

124 "a cowherd, . . . a servant's blunder," I: 26, S 112, 114, OC 151–2, 155.

124 and envies those . . . own servants." III: 3, S 623, OC 799.

124 Cannot remember servants' names. II: 17, S 494, OC 634.

124 Montaigne scolding his valet. I: 38, S 173, OC 230.

124 Servant who had known cannibals. I: 31, S 150–2, 154, OC 200, 202–3, 205.

124 He has taken . . . as the rich, III: 13, S 829–30, OC 1060.

124 Beggar at Montaigne's door. I: 39, S 179, OC 238.

124 French pages. III: 5, S 674, OC 862.

124 Montaigne's Italian page killed. II: 5, S 264, OC 346.

124 Montaigne's handling of money. I: 14, S 43–6, OC 63–6. It seems likelier that he came into money at his father's death in 1568. But *"enfance"* (childhood) is a vague word in Montaigne and in his time; he came into some money when he married in 1565; and the costly trip may have been the one to Paris in 1570 to publish La Boétie's works.

124 "vile and stupid" "What would I . . . to my affairs?" III: 9, S 727–8, OC 930–1.

124–125 "I cannot reckon . . . I shall starve." II: 17, S 495, OC 636.

125 Montaigne's house unguarded. II: 15, S 467–8, OC 600.

125 "virgin of blood and pillage, III: 9, S 737, OC 943.

125 House unguarded in plague.   III: 12, S 801, OC 1024.

125 Threatened in his house.   III: 9, S 741, OC 948.

125 "For what if . . . time of need.' "   III: 9, S 738, OC 943–4.

125 Carefully trained . . . to our lair."   I: 13, S 32, OC 48–9.

125 Indolence of taste . . . taking offense.   III: 3, S 625, OC 801–2.

126 Like the long . . . our etiquette."   I: 40, S 186–7, OC 246–7.

126 Unable to talk . . . telling stories."   II: 17, S 483, OC 620–1.

126 Conversations must . . . man whatever."   III: 3, S 622, OC 797.

126–127 He devotes one . . . dagger in hand."   III: 8, S 704–7, 715, OC 900–4, 914.

127 "This man must . . . as before.   III: 13, S 823, OC 1053.

127 . . . Obstinacy . . . as an ass?"   III: 8, S 717, OC 917.

127 Montaigne seeks . . . and friendliness."   III: 3, S 625, OC 802.

127 He thinks . . . often indiscreet;   II: 17, S 484, 492, OC 621–2, 632.

127 often they . . . before a meal."   III: 13, S 834, 844–5, OC 1065–6, 1080.

127 Despite his scruples . . . or padding."   III: 11, S 786, OC 1005.

127–128 Florimond de Raemond.   *Histoire de la papesse Iane* (Lyons: Rigaud, 1595), p. 159; see Villey, *Les Sources et l'évolution . . .* , 1933 ed., II, 458.

128 "seek business only for busyness";   III: 10, S 767, OC 981.

128 Inept at checkers and chess.   II: 17, S 494, OC 635.

128 Once liked cards and dice.   III: 10, S 776, OC 992.

128 Cards with wife and daughter.   I: 23, S 79, OC 108.

128 Game of extremes that meet.   I: 54, S 226, OC 298.

128 Trick dancers.   II: 10, S 300, OC 391–2.

128 The blind gentleman.   II: 12, S 445, OC 573–4. For his name, see Pierre Bonnet, "Une Nouvelle Série d'annotations de Florimond de Raemond aux *Essais* de Montaigne," in *BSAM* III: 10 (April–June, 1959), p. 12.

128 The two armless men.   I: 23, S 79, OC 108–9.

128 Performing dogs, blind men's dogs.   II: 12, S 340, OC 441.

128–129 The Brazilian cannibal.   I: 31, S 159, OC 213.

129 The "monstrous child."   II: 30, S 538–9, OC 690–1.

129 The tortured peasant.   II: 32, S 548, OC 702.

129–130 Villager, woman of Bergerac.   II: 29, S 534, OC 684–5.

130 The impotent gentleman.   III: 5, S 659–60, OC 844.

130 Montaigne has seen . . . by a strange spirit!   III: 11, S 787–9, OC 1006–7, 1009.

130 "When the vines freeze . . .   I: 26, S 116, OC 156.

130–131 "He chooses . . . and strangeness."   I: 28, S 135, OC 181.

131 Montaigne once persuaded . . . a similar disease."   II: 37, S 587, 592, OC 753, 759.

131 "the cries of mothers . . . around us." I: 20, S 68, OC 94.

131 Some peasants . . . into trouble. III: 13, S 819, OC 1047.

131–132 Montaigne held up on the road and at home. III: 12, S 812–4, OC 1037–40.

132 "backward region . . . or even French, III: 5, S 666–7, OC 853.

132 Montaigne with La Brousse. II: 5, S 264, OC 346.

132 The Thief. III: 2, S 616, OC 789–90.

132–133 Mourning widow. III: 4, S 630–1, OC 808.

133 Visit from Madame de Duras. II: 37, S 595, 597, OC 763, 765. For her husband and the Gramonts, see Raymond Ritter, "Un Ami de Montaigne: Philibert de Gramont (1552–1580)," in Georges Palassie, *Mémorial du Ier Congrès International des Etudes Montaignistes* (Bordeaux: Taffard, 1964), p. 141.

133 Reader of "Pedantry." I: 26, S 109, OC 147.

133 Madame d'Estissac. II: 8, S 278–9, OC 364–5.

133 Monluc. II: 8, S 287, OC 375–6.

133 The benign medal. I: 21, S 70–1, OC 98–9.

133–134 Children and fathers. II: 8, S 280–1, 283–4, OC 367–8, 370–2.

134–135 Raemond's identifications. See Alan M. Boase, "Montaigne annoté par Florimond de Raemond," *Revue du Seizième Siècle*, XV (1928), 237–78; and Bonnet article in *BSAM* III: 10, pp. 10–23.

134 René de Valzargues. I: 14, S 36, OC 54.

134 François de La Rochefoucauld. I: 23, S 80, OC 109.

134 Antoine Prévost de Sansac. I: 14, S 46, OC 67.

134 François de Candale. II: 12, S 442, OC 570.

134 The pregnant widow. II: 2, S 246, OC 323–4.

134 François de Montmorency. II: 8, S 288, OC 376–7.

134 Poyanne. I: 46, S 202–3, OC 268.

134 Louis de Montpensier. II: 33, S 550–1, OC 706.

134 Pardaillan. III: 10, S 771, OC 985–6.

134 Margaret of Valois. III: 5, S 670, OC 857.

134 Monsieur de Nemours. III: 11, S 787, OC 1006.

134–135 Pisani, Matignon. III: 13, S 829, 831, OC 1059, 1062.

135 Ventadour. I: 21, S 73, OC 101.

135 marquis de Trans, . . . mayor of Bordeaux. Nicolaï, *Les Belles amies de Montaigne*, pp. 135–45.

135 Trans and sons' death. I: 14, S 42, OC 61.

135 Trans in his household. II: 8, S 285–6, OC 373–4.

135 Subject to . . . imagination, I: 21, S 68, OC 95.

135 Likes foreign things. II: 17, S 480, OC 617.

135 would weep, if he could, II: 11, S 314, OC 409.

135 Moved by music. II: 12, S 448, OC 577.

136 Pained by names of dear ones lost. III: 4, S 635, OC 814–5.

136 Avoids commitments. III: 9, S 738, OC 944.

136 Never takes advice. III: 2, S 618, OC 792–3.

136 Has affection, not esteem, for himself.   II: 17, S 499, OC 641.

136 Opinions worse than conduct.   II: 11, S 312, OC 407.

136 . . . better defend a position . . .   II: 17, S 496, OC 637.

136 Hates no one.   III: 12, S 814, OC 1040. Cf. II: 11, S 315–8, OC 411–5; III: 1, S 609–10, OC 779–81.

136 "moderate in . . . the occasion."   II: 17, S 491, OC 630.

136 "If anyone . . . paying his wages."   III: 2, S 612, OC 784–5.

136 Avoids seeing others' letters.   II: 4, S 263, OC 345.

136 Can be cheated.   II: 17, S 488, OC 627.

136 when falsely accused . . .   III: 12, S 799, OC 1021.

136 Lets his friends lecture him.   III: 2, S 613, OC 785.

136 Never imprisoned.   III: 13, S 820, OC 1049.

136 He strongly . . . bad breath?"   III: 10, S 774–5, OC 990.

136 His variability.   Roger Trinquet, rightly disagreeing with the analyses of Montaigne by modern French characterologists but using theirs and many other modern instruments for psychological analysis, lays heavy stress on Montaigne's frustrations in all domains except self-study and the *Essays,* and types him as a cyclothymic, characterized by marked alternations between despondent inactivity and active blitheness. "Le Vrai Triomphe de Montaigne," in Georges Palassie, *Mémorial du Ier Congrès International des Etudes Montaignistes* (Bordeaux: Taffard, 1964), pp. 190–9. I am too impressed with Montaigne's representativeness to follow M. Trinquet all the way in this view.

136–137 I who spy . . . sects and divisions.   II: 12, S 425, 428, OC 548–9, 553.

137 Holds services in his chapel.   III: 9, S 738, OC 943.

137 Swearing only "Par Dieu!"   III: 5, S 667, OC 854.

137 Crossing himself, loving the Lord's Prayer.   I: 56, S 229–31, OC 303–4.

137 Healthy because free from medicine.   III: 13, S 833–6, 839–40, OC 1064–9, 1072–4. Cf. II: 37, S 581, OC 745, and *passim.*

137 His quarrel . . . agrees with him.   II: 37, S 593, OC 760; and S 580–98, OC 743–66, *passim.*

137–138 His faith in . . . as gay as before.   III: 13, S 827, 830–1, OC 1057, 1061–2.

138–139 He rises at seven . . . old age of my sight."   All this, with the four exceptions that follow this note, is from III: 13, S 828–32, 840–8, OC 1058–64, 1074–85.

138 Prefers fish to meat.   I: 49, S 218, OC 287.

138 . . . he could not swallow a drop.   II: 17, S 493, OC 633.

139 Venice and Paris.   I: 55, S 229, OC 302.

139 He dresses in black and white.   I: 36, S 168, OC 223.

139 Wants as many years more.   I: 20, S 58, OC 82.

139 He writes, . . . several months."   II: 37, S 574, OC 736.

139–140 To Paris in 1571.   Nicolaï says he went ("Les Grandes Dates de la vie de Montaigne," *BSAM* II: 13–14 [Oct. 1948–Jan. 1949], p. 32), but gives no evidence.

140 Order of Saint Michael. *Ephemeris*, Oct. 28; OC 1407. The text of Charles IX's letter notifying Montaigne of this honor is reproduced by J.-F. Payen (after Canon Prunis) in *Nouveaux Documents inédits ou peu connus sur Montaigne* (Paris: Jannet, 1850), pp. 47–8.

140 Gentleman in ordinary by 1573. The earliest known reference to Montaigne as gentleman of the chamber to Charles IX is dated Oct. 5, 1573. See Malvezin, p. 303; Nicolaï, "Les Grandes Dates . . . ," p. 32.

140 . . . eminent persons like Trans . . . Trinquet, "Problèmes . . ."

140 In May 1574 . . . and went out. Paul Courteault, "Une Mission de Montaigne en 1574," *BSAM* II: 8 (March 1, 1940), p. 4.

140–141 De Thou's account. *Historiarum* . . . , VII, *De vita sua*, p. 88.

Chapter 9: *The Early* Essays

The main source here besides the *Essays,* especially for the composition and dating of Montaigne's early chapters, is Pierre Villey's *Les Sources et l'évolution des Essais de Montaigne* (Hachette, 2nd ed., 1933, 2 vols.). See also Richard A. Sayce, "L'Ordre des *Essais* de Montaigne," *BHR*, XVIII (1956), 7–22. I have drawn on ch. 2 ("The Apprehensive Humanist," pp. 30–48) of my book *Montaigne's Discovery of Man* (New York: Columbia University Press, 1955). In this chapter and the next two, wherever Montaigne later changed his original (1580) text, my primary reference is to the Dezeimeris and Barckhausen (DB) reproduction of the 1580 ed.

Page

142–143 "It is at my side . . . human journey." III: 3, S 628, OC 805–6.

143 Readings as a child. I: 26, S 130, OC 175.

143 Complete Virgil before sixteen. Villey, *Les Sources et l'évolution* . . . , I, 265.

143 Nicole Gilles's *Annals* . . . Montaigne, *Œuvres complètes*, Armaingaud ed., XII (1941), 16–222. The comment on Sauvage is p. 57, the longer quotation p. 94. The same text, edited by Reinhold Dezeimeris, first appeared in *RHLF*, 1909, 1912–4.

143 Du Bellay, Guicciardini, Commines. II: 10, S 305–6, OC 398–400.

143–144 "melancholy humor . . . some years ago" II: 8, S 278, OC 364.

144 Lately when . . . ashamed of itself. I: 8, S 21, OC 34.

144 Antecedents of earliest essays.   Villey, *Les Sources et l'évolution* . . . , II, 3–33 and *passim.*

145 whose heads he had cut off,   Clause suppressed after 1580, here supplied from DB I, 17–18.

145 Lost third edition of *Essays.*   No trace of a third edition has been found; but the third that we know of is not numbered, the fourth that we know of (1588) is labeled "fifth," and Montaigne changed this to "sixth" on the Bordeaux Copy, which was to provide the fifth edition that we know of.

146 Reproductions of Bordeaux Copy.   Especially the Ed. Munic., and the Edition Phototypique (Hachette, 1912).

146 Montaigne's use of the term "essays."   See below, ch. 11.

147 Strowski (1906)   In his *Montaigne* (Alcan, 1906).

147 Villey took pains, . . . often spoke . . .   *Les Sources et l'évolution* . . . , I, v–vi; but cf. II, 77, 89–92, 128–9, 138–43, 206–24, and *passim.*

147 consubstantial with its author,   II: 18, S 504, OC 648.

147 Continuing debate over change in Montaigne.   See my article "What Next in Montaigne Studies?" *French Review,* XXXVI (May, 1963), 579–82.

148 death the goal . . . learning to die;   I: 20, title and S 57, OC 81.

148 philosophy . . . teaches us to live,   I: 26, S 120, OC 162.

148 death . . . not the goal of life.   III: 12, S 805, OC 1028.

148 the privation of being ill;   II: 12, S 364, OC 472.

148 God has made all things good,   III: 13, S 855, OC 1094.

148 After urging a tense defense . . .   I: 14, S 39, OC 58, and *passim.*

148 better to relax . . .   III: 12, S 803–5, OC 1026–8.

148 Diversity and unity.   See conclusion of II: 37; and III: 13, S 815–9, OC 1041–7.

148 "I am nearly . . . inert bodies. . . .   III: 2, S 615, OC 789.

148 . . . The firmest . . . born with me."   II: 17, S 499, OC 641.

148 "I do not . . . my mutations."   II: 37, S 574, OC 736–7.

148–149 "I aim here . . . changes me."   I: 26, S 109, OC 147.

149 "I do not portray . . . and aspects."   III: 2, S 611, OC 782.

149 "I hope that . . . enough prepared."   II: 6, S 268, OC 352.

149 In between his . . . such accidents."   II: 37, DB II, 331; cf. S 577–8, OC 740.

150 Montaigne's Pyrrhonism largely paradox.   See below, ch. 10.

150 "if simplicity . . . annihilate man."   II: 12, S 364, OC 473.

150 "Since then I . . . cannot say."   III: 9, S 736, OC 941.

150 "The wretchedness . . . can hope for."   II: 12, DB II, 82–3; cf. S 363–4, OC 472.

151 "With such . . . by the throat?"   I: 20, S 59, OC 84.

151 "Since the day . . . a weary life."   I: 28, S 143, OC 192.

151 " 'My poor . . . sweet daughter!' "   III: 4, S 635, OC 814.

151 We must reserve . . . flesh as well.   I: 39, S 177–8, OC 235–6.

151 Contempt, poverty, pain, and death.   Death, poverty, contempt, and disease: I: 39, S 179, OC 238. Death, poverty, and pain: I: 14, S 33, OC 50. Pain: I: 14, *passim*. Death: I: 20, *passim*.

151 Relies on his own laws.   III: 2, S 613, OC 785.

151 He knew that . . . even in death.   I: 14, S 37–8, OC 55–6.

151 Pain, magnified . . . of suicide;   II: 37, S 575, OC 737. See below, ch. 11.

152 we cannot give . . . truth and essence."   II: 6, S 268, OC 352.

153 "brutish stupidity"   I: 20, S 58, OC 82.

153 "what torments . . . make an effort."   I: 20, S 59–60, OC 84–5.

153 "Here all does . . . judges of it."   I: 14, S 37, OC 55.

153 "we must resist . . . against it."   I: 14, S 39, OC 58.

154 In what is probably . . . has no remedy."   I: 24, S 97, OC 131–2.

154 body to help the soul;   I: 39, S 182, OC 241.

154 he welcomes . . . ills of life;   I: 12, S 30, OC 46.

154 would hide under a calf's skin . . .   I: 20, S 59, OC 84.

154 "man of understanding . . . effects of habit."   I: 39, S 177, 179, OC 235, 238.

154–155 If reason fails . . . the common herd"?   I: 14, S 36–8, OC 54–6.

155 "a harmony . . . us and others."   II: 1, S 240–1, 244, OC 316–7, 321.

155–156 Greater even . . . heaven and earth.   I: 42, DB I, 215–8; cf. S 189–91, OC 250–3.

156 "impotence and . . . the strong."   F. J. Billeskov Jansen, *Les Sources vives de la pensée de Montaigne* (Copenhagen: Levin and Munksgaard, E. Munksgaard, 1935), pp. 56–7.

157 "Crawling in . . . heroic souls."   I: 37, DB I, 193; cf. S 169, OC 225.

157 responsible only for intentions,   I: 7, S 20, OC 32. This chapter of Montaigne's is quoted above in the present chapter.

157 Seeks harmony within.   II: 11, S 311, OC 406.

157 By around 1573 . . . and feel it."   II: 3, DB I, 289; cf. S 254, OC 334.

157 "Even if we . . . our own wisdom."   I: 25, DB I, 94–5; cf. S 101, OC 137.

157–158 The male member, . . . not omnipotent;   I: 21, S 72–3, OC 100–1.

158 but he finds . . . and confuses it."   I: 10, DB I, 25; cf. S 26, OC 41.

158 When we hear . . . measure and proportion.   II: 2, DB I, 283–4; cf. S 250–1, OC 329–30.

158–159 Posidonius.   I: 14, S 37, OC 55.

159 "Stoical harshness . . . Christian moderation."   I: 33, S 162, OC 216.

159 Out of a thousand . . . not in him.   II: 2, DB I, 282–3; cf. S 249–50, OC 328.

159 Montaigne often echoes this view . . .   I: 14, S 33–4, 36, OC 50–1, 54; and *passim.*

159–160 In the first place . . . and combat himself."   II: 3, DB I, 287–9; cf. S 253–4, OC 332–4.

160 "A man may . . . augments his misery."   I: 30, DB I, 163, 165; cf. S 146, 148, OC 195, 198.

Chapter 10: The "Apology for Raymond Sebond"

The main source is of course the chapter itself. Zeitlin's treatment (II, 481–519) is very good. I have drawn on my article "Did Montaigne Betray Sebond?" in *Romanic Review,* XXXVIII (Dec., 1947), 297–329, and on ch. 3 ("The Skeptical Revolt," pp. 49–73) of my book *Montaigne's Discovery of Man* (New York: Columbia University Press, 1955).

Page

162 In its final . . . 1580 edition.   In the Pléiade *Œuvres complètes* it occupies 174 pp. out of 1089, as against 58 pp. for each of the two next-longest, III: 5 and III: 9. In the DB ed. of the original text it fills 170 pp. out of 722 in all; the next-longest (II: 37) is 38 pp. long.

162 "What do I know?"   II: 12, S 393, OC 508.

162 Montaigne's fortunes.   For France, 17th century: Alan M. Boase, *The Fortunes of Montaigne: A History of the Essays in France, 1580–1669* (London: Methuen, 1935), and Pierre Villey, *Montaigne devant la postérité* (Boivin, 1935); 18th century, Maturin Dreano, *La Renommée de Montaigne en France au XVIIIe siècle, 1677–1802* (Angers: Editions de l'Ouest, 1952). There is no adequate study of Montaigne's fortunes in England before 1760; but see Villey, "Montaigne en Angleterre," in *Revue des Deux-Mondes,* Sept. 1913, pp. 113–50.

162–163 Sainte-Beuve.   *Port-Royal* (3rd ed., Hachette, 1867–71, 7 vols.), II, 395–453.

163 Gide.   *Essai sur Montaigne* (Schiffrin, 1929).

163 Montaigne opens . . . yet be useful.   II: 12, S 319–27, OC 415–25.

163 The second objection . . . divine majesty."   II: 12, S 327–8, OC 425–6.

163–164 His introduction . . . to infinity,   II: 12, S 328–30, OC 426–9.

164 forty-three-page romp   II: 12, DB II, 32–75; cf. S 330–58, OC 429–65.

164 He presents as true . . . by Montaigne.   See Zeitlin, II, 496–7.

164 Jacques Amyot on the "Gryllus."   Plutarch, *Œuvres morales* (Gouffier, 1612 ed., 2 vols.; Amyot tr.), I, 952–4. A century after Amyot Bossuet will adopt the opposite view.

164–166 Suppose, however, . . . obedience and submission."   II: 12, DB II, 75–90; cf. S 358–70, OC 465–80.

166–167 "Yet must I see . . . instruction and belief."   II: 12, DB II, 90–6; cf. S 370–5, OC 480–6.

167 Most of the dogmatists . . . theorizing anyway.   II: 12, S 375–80, OC 486–93.

167 Montaigne now examines . . . body (one page).   II: 12, DB II, 100–113–121–135–136; cf. S 380–400–405–417–418, OC 493–517–523–539–540.

167 "For what is . . . and our laws?"   II: 12, DB II, 100; cf. S 380, OC 493.

167 The most excusable . . . within his reach.   II: 12, DB II, 100–6; cf. S 380–7, OC 493–501.

167–168 Turning to our . . . he does of God.   II: 12, S 400–18, OC 517–40.

167 "god of scholastic knowledge"   II: 12, S 403, OC 521.

168 The two-page warning.   II: 12, DB II, 136–8; cf. S 418–20, OC 540–2.

168–169 The Academic . . . and universal."   II: 12, S 421–36, OC 544–62.

169 Our senses are . . . resembles him."   II: 12, S 443–54, OC 571–85.

169–170 Finally, we can . . . not otherwise."   II: 12, DB II, 182–6; cf. S 455–7, OC 586–9.

170 "supports Sebond . . . hanged man."   Louis Cons, *Anthologie littéraire de la Renaissance française* (New York: Holt, 1931), p. 143.

170 Montaigne protests his truthfulness.   III: 2, S 611, OC 782; III: 5, S 677, OC 866; III: 9, S 751, OC 961; and *passim*.

170 His fideism . . . in 1580–81;   See below, ch. 12.

171 Even when . . . extravagant claims.   See above, ch. 5.

171 In the "Apology" . . . himself from him.   See above, ch. 7; S 319–27, OC 415–25; and note two other things. Montaigne never claims Sebond or his book as his own; but in speaking of the ladies, calls it "their book," and in addressing the princess, calls him "your Sebond" (S 320, 418, OC 417, 540). Note also the apologetic reservations in the passage that is as much of a defense of Sebond as he offers: "Sebond's arguments . . . are capable of serving as a start and a first guide to an apprentice to set him on the road to this knowledge [of God]; they fashion him to some

extent and make him capable of the grace of God . . ." (S 327, OC 425).

171 It is about . . . salvation and yours."   II: 12, S 418, 420, OC 540, 542.

171 Margaret of Valois and the "Apology."   *Mémoires,* ed. Bonnefon (Bossard, 1920), p. 115. Cf. Jean-H. Mariéjol, "Marguerite de Valois, Reine de Navarre, en Gascogne," *Revue de Paris,* XXIX(1) (Feb., 1922), 528–9; Joseph Coppin, "Marguerite de Valois et le Livre des Créatures de Raymond Sebon," *Revue du Seizième Siècle,* X (1923), 57–66. Zeitlin provides a good summary (II, 509–11).

171 "Because many . . . against it."   II: 12, S 320, OC 416–7.

171 with Villey and Zeitlin,   Villey, *Les Sources et l'évolution . . . ,* I, 375–82; cf. II, 171–2. Zeitlin, II, 494–519.

171 "to extend . . . to my custom."   II: 12, S 418, OC 540.

174 inequality of men as . . . already treated   II: 12, S 342, OC 444. Montaigne claims that if he wanted to list all known examples of elephant intelligence, "I should easily win the argument that I ordinarily maintain, that there is more difference between a given man and a given man than between a given animal and a given man."

174 Brazilian cannibals as . . . not yet written.   "These nations that we have just discovered to be so abundantly furnished with food and natural drink, without care or preparation, have now taught us . . . that without plowing, our mother Nature had provided us in plenty with all we needed . . ." (S 334–5, OC 435).
    "I once saw among us some men brought by sea from a far country. Because we did not understand their language at all, and because their ways . . . were totally remote from ours, which of us did not consider them savages and brutes?" (S 343, OC 445.)

174 He acknowledges . . . his compilation."   II: 12, DB II, 137; for the context, cf. S 419; OC 541, 1571. This statement is a real puzzler for the chronology of the chapter. By most theories (including mine), Montaigne wrote this bit around 1579, when he had contracted a heavy debt to Pyrrho via Sextus Empiricus. Some time between 1580 and 1588 he deleted it.

174–175 The two Pyrrhonian medals.   Alain Brieux, "Autres Souvenirs see de Michel de Montaigne," *BHR,* XX (1958), 370–1.

175 Ἐπέχω   Another chronological puzzler: Montaigne writes only after 1580 of using such a motto (S 393, OC 508), and then says the motto is "Que sçay-je?" (not Ἐπέχω), inscribed over a pair of scales. Of course, he may simply have forgotten by then which one he had used earlier.

176 "They do not . . . believe in."   II: 12, S 372, OC 483.

176 Montaigne's talk with the innovation-monger.   II: 12, DB II, 153–4; cf. S 430, OC 554–5.

176 "For every human . . . between them."   II: 12, S 404, OC 522.

177 In a passage . . . displays in it.   II: 11, S 317–8, OC 414. See below, ch. 11.

177 Pyrrho's science of ignorance.   II: 29, S 533, OC 683. See below, ch. 11.

177 "reason alone . . . our inclinations."   II: 8, S 279, OC 366. See below, ch. 11.

177 wise at our own expense."   II: 12, S 423, OC 546.

177 Pyrrho's eccentricities.   II: 29, S 533, OC 683–4.

177–178 As for the actions . . . and gave up.   II: 12, DB II, 95; cf. S 374, OC 485–6.

178 For the common herd . . . their consent.   II: 12, DB II, 18–9; cf. S 320, OC 416.

178 Montaigne and the Counter Reformation.   Richard H. Popkin, *The History of Scepticism from Erasmus to Descartes* (Assen: Van Gorcum, 1960), pp. 56–7, 66–7, and *passim*.

179 Holding back La Boétie's works.   I: 28, S 144, OC 193. Letters, August 10, 1570; S 1061, OC 1719.

179 His man without divine grace . . .   II: 12, S 328, OC 427.

Chapter 11: *The Writer Finds His Theme*

The main source is again the *Essays;* for composition and dating of the chapters, Villey, *Les Sources et l'évolution* . . . , and Sayce, "L'Ordre des *Essais* de Montaigne," *BHR*, XVIII (1956), 7–22. I have drawn on chapters 4–5 ("Self-Discovery and Liberation" and "The Free Man"; pp. 74–109) of my book *Montaigne's Discovery of Man.*

Page

182 If he had . . . excuse to infringe.   For his sense of God's moral inaccessibility, the clearest statement, written later, is III: 2, esp. S 617, 620, OC 791, 795. For the rest, II: 12, especially S 321–5, 368–70, 380–1, 386–7, 455–7, OC 418–23, 477–80, 493–4, 500–1, 586–9.

182 Even Calvin . . . *Institutes.*   Book I, ch. 1.

182 "Since nothing . . . back home."   Montaigne, *Œuvres complètes,* Armaingaud ed., IX, 2.

182 "lofty and hazardous . . . men in motion."   II: 1, S 244, OC 321.

183 "This account . . . is for me."   II: 6, S 272, OC 357.

183 The know-it-alls who criticize Sebond . . .   II: 12, S 402, OC 520.

183 If man can . . . most accessible.   II: 12, S 405, 418, 421, OC
523, 539–40, 543.

183 "I who spy . . . in myself."   II: 12, S 425, OC 548.

183 "each man . . . as he pleases."   II: 12, S 447, OC 576.

183 "perch astride the epicycle of Mercury"   II: 17, S 481, OC 617.

183 For this, . . . scholastic logic;   II: 12, S 400–1, OC 517–8.
This is stated best later: III: 5, S 666, OC 852.

183 "vain, diverse, and undulating."   I: 1, S 5, OC 13.

183 What truly reveals . . . the everyday.   I: 50.

183 "there is no . . . to himself."   II: 16, DB II, 206; cf. S 474,
OC 609.

184 it has no necessary connection with it.   II: 10, S 297, OC 388.

184 . . . the heart of education.   I: 26, S 111, OC 151.

184 "I find my . . . to myself."   II: 17, DB II, 236–7; cf. S 499,
OC 641.

184 Montaigne approves Socrates' view.   II: 12, S 376, OC 488; cf.
I: 26, S 117, OC 158.

184 "I make no account . . . and my work."   II: 37, S 596, OC
764.

184 The name may . . . impromptu poem.   See John Charles Daw-
son, *Toulouse in the Renaissance* (New York: Columbia University Press, 1921), pp. 12–3.

185 *Essays* as trials, tests, attempts, samplings.   See Andreas Blink-
enberg, "Quel sens Montaigne a-t-il voulu donner au mot *Essais*
dans le titre de son œuvre?" *BSAM* III: 29 (Jan.–March, 1964),
22–32.

185 "Having *found* . . . cannot discover."   II: 12, S 421, OC 543.

185 "I have *experienced* . . . than near."   I: 20, S 63, OC 89.

185 "The reason why . . . common opinions."   II: 12, DB II, 116;
cf. S 403, OC 521.

185 "And whoever . . . surer status."   I: 23, DB I, 77; cf. S 84–5,
OC 116.

185 The verb *essayer* in II: 6.   DB I, 303–5, 309; cf. S 267–8, 271,
OC 350–2, 355. In the third of these instances (when Montaigne
came to *experience* illness) he originally wrote *"essayer,"* then
(after 1588) changed this to *"experimenter."*

185 "If these essays . . . being judged . . ."   I: 54, S 227, OC 300.

185 once adding . . . acquired ones";   II: 10, S 296, OC 387. Cf.
the second note after this one.

185 *essais* of his judgment.   I: 50, S 219, OC 289; II: 17, S 495,
OC 637.

185–186 "As for the . . . and blundering."   I: 26, S 107, OC 145.

186 Judgment is a tool . . . make us known.   I: 50, DB I, 252–3;
cf. S 219, OC 289, 1516.

186 he recognizes . . . moral science,   II: 10, DB I, 351; cf. S 303,
OC 396, 1538, where this phrase has been deleted.

186 subject of his study is man,   II: 17, S 481, OC 617.

186 his general ordinariness . . . judgment.   II: 17, DB II, 235; cf. S 498, OC 640. After 1580 Montaigne changed the quality he claimed from "judgment" to "sense."

186 the first . . . to be studied,   III: 2, S 611, OC 782. Cf. II: 18.

186 while the second . . . impartiality.   II: 17, S 480–1, OC 616–8. Cf. II: 6, S 273–5, OC 357–60; III: 5, S 641–2, OC 822–3.

186–187 "If strangeness . . . monstrous plan."   II: 8, DB I, 317–8; cf. S 278, OC 364.

187 What he aims . . . I am treating."   II: 10, DB I, 340, 342; cf. S 296, 298, OC 387, 389.

187 "For likewise . . . to be believed."   I: 26, S 108, OC 147.

187 He likes his language . . . movements."   II: 17, DB II, 218; cf. S 483, OC 621.

187 "I have no other . . . go as I am."   II: 10, S 297, OC 388.

187 Montaigne wants . . . begun earlier.   II: 37, S 574, OC 737.

187 If something new . . . but mine. . . .   I: 26, S 108–9, OC 147.

187 . . . Even if I . . . have done it. . . .   II: 37, S 595, OC 763.

187 . . . I want to be . . . I portray."   "To the Reader," I, S 2, OC 9.

187 He knows that . . . in "Presumption."   II: 17, S 478–9, OC 614–5. Cf. II: 6, S 273, OC 358–9.

188 "the meanness of . . . them as such."   II: 17, DB II, 231–2; cf. S 495–6, OC 636–7.

188 "these stupidities";   II: 37, S 596, OC 764.

188 Now, however, . . . contempt for it."   II: 15, S 464–5, OC 597.

188 He devotes . . . and resist.   I: 14, S 39, OC 58, and *passim.*

188 "Our conception . . . own impressions."   II: 12, S 454, OC 585.

188–189 "The privilege . . . to the beasts."   II: 12, S 354, OC 460–1.

189 "That things . . . as we please."   II: 12, DB II, 142–3; cf. S 422, OC 545.

189 For cognition . . . their own essence."   II: 12, S 443, OC 572.

189 "Moreover . . . as our sickness?"   II: 12, DB II, 180; cf. S 453, OC 584.

189 "The soul . . . ills and pains."   I: 14, S 39, OC 57.

189–190 "Things in themselves . . . ourselves alone."   I: 50, S 220, OC 290.

190 "I, who have . . . bodily comforts."   I: 39, DB I, 207; cf. S 182, OC 241.

190 "We must order . . . husband to it."   II: 17, DB II, 220; cf. S 484–5, OC 622–3.

190 Michelet on Montaigne.   *Histoire de France,* X (*La Ligue et Henri IV,* Chamerot, 1856 ed.), 400–1.

190 "blithe and ebullient."   II: 6, S 268, OC 352.

191 Pliny on suicide.   II: 3, DB I, 291; cf. S 256, OC 336.

191 His *Travel Journal* . . . consider suicide.   Three stones in two
   days: *TJ*, Ponte a Elsa-Lucca, October 19 (P.M.)–21 (A.M.),
   1581; S 1029–30, OC 1327–8. Often every few days: *TJ*, Pisa-
   Lucca, July 26–7, 1581; S 1013–4, OC 1303–5. Considered suicide: *TJ*, La Villa, Aug. 24, 1581; S 1018, OC 1311. Intense pain,
   pain even without a stone: *TJ*, La Villa, Aug. 14–Sept. 12, 1581;
   S 1016–21, OC 1308–15, and *passim.*

191 The stone . . . feared most,   II: 37, S 575, OC 737.

191 knowing it . . . not bear it.   III: 13, S 836, OC 1069.

191 His father . . . in great pain;   II: 37, S 578–9, OC 742.

191 "I felt and . . . vain propositions."   II: 37, DB II, 327–8; cf.
   S 575, OC 737.

191 Montaigne got some . . . very bad bout.   II: 37, DB II, 351–2;
   cf. S 589 fn., OC 755, 1616–7.

191 After a year and . . . a beginner,"   II: 37, S 575, 578, OC
   737, 741.

191–192 "I was so far from . . . countless healthy men.   II: 37, DB II,
   328–32; cf. S 575–8, OC 737–41.

192 his view of life . . . to happiness.   III: 13, S 835, OC 1068.

193 Now he reveals . . . teaches us to live."   I: 26, DB I, 114–5;
   cf. S 118–20, OC 159–62.

193 In this he is . . . Stoicism."   See especially Hiram Haydn, *The
   Counter-Renaissance* (New York: Scribner's, 1950), pp. 468–97.

194 "But when . . . other creatures."   II: 11, DB II, 16; cf. S
   317–8, OC 414.

194–195 They are wild . . . don't wear breeches."   I: 31, DB I, 170–1,
   174, 177–82, and *passim;* cf. S 152–3, 156, 158–9, OC 203–4,
   209, 212–3; and *passim.*

195 "It is an absolute . . . being rightfully";   III: 13, S 857, OC
   1096.

195 "Had I been . . . wholly naked."   I, "To the Reader," S 2,
   OC 9.

195 "Since it has . . . our inclinations."   II: 8, S 279, OC 366.

196 The simple take . . . human levels.   II: 12, S 367–70, 375, OC
   477–80, 486–7.

196 Stupidity and . . . cannot endure them.   I: 54, S 226, OC
   298–9.

196–197 Montaigne's fullest . . . tragedy and tension.   II: 11, DB II,
   1–6, 8–10; cf. S 306–12, OC 400–8.

197–198 "Of all the opinions . . . of himself."   II: 17, DB II, 214; cf.
   S 480–1, OC 617.

198 Our capacity for . . . inconstancy.   III: 4, S 635, OC 813.

198 Those tyrants . . . highest virtue.   I: 23, S 77, 82, OC 106,
   113; II: 11, S 310, OC 404–5.

198 The mutability . . . is wisdom,   II: 12, S 423, OC 546.

198 Our ephemerality . . . our pleasure.   II: 15.

198 Ignorance may lead to happiness . . .   II: 12, S 358–70, OC 465–80.

198 The soul no . . . husband to it.   II: 17, S 484–5, OC 622–3.

198 makes us our own best judges;   II: 16, S 474, OC 608–9.

198 contempt as a thing to fear;   I: 39, S 179, OC 238.

199 "a well-made . . . well-filled head"   I: 26, S 110, OC 149.

199 "I welcome health . . . with me. . . .   II: 12, DB II, 81; cf. S 362, OC 471.

199 . . . I am at grips . . . their reasoning."   II: 37, S 576, 578, OC 738, 741.

199 Only nobler beings . . . than we are.   II: 3, S 254, OC 334.

200 "The greatest thing . . . to oneself."   I: 39, S 178, OC 236.

200 "a marvelously . . . uniform judgment."   I: 1, S 5, OC 13.

200 "I do not . . . diversity and discord."   II: 37, DB II, 364; cf. S 597–8, OC 766.

Chapter 12: Travel in Italy

The main texts here are the primary ones: Montaigne's *Travel Journal* and his chapter "Of Vanity" (III: 9). Sainte-Beuve's article "Montaigne en voyage" (*Nouveaux Lundis*, II, 156–77; March 24, 1862) is perceptive and delightful; Charles Dédéyan's complementary dissertation, *Essai sur le Journal de Voyage de Montaigne* (Boivin, ca. 1946) is sometimes useful. The best book on the subject is Imbrie Buffum's *L'Influence du voyage de Montaigne sur les Essais* (Princeton, N.J., 1946). On Montaigne and Venice, see Roger Trinquet's masterly article "Montaigne et Venise, ou le mythe de la liberté," *Mercure de France*, Vol. 327 (June 1, 1956), 293–323.

Page

201 Writing at first . . . mind behave,   I: 8, S 21, OC 34.

201 Now it is . . . my plan."   II: 18, S 503, OC 647.

201–202 "If strangeness . . . with honor."   II: 8, S 278, OC 364.

202 "I am myself . . . So farewell."   I, "To the Reader," S 2, OC 9.

202 Diplomatic mission.   For the conjectures, Dédéyan, *Essai* . . . , pp. 30, 98–105; for their lack of support, Trinquet article.

202 Montaigne's reasons for his trip.   For all but the third, see *Travel Journal*; for the first, II: 37, for all, III: 9.

202 Aigues-Caudes and Bagnères.   II: 37, S 589 fn., OC 1616.

202 Mistrustful of medicine.   II: 37, *passim*.

202 His own best doctor.   III: 13, S 826–7, OC 1056–7.

202 At times . . . in his nostrils."   III: 9, S 721, OC 922–3.

202 count of what you piss."   *TJ*, La Villa, May 10, 1581; S 988, OC 1270.

202–203 if anyone . . . of soldiers.   II: 12, S 323, OC 420–1.

203 "I see not one . . . like our own.   III: 9, S 729–30, 737–8, 741, 743, OC 933–4, 943, 948–50.

203 "In truth . . . considerations."   *TJ*, Lindau, Oct. 10, 1580; S 892, OC 1146.

203–204 Some people complain . . . and product.   III: 9, S 744, 746–8, 750–1, 755, OC 952, 954–7, 960, 965–6.

204 Domestic matters importunate.   I: 39, S 175, OC 233.

204 "In the midst . . . think about."   III: 9, S 725, 728–9, OC 928, 931–2.

204–205 Rome's endurance . . . their writings."   III: 9, S 725, 728–9, 733, 745, 762–3, OC 928, 931–2, 937, 953, 975–6.

205 It is no surprise . . . recently demolished.   *TJ*, Ronciglione-Rome, Nov. 30, 1580; S 935, OC 1202–3. Rome, April 5, 1581; S 962, OC 1236. Rome, Jan. 26, 1581; S 943, OC 1212–3.

205 But he loves . . . as if at home."   *TJ*, Rome, March–April, 1581; S 960–1, OC 1235–6.

205 Montaigne's love of Venice.   See Trinquet article.

205 La Boétie on Venice as symbol.   *Discours de la Servitude volontaire*, Bossard, 1922 ed., pp. 69–70; M. Rat ed., Colin (Bibliothèque de Cluny), c. 1963, p. 65.

205 Montaigne on La Boétie.   I: 28, S 144, OC 193.

206 Montaigne's visit to Venice.   *TJ*, Volargne-Venice-Padua, Oct. 31–Nov. 13, 1580; S 916, 920, 922, OC 1178, 1183, 1185.

206 Florence inferior to Venice.   *TJ*, Florence, Nov. 23, 1580; S 930, OC 1196–7.

206 Rome and Venice.   *TJ*, Rome, Nov. 30, 1580, S 936–7, OC 1204–5; April 2, 1581, S 961–2, OC 1236.

206 Ancona, La Villa.   *TJ*, Ancona, April 26, 1581; S 974, OC 1252. La Villa, Sept. 1, 1581; S 1019, OC 1313.

206 Venice and Paris.   I: 55, S 229, OC 302.

206 Venice for retirement.   III: 9, S 750, OC 960. The words "to myself" were added after the trip.

206 Montaigne, de Thou, and Venice.   De Thou, *Historiarum* . . . , VII, *De vita sua*, p. 88; *Mémoires*, Buchon ed., p. 628. Later on (p. 97; *Mémoires*, p. 637) de Thou tells how he and Schomberg, on a mission for Henry III seeking troops in Germany and funds in Italy, stopped at Montaigne's château to see him, but learned from his wife that he was in Bordeaux. He may have been hoping to go along with them.

206 Recommended for his pupil.   I: 26, S 112, OC 152.

206–207 "I know no . . . our nature."   III: 9, S 744, OC 951.

207 I . . . travel . . . satisfies me.   III: 9, S 753, 755–6, OC 963, 966.

207 Sainte-Beuve's disillusionment.   The full text, *Pensée* XXXI of
the *Portraits contemporains* (V, 465) is this:

"Why don't I love nature, the country, any more?
Why don't I love to walk down the little path any more?
I know very well that it is the same, but *there is nothing on
the other side of the hedge any more.*

Earlier, there wasn't anything most of the time, but there
might have been something."

207 Sainte-Beuve on Montaigne the traveler.   "Montaigne en voyage," *Nouveaux Lundis,* II, 162, 169, 177.

207–208 I truly believe . . . get away alone.   *TJ,* Rovereto, Oct. 29,
1580; S 915, OC 1176–7.

208 His secretary.   For his working for Montaigne before, see the
previous quotation: "I never saw him less tired. . . ." As a man
of breeding, see his remark that "a train of valets is of no use to
us at all here" (Venice, Nov. 5–12, 1580; S 921, OC 1184). On
his intelligence, *TJ, passim.*

208 Secretary dismissed.   *TJ,* Rome, Feb. 15, 1581; S 947, OC 1219.

208 Montaigne leaving home June 22, 1580.   *TJ,* Montaigne, Nov.
30, 1581; S 1039, OC 1342. *Ephemeris,* Nov. 30, OC 1409. The
Ephemeris dates Montaigne's departure June 22, 1579; but the
TJ corrects this not only by giving the right year (1580) but also
by adding that he was gone just over seventeen months.

208–209 Montaigne at court and at La Fère.   The *TJ* shows Montaigne
leaving home June 22, 1580 for La Fère; the *Ephemeris* shows him
leaving home June 22 (1579, for 1580), and Gramont dying at
La Fère on Aug. 6; the *Essays* show him escorting Gramont's
body from La Fère to Soissons (III: 4, S 637, OC 816). La Croix
du Maine (*Bibliothèque françoise,* 1584; in 1772–3 ed., 2 vols.,
II, 130–1) reports Montaigne's conversation with Henry III. We
do not know that their talk took place in 1580 when Montaigne
was on his way to La Fère, or that—as most critics assume—he
had presented a copy of the *Essays* to the king; but all this seems
most likely. Though the episode seems almost too pat, it fits Montaigne around 1580 pretty well.

209 "a human disease,"   I: 31, S 156, OC 208.

209 . . . military life . . . devoted to them."   III: 13, S 841, OC
1075–6.

209 Mme d'Estissac and Charles.   For her true identity see Roger
Trinquet, "En marge des *Essais.* La Vraie Figure de Madame d'Estissac ou les pièges de l'homonymie," *BHR,* XVIII (1956), 23–36.

209 Monsieur de Cazalis.   Bernard de Cazalis married Montaigne's
sister Marie on Sept. 28, 1579. Since in 1600 he married off a
daughter by his second wife (Malvezin, pp. 162–3 for both these
facts), it is likely that Marie died soon after their marriage. M.

Maurice Rat states (OC 1102) that she died two or three months before the start of the trip; but I do not know what his evidence is.

209 All four not over twenty.   This at least is the usual conjecture, found in Sainte-Beuve and passed along by most modern editors (Pilon, Dédéyan, Rat). It is not known, but seems very likely.

209 Cazalis to Padua to study.   Montaigne says that many foreigners —not only students—stay at Padua because of the low cost of living. He speaks as though Cazalis is a student. (*TJ*, Padua, Nov. 12, 1580; S 921, OC 1184.)

209–210 Itinerary of Mattecoulon and the others.   Montaigne mentions Mattecoulon as staying at La Villa during his first sojourn (*TJ*, May 20, 1581; S 993, OC 1276) and remaining in Rome after he himself went home (*TJ*, Oct. 15, 1581; S 1029, OC 1326). D'Estissac and others saw Montaigne off (*ibid.*).

211 Initial reception of the *Journal*.   See Dédéyan, pp. 165–6; OC 1105.

211 Details about Basel.   *TJ*, Basel, Sept. 29–Oct. 1, 1580; S 877–81, OC 1128–32.

211 Inn of the Rose.   *TJ*, Innsbruck, Oct. 23, 1580; S 906, OC 1165.

211 Montaigne's interest in machines and gadgets.   *TJ* in S 871, 887–8, 899–902, 928, 931–2, OC 1120, 1140, 1142, 1155–60, 1193–4, 1197–8.

211–212 The Villa d'Este at Tivoli.   *TJ*, Tivoli, April 3, 1581; S 962–4, OC 1237–9.

212 Landscape near Thann.   *TJ* in S 877, OC 1127. Cf. near Innsbruck, S 908, OC 1167–8; near Bressanone, S 910–1, OC 1170–2.

212–213 Landscape near Foligno.   *TJ* in S 969, OC 1245–6.

213 Choice of room at La Villa.   *TJ* in S 983–4, OC 1264.

213 Narni.   *TJ* in S 967, OC 1243.

213 Mulhouse.   *TJ* in S 877, OC 1127.

213–214 Protestantism: visits, discussions, comments, at Basel, Baden, Lindau, etc.   *TJ* in S 878 (Basel), 885 (Baden), 891 (Lindau), 893 (Isny), 894–5 (Kempten), 898 (Augsburg), OC 1129, 1138, 1145, 1148, 1149–51, 1154–5. It is in Basel that he remarks on their sectarian disputes. His note in Lindau is developed thus in the *Essays* (III: 13, S 818, OC 1046): "I have observed in Germany that Luther has left as many divisions and altercations over the uncertainty of his opinions, and more, as he raised about the Holy Scriptures."

214 High Mass in Verona.   *TJ* in S 917, OC 1179.

214 The Pope's Mass in Rome.   *TJ* in S 938, OC 1206.

214 Italian people less devout than French.   *TJ*, Rome; S 949, 960, OC 1220, 1234. Maldonado added that against the Spanish charge "that France was totally lost in heresy," he maintained that there were more "truly religious" men "in the city of Paris alone than in all Spain put together."

214 Rome's "ecclesiastical idleness." *TJ* in S 954, OC 1226.

214 The flagellant Penitents. *TJ* in S 959, OC 1232–3.

214 Miraculous cure, ugly squabble, miracle of Loreto. *TJ* in S 973, 1012, OC 1250–1, 1303.

214–215 An exorcism in Rome. *TJ* in S 947–8, OC 1219–20.

215 Generally, however, . . . heretics of our time." *TJ* in S 956–7, OC 1230.

215 Lancre on Maldonado. Quoted by Villey, *Montaigne devant la postérité*, p. 368, from *Tableau de l'inconstance des mauvais anges et démons* (Berjon, 1612), p. 81.

216 Montaigne and Maldonado. See Clément Sclafert, "Montaigne et Maldonat," *Bulletin de Littérature Ecclésiastique*, 1951, pp. 65–93, 129–46; and especially Camille Aymonier, "Un Ami de Montaigne: le jésuite Maldonat," *RHB*, XXVIII (1935), 5–35. Montaigne's stress on disciplined submission to Church doctrine (I: 56; III: 2) seems close to the statement of Saint Ignatius of Loyola in his *Spiritual Exercises* that if the Church defines as black something that to us appears white, we must ourselves pronounce it black. However, Montaigne stresses mainly how things appear to him, and at times (as on torture) sticks to his guns when he thinks the Church is wrong.

216 Montaigne's meetings with Maldonado. *TJ*, Epernay, Sept. 8, 1580, and Rome, March 29, 1581; S 868–9, 960, OC 1117, 1234.

216 Pope Gregory XIII. *TJ* in S 938–40, 962, OC 1206–8, 1236–7.

216–217 Montaigne's religious practice. In an urbane debate in *BHR*, XVI (1954), 86–95, 213–7, Maturin Dreano showed how regular Montaigne's practice was on his trip, while Henri Busson cast doubt on some of his conclusions.

217 Communion at Loreto. *TJ* in S 971, OC 1248.

217 "God knows! *TJ*, Lucca, July 27, 1581; S 1014, OC 1305.

217 Books taken for scrutiny. *TJ*, Rome, Nov. 30, 1580; S 937, OC 1205.

217–218 The *Essays* examined in Rome. *TJ*, March 20 and April 15, 1581; S 955–6, 965, OC 1228–9, 1240. The passages criticized in the *Essays* are these, or others like them: Fortune: II: 4, S 263, OC 346, and *passim*. Heretic poets (Beza and Buchanan): II: 17, S 502, OC 645. Julian the Apostate: II: 19, *passim*. Praying: I: 56, *passim*. Torture: I: 31, S 155, OC 207–8; II: 11, S 314, OC 410. Training a child: I: 26, S 123, OC 166.

For Montaigne's negligible use of the suggestions, see below, ch. 16.

218 Montaigne in Switzerland. *TJ*, Baden, Oct. 4, 1580; S 884, OC 1136.

218 Montaigne in Germany. *TJ*, Lindau, Oct. 10, 1580; S 892, OC 1146.

218–219 Montaigne in Augsburg. *TJ*, Aug. 16, 1580; S 900, OC 1156–7.

219 Montaigne's Italian. III: 5, S 665, OC 851.

219 Vexed at silly reports.   *TJ*, Bressanone, Oct. 26, 1580; S 910, OC 1170.

219 The good Swiss.   *TJ*, Baden, Oct. 4, 1580; S 884, OC 1136.

219 The good Lorrains.   *TJ*, Plombières, Sept. 16, 1580; S 873, OC 1123.

219 Letter to Hotman.   *TJ*, Bolzano, Oct. 27, 1580; S 912, OC 1173.

219 Roman upper classes.   *TJ*, Rome, Feb. 12, 1581; S 947, OC 1217.

219 Florence the beautiful.   *TJ*, June 22–July 2, 1581; S 1006, OC 1295.

219 Well lodged in Italy.   *TJ*, Lucca, July 28, 1581; S 1014, OC 1306.

219 The Vatican Library.   *TJ*, Rome, March 6, 1581; S 949–50, OC 1221–3.

219 Medical consultant.   *TJ*, La Villa, May 31, 1581; S 999–1000, OC 1285.

219–220 Leaving La Villa and returning.   *TJ*, La Villa, June 21 and Aug. 14, 1581; S 1003, 1016, OC 1290, 1308.

220 "After dinner . . . too reserved."   *TJ* in S 991, OC 1274.

220–221 Montaigne gave a big dance.   *TJ* in S 993–5, OC 1277–9.

221 One of his worst attacks.   *TJ* in S 1018, OC 1311. For the Italian, see Dédéyan ed. of the *Journal* (Les Belles Lettres, 1946), p. 385.

222 Imbrie Buffum.   See *L'Influence du voyage . . .* , pp. 27–133 and *passim*.

222 Socrates above Cato.   II: 11, S 308–10, OC 402–5.

222 Montaigne on diversion.   III: 4, *passim*.

Chapter 13: Mayor of Bordeaux

The primary texts are Montaigne's letters (especially to Matignon) from 1581 to 1585 (S 1066–89, OC 1372–94) and his chapter "Of Husbanding Your Will" (III: 10). There are revealing glimpses in some letters of Matignon and Henry of Navarre, and especially of Philippe de (Duplessis-) Mornay.

The most useful old sources are the *Chronique bourdeloise* of Gabriel de Lurbe, the *Chronique bordeloise* of Jean de Gaufreteau, and especially the *Supplement* to de Lurbe by Jean Darnal. The best modern source, which uses all these, is Paul Courteault's thorough study, "Montaigne, maire de Bordeaux," in *IVe Centenaire de la naissance de Montaigne*, *1533–1933* (Bordeaux: Delmas, 1933), pp. 71–162. For the events leading to Montaigne's election, see Nicolaï, *Les Belles Amies de Montaigne* (Dumas, c. 1950), pp. 135–45; for his re-election, Xavier Védère, "Deux Ennemis de Montaigne: le sénéchal Merville et le capitaine Vaillac," *RHB*, XXXVI (July–Dec., 1943), 88–97; for Matignon and Vaillac, Jacques de Callières (or Cailliere), *Histoire du mareschal de Matignon* (Courbe, 1661), pp. 156–9.

Page

223–224 The end of Montaigne's trip.   *TJ*, Sept. 1, 1581, S 1019, OC 1313; Sept. 7, S 1020, OC 1314–5; Oct. 1, S 1027, OC 1324. "Nothing but my return home on my mind": Sarzana, Oct. 22; S 1032, OC 1330.

223 Monsieur de Tausin.   Probably the same Bordeaux banker who was to handle Marie de Gournay's mail fifteen years later. See J.-F. Payen, "Recherches sur Michel Montaigne. Correspondance relative à sa mort," *Bulletin du Bibliophile*, 1862, pp. 1304, 1306.

224 Henry III's letter.   Reproduced in Payen, *Documents inédits ou peu connus sur Montaigne* (Techener, 1847), p. 28; and (after Payen) in *BSAM* I: 2 (1913), 198. For its being sent to Rome, see Gaufreteau, *Chronique bordeloise*, I, 233.

224 "Messieurs of . . . the matter."   III: 10, S 768, OC 982.

224 thinking he was still in Rome;   *Ephemeris*, Nov. 26, OC 1409.

224 "knowledge of . . . them to this";   III: 10, S 768, OC 982–3.

224 Montaigne chosen to be mayor.   Nicolaï, *Les Belles Amies de Montaigne*, pp. 135–45; Courteault article, pp. 73–5. The election by the jurats may have been unanimous; this may be the meaning of Montaigne's phrase "d'un publico consentimento" (*TJ*, Dédéyan ed., p. 393), which I translated "by general consent."

225 Henry IV escaped from court.   Raymond Ritter now says he did so with the connivance of Catherine de' Medici. See "Un Ami de Montaigne: Philibert de Gramont (1552–1580)" in Georges Palassie, *Mémorial du Ier Congrès International des Etudes Montaignistes* (Bordeaux: Taffard, 1964), p. 139.

226 Guise sought Navarre's friendship.   De Thou reports that Montaigne told him this. See above, ch. 8, end.

227 The jurats of Bordeaux.   The following were the jurats during Montaigne's mayoralty: 1580–2, Gabriel de Lurbe, Treilles, Pierre Dupérier; 1581–3, Mathelin Fort, Jean Turmet, Guillaume Cursol; 1582–4, Geoffre d' Alesme, Jean de Galopin, Pierre Régnier; 1583–5, Jean de Lapeyre, Jean Claveau, Baude de Moncuq, seigneur de Lamothe; 1584–6, Guillaume Collond, Casaus, Louis de Lafourcade. ("Registre du Clerc de Ville de Bordeaux," *AHG*, XLVI, 1911, 162–71.)

227–228 The mayor, says . . . Lordship the Mayor.   Jean Darnal, *Supplément des Chroniques de la noble ville et cité de Bordeaux* (Bordeaux: J. M. Millanges, 1666), pp. 16–7, 30, 39–40; good summary in Courteault, pp. 83–5.

228 Though chosen, . . . to follow it.   III: 10, S 768–9, OC 982–3.

228 February 8, 1582.   "Journal de François de Syrueilh," *AHG*, XIII (1871–2), 342–3; Philippe Lauzun, *Itinéraire raisonné de Marguerite de Valois en Gascogne d'après ses livres de comptes* (Picard, 1902), p. 196; Courteault, pp. 89–90.

228–241 Montaigne's years as mayor.   Where other sources are not given, see Courteault.

229 De Thou and Montaigne.   De Thou, *Historiarum . . .* , VII, *De vita sua*, p. 39; *Mémoires*, Buchon ed., p. 592.

229 Montaigne's inscription to Loisel.   S 1091, OC 1396–7.

230–241 Montaigne's letters while mayor.   S 1066–89, OC 1372–94. These include the two letters of remonstrance to Henry III and Henry of Navarre.

230 Montaigne's sixth daughter.   *Ephemeris*, Feb. 21, OC 1409.

230 Montaigne in Paris (August, 1582).   Courteault, p. 96; based on Darnal, p. 95.

230 Montaigne's re-election disputed.   Xavier Védère, "Deux ennemis de Montaigne . . . ," *RHB*, XXXVI, 88–97; cf. *AHG*, New Series, I (1933–6), 63.

232 Elie Vinet's letter.   *AHG*, XXX (1895), 73.

232 Godfather to a marrano.   See above, ch. 2.

232 Conferring with Margaret of Valois.   See her letter of Dec. 3, 1583 to Matignon in Lauzun, *Itinéraire . . .* , p. 257.

232–234 Letters from Duplessis-Mornay.   Philippe de Mornay, *Mémoires et correspondance* (Treuttel and Würtz, 1824–5, 12 vols.), II, 382–3, 385–7, 393–4, 401–2, 518–9. This edition leaves the last letter undated; Courteault (p. 113) dates it Jan. 25, 1584.

232 Three days later Navarre . . .   Henry IV, *Recueil des Lettres missives* (ed. Berger de Xivrey, Imprimerie Royale and Imprimerie Nationale, 1843–76, 9 vols.), I, 601–2.

234 Here the correspondence as we have it ends.   In his letter to Matignon of Jan. 26, 1585, Montaigne offers to show him a letter just received from Mornay (S 1078, OC 1384). In all probability they exchanged many others.

234 Navarre's letter of May 10, 1584.   *Recueil des Lettres missives*, I, 661.

234 An invitation from the Dutch.   This reading of "la requeste, que ceus du bas païs lui font" (OC 1381) departs from my earlier assumption (S 1076 fn. 62) that these are Protestants of lower Guienne, to the north.

234 Montaigne's letter of August 19.   Courteault (p. 114) dates it April 19, but does not explain why.

235 Navarre's visit to Montaigne.   *Ephemeris*, Dec. 19, OC 1409–10. Montaigne had help as host not only from his wife but also from his able steward, Pierre de Lagreau; see Nicolaï, "Le Maître d'hôtel de Montaigne: M. de Lagreau," *BSAM* II: 15 (1949–52), 24–28.

235 What we hear in 1588.   See below, ch. 15.

235–236 Montaigne's letter about Corisande.   Dated Jan. 18, 1585; S 1077, OC 1383. The text reads "Bissonse," but probably refers to one of Montaigne's visitors of a month earlier in his château, Raymond de Bissouse (or Vissouse, Vysouze, or Viçoze), financial secretary to Henry of Navarre. Henri de La Tour d'Auvergne, vicomte de Turenne (1555–1623), by his second marriage father of the great marshal, was one of Navarre's chief followers and another recent visitor at Montaigne.

236 Turenne's letter to Montaigne.   Published (after Canon Prunis) by Payen, *Nouveaux Documents inédits ou peu connus sur Montaigne* (Jannet, 1850), pp. 49–50.

236 The background of Montaigne's letter to the jurats (Feb. 8, 1585). See Trinquet, "Quand Montaigne défendait les privilèges des vins bordelais," *RHB*, New Series, V (Oct.–Dec., 1956), 263–6.

237 Matignon's pressure, League stirrings.   By April 3 Navarre alerts Matignon and the mayor and jurats of Bordeaux to the dangers from Vaillac in Bordeaux, of which he has apparently already warned Henry III (*Recueil des Lettres missives*, II, 26–7, 29).

238 "to oppose . . . the state."   Quoted in Lavisse, *Histoire de France*, VI, 244.

238 Soon after mid-April.   The date is uncertain. Strowski says April 25, but gives no evidence. It seems to me likelier that Navarre's allusion of April 24 is to an accomplished fact.

238 Matignon and Vaillac.   Jacques de Callières (or Cailliere), *Histoire du mareschal de Matignon* (Courbe, 1661), pp. 156–9.

238 Navarre to Matignon, April 24.   *Recueil des Lettres missives*, II, 45. Another letter (IX, 95), undated but probably of about the same time, again sends news and recommendations to Matignon via Montaigne, saying that "I shall rely on him for this, asking you to believe him just as you would / Your most affectionate cousin and perfect friend, / Henry." Soon after (end of April) there are several letters of commendation from both Henry III and Navarre to Matignon and to the mayor and jurats of Bordeaux.

238–239 The time came . . . mutual confidence.   I: 24, S 95–6, OC 129–30. As for the date, this is probably the general review that Gabriel de Lurbe places in May 1585 (*Chronique bourdeloise*, Bordeaux: Boé, 1703 ed., p. 34 recto and verso).

239 I am telling . . . to the King.   For the duty of ambassadors (and subordinates in general) to tell everything and leave the assessment to their superiors, see *Essays*, I: 17, end.

240 With Navarre at Sainte-Foy.   Henry IV, *Recueil* . . . , II, 69–70.

240 Matignon reluctant to meet Navarre.   See Turenne's letter to Montaigne, quoted earlier in this chapter; also Grün, *La Vie publique de Michel Montaigne*, p. 342; and Nicolaï, "Les Grandes

Dates de la vie de Montaigne," *BSAM* II: 14–15 (Oct. 1948–Jan. 1949), 55.

240 Matignon's letter to Montaigne.   *AHG*, X (1868), p. 402.

240 The plague in Bordeaux.   Courteault is the best of many sources. In "Les Grandes Dates . . ." Nicolaï tells of a letter of July 25 from the jurats urging Montaigne to return, but gives no evidence.

241 Sainte-Beuve.   "Montaigne, maire de Bordeaux," *Nouveaux Lundis*, VI, 260–2.

241–242 "I went about it . . . easy and light."   III: 10, S 781–3, OC 998–1000, 1002.

242 He has trouble . . . conducts us."   III: 10, S 766–70, OC 980–1, 984–5.

242–243 Its excessiveness . . . clear separation."   III: 10, S 770, 773–5, 777–8, OC 984–5, 989–90, 994.

243 He had been . . . required of me."   III: 10, S 781–2, OC 999.

243–244 "I had nothing . . . care about that.   III: 10, S 783–4, OC 1001–2.

244 "produces Essays . . . produce results."   III: 9, S 759, OC 971.

244–245 His natural languor, . . . well guided.   III: 10, S 781, OC 998–9.

Chapter 14: *The* Essays *of 1588*

The source here is the 1588 material itself: Book III of the *Essays* (minus the post-1588 additions) and the 1588 ("B") additions to Books I and II. For chronology see Villey, *Les Sources et l'évolution des Essais de Montaigne* (Hachette, 1908, 2 vols.; 2nd ed., 1933) and the necessary corrections offered by Trinquet, "Du nouveau dans la biographie de Montaigne," *RHLF*, LIII (1953), 5–16, LIV (1954), 1–22. Quotations from the *Essays* are of course given here in the form in which they first appeared in 1588, regardless of later additions or modifications.

Page

246–247 The first year . . . at Saint-Brice.   For the text, Trinquet, "Du nouveau dans la biographie de Montaigne." For the Montaigne quotations, III: 12, S 796, 798–9, 801–2, OC 1017–8, 1020–2, 1024–5.

248 Now, what example . . . of stupidity.   III: 12, S 802–5, OC 1025–6, 1028–9.

248 "We are each . . . by itself."   III: 12, S 794, OC 1015–6. In the text, the third sentence quoted here immediately precedes the first.

248 A third edition (Rouen, by 1584).   La Croix du Maine, *Bibliothèque françoise*, Rigoley de Juvigny ed., 1772–3, II, 130.

249 A joke in Gascony.　III: 2, S 614, OC 786.

249 The initial reception of the *Essays*.　See Villey, *Montaigne devant la postérité* (Boivin, 1935), pp. 20–8, 343–8.

250 Villey's count of the additions.　*Les Sources et l'évolution* . . . , 2nd ed., 1933, I, 412, fn. 1.

250 Times of composition.　Villey, *Les Sources et l'évolution* . . . , 2nd ed., I, 403–22; to be corrected on the chronology of the plague by Trinquet, "Du nouveau dans la biographie de Montaigne."

251–252 "I set forth . . . that oppose it."　III: 2, S 611, 615, OC 782, 789.

252 Events, he says, . . . man from man."　III: 13, S 815, 819, OC 1042, 1047.

252 "I speak the . . . grow old."　III: 2, S 611, OC 783.

252 "the favor . . . I expected."　III: 9, S 736, OC 942.

252 He wants . . . unpublishable."　III: 5, S 642, OC 822–3.

252 He blames Tacitus . . .　III: 8, S 720, OC 921.

253 taste in fruit . . . defecation.　III: 13, S 831–2, 840–1, 845–6, OC 1063, 1074–5, 1081–2.

253 "humorous and familiar style"　I: 40, S 186, OC 246.

253 Rich but unformed language, backward region.　III: 5, S 665–6, OC 851–3.

253 "for few men and for few years,"　III: 9, S 751, OC 960.

253 "I go out of . . . sidelong glance."　III: 9, S 761, OC 973.

253 He adds . . . the public.　III: 9, S 736, OC 941.

253 He studies . . . good scholar."　III: 13, S 821–2, OC 1050–1. The 1588 edition read "Plato," which Montaigne later changed to "Cicero."

253 Fortune has . . . his thoughts.　III: 9, S 721, OC 922.

253 "I speak . . . piteously."　III: 12, S 809, OC 1034.

253 "the essays of my life,"　III: 13, S 826, OC 1056.

253 "this essay of myself," "this third extension . . . painting."　III: 9, S 736, OC 941.

253–254 His chapter titles . . . give him anything.　III: 9, S 761–2, OC 973–4.

254 He warns us . . . if he had one.　III: 11, S 790–1, OC 1011.

254 Though he knows . . . than candor.　III: 13, S 818, OC 1046.

254 He finds his . . . and uncertainly."　III: 8, S 718, OC 918.

254 He regrets . . . own person.　III: 12, S 808, OC 1033.

254 His memory weakens.　III: 9, S 734–5, OC 939.

254 How much he still has to learn.　III: 13, S 823, OC 1052.

254 "I have seen . . . understand myself."　III: 11, S 787, OC 1006.

254 "I leave nothing . . . or guessed."　III: 9, S 751, OC 961.

254 By mirroring . . . about himself.　III: 13, S 824, OC 1053.

254 The honesty . . . so in action."　III: 5, S 642, OC 822.

254 Publication as a rule of conduct.　III: 9, S 749, OC 958.

255 The most honorable . . . out of laziness."   III: 9, S 727, OC
      929–30.
255 Dislike of mastery.   III: 7, S 700, OC 896.
255 Public life morally debilitating.   III: 1, *passim*.
255 Disgusted with public life. . . . The virtue . . . to the business.
      III: 9, S 758–9, OC 970.
255 but would rather . . . worse for it.   III: 1, S 604–5, OC 774.
255–256 Private life is less . . . to judge us.   III: 2, S 613–4, OC 785,
      787.
256 His ideal . . . our happiness."   III: 10, S 769, OC 983–4.
256 The rounded man who will do good by choice.   I: 26, S 123,
      OC 166.
256 The decaying body . . . than does folly."   III: 5, S 638–9,
      OC 818.
256 "We call 'wisdom' . . . rheumatic virtue."   III: 2, S 619–20,
      OC 793–5.
256 To keep . . . dead tree."   III: 5, S 641, OC 821.
256–257 Above all, we . . . he were in it.   III: 2, S 619, OC 793.
257 Habit may make us adaptable.   III: 13, S 830, OC 1061.
257 "The fairest souls . . . and a gardener."   III: 3, S 621, 623,
      OC 796, 799.
257 The conclusion . . . of perfection."   III: 13, S 850–2, OC
      1088–90. After 1588 Montaigne incorrectly changed "Scipio the
      Younger" to "Scipio the Elder."
257 Concern with conduct.   III: 10, S 769–70, OC 984.
257 He finds men addicted . . . is our condition."   III: 9, S 756–8,
      OC 967–9. For abandoning moral effort and changing into beasts
      not angels, III: 13, S 856, OC 1096.
257 Unjust self-condemnation.   III: 13, S 852, OC 1091.
257–258 "Alas, poor . . . by art."   III: 5, S 670, OC 857–8. After 1588
      Montaigne changed "natural" to "necessary."
258 In an early . . . than we are.   II: 3, S 254, OC 334.
258 Now, convinced . . . do no better."   III: 2, S 617, OC 791.
258 Religion proven ineffective as a moral force.   This is conjecture,
      based largely on two things: Montaigne's shocked revulsion at
      what men of his time do to their religion (III: 9, and especially
      II: 12, beginning) and on the absence of elements in his moral
      code that are specifically Christian.
258 He takes for granted . . . our appetites."   III: 2, S 612, 620,
      OC 784, 795.
259 . . . rejecting Plato's belief . . . our being,   II: 12, S 386,
      OC 500.
259 "these parts must not be separated."   I: 26, S 122, OC 164.
259 He finds nothing . . . or spiritual,   III: 5, S 681, OC 871.
259 "dismember . . . correspondence,"   III: 13, S 855, OC 1094.
259 "It is still . . . corporeal movement."   III: 8, S 710, OC 909;
      III: 9, S 756, OC 967.

259 Montaigne on the body and the soul.   For most of this the reference must be to *Essays, passim*. However, here are a few key passages: III: 2, S 616, OC 790; III: 4, S 637–8, OC 816–7; III: 10, S 770, OC 984; III: 13, S 823, 836, 842, 849, 855, OC 1052, 1068, 1077, 1086, 1094–5.

260 We have in us . . . comfortably.   III: 12, S 794, OC 1015–6; III: 13, S 822, OC 1051.

260 Divert the ailments of the soul.   III: 4, S 632, OC 810.

260 Direct mind to help body.   III: 5, S 641, OC 821.

260 . . . to fool . . . about pain;   III: 13, S 836–7, OC 1068–9.

260 . . . train our soul . . . pass without hurt.   III: 13, S 853–4, OC 1091–3.

260 "that inhuman wisdom"   III: 13, S 849, OC 1086.

260 For our being . . . virtually divine."   III: 13, S 855–7, OC 1095–6. After 1588 Montaigne changed "simple, natural" and "seriously and expressly" to "express, simple" and "seriously and sternly."

260–261 Evil too . . . of our life.   III: 1, S 599–600, OC 767–8.

261 However, we . . . night the day.   III: 2, S 612, OC 784.

261 "I do not . . . of inanity."   I: 50, S 221, OC 291.

261 Aware as he . . . and pastime,   III: 3, S 629, OC 807.

261 "vanity itself . . . are pleasant."   III: 9, S 762–3, OC 974–6.

261 "Our follies . . . wisdom does,"   III: 3, S 625, OC 801.

261 "Is there . . . its power?"   III: 4, S 637–8, OC 817.

261 Plaything of the gods.   III: 5, especially S 652, 668–9, OC 835, 855.

261 There is vanity . . . is vanity."   III: 9, S 756, OC 967.

261 If others . . . of the farce."   III: 9, S 766, OC 979–80.

261 "Things that . . . despise ourselves."   II: 3, S 254, OC 334.

261–262 "There is . . . disdain our being."   III: 13, S 852, OC 1091. After 1588 Montaigne changes "hate and disdain" to "despise" and adds "and naturally" after "well."

262 "We must slide . . . on the surface. . . .   III: 10, S 768, OC 982.

262 Oh, what . . . well-made head!"   III: 13, S 822, OC 1050–1.

262 "Nature," he . . . wise and just. . . .   III: 13, S 855, OC 1094.

262 We cannot . . . following nature."   III: 12, S 811, OC 1036–7.

262 that "disdainful . . . peg lower."   III: 9, S 748, OC 956.

262 He mistrusts . . . troublesome.   III: 13, S 851, OC 1089.

262 He lets . . . combat nothing."   III: 12, S 811, OC 1037.

262 If he does not . . . as I could."   II: 11, S 311–2, OC 406–8.

262 not be slaves . . . reason alone.   II: 8, S 279, OC 366.

262 Now he wants . . . every direction,   III: 5, S 639, OC 818.

262 that alone gives true freedom;   III: 12, S 800, OC 1022.

262 A slave only to reason.   III: 1, S 603, OC 772.

262–263 "the inventions . . . or bounds."   II: 37, S 580, OC 744.

263 His plan . . . with my feet."   III: 9, S 749, 758, OC 958, 969.
263 After Aristotle . . . into nature."   III: 10, S 772–3, OC 987–8.
263 We have only . . . in that."   III: 13, S 827, 830, OC 1058, 1061.
263 "What those . . . [*complexion*]"   III: 10, S 780, OC 997.
263 "school of stupidity,"   III: 12, S 805, OC 1029.
263 "He . . . raised . . . their strength."   III: 12, S 793–4, OC 1014–5.
263 "refrain . . . one's power."   III: 3, S 622, OC 798.
263–264 His defense . . . to myself."   III: 2, S 613, OC 785.
264 "those that . . . our own."   III: 13, S 855, OC 1094.
264 Epaminondas . . . and humanity."   III: 1, S 609, OC 780.
264 "a humanity truly more than human."   III: 5, S 658, OC 842.
264 "There is nothing . . . and properly."   III: 13, S 852, OC 1091.
264 "Our well-being . . . being ill."   II: 12, S 364, OC 472.
264 We need little learning . . .   III: 12, S 794, OC 1016.
264 Diversion a benefit.   III: 4, S 635, OC 813.
264 Nature gently leads us.   I: 20, S 63, OC 89.
264 we can control . . . from experience.   III: 13, S 834, 836, OC 1066, 1068; and *passim*.
264 Virtue once a struggle.   II: 11, S 307, OC 401.
264 pleasant and gay, like the wisdom Montaigne loves.   III: 5, S 641, OC 822.
264 Socrates in the *Phaedo*.   III: 13, S 838, OC 1072.
264 "Our life is . . . than the other."   III: 13, S 835, OC 1068.
264–265 Some "wise . . . all things good."   III: 13, S 853–5, OC 1091–4.

Chapter 15: Among the Great

Bonnefon is completely reliable but now outdated on many points by new documents; Strowski is much more up-to-date but overeager to exaggerate Montaigne's role. For material on Marie de Gournay, see Marjorie H. Ilsley, *A Daughter of the Renaissance. Marie Le Jars de Gournay. Her Life and Works* (The Hague: Mouton, 1963). For the historical background, Lavisse's *Histoire de France*, Vol. VI is still very valuable. Other sources are listed below as appropriate.

Page
267–269 The Conferences at Saint-Brice.   See Trinquet, "Du nouveau dans la biographie de Montaigne," *RHLF*, LIV (1954), 1–22; and my "New Light on Montaigne's Trip to Paris in 1588," *Romanic Review*, LI (1960), 163–6.
267 Catherine de' Medici's letters.   *Lettres* (Imprimerie Nationale, 1880–1943, 11 vols.), IX, 132 (Dec. 31, 1586), 176 (Feb. 18, 1587). For the four mentions of François Montaigne, II, 95

(1563); VI, 201 (1579); VII, 133 (1579); VIII, 179 (1584). The 1584 letter is the one that interests Catherine and Henry III.

268 Montaigne's sketch of Henry of Navarre. I: 24, S 94–5, OC 128.

268 "I still . . . succumb to them." III: 12, S 800, OC 1022.

269 L'Estoile quotation. Pierre de L'Estoile, *Journal de L'Estoile pour le règne de Henri III*, Lefèvre ed. (5th ed., Gallimard, c. 1943), p. 510.

269–270 Navarre, Corisande, and Montaigne. Raymond Ritter, *Cette Grande Corisande* (Michel, c. 1936), pp. 232–55. (Later republished, c. 1959, as *Une Dame de Chevalerie*.)

270–276 Montaigne's trip to Paris in 1588. See my article, listed above.

271 Mornay's letter. Madame de Mornay, *Mémoires* (Renouard, 1868–9, 2 vols.), II, 148.

271–272 Stafford's letters. *Calendar of State Papers, Foreign Series, of the Reign of Elizabeth, 1586–1588*, Vol. XXI, part I (London: Stationery Office, 1927), pp. 488, 510.

271–272 Montaigne's letter of February 16, 1588. S 1090, OC 1395–6.

272–273 Mendoza's letters. Ritter (pp. 254–5) was the first to publish these, in French translation. The Spanish text, and a bit of the context, is given in my article "New Light . . ."

273 Marie de Gournay's account. Quoted by Nicolaï, *Les Belles Amies de Montaigne*, pp. 174–5, from the "Copie de la Vie de la demoiselle de Gournay," pp. 992 ff. of the extremely rare 1641 (Du Bray) ed. of her *Les Advis ou les Presens de la Demoiselle de Gournay*.

274 Thorigny's trip to Moissac. Jacques de Callières (or Cailliere), *Histoire du mareschal de Matignon* (Courbe, 1661), pp. 216–7.

276 His holdup like an earlier one. See *Essays*, III: 12, S 813–4, OC 1039–40. My main reasons for thinking that the two accounts are not of the same holdup are these: 1) the details do not seem to me to tally very well; 2) it seems unlikely that Montaigne added the account in III: 12 to the *Essays* between February and June, 1588; 3) he speaks of the leader of the holdup in III: 12 (S 814, OC 1040), in a passage that had to be written within months if the holdup is the same one, as being "still on his feet to tell the tale. . . ."

276 Some inferences from our knowledge of Montaigne's trip. In his article "Problèmes . . . ," Roger Trinquet infers, from two facts about our evidence on this trip, that the theories of Strowski, Nicolaï, and others, that Montaigne played a really extensive role as secret negotiator are probably ill-founded. If we have this many reports of one known trip, he argues, it is unlikely that many others would leave us no trace. Moreover, "Montigny" at the age of fifty-four is an unknown to Stafford and his well-informed agents, for his first comment is "I never heard of the man afore in my life."

276 A Guelf to the Ghibellines.   III: 12, S 798, OC 1021.

276 "I do not want a man to refuse,"   III: 10, S 770, OC 984.

276–283 Marie de Gournay.   See Ilsley, *A Daughter of the Renaissance*, pp. 22–35, 44, 50, 135–43.

277 Gournay quotation.   Quoted by Nicolaï, *Les Belles Amies de Montaigne*, p. 175, from the "Copie de la Vie . . ."

277 Marie's adulation of Montaigne.   See especially the Preface to her 1595 (L'Angelier) edition of the *Essais*.

277 I have seen a girl . . . in good earnest.   I: 14, S 41, OC 60; cf. Ed. Munic., I, 72.

277–278 Montaigne's tribute to Marie de Gournay.   II: 17, S 502, OC 645–6. For the page in the Bordeaux Copy, see Edition Photo-typique, plate 596.

278–279 Marie's revised tribute in 1635.   *Essais*, Camusat, 1635, p. 517. Her acknowledgment of the revision is p. ¶¶¶ii recto.

279 And if I had not supported . . . carried it away.   III: 9, S 752, OC 961. Cf. Ed. Munic., III, 255; Edition Phototypique, plate 895.

280 "I would willingly . . . to honor me."   III: 9, S 751, OC 961.

280 "My Father told . . . minds as he."   1595 Preface, 14th page (unnumbered).

280 Montaigne with the king in Chartres and Rouen.   De Thou reports his being at Chartres and Rouen; the *Ephemeris* shows him having come from Rouen to Paris in July.

280 A first trip to Gournay-sur-Aronde.   Pasquier says he spent about three months there on two or three trips (*Lettres*, XVIII, i; *Choix de Lettres*, Thickett ed., Droz, 1956, p. 49). Marie writes of enjoying Montaigne only two or three months; see Payen, "Recherches sur Michel Montaigne. Correspondance relative à sa mort," *Bulletin du Bibliophile*, 1862, p. 1293.

280–281 Montaigne in the Bastille.   The revised account, entered in the *Ephemeris* for July 10, adds that Montaigne was staying in the Faubourg Saint-Germain; that his malady was indeed a sort of gout; that he learned at the Bastille of Elbeuf's role, and that the man imprisoned in Rouen was a relative of Elbeuf's (probably, we gather from a letter of Catherine's to Henry III in Rouen, on the same day, a M. de Chaumont); and that *secrétaire d'Etat* Pinart had notified the queen mother. The Provost of Merchants, who had to endorse Montaigne's release, was an old acquaintance from Montaigne's Italian trip, Michel Marteau, seigneur de la Chapelle, who had experienced a marvelous cure at Loreto (*TJ*, Loreto, April 23–6, 1581; S 973, OC 1250).

281–282 Montaigne's illness and Brach's account.   Payen, "Recherches sur Michel Montaigne. Correspondance relative à sa mort," *Bulletin du Bibliophile*, 1862, p. 1293. Note that Montaigne's illness could hardly have occurred earlier in that year without Brach's mentioning it (as he does not) to Lipsius in his letter of July 8.

Other information on Brach is drawn from Dezeimeris' Preface to Brach's *Œuvres poétiques* (Paris: Aubry, 1861–2, 2 vols.).

282 Montaigne left Gournay for Blois on November 23.   So Marie clearly implies in her letter to Montaigne that serves as Preface to the 1594 (L'Angelier) ed. of *Le Proumenoir de Monsieur de Montaigne* (*Monsieur de Montaigne's Walk*), pp. 2 recto, 5 recto and verso; see Jean Marchand, "*Le Proumenoir de Monsieur de Montaigne, par sa fille d'alliance.* Etude bibliographique," in *BSAM* II: 13–14 (Oct. 1948–Jan. 1949), pp. 69–70. The expanded story of the Picard girl with the bodkin (see above) says that Montaigne saw her just before attending the Estates. He may well have gone to Blois via Paris, of course. I doubt that he made two trips to Blois; and if not, he apparently did not go there until late November.

282–283 Montaigne at Gournay, and the *Proumenoir.*   Again, see the prefatory letter to the 1594 *Proumenoir*, pp. 2–5 recto and verso; quoted in part in the Marchand article and in Ilsley, pp. 32–4, 48–50.

282 Plutarch's "Love Stories"   So titled in the Loeb; the Ἐρωτικαὶ διηγήσεις, which Amyot called "Estranges Evenemens advenus pour l'amour."

283 Montaigne on Guise's boldness.   I: 24, S 94, OC 128; cf. Edition Phototypique, plate 96.

283–284 Montaigne and Pasquier at Blois.   Pasquier, *Lettres*, XVIII, i, "A M. de Pelgé"; in *Choix de Lettres*, ed. Thickett, pp. 45–6.

284 When I have been . . . my book in me."   III: 5, S 667, OC 853.

284 Montaigne back in Guienne.   Marie de Gournay, quoted by Bonnefon, p. 442, and Dreano, p. 166.

284 Montaigne collaborating with Matignon.   De Thou, *Historiarum* . . . , V, 180; *Histoire universelle* (Basel: Brandmuller, 1742), VIII, 146.

284 Marie sent *Proumenoir* in second half of December.   Ilsley, p. 28, fn. 13.

284 De Thou and Schomberg at Montaigne.   De Thou, *Historiarum* . . . , VII, *De vita sua*, p. 97; *Mémoires*, ed. Buchon, p. 637.

284 Matignon in Bordeaux.   Callières, *Histoire du Mareschal de Matignon*, pp. 246–67; Devienne, *Histoire de Bordeaux*, p. 187; Boscheron des Portes, *Histoire du Parlement de Bordeaux*, pp. 293–6.

285–288 Montaigne's two letters to Henry IV.   S 1091–4, OC 1397–1400.

285–286 Montaigne's hope to be a candid adviser.   III: 13, S 825–6, OC 1055–6.

288 Montaigne a devoted loyalist to the very end.   Roger Trinquet ("Le Dernier Message politique de Montaigne," *Mercure de France*, Vol. 329, April 1957, pp. 612–9) argues that the marquis de Trans's will, signed March 26, 1591, is in large part the work

of Montaigne, who was a signer and one of three executors. Its most striking provision is that the young grandson Frédéric de Foix shall be the universal heir on condition that he be a Catholic, as shall his heirs if they are to inherit; but that they shall bear arms for the king and serve him faithfully regardless of his religion or opinion. Mme Léonie Gardeau, who first published the will, gives cogent reasons for believing it to be fully Trans's own; see *Bulletin de la Société Historique et Archéologique du Périgord,* LXXXIV (1957), pp. 98–103 ("En marge d'un testament"); LXXXIII (1956), 125–32; and *BSAM* IV: 2 (April–June, 1965), 29–36.

Chapter 16: The Final Additions

The additions themselves are the source.

Page

289 Long before . . . ready to go.   I: 20, S 61, OC 86.

290 Description of his library.   III: 3, S 628–9, OC 806–7; see above, ch. 8.

290 Reluctance to take advice.   III: 2, S 618, OC 792–3.

290 Equanimity over loss of children.   I: 14, S 42, OC 61.

290 Equanimity over plight of France.   III: 12, S 800, OC 1023.

290 " 'Idle. . . . their reproaches.   I: 26, S 130–1, OC 175–6.

290 His errors as object lessons.   III: 8, S 703, OC 899.

290 Lied about money.   I: 14, S 44, OC 65.

290 "Guide me . . . emptied"   III: 10, S 772–3, OC 987–8.

290 "Myself now . . . dizzy, wobbling."   III: 9, S 736, OC 941–2.

290–291 "When I call . . . my definition."   I: 38, S 173, OC 230.

291 "peacock's feet."   III: 5, S 669, OC 855.

291 a certain part lower down."   II: 12, S 402, OC 520.

291 "the unruly liberty of this member,   I: 21, S 72–3, OC 100–1.

291 Love, he . . . our vessels."   III: 5, S 668, OC 855.

291 "Each one of . . . this one."   III: 5, S 677, OC 866.

291 "We imagine . . . his ability."   III: 2, S 615, OC 788.

291 "Shit in the basket . . .   III: 5, S 649, OC 831.

291 "Won't they . . . on their wives?"   III: 13, S 850, OC 1087.

291 "On the loftiest . . . own rump."   III: 13, S 857, OC 1096.

291 To the ancient . . . in private"   II: 12, S 440, OC 568.

291–292 I owe a . . . half of it.   III: 5, S 677–8, OC 866–7.

292 Now he dares . . . or a tree."   III: 8, S 720, OC 921.

292 "And he who . . . he understand?"   II: 12, S 418, OC 539.

292 "man in general . . . I seek."   II: 10, S 303, OC 396.

292 As a dispassionate . . . can happen."   I: 21, S 75–6, OC 104–5.

292 "We *naturalists*"   III: 12, S 809, OC 1034. Italics mine.

292 ". . . *naturalize* art"   III: 5, S 666, OC 852. Italics mine.

292 He has noted . . . be portrayed.   III: 13, S 818, OC 1046.

292 A memory of paper. III: 13, S 837–8, OC 1071.

292 His gifts to . . . richer than I." II: 8, S 293, OC 383.

292–293 Those who praise . . . get my drift." I: 40, S 184–5, OC 245.

292 . . . or plucked it cleaner. III: 2, S 611, OC 783.

293 Order is . . . sow them." II: 27, S 528–9, OC 678.

293 His book is . . . ambitious subtlety." III: 9, S 736, OC 941.

293 "Of Practice" (additions) II: 6, S 272–5, OC 357–60.

293–294 "Of Giving the Lie" (additions) II: 18, S 503–5, OC 647–9.

294 Added two notes. On his casual use of such terms as "fortune": I: 56, S 234, OC 308. On his refusal to concede to his censor that he was wrong to praise a heretic for his poetry: III: 10, S 775, OC 990.

294 Disclaimer in "Prayers." I: 56, S 229, OC 303.

294 "that he was . . . divine word." III: 12, S 798, OC 1020.

294–295 Both sides twist . . . incites them." II: 12, S 323–4, OC 420–1.

295 "Since philosophy . . . individually." II: 16, S 471, OC 605–6.

295 "our own affairs and Michel, III: 9, S 726, OC 929.

295 Offices of friendship. I: 39, S 178, OC 237.

295 Anyone who . . . anything else." I: 3, S 9, OC 18.

295 Pleasure a form of profit, to be treasured. III: 13, S 834, 849, OC 1067, 1086–7; and *passim.*

295 Voluptuousness the goal of virtue. I: 20, S 56, OC 80.

295 Equanimity in pain and pleasure. III: 13, S 853, OC 1091.

295 "Let him . . . without shame." I: 39, S 178, OC 237.

295–296 When he speaks . . . to penance. I: 20, S 56, OC 80.

296 Virtue . . . is not, . . . those monsters. I: 26, S 119–20, OC 160–2.

296 Refuses to break a promise. III: 1, S 608, OC 779.

296 Even a weak man. II: 29, S 533, OC 683.

296 "saying anything . . . already said." I: 7, S 20, OC 33.

296 Truth the wisdom of his lesson. III: 5, S 677, OC 866.

296 His soul hates . . . for itself." II: 17, S 491, OC 631.

296–297 "In this universe . . . trust to her." III: 13, S 821–2, OC 1050.

297 Fools who regard our being as vice. III: 5, S 670, OC 857.

297 "supercelestial thoughts . . . Socrates alarm him. III: 13, S 856, OC 1095–6.

297 our conduct is why we are here; III: 10, S 769–70, OC 984.

297 Shall I say . . . and conscience. III: 12, S 811, OC 1037.

297 His pride in . . . it is naturally. III: 2, S 612, 619–20, OC 784, 794.

297–298 We are great . . . at most. III: 13, S 850–1, OC 1088.

298 Spurina. II: 33, S 555, OC 712.

298 Cato the Elder. II: 2, S 246, OC 324.

298 "The greatest . . . to oneself," I: 39, S 178, OC 236.

298 "He who lives . . . unto himself."   III: 10, S 769, OC 984.

298 He no longer . . . we employ them."   II: 37, S 575, OC 738.

298 Opinion gives value to things.   I: 14, S 42, OC 62.

298–299 The soul is . . . unhappy condition."   I: 14, S 39, 46, OC 57, 67.

299 Things in themselves . . . ourselves alone.   I: 50, S 220, OC 290.

299 "The goal of our career is death.   I: 20, S 57, OC 82.

299–300 If we . . . give it weight.   III: 12, S 805, OC 1028–9.

300 "The wretchedness . . . to pursue."   II: 12, S 363–4, OC 472–3.

300 The two passages.   II: 12, S 320, 429, OC 416, 554. Cf. DB II, 18, 152–3; and Edition Phototypique, plates 369, 508–9.

301 Democratic rule the most equitable.   I: 3, S 12, OC 23.

301 Goodness commonest among the humble.   II: 35, S 564, OC 724.

301 bravery . . . the crude herd,   I: 23, S 82, OC 113.

301 . . . goodness . . .   II: 35, S 564, OC 724. Not all the references in this paragraph are specifically to the *vulgaire,* but all seem to be applicable.

301 the soft and effeminate mob.   II: 32, S 547, OC 702.

301 As gullible as children.   I: 27, S 132, OC 177–8. Cf. I: 51, S 222, OC 293.

301 Prey to delusions.   I: 21, S 70, OC 97; II: 12, S 365, OC 474.

301 Prey to imaginings.   I: 18, S 52, OC 75.

301 Opinions and complaints to be shunned.   I: 31, S 150, OC 200; II: 12, S 333, OC 433.

301 Slaves to custom.   I: 49, S 215, OC 284–5.

301 "brutish stupidity."   I: 20, S 58, OC 82.

301 The cruelty . . . of cowardice.   II: 27, S 524, OC 672.

301 Base and vile.   I: 25, S 99, OC 134; cf. S 97–8, 104, OC 132, 141.

301 "the people . . . faculties idle."   II: 12, S 371, OC 481.

301 "more distance . . . on others."   I: 42, S 191, OC 252. It was only after 1588 that Montaigne cut down these amenities (deleting "ignorant," "asleep," and "full of fever and fright") to read simply: "stupid, base, servile, unstable . . ."
     On the vulnerability of the vulgar to external impulsion, see I: 1, S 4, OC 12; II: 29, S 533, OC 683.

301 Less criticism after 1580.   He notes that they are ignorant and easily led (I: 26, S 108, OC 146; II: 16, S 473, OC 607) and less patient of pain than he is (III: 9, S 725, OC 927); but his criticisms are generally mild and seem a bit reluctant. One curious case is in I: 51 (S 222, OC 293; cf. DB I, 255), where in 1580 he had stated that orators throve in poorly regulated states in which "the people, or the ignorant, or all men held all power"; after 1588 he changes "the people" to "the vulgar."

301 He recognizes . . . subtler ones."   III: 3, S 622, OC 797–8; cf. III: 8, S 713, OC 912.

301–302 From the most . . . school of it.   III: 12, S 793, 803, 805, OC
  1014–5, 1026, 1029.

  302 Peasants the true philosophers.   II: 17, S 501, OC 644.

  302 "of the common sort,"   III: 11, S 790, OC 1010 (*"homme du
  commun"*); II: 17, S 481, OC 618 (*"de la commune sorte, sauf
  en ce que je m'en tiens"*).

  302 His life is "common and private,"   III: 2, S 611, OC 782.

  302 his soul "low and common,"   "Low and common": III: 13, S
  824, OC 1054. "Common": III: 10, S 777, OC 993.

  302 opinions and conduct "low and humble."   III: 13, S 855, OC
  1094.

  302 "take refuge . . . of mine."   III: 10, S 780, OC 997. Cf. II:
  17, S 480, OC 617.

Chapter 17: Death and Survival

The main sources are listed individually.

Page

  303 Visitors.   Brach, Charron, and Raemond are simply very strong
  probabilities. For Bacon, see Brach's letter to him, and the comment on it, in Sidney Lee, *The French Renaissance in England*
  (New York: Scribner's, 1910), pp. 173–4.

  303 Correspondents.   For herself and Ossat, Marie de Gournay is
  our witness; see her Preface to the 1595 *Essays*, p. ã ii, verso.

303–304 Léonor's marriage and child.   *Ephemeris*, May 27, June 23
  (1590) and March 31 (1591); OC 1412.

  304 "colds, . . . pleasure and painlessness."   III: 13, S 834–9, OC
  1066–73.

  304 In his final . . . it is naturally."   III: 2, S 620, OC 794.

304–305 Pasquier's account of Montaigne's death.   *Lettres*, XVIII, i; in
  Choix de lettres, Thickett ed., pp. 48–9.

  305 Automne's account of Montaigne's death.   Bernard Automne,
  *Commentaire sur les coustumes génèralles de la ville de Bourdeaus
  et pays Bourdelois* (Bordeaux: Millanges, 1621); quoted in Zeitlin,
  I, xlvi, and in Feugère's ed. of Estienne Pasquier, *Œuvres choisies*
  (Didot, 1849, 2 vols.), II, 397 fn. We do not have Montaigne's
  will or know who his heirs were.

  305 Brach to Anthony Bacon.   See Sidney Lee's book, above.

  305 Brach to Lipsius, Lipsius to Gournay.   See Payen, "Nouveaux
  Documents sur Michel Montaigne. Correspondance relative à sa
  mort," *Bulletin du Bibliophile*, 1862, pp. 1292–1311.

  305 Marie adds . . .   Preface to 1595 *Essais*, p. ĩ verso.

  305 Raemond on Marie de Gournay's grief.   Alan M. Boase, "Montaigne annoté par Florimond de Raemond," *Revue du Seizième
  Siècle*, XV (1928), 240.

  305 Pasquier on Marie de Gournay's grief.   *Choix de Lettres*, p. 49.

306 Marie de Gournay to see Bussaguet.   Preface to 1595 *Essays*, p. ĩ ii recto.

306 De Thou.   *Historiarum* . . . , V, 180.

306 Malvin de Cessac.   Payen article; also *AHG*, XXXIV (1899), p. 323.

306 Raemond on Montaigne.   *Erreur populaire de la papesse Iane* (Lyons: Rigaud, 1595), 159–60.

306 Funeral arrangements noted.   *Ephemeris*, Sept. 13 (1592), OC 1415.

306–308 History of Montaigne's remains.   Nicolaï, "L'Odyssée des cendres de Montaigne," *BSAM* II: 15 (1949–52), 31–45; especially Paul Roudié, "Précisions et réflexions au sujet de la sépulture de Montaigne," in Georges Palassie, *Mémorial du Ier Congrès International des Etudes Montaignistes* (Bordeaux: Taffard, 1964), pp. 108–22; also Bonnefon, pp. 487–92, and Malvezin, pp. 308–9, 323.

307 The contretemps during the Revolution.   *AHG*, XIV (1873), 551–7; Malvezin, pp. 158–9, 179–80; Dreano, *La Renommée de Montaigne en France au XVIIIe siècle* (Angers: Editions de l'Ouest, 1952), pp. 499–502.

307 The fire in 1871.   Malvezin, p. 181.

307–308 Montaigne's epitaphs.   Bonnefon, pp. 490–1.

308 As Marie de . . . months with them."   Preface to 1595 *Essays*, pp. â ii verso, ĩ ii recto; and "Copie de la vie . . ." in *Advis ou Presens* . . . , 1641 ed., quoted by Bonnefon, p. 482.

308 "other copy . . . in his house"   Preface to 1595 *Essays*, p. ĩ ii recto.

308–309 The copy Marie de Gournay used.   Zeitlin, I, 421–34.

309 The Bordeaux Copy in the 18th century.   Dreano, *La Renommée* . . . , pp. 345–7.

309–310 The Bordeaux Copy in the 19th century.   See my *Montaigne in France, 1812–1852* (New York: Columbia University Press, 1940), 207–8. The Naigeon comment is in his edition (Didot, 1802, 4 vols.), I, 178 fn.; that of de l'Aulnaye, in each of his three Desoer eds. (1818, 4 vols., I, 246 fn.; 1818, 1 vol., p. 47 fn.; 1819, 9 vols., II, 228 fn.); that of Lefèvre in his (1818, 5 vols.), I, 254 fn.

309 Montaigne on strangling the pupil.   I: 26, S 120, OC 162.

310 Dezeimeris.   *Recherches sur la recension du texte posthume des Essais de Montaigne* (Bordeaux: Gounouilhou, 1866; extract from *Actes de l'Académie de Bordeaux*, XXVIII, 1866).

310 Reception gratifying to Montaigne.   III: 9, S 736–7, OC 942.

310 Reception disappointing to Marie de Gournay.   Preface to 1595 *Essays*, beginning and *passim*.

310–311 Pasquier on Montaigne.   Pasquier, *Lettres*, XVIII, i; in *Choix de lettres*, Thickett ed., pp. 42–4, 46–8. The letter, to Claude de Pellejay (or Pelgé) was written around 1602 but published only in 1619.

311   Six criticisms reported by Marie de Gournay.   1595 Preface, pp.
ã iii verso–ẽ iii recto; cf. 1635 Preface (mainly unpaginated), 3rd
to 16th pages.

311   Master of the Sacred Palace.   See above, ch. 12.

311–315   Reception in 16th and 17th centuries.   See Alan M. Boase, *The
Fortunes of Montaigne. A History of the Essays in France, 1580–
1669* (London: Methuen, 1935); and for the period up to about
1620, Pierre Villey, *Montaigne devant la postérité* (Boivin, c.
1935).

312   Montaigne in England.   Villey, "Montaigne en Angleterre," *Revue des Deux-Mondes*, Sept., 1913, pp. 113–50. Jonson's remark
(*Volpone*, Act III, sc. ii) is that "All our English writers /
Will deign to steal out of this author [Guarini], mainly, / Almost
as much as from Montaignié." Shakespeare seems probably to owe
Montaigne much, but the question is vague and mooted. His one
clear borrowing is Gonzalo's speech beginning "I' the commonwealth I would by contraries" in *The Tempest*, Act II, sc. ii,
which he takes from Montaigne (I: 31, S 153, OC 204), "This
is a nation, I should say to Plato . . . ." For Montaigne's impact
on Elizabethan and Jacobean England, see Hiram Haydn, *The
Counter-Renaissance* (New York: Scribner's, 1950), *passim*.

313–314   Montaigne and Charron.   See Pierre Spriet, "Montaigne, Charron
et la crise morale provoquée par les guerres de religion," *French
Review*, XXXVIII (April, 1965), 587–98.

313–314   Charron's *Wisdom* on Index.   Curiously, Boase mentions this
fact about Charron rather in passing, Villey not at all. Boase dates
it at 1606 (p. 129); but all the editions of the *Index librorum
prohibitorum* that I have seen give the date as 1605, either Dec. 16
(1881 ed., Rome: Typographia Polyglotta; and 1892 ed., Mechlin:
Dessain), or, apparently more officially, Sept. 9 (1900 ed., Rome:
Typis Vaticanis; and 1930 ed., in Italian, Rome: Tipografia Poli-
glotta Vaticana).

314   Descartes.   See the *Discourse on Method*, and Léon Brunschvicg,
Descartes et Pascal, lecteurs de Montaigne (New York and Paris:
Brentano, 1944).

314   Pascal.   See the *Pensées* and the *Entretien avec M. de Sacy;* also
the Brunschvicg book.

314   Voltaire takes Montaigne's side.   See the *Remarques sur les
Pensées de M. de Pascal* (1734).

315   Thibaudet.   See his *Montaigne* (Gallimard, c. 1963), p. 49.

315–316   Montaigne in the 18th century.   See especially Dreano, *La Renommée de Montaigne en France au XVIIIe siècle* (Angers: Editions de l'Ouest, 1952).

316   Montesquieu.   *Œuvres complètes* (Garnier, 1875–9, 7 vols.),
VII, 162, 171.

316–318   Montaigne in the 19th century.   See my *Montaigne in France,
1812–1852* (New York: Columbia University Press, 1940).

317 "I am rereading Montaigne . . . better chat with." *Correspondance* (Librairie de France, 1922–4, 4 vols.; listed as Vol. V parts 1–4 of *Œuvres complètes*), II, 147 (Oct. 28–9, 1853).

317 Montaigne in 19th-century England and America.   See Dédéyan, *Montaigne chez ses amis anglo-saxons* (Boivin, c. 1946, 2 vols.).

317 Emerson.   See Charles Lowell Young, *Emerson's Montaigne* (New York: Macmillan, 1941). "Wild and savoury as sweet fern" and "It seemed to me . . . thought and experience" are in Bliss Perry, ed., *The Heart of Emerson's Journals* (Boston and New York: Houghton Mifflin, c. 1926), p. 45. "Gross, semi-savage indecency," and "The sincerity . . . vascular and alive" are in *Representative Men* (Houghton Mifflin, 1903 ed.), pp. 162, 166, 168.

317–318 Sainte-Beuve.   See especially *Port-Royal* and *Nouveaux Lundis*, II, 156–77.

317 Sainte-Beuve on Montaigne's style.   *Port-Royal* (Hachette, undated, 8th–9th eds., 7 vols.), II, 443.

318 "Nature complete without Grace."   *Port-Royal*, II, 409.

318 "the skepticism . . . of its dream."   *Causeries du lundi*, XI, 515.

318 "I have reached . . . can die."   *Table générale et analytique des lundis*, p. 45.

318 It is never a waste . . . ever lived."   *Nouveaux Lundis*, II, 177 (March 24, 1862).

318 *Travel Journal* in Italian.   Alessandro d'Ancona's ed. (Città di Castello: Lapi, 1889), entitled *L'Italia alla fine del secolo XVI. Giornale del Viaggio di Michele di Montaigne in Italia nel 1580 e 1581.*

318 one of the best books . . . in German;   Hugo Friedrich, *Montaigne* (Berne: Francke, 1949).

318–319 Read in Polish, Russian, Turkish, Japanese.   The translation into Turkish by Sabahattin Eyüboğlu (1947) is of selections only, but those into Polish by T. Zelenski (3rd ed., 1957), into Russian by A. S. Bobovich (1960), and into Japanese by Professor Sekine are complete.

319 Japanese scholars.   Professor Yoichi Mayeda, Hiroshi Yamagishi, Miss Michiko Ishigami.

319 André Gide's selections.   Published in English as *The Living Thoughts of Montaigne* (New York and Toronto: Longmans Green, 1939).

319 Salvador Dali's selections.   Published in English as *Essays of Michel de Montaigne* (Garden City: Doubleday, 1947).

319 Albert Thibaudet.   See his *Montaigne* and his editions of Montaigne in the Pléiade series (Gallimard, 1933 and later).

319 Stefan Zweig.   See his "Montaigne" in *Age Nouveau*, XXXI (1948), p. 13 and pp. 8–15, *passim;* and his nine chapters on

Montaigne (pp. 7–81) in *Europäisches Erbe* (Frankfurt: Fischer, 1960). Cf. Margaret Marshall in *The Nation*, March 14, 1942, p. 314.

319 Justice Holmes. *Holmes-Pollock Letters. The Correspondence of Mr. Justice Holmes and Sir Frederick Pollock, 1874–1932* (Cambridge, Mass.: Harvard University Press, 1941, 2 vols.), II, 116; cf. I, 229; II, 169.

319 T. S. Eliot. Introduction to Pascal, *Pensées* (Everyman ed.), pp. xiv–xv; also in *Essays Ancient and Modern.*

319 Aldous Huxley. *Collected Essays* (New York: Harper, 1958), Preface, p. vii.

319 Virginia Woolf. *The Common Reader* (First and Second Series, New York: Harcourt, Brace, 1948 ed.), pp. 87, 100.

319–320 Gide. "To what a point . . . a great virtue" are in Gide, ed., *The Living Thoughts of Montaigne*, pp. 6–7. (The translation, however, is my own.) "Derived a little . . . and joy" is from *Journals* (Justin O'Brien tr., New York: Knopf, 1947–51, 4 vols.), III, 382; Jan. 18, 1938.

320 Thibaudet on Montaigne's "mobilism." See his *Montaigne*, pp. 191–2, 198; and, for the quotation, p. 222.

321 "I customarily do . . . in one piece,"   III: 2, S 616, OC 790.

321 "I do not know . . . within me,"   II: 11, S 311, OC 406.

321 We are not, . . . to be laughed at.   I: 50, S 221, OC 291–2.

321 Man, who . . . fool of the farce."   III: 9, S 766, OC 980.

321 It is an absolute . . . our own rump.   III: 13, S 857, OC 1096.

321 The beggar at his door.   I: 39, S 179, OC 238.

321 even of his cat—   II: 12, S 331, OC 430.

322 When he tells . . . to your own."   III: 2, S 613, OC 785.

322 "not so much say his lesson as do it."   I: 26, S 124, OC 167.

322 . . . to make him better and wiser,   I: 26, S 112, OC 151.

322 "Among the liberal . . . liberates us."   I: 26, S 117, OC 158.

323 "Let him be able . . . only the good."   I: 26, S 123, OC 166.

323 "Truth . . . fundamental part of virtue. . . .   II: 17, S 491, OC 631.

323 We are men . . . only by our word. . . .   I: 9, S 23, OC 37.

323 He who breaks . . . of each other."   II: 18, S 505, OC 650.

323 On the truth of Montaigne's portrait. See Herbert Lüthy, "Montaigne, or the Art of Being Truthful," *Encounter*, Nov. 1953, pp. 33–44; also in Quentin Anderson and Joseph A. Mazzeo, eds., *The Proper Study* (New York: St. Martin's Press, c. 1962), pp. 319–36.

323 where he finds himself mixed and variable,   II: 1, S 242, OC 319.

323 "If I had to live . . . for the future."   III: 2, S 620, OC 794.

323 A generous heart . . . everything is human.   II: 17, S 491, OC 630.

Index

Academic(s), 166, 168
Academy of the Palace, 117
Academy of Poetry and Music, 117
Adages (Erasmus), 144
Adler, Alfred, 320
Aeneid (Virgil), 41, 143
Aesculapius, 219
Affair of the Placards, 36
Africa, 19
Agen, 4, 71, 232, 234
Agenais, 77
Agrippa, Cornelius, 62
Aigues-Caudes, 191, 202
Aiquelini, Remundus, 7
Aire, 52, 134
Alain, 319
Alcestis, 86
Alcibiades, 76
Alexander the Great, 119, 255, 257
Alps, 210
Alva, duke of, 145
Amadis de Gaule, 41
Amboise, 36
Amboise, Peace of, 53
America, 317
Amerisks, 56
Amyot, Jacques, 109, 164, 170
Ancient Lessons (Coelius Rhodiginus), 144
Ancona, 206
Andoins, Corisande d'; see Gramont, Diane de
Anglo-Saxons, 318
Angoulême, 274
Anjou, François, duke of, 224–5, 234
Annals and Chronicles of France (Gilles), 143
Anti-Dictator; see Voluntary Servitude (La Boétie)
Antipodes, 204, 213
Antwerp, 4, 22–3
Apennines, 213
Apollo, 182, 261
Apology for Herodotus (Estienne), 172
Arabic, 40
Aragon, 21
Archives Historiques de la Gironde, 49
Archytas, 81
Ariosto, 221
Aristophanes, 45
Aristotle, 40, 60, 91, 158, 165–8, 197, 248, 263, 292
Armada, 275
Armagnac, 132
Armaingaud, Arthur, 147, 318

Arnaldi, Aiquelmus, 7
Arnauld, Antoine, 315
Aronde (stream), 282
Arques, 285
Arsac, 31, 70
Arsac, Jacquette d', 30–2, 70, 78, 80
Arsac, Jean d', 70
Athens, 76, 119, 167
Atlantic Ocean, 4
Attic Nights (Aulus Gellius), 144
Auch, 21, 23
Auctoville, Le Londel d', 238
Augsburg, 202, 210–1, 213, 218–9
Augsburg Confession, 141
Augustine, Saint, 143
Aulnaye, F.-H.-S. de l', 309
Aulus Gellius, 144, 178
Austria, 202, 210
Automne, Bernard, 305–6
Auvergne, 47
Auxerre, 164
Ayquem (Aichelmus, Aiquelini, Aiquelinus, Aiquem, Ayquelmus); see Eyquem
Ayquem de la Rossella, Pey, 7

Bacon, Anthony, 303, 305
Bacon, Francis, 162, 181, 184, 312
Baden, 202, 210–1, 213
Bagnères, 191, 202
Baïf, Jean-Antoine de, 71, 282
Baptistes (Buchanan), 40
Baralipton, 193
Barbarin, Jean, 48
Barckhausen, Henri, 163, 172, 174–5
Bar-le-Duc, 57, 210
Baroco, 193
Barrault, Monsieur de, 271
Barricades, Day of the, 276, 280
Barrois, 209
Basel, 210–1, 213
Basques, 307
Bastien, J.-F., 315
Bastille, 281
Baudier, Michel, 312
Bayle, 318
Bayonne, 236–7
Bazas, 232, 234
Béarn, 209, 237, 273
Beaumont-sur-Oise, 209–10
Beauregard (estate), 31, 113
Beauregard, Thomas de (brother of M.): urged by the dying La Boétie to maintain family unity, 15, 29–30, 78; remembered in his mother's will, 26; mar-

ries La Boétie's stepdaughter, 30, 70;
brings suit against M.'s widow and daughter, 30; tries to make young Jeanne de
Lestonnac a Protestant, 32; inherits noble
house of Beauregard, 113; other references, 24, 35, 89, 247
Béda, Noël, 36
Belbeys, 7
Belcier, Antoine de, 25
Bellièvre, Pompone de, 232–3, 272
Belot, Jean de, 54, 75, 78
Belzunce (or Belsunce), Henri-François-
Xavier de, 241
Benedictines, 32
Béraud, Fronton de, 48, 50
Bergerac, 37, 48, 129, 237–8
Bergson, Henri, 319–20
Beringuiet, 56
Beuther, Michael, 35, 94
Bèze (Beza), Théodore de, 117
Bible, 36, 104, 108, 160. *See also* Scripture
Bibliothèque du Roi, 208
Biron, Armand de Gontaut, baron de, 227
Bishe; *see* Gramont, Diane de
Bissouse, Raymond de, 235
Blanchier, Pierre, 48
Blanquefort, 7
Blaye, 85
Blois, 140, 276, 282–4. *See also* Estates General of Blois
Blount, Charles, 162
Boleyn, Anne, 36
Bologna, 210–1
Bolzano, 210
Bonnefon, Paul, 318
Book of Creatures; see Natural Theology
(Sebond)
Bordeaux: in M.'s time and earlier, 3–5;
M.'s ancestors prominent in, 8, 10, 23;
Jews in, 19–21; Lutherans executed, 35;
salt tax revolt, 42; in danger from Protestant troops (1562–3), 53; visited by
Charles IX (1565), 55–6; Pierre de M.
mayor of, 109, 112; M. mayor of, 135,
210, 223–45, 266, 269, 272, 276; trouble
spot in civil wars, 226–7; how mayor and
jurats elected, 227–8; meeting of Court
of Justice of Guienne, 228–9; M.'s re-
election as mayor disputed, 230; M. and
jurats send letters of remonstrance, 230–2;
League stirrings in, 237–9; plague in
1585, and M.'s failure to return, 240–1;
virtues of its people, 244–5; M. there in
1588–9, 284; other references, 6–7, 12,
22, 25–7, 31, 34, 37, 40, 48, 52, 54, 59,
62, 77, 85–8, 134, 140, 145, 151, 163,
216, 246, 268, 274, 306–7, 309, 312.
See also Burdigala
Bordeaux Academy (Society of Sciences,
Letters, and Arts of Bordeaux), 307
Bordeaux, University of, 43, 56, 307

Bordeaux Copy (of *Essays*), 145–6, 277–9,
283, 289–90, 308–10
Bordeaux Municipal Edition (of *Essays*),
310
Bordeaux Municipal Library, 309
Bordelais(es), 5, 8, 20, 229
Bossuet, 162, 315
Bouchet, Guillaume, 249
Bouilhonnas, 70
Bourbon, Catherine de, 273
Bourbon, Charles, cardinal de, 237–8
Bourdeille, sieur de, 140
Bourg, Anne du, 70
Boyssoné, Jean de, 43
Brach, Anne de, 282
Brach, Pierre de: law student at Toulouse,
45; reports M.'s grave illness, 276, 281–
2; may have seen 1588 *Essays* through
the press, 280; role in publication of 1595
Essays, 289, 308–9; visits the aging M.,
303; letter on M.'s death, 305–6
Brantôme, Pierre de Bourdeilles, seigneur de,
6, 34, 117–9, 140
Brazil, 124
Brazilian(s), 17, 56, 128–9, 174, 194
Brenner Pass, 210
Brian, Marie de, 307
Brisson (tower), 10
Brittany, 6
Browne, Thomas, 162
Brunet, Gustave, 318
Brusac, Jacques, 48
Brussels, 145
Buchanan, George, 40
Budé, Guillaume, 12, 36
Buffum, Imbrie, 221
Bunel, Pierre, 35, 44, 106, 109, 163
Buoncompagno, Ugo; *see* Gregory XIII, Pope
Burdigala, 5, 19
Burghley, William Cecil, Lord, 272, 275
Burgundy, 4–5
Burie, Charles de Coucy, sieur de, 31, 52,
71
Burton, Robert, 312
Bussaguet (cousin of M.), 306
Bussaguet, Joseph de, 87–8
Bussaguet, Raymond de (uncle of M.), 9,
14, 24, 30, 50, 85, 88
Byron, 317

Cadillac, 228
Caesar, 119, 257
Caila, baron de, 307
Calatayúd, 21
Calvin, Jean, 36, 182
Calvinism, 36
Calvinist(s), 32, 213, 222
Camain, Jeanne de, 26, 33
Camain, Léonor de (sister of M.), 24–6, 29,
33, 94, 113, 313
Camain, Thibaud de, 33
Camus, Jean-Pierre, 162, 312

Canadians, 56
Candale, Christophe de Foix de, 52
Candale, Fédéric de Foix de, 52–5
Candale, François de, 117, 134
Capitol (Rome), 204
Caplong, 9
Carle, Lancelot de, 70
Carle, Marguerite de, 70
Carle, Pierre de, 48, 70
Carlyle, 317
Carneades, 166
Casteljaloux, 34
Castello, 211
Castera, 31
Castiglione, 117, 315
Castillon, 37, 246–7, 250, 276, 313
Catechism (Ochino), 313
Catherine de' Medici: her tolerant religious
  policy of 1562, 52, 72; weakens the
  French nobility, 117; helps select M. as
  mayor, 225, 266; sketched, 225; summons
  M. to conferences with Navarre at Saint-
  Brice, 247, 267–8; procures M.'s release
  from Bastille, 281; other references, 37,
  224, 237
Catholic(s), 19, 23, 28, 30–2, 34, 37, 52,
  58, 78, 170, 213, 216, 222, 266, 271–3,
  275, 284, 295, 306
Catholicism, 170, 178, 275, 313
Cato the Elder, 257, 262, 298
Cato the Younger (of Utica): an early hero
  of M., 144, 152, 155–6, 196–7, 200; his
  heroic death, 152, 196–7, 299; a model of
  consistency, 155; supplanted as M.'s hero
  by Socrates, 196–7, 222, 262; enjoyed
  natural pleasures, 257; M. neither angel
  nor Cato, 258
Catullus, 77
Cazalis, Bernard (or Bertrand) de, 33, 209
Cazalis, Marie de (sister of M.), 24–5, 29,
  33, 94, 113, 209
Cemetery of the Jews (Bordeaux), 19
Cesi, cardinal, 219
Cesi, Paolo, 219
Ceylonese, 56
Chalons, 210
Chambéry, 210
Chambre des Enquêtes (Parlement of Bor-
  deaux), 49, 57–8, 114
Chambre des Requêtes (Parlement of Bor-
  deaux), 47–51, 57
Chambre des Vacations (Parlement of Bor-
  deaux), 49
Champagne, 117
Charles V, Emperor, 145
Charles VII, king of France, 5, 49, 227
Charles IX, king of France, 51, 55–7, 71,
  117, 266
Charron, Pierre, 33, 162, 303, 312–4
Chartres, 276, 280, 306
Château de Montaigne; *see* Montaigne (châ-
  teau and noble land of)

Château du Hâ, 5, 230
Château Trompette, 5, 230, 238
Chateaubriand, François-René de, 317
Christ, 104–5, 110–1, 137, 179, 214, 307,
  320
Christendom, 19, 215
Christian(s), 19, 21, 78, 105, 111, 163, 166
Christianity, 21, 103–4, 144, 159–60, 163–4,
  167, 170, 180, 182, 258–9, 314
Cicero, 45, 84, 152, 253, 299
Circe, 164
Civil Conversation (Guazzo), 315
Cléandre ("Cleander, or Honor and Valor,"
  by La Chassaigne de Pressac), 86, 249
Clement VII, Pope, 36
Clermont, Thomas Pons, sieur de, 7–8
Clermont-Ferrand, 210
Clitomachus, 166
Cognac, 267–8
Coignet, Matthieu, 249
Collège de France, 36, 43
Collège de Guyenne, 12, 20, 32, 39–40, 70
Colloquies (Erasmus), 144, 184
Commines, Philippe de, 143
Concordat (of 1516), 36
Condé, Henri I, prince of, 226, 235–6, 271,
  274
Condom, 232, 234
Confessions (Rousseau), 316
Constance, 210–1
*Contr'Un; see Voluntary Servitude, Discourse
  on* (La Boétie)
Coppin, Joseph, 111
Cordouan Tower, 231–2
Corisande; *see* Gramont, Diane de
Corras, Jean, 43–4
Corso (Rome), 17
Costa, Jean da, 20
Costa, Matthieu da, 20
Coste, Pierre, 315
Cotgrave, Randle, 267
Council of Trent, 72
Counter Reformation, 178, 312
Cour des Aides (Montpellier), 47–8
Cour des Aides (Paris), 47
Cour des Aides of Périgueux, 45–8, 50–1
Courtezelles, 33
Courtier, The (Castiglione), 117, 315
Coutances, 274
Coutras, 269–70, 274–5
Cracow, 207
Crinito, Pietro, 144
Cujas, Jacques, 43
Cyclops, 76
Cyrus, 119

Dacosta, Diogo, 17
Dacosta, Fernandès, 20
Dacosta, Guiomar, 17
Dacosta, Michel, 17, 232
Dali, Salvador, 319
Dampierre, Françoise de, 31

Daringes, Etienne, 48
Darnal, Jean, 227–8
Dax, 237
Delacroix (Prefect of the Gironde), 307
Delphi, 182, 261
Democritus, 167
Demosthenes, 45
Depository of the Charterhouse (Bordeaux), 307
Descartes, 162, 181, 314–5
Devise (stream), 10
Dewey, John, 198
Dezeimeris, Reinhold, 163, 172, 174–5, 310, 318
Dialogi de Natura Hominis (Dorland), 110
Diane de Poitiers, 225
Diderot, 162, 309, 316
Dieppe, 285
Discourse on Method (Descartes), 314
Discourses (Machiavelli), 144, 184
Divizia, 221
Dolet, Etienne, 44
Dominican Order, 217
Domrémy, 210
Dorat, Jean, 71, 282
Dordogne river, 4, 37, 70, 235–6, 246
Dorland, Pierre, 110
Dreux, 241
Du Bellay, Joachim, 39, 117
Du Bellay, Martin, 143
Duboys, Guillaume, 7–8
Duhamel, Georges, 319
Dumas (royal notary), 89
Duplessis-Mornay; *see* Mornay, Philippe de
Du Puy, Claude, 312
Duras, Marguerite de, 133
Dutch, 234
Du Tillet, Jean, 143
Du Verdier, Antoine, 249

Egmont, count of, 145
Egypt, 145
Elbeuf, Charles I, duc d', 239, 281
Eleanor of Aquitaine, 5
Eliot, T. S., 319
Elizabeth I, queen of England, 272, 274–5
Emerson, Ralph Waldo, 121, 317
England, 4–5, 19, 52, 135, 145, 162, 227, 272, 275, 285, 315, 317
English, 6, 271, 275
Epaminondas, 101, 119, 257, 264
Epernay, 210, 216
Epernon, Jean-Louis, duc d', 234
Ephemeris historica (Beuther), 35, 94, 208, 235, 281, 284, 306
Epictetus, 314
Epicurean(s), 168–9, 196
Epicureanism, 193
Epicurus, 158–9, 166
Epinal, 210
Erasmus, 36, 41, 144, 184
Escars, François de Péruse d', 53–5

Espaigne, 31
Esparezat, 34
Essays (Montaigne): examined by the papal censors in Rome, 17, 217–8; Pius XII hoped to see them removed from Index, 32; a compensation for the loss of La Boétie, 63, 81–3; Raemond's notes on his copy, 93, 134–5; whether M.'s wife read them, 102; M. seeks plan of, 144, 146, 184–6, 201; impersonal and pessimistic at first, 145–7, 149; basic editions of, 145–6, 199–200, 228, 248; praised by Henry III, 208; changes in those of 1588, 221, 252–3; early reception of, 222, 249, 310–2; when those of 1588 composed, 250, 269; M.'s remarks on, 251, 253–4; final message of, 261–2, 264, 321; read and edited by Marie de Gournay, 273, 277–8, 280, 283, 289, 308–9; took an effort to create, 276; final additions, 289–90, 303; fortunes of, 310–20; placed on the Index, 314–5; other references, 18–9, 30–1, 59, 71, 80, 86, 109, 111–2, 115, 118, 130, 133, 141–2, 154, 156, 163, 181, 202, 205, 213, 229, 241, 244, 246, 266, 268, 279, 284–5, 287, 305
Estates General of Blois (1588), 140, 226, 276–7, 282–4
Estève, Serène, 31
Estienne (Stephanus), Henri, 12, 172, 175
Estissac, Charles d', 209, 213, 216
Estissac, Geoffroy d', 209
Estissac, Louise de la Béraudière d', 133, 209
Euripides, 45
Europe, 4, 249
Evenings (Bouchet), 249
Eymar, Etienne, 22
Eymar, Madame d', 134
Eymar, Charlotte d', 35
Eymar, Joseph d', 22–3, 35, 50, 54, 134, 237
Eyquem (name and family), 3, 6–17, 27–8, 118–9
Eyquem, Pierre (great-uncle of M.), 8
Eyquem de Montaigne, Grimon (grandfather of M.), 8–9
Eyquem de Montaigne, Raymond or Ramon (great-grandfather of M.), 7–8
Eyquem-de-Montaigne, Tower of, 10

Fabri, Sisto (Master of the Sacred Palace), 17, 217–8, 248, 311–2
Fauguerolles, 54
Faure, Jean, 48
Fayard, François, 48, 56
Ferdinand V, king of Spain, 18
Féron, Raoul, 267
Ferraignes, Isabeau de, 7
Ferrand (messenger for Margaret of Valois), 237
Ferrand, Bertrand de, 22
Ferrand, Pierre de, 22
Ferrara, 208, 210–1

Ferrara, cardinal of, 211
Ferrier, Arnaud du, 43–4, 206, 236–7
Ferron, Arnould du, 143
Feuillants (church and order of), 31, 87, 306, 309
Feuillas, 241
Fitzgerald, Edward, 317
Flaubert, 317
Fleix, Le, 224, 228, 236–7
Floral Games (Toulouse), 184
Florence, 202, 206, 208, 210–1, 219
Florence, duke of, 211
Foix, Diane de, comtesse de Gurson, 133, 228
Foix, Louis de, 231–2
Foix, Louis de, comte de Gurson, 133, 228
Foix, Paul de, 6, 44, 117, 224
Foligno, 212
Forest of Varied Lessons (Mexia), 144
Four, Grimon du, 8
France, 4–6, 11, 19–20, 32, 34, 36, 39–41, 44, 48–9, 57, 59, 73, 75, 103, 114, 117, 119, 121, 128–9, 143, 162–4, 195, 202–4, 210, 214, 223–7, 229, 234, 250, 269–72, 275–6, 283–4, 286, 290, 305, 308, 312, 314–5
France, Anatole, 319
Francis I, king of France, 11, 36, 47, 52, 117
Francis II, king of France, 37, 57
French (Frenchman, Frenchmen), 6, 39, 136, 200, 207, 217–9, 222, 269, 283, 318
French (language), 39–40, 71, 106, 112, 132, 152, 163, 168, 185, 208, 249, 315
French Bibliography (Du Verdier), 249
French Bibliography (La Croix du Maine), 249
Freud, Sigmund, 320
Freyche, 33
Froissart, Jean, 143
Fugger (family), 211

Gaguin, Robert, 143
Gaillac, 4
Gamaches, Charles de, 34, 87
Gamaches, Marie de (granddaughter of M.), 86–8, 304
Garasse, François, 162
Garcilopez de Villanueva, 21
Garda, Lake, 34, 210
Garonne river, 4, 10, 37, 231–2, 236
Gascon(s), 5–6, 44, 212, 284
Gascony, 5–6, 19, 28, 89, 171, 249, 308
Gaujac, Pierre Eyquem de (uncle of M.): his life, 9; M. a favorite nephew, 9; studies law at Toulouse, 9, 43; left as a foster father by Pierre de M., 14, 24–5, 30; gives M. his post in Cour des Aides of Périgueux, 46, 48; helps baptize M.'s daughter Léonor, 94
Gaujac, Ramon de, 7

Gautier (councillor in Parlement of Bordeaux), 54
Gelida, Jehan, 20
Gellius, Aulus; *see* Aulus Gellius
Geneva, 36
German(s), 6, 222, 269
German (language), 318
Germany, 103, 202, 210, 218–9, 271, 318
Germignan, 77
Ghibelline, 247, 276
Gide, André, 163, 310, 319–20
Gilles, Nicole, 143
Gironde (department), 307
Gironde river, 4
Glanvill, Joseph, 162
Golden Epistles (Guevara), 144
Gospel; *see* Scripture
Gounouilhou, 163
Gourgues, Ogier de, 231
Gournay, Marie le Jars de: her quatrains to M.'s family, 30–1, 33, 35, 86; M.'s *fille d'alliance*, 82, 273, 277; a welcome friend but no La Boétie, 82, 279–80; spent 15 months at M. after M.'s death, 86, 308; editor of 1595 *Essays*, 146, 283, 289, 308–9; M.'s trip to Paris in 1588 and their first meeting, 273, 275–7; devotion to M., 277, 303, 305–6; M.'s feeling toward her and references to her, 277–80; in 1635, reduces M.'s tribute to her, 278–9; visited by M., 282–3; sends M. her *Proumenoir*, 284; mourns M.'s loss, 305–6; disappointed at reception of *Essays*, 310; stanch defender of M., 311–2
Gournay-sur-Aronde, 280, 282
Gouvéa (Goveanus), André de, 12, 20, 40–1
Gramont, Diane ("Corisande") d'Andoins, comtesse de Guissen (or Guiche): husband killed at La Fère, 209; becomes mistress to Henry of Navarre, 232; advised by M. to consider welfare of Navarre and of France, 235–6, 270, 286; Navarre with her after Coutras, 269–70; M.'s reported influence on her and through her on Navarre, 272–3, 275, 286; other references, 133, 237
Gramont, Philibert de, comte de Guissen (or Guiche), 133, 209
Grand' Chambre (Parlement of Bordeaux), 49–50, 57–8, 114
Granollers, Ramon de, 20
Greece, 207
Greek(s), 39, 86
Greek (language), 32, 40, 45, 120, 175, 307, 315
Gregorian calendar, 271
Gregory XIII, Pope, 34, 214–6, 219
Grouchy, Nicholas, 40
Gryllus, 164
Guazzo, Stefano, 315
Guelph, 247, 276
Guémené, Louis VI de Rohan, prince de, 128

Guerente, Guillaume, 40
Guerre, Martin, 43
Guevara, Antonio de, 144
Guicciardini, Francesco, 143
Guiche; *see* Gramont
Guienne, 5–7, 20, 31, 42, 47–9, 52–3, 62, 227–30, 284
Guilhelmi, Aiquelmus, 6
Guise, François, duc de, 37, 53, 119, 226
Guise, Henri, duc de: M.'s attempt to mediate between him and Navarre, revealing Guise's religious indifference, quest of Navarre's friendship, 140–1, 226, 266, 283; Margaret of Valois once drawn to him, 225; his career, 226, 283; head of the League, national hero, 226; his grace, 242; sent to fight German invaders, 269; summoned to court, 272; bought information from Stafford, 275; assassinated at Blois, 276, 283–4, 312; signed order releasing M. from Bastille, 281; other references, 135, 238
Guissen; *see* Gramont
Gurson; *see* Foix
Gurson, countess of, 87

Hagetmau, 270
Hakluyt ("Hacklytt"), Richard, 272
"Harangue of the Duke de Guise to the Soldiers at Metz" (Ronsard), 278
Hautoy, Monsieur du, 209–10
Hazlitt, William, 317
Hebrew, 315
Hechelmus, 7
Helen of Troy, 86
Henry VII, king of England, 145
Henry VIII, king of England, 36
Henry II, king of France, 20, 37, 47, 52, 57, 225–7
Henry III, king of France: compliments M. on *Essays*, 206, 208, 248, 266; summons M. to duties as mayor, 224, 228; helps select M. as mayor, 224; sketch of, 225–6; confirms privileges of Bordeaux, 230; sent remonstrances by mayor and jurats of Bordeaux, 230–1, 244; seeks Henry of Navarre's conversion, 234; morals open to criticism, 242; capitulates to League, 246; eager for peace, 267; seeks to pit enemies against each other, 269; M.'s trip seeks to bring him and Navarre closer together against the League, 270–6; has Guise assassinated, 284; other references, 6, 34, 117, 135, 171, 209, 216, 232, 238–9, 268, 280–1, 294
Henry IV, king of France; *see* Navarre, Henry, king of
Henry Plantagenet, king of England, 5
Hercules, 35, 75–6
Herodotus, 145, 164, 172, 321
Hitler, Adolf, 72
Holland, 103, 318

Holmes, O. W., Jr. (Justice), 319
Holy League; *see* League
Holy Writ; *see* Scripture
Honorable Teaching (Crinito), 144
Horace, 45, 67, 318
Horn, count of, 145
Horstanus, 27, 39
Hotman, François, 219
Huguenot(s), 205, 242, 268
Hundred Years' War, 5
Huon de Bordeaux, 41
Huxley, Aldous, 319, 322

Index of Prohibited Books, 32, 108, 170, 313–5
Indians, 56
Innsbruck, 210–1
Inquisition, 17, 21
Institutes (Calvin), 36, 182
Instruction for Princes (Coignet), 249
Isabella, queen of Spain, 18
Isle river, 37
Isny, 213
Italian(s), 217, 222
Italian (language), 9, 12, 106, 208, 219, 318
Italy, 10, 13, 18, 33–4, 44, 117, 202, 206–7, 210, 219–20
Ivry, 285

Jansenism, 317
Japanese, 319
Javerlhac, lord of, 95
Jephthes (Buchanan), 40
Jesuit(s), 214–6, 229
Jesuitines, 32
Jews, 17–21, 215, 222
Joachim (name), 6
Johanneau, Eloi, 309–10
John II, king of Portugal, 18–9
Jonson, Ben, 312
Joubert, Laurent, 174
Joyce, James, 320
Joyeuse, Anne, duc de, 269–70, 272, 274
Judaic Street (Bordeaux), 19
Julian the Apostate, Emperor, 217
Julius Caesar (Muret), 40
Jung, Carl Gustav, 320
Jurade (of Bordeaux), 53

Karenty, 93
Kelso, Ruth, 90
Kempten, 210, 213

La Boétie, Etienne de (uncle of M.'s friend), 70, 77–8
La Boétie, Etienne de: his poetry admired by M., 6; friend of Bussaguet, 9; his love for M.'s family, 15; urges Beauregard not to split family, 29–30; death, 29–30, 76–9, 150–2, 276; family, 30, 70, 77–9; set freedom of conscience first, 36; works

La Boétie, Etienne de (cont.)
  published with dedications by M., 44, 110,
  114, 117; friend of d'Escars, 54–5; advocate of firmness toward Protestants, 55,
  58; enjoyed Parlement more than M. did,
  57; friendship with M., 63, 69–70, 73–
  84, 200, 220, 301; M.'s *Essays* a compensation for his loss, 63, 81–3; sketch,
  69–73, 76; works, 71–3; his testimony on the friendship, 74–6; M.'s account of his death, 76–80, and memorial
  inscription, 80; M.'s sense of loss, 80–4,
  91, 142, 277; his influence on M., 83–4,
  151–2, 156–7; gave M. his papers and
  books, 93; thought of fleeing Old World
  for New, 194; admired Venice, 205; not
  replaced by Marie de Gournay, 279–80;
  M.'s death worthy of him, 282; other
  references, 48, 50, 56, 62, 98, 113, 130,
  139–40, 179, 206
La Boétie, Marguerite de Carle, madame de,
  77, 79
La Brousse (estate), 113
La Brousse, Pierre de (brother of M.), 29,
  31, 89, 113, 132, 305–6
La Bruyère, 315
La Chassaigne, Adrienne de, 9, 85, 88
La Chassaigne, Françoise de; *see* Montaigne,
  Françoise de La Chassaigne de (wife of
  M.)
La Chassaigne, Geoffroy de (President), 9,
  54, 85
La Chassaigne, Geoffroy de, sieur de Pressac,
  86–7, 102, 117, 249
La Chassaigne, Joseph de, 57, 85, 94
La Croix du Maine, 249
Laertius, Diogenes, 178
La Fère, 208–9, 225
La Fontaine, 315
Lagebaston, Jacques-Benoist de, 52–6, 85
Lagreau (M.'s steward), 98
La Guiche, Philibert de, 272
La Guyonie, 54, 56
Lahontan, 9
Lalanne, Sarran de, 51–2
La Marsillière, Hurosius Berziau, seigneur
  de, 237
Lamartine, 316
Lambert, Bertrand, 48
Lamothe, Baude de Moncuq, seigneur de,
  237, 240–1
La Mothe Le Vayer, 162
Lancre, Pierre de, 20, 215–6
Landes, Les, 4
Landiras, 32
Landor, Walter Savage, 317
L'Angelier, Abel, 145, 250, 280, 283, 308
Languedoc, 4, 6
La Noue, François de, 117–8
La Primaudaye, Pierre de, 174
La Rochefoucauld, François IV, duc de, 134,
  271

La Rochefoucauld, François VI, duc de (au-
  thor of *Maxims*), 315
La Rochelle, 269–70
Lataste, 56
Latin, 6, 12–3, 16, 18, 27, 32, 39–41, 43,
  45, 71, 109, 120, 132, 307, 311, 314
Latinist, 249
La Tour (estate), 304
La Tour, François de, 86, 303
La Tour, Françoise de, 86, 304
La Tour, Léonor de; *see* Montaigne, Léonor
  de (daughter of M.)
La Tour de Camet, 33
Lautrec, Odet de Foix, vicomte de, 10
La Villate, 34
League, 20, 226, 229, 234, 237, 239, 242,
  246–7, 267–9, 274, 276, 281, 284–5, 312
Leaguer(s), 238, 271, 274, 276, 281
Le Clerc, 281
Lecomte, 54
Lefèvre (publisher), 310
Lefèvre, Noël, 229
Lefèvre d'Etaples, Jacques, 36
Leo X, Pope, 36
Leonidas, 119
Lestonnac, Guy de, 307
Lestonnac, Jeanne de (sister of M.), 26, 29–
  32, 35, 50, 77, 113, 247
Lestonnac, Saint Jeanne de (daughter of the
  preceding), 30–2
Lestonnac, Richard de, 30–2, 50, 57, 77,
  230
"Letter of Consolation to His Wife" (Plu-
  tarch), 71, 93
L'Hôpital, Michel de, 52, 56, 72, 114, 117
Libourne, 37, 240–1
Lidoire (stream), 38
Liége, 216
"Life of Aemilius Paulus" (Plutarch), 98–9
"Life of the Demoiselle de Gournay" (Gour-
  nay), 273
Lilhan, 31
Lima (river), 213
Limeuil, sieur de, 140
Limoges, 210, 224
Lindau, 213
Lipsius, Justus, 12, 249, 277, 281–2, 303,
  305
Lisbon, 134
Loirac, 31
Loire river, 269
Loisel, Antoine, 62, 229, 232
London, 4, 22–3
Lopès (family), 21
Lopez de Villanueva (name and family),
  16–28. *See also* Louppes de Villeneuve,
  Villeneuve
Lopez de Villanueva (individual members
  of the family): Antonio, Eleanora, Garcia
  (Garcilopez de Villanueva), Garcia (the
  younger), Juan (elder and younger), Juan
  Fernando (elder and younger), Martin

(?), Martin (of London and Antwerp, the elder), Martin (son of the preceding), Martin Pablo, Micer Fernando, Micer Pablo, Dr. Pablo, and Ramon, 21–3

Lord's Prayer, 132, 137

Loreto, 202, 210–1, 214, 216

Lorrain(s), 219, 226

Lorraine, 269

Lorraine, Charles, cardinal of, 141

Losse, sieur de, 140

Louis XI, king of France, 5, 49

Louis XII, king of France, 20

Louppes de Villeneuve (family), 16–28. *See also* Lopez de Villanueva, Villeneuve

Louppes de Villeneuve, Antoine, 22–3, 25

Louppes de Villeneuve, Antoinette de; *see* Montaigne, Antoinette de Louppes de (mother of M.)

Louppes de Villeneuve, Beatrix, 22

Louppes de Villeneuve, Catherine, 22

Louppes de Villeneuve, Pierre de (grandfather of M.), 22–4

"Love, On" (Plutarch), 71

"Love Stories" (Plutarch), 282

Louvre, 204

"Lovers' War," 225

Low Countries, 145

Lucca, 81, 202, 210, 219–20

Lucian, 178

Lucilius, 159

Lucretius, 84, 152

Lucullus, 14, 204

Lur, Guillaume de (de Longa), 70

Lur-Saluces, Charles de, 88

Lurbe, Gabriel de, 232

Luther, 72, 106, 213

Lutheran(s), 213, 222

Lutheranism, 35, 163

Lycurgus, 194

Lyons, 5, 49, 210–1, 224

Macanan, Bertrand, 48, 56

Macau, 113

Macei, 56

Machiavelli, 144, 184, 287

Madrid, 21, 134

Maldonado, Juan, 214–6

Malebranche, 162, 315–6

Malherbe, 278

Malicorne, Jean de Chourses, seigneur de, 267

Malraux, André, 319

Malvezin, Théophile, 89, 318

Malvin de Cessac, Charles de, 53–4, 86–7, 306

Manuel, king of Portugal, 19

Marivaux, 316

Marmande, 240

Marot, Clément, 36

Marseilles, 241

Marston, John, 312

Martin, Jean, 110

Mary Queen of Scots, 275

Mas-de-Verdun, 232

Mass, 36, 45, 78, 214, 216, 305–6

Master of the Sacred Palace (Sisto Fabri), 17, 217–8, 248, 311–2

Matignon, Jacques de Goyon, comte de (Marshal): commands siege of La Fère, 208; becomes lieutenant general in Guienne, 227; an astute diplomat, 227; M.'s letters show their collaboration, 232–41, 271–2, 284–5, 287; jockeying with Henry of Navarre, 232–5; M.'s efforts, finally successful, to bring him and Navarre together, 235–6, 240; takes Château Trompette from Vaillac, 238; succeeds M. as mayor of Bordeaux, 240–1; joined by Mayenne, 246; at Coutras after the battle, 269–70; sponsors M.'s trip to Paris in 1588 escorted by his son, 271–5; other references, 134–5, 244, 266

Matignon, Lancelot de, 274

Matignon, Odet de Thorigny, comte de; *see* Thorigny

Mattecoulon (estate), 33

Mattecoulon, Bertrand Eyquem de (brother of M.): remembered in his mother's will, 26; sketch, 33–5; travels with M., 33–4, 209; his duel in Rome, 34, 118; in service of Henry of Navarre, 34–5; his epitaph to his son, 35; hailed in verse by Marie de Gournay, 35; helps baptize M.'s fifth daughter, 94; other references, 24, 29, 113

Maurois, André, 319

Maximilian I, Emperor, 145

Maximus, Valerius; *see* Valerius Maximus

Mayenne, Charles de Lorraine, duc de, 239, 246, 285

Meaux, 210

Mediterranean, 4

Médoc, 4, 30, 77, 129

Melanchthon, 141

Memoir concerning the Edict of January 1562 (La Boétie), 72–3, 179

Memoirs (Commines), 143

Memoirs (Margaret of Valois), 171

Memorable Deeds and Words (Valerius Maximus), 144

Menander, 74

Mendoza, Don Bernardino de, 272–3, 275–6

Mercoeur, Philippe Emmanuel de Lorraine, duc de, 239

Mercury (planet), 183

Mérimée, 317

Merle, François, 48

Merville, Jacques d'Escars, sieur de, 230

Mesmes, Henri de, 44–5, 110, 114, 117

Mesnil, Baptiste du, 53

Metamorphoses (Ovid), 41, 143

Metellus, 14, 204

Mexia, Pedro de, 144

Micheau (M.'s nickname), 38–9, 42
Michelet, Jules, 190, 317
Milan, 210, 224
Milan, duke of, 118
Millanges, Jean, 20
Millanges, Simon, 20, 145
Moissac, 4, 270, 273–4
Molière, 315
Moneins, Tristan de, 42, 238–9
Monluc, Blaise de, 52, 55, 117–8, 133
Mons, Jeanne de, 94
Monsieur de Montaigne's Walk; see Proumenoir
Montaigne, Anne de (daughter of M.), 94, 151
Montaigne, Antoinette de Louppes de (mother of M.): barely mentioned by M., 16; Jewish ancestry of, 16–7, 21–3; marriage, 23–4; place in her husband's wills, 24–5; arrangement with M. over will, 25, 113; relationship with M., 25, 27–8; sketch, 25–8; her will, 26–7, 33; carried M. eleven months, 38; learned some Latin to use with infant M., 39; role in incident of gold chain, 89–91; helps name M.'s first child, 94; other references, 29–30, 35, 184, 230
Montaigne, Blanquine Eyquem de (aunt of M.), 25
Montaigne (brothers): see Beauregard; La Brousse; Mattecoulon; Saint-Martin
Montaigne (château and noble land of): M.'s retreat, 3; purchased by M.'s great-grandfather, 7–8; description, 37–8; M. hopes to complete building of it, 115; tower and view, 120–1; *Travel Journal* discovered there, 208; visited twice by Henry of Navarre, 235, 270; camped on during siege of Castillon, 246–7; M.'s last years and death there, 303, 305; Charron a guest there, 313; other references, 5, 9, 26, 35, 54, 70, 86, 89, 94, 105, 112–4, 117, 123, 125, 130, 144, 266, 274
Montaigne, François, 267–8
Montaigne, Françoise de La Chassaigne de (wife of M.): unmentioned in M.'s mother's will, 26; gold chain, worn by M.'s brother Arnauld, found in her coffers, 33, 89–91; daughter and granddaughter of Presidents in Parlement, 50; marriage, 85–100; sketch of life, 85–7; letters written in her seventies, 87–9; conjecture of her infidelity, 89–91; M.'s comments on her and on marriage, 91–5; on vexations of domesticity, 95–99, on its values, 99–100, on marriage and wives in general, 100–2; whether she read the *Essays*, 102; M., semi-conscious, orders a horse for her, 114, 122; probably blames M. for love of travel, 203; summoned, with M., to Saint-Brice, 267; entertains de Thou and Schomberg, 284; names

granddaughter after self, 304; her care for M.'s remains, 306–8; buried with him, 307; her care for M.'s literary remains, 308–9; other references, 30, 37, 57
Montaigne, Geoffroy de (cousin of M.), 230
Montaigne, Grimon Eyquem de; see Eyquem de Montaigne, Grimon (grandfather of M.)
Montaigne, Jeanne de (sister of M.); see Lestonnac, Jeanne de
Montaigne, Joseph, 307
Montaigne, Léonor de (sister of M.); see Camain, Léonor de
Montaigne, Léonor de (daughter of M.): bequeathed little in her grandmother Antoinette's will, 26–7; sketch of her life, 86; birth, 94; plays cards with parents, 95; taught to avoid the word *fouteau*, 95–6; first marriage, 303–4; first child, 304; buried with parents, 307; widowed in 1584, 308; her concern for M.'s book, 308; other references, 30, 87, 150
Montaigne, Marie de (sister of M.); see Cazalis, Marie de
Montaigne, Marie de (daughter of M.), 95, 151, 230
Montaigne, Michel de: The Eyquems of Bordeaux (paternal ancestors), 1–15: "best father there ever was," 9–15. The Lopez de Villanueva (maternal ancestors), 16–28: M. and the Jews, 16–21; mother's family tree, 22; mother, 23–8; settlement of father's will, 24–5. The early years, 29–45: birth, 29; brothers and sisters, 29–35; tolerant family atmosphere, 35–6; to nurse with humble folk, 38–9; taught Latin from cradle, 39–40; at Collège de Guyenne, 40–2; learned to love books, 41; unknown years, 42–5; may have studied law at Toulouse, 43–5. The magistrate, 46–62: whether at Cour des Aides of Périgueux, 46, 48; in Parlement of Bordeaux, 48–62; relatives there, 49–50; reception, 50–2; maiden speech, 51–2; profession of faith, in Paris Parlement, 53; counter-challenge to Lagebaston, 54–5; suggests remarks to Charles IX, 55; report on a case, 56; at court of France, 57; request to rise to a higher chamber, refusal, resignation, 57–8; "a most worthy magistrate," 58; impact of legal service on style, 58–9; dim view, but constructive criticism, of French law, 59–62; learns tough-minded skeptical temper, 62. Friendship with La Boétie, 63, 69–70, 73–80: M. at thirty, 63–9, 72–3; influence of La Boétie: the *Essays* a compensation for his loss, 80–4. Marriage, 85– 102: theory of cuckoldry ill-founded, 89–91; M. on the marriage, 91–5; children's births and deaths, 94–5; house-

hold, 95–8; vexation with domesticity, 98–9; values of marriage, 99–100; wives and marriage in general, 100–1; conclusion, 101–2. Translation of Sebond, inheritance, retirement, 103–15: changes in Sebond's Prologue, 107–8; how M. came to translate him, 109–10; expansions and improvement in text, 110–2; father's death, 112–3; M.'s retirement, 114–5. At home, 116–41: in his study, 120–1; on horseback, 121; knocked from horse, 121–3; surrounded by animals, 123, by servants, 123–4; house always open, 125; trained in etiquette, 125; loves discussion, 126–8; diversions—incidents, tales, persons, 128–35; M. in his forties, 135–9; often away from home, 139–41; brings report from Montpensier to Parlement, 140; attempt to mediate between Navarre and Guise, 140–1. The early *Essays*, 142–61: early readings, 143; how M. comes to write, 144–5; question of changes in attitude, 147–50; early *Essays* Stoical, pessimistic, 150–6; those of 1573–4 react against this, 156–61. The "Apology for Raymond Sebond," 162–80: summary, 163–70; a puzzling chapter, probably composed in different strata, 170–5; plan of its contents, 172–3; a repudiation of Stoicism, 175, 178–80; M.'s Pyrrhonism limited, 175–8. The writer finds his theme, 181–200: the years 1577–80 productive, 181; self-study, 182–4; the term and concept "essay," 184–6; self-portrayal, 186–8; optimism, 188–90; illness and liberation from fear, 190–3; for nature against art, 193–5, but nature guided by reason, 195–7; man's resources, 197–9; still little sense of human unity, 199–200. Travel in Italy, 201–24: motives, 202–8; love of Rome and Venice, 204–6; the *Travel Journal*, 208, 211–21; the trip in outline, 209–11; M.'s interest in gadgets, 211–2, in all signs of man's ingenuity, 212–3, in religious matters, 213–7; *Essays* examined by papal censors in Rome, 217–8; M.'s enjoyment of foreign people and ways, 218–20; gives a dance at La Villa, 220–1; hard hit by the stone, 221; influence of trip on M., 221–2. M. mayor of Bordeaux, 223–45: return from Italy, 223–4; summoned to duties by Henry III, 224; probable reasons for M.'s election, 224; political rivalries and personalities, 224–6; role of mayor and jurats, 226–8; calm first term, 228–30; re-election disputed, 230; remonstrances to Henry III and Henry of Navarre, 230–2; letters from Mornay, 232–4; M. host to Navarre, 235; advice to Diane de Gramont, 235–6; vigilance shown in letters of 1585 to

Matignon, 236–41; ouster of Vaillac from Château Trompette, 238; M.'s failure to return into Bordeaux during plague, 240–1; M.'s reflections on his mayoralty, 241–5; a detached but efficient mayor, 244. The *Essays* of 1588, 246–65: siege of Castillon and plague, 246–8; success of 1580 *Essays*, 248–9; composition of 1588 materials, 250; summary of Book III, 251; sense of unity, 251–2; freedom and frankness, 252–4; man and society, 254–6; stress on wholeness, 256–7; concern with effective moral code, 257–8; man part body, part soul, 258–60; human vanity, 260–2; seeks control as well as acceptance, 262–4; the joys of living, 264–5. Among the great, 266–88: at Saint-Brice, 267–9; Coutras, 269–70; mission in 1588 from Henry of Navarre to Henry III in Paris, 270–6; noted by Stafford, Mendoza, and others, 271–6; M.'s year in north of France, 276–84; meets Marie de Gournay, 276–80; in the Bastille, 281; gravely ill, 281–2; at Gournay, 282–3; at Blois, 283–4; Pasquier's suggestions, 283–4; back to Guienne, 284; letters to Henry IV, 285–8; hope of being his adviser, 285–6. Final additions to the *Essays*, 289–302: general, 289–90; self-revelation, 290–1; obscenity, 291–2; clearer sense of plan, 292–4; self-portrayal as self-formation, 294; religion, 294–5; independent morality, 295–8; humanness, 297–8; contradicts some earlier views, 298–300; "we are all of the vulgar," 300–2. Death and survival, 303–23: late years, 303–4; a grandfather, 303–4; death, 304–6; sites of his remains, 306–8; *Essays* of 1595 and Bordeaux Copy, 308–10; fortunes, 310–20; appeal today, 320–3

Montaigne, Pierre Eyquem de (M.'s father): ancestry, 7–9; sketch, 9–15; mayor of Bordeaux, 10, 12, 227–8, 244; suffers from kidney stone, 13, 112, 150, 191; marriage, 23–4; wills, 24–5; failed to invest wife's dowry as agreed, 26–7; given Sebond's book, 35, 163; tolerance, 35–6; gives M. excellent upbringing, 38–9; sends him to Collège de Guyenne, 40, and probably to law school, 43; probably not in Cour des Aides of Périgueux, 46; death, 57, 91, 112–3, 150, 191, 204; M. imitates his dress, 64, 139; wedding present to M., 86; has M. translate Sebond, 103, 105–6, 108–9, 163; wanted M. to be learned, 118; first of family born at M., 119; observes cat and bird, 123; other references, 22, 28–9, 75, 77

Montaigne, Raymond Eyquem de; *see* Eyquem de Montaigne, Raymond (great-grandfather of M.)

Montaigne, Thoinette de (daughter of M.), 93–4, 114, 150
"Montaigne; or, the Skeptic" (Emerson), 317
Montaigne's secretary, 18, 203, 208, 211
Montaigne's two unnamed daughters, 33, 94, 151
Montalcino, 34
Montauban, 237, 271
Mont-de-Marsan, 232–4
Montesquieu, 316
Montferrand, Charles de, 140
Montferrand, Gaston de, 32
Montherlant, Henry de, 319
Montigny; see Montaigne, Michel de
Montmorency, Anne de, Constable, 117–8, 134
Montmorency, François de, 134
Montpellier, 47–8
Montpensier, Louis, duc de, 134, 140
Montravel, 7
Montrésor, 272, 274
Moral Distichs (attributed to Cato), 144
Moral Essays or *Moralia* (Plutarch), 144, 174, 184, 249
Mornay, Charlotte Arbaleste, madame de, 271
Mornay, Philippe de (Duplessis-Mornay): letters to M. defending Protestant actions, 232–4, 266; letter to wife mentioning M.'s trip (1588), 271; unaware of just what message M. bore, 272, 274; other references, 117, 236, 247, 313
Mulhouse, 210, 213
Munich, 210
Muret, Marc-Antoine, 40, 43
Muses, 115, 142, 256
Mussolini, Benito, 72

Naigeon, Jacques-André, 309–10
Nantes, 128
Narni, 213
Natural Theology (Sebond), 13–4, 35, 44, 57, 103–13, 182
Navarre, 34
Navarre, Antoine de Bourbon, king of, 53–4
Navarre, Henry, king of (Henry IV of France): Mattecoulon in his service, 34, 247; consults M. on judiciary reform, 62; M.'s attempted mediation between him and Guise, 140–1, 266, 281, 285; friendship sought by Guise, 140–1, 226, 283; religious indifference, 141, 226; esteem for Maldonado, 215–6; helps select M. as mayor, 224; sketch, 225; opposed by Biron, 227; seizure of Mont-de-Marsan, 232–4; M. sees him about Mas-de-Verdun, 232; relations with wife, Margaret of Valois, 232, 234, 236–7; relations with Diane de Gramont, 232, 235–6, 269–70, 286; relations with Matignon and M., 232–8, 240; M. an intermediary between him and Matignon, 232–8, 240, 266; his conversion sought by Henry III, 234; two visits to M., 235, 270; his activity, 242; M. gentleman of his chamber, 266; at Saint-Brice, 267–8; sketch of him by M., 268; at Coutras and after, 269–70; M. his emissary to Henry III in 1588, 271–5; invites M. to join him, 276, 285; M.'s letters of 1590 to him, 284–8; M.'s hopes of being a candid adviser to him, 285–7; other references, 134–5, 171, 228, 244, 295, 303, 313
Navarre, Margaret of Angoulême, queen of, 36, 117
Navarre, Margaret of Valois, queen of; see Valois, Margaret of
Navarrenx, 270
Nemours, duke of, 134
Nemours, Treaty of, 246
Nérac, 225, 227, 232, 237, 271
Nesmond, François de, 231
Neufchâteau, 211
New Christians, 18–21, 28
New Testament, 40
New World, 56, 75, 165, 194, 251
Newfoundland, 4
Nicolaï, Alexandre, 89–90
Nicole, Pierre, 315
Nile, 183
Niort, 267
Nodier, Charles, 317
Nominalists, 103
Normandy, 49, 208, 272
Notre-Dame de Paris (cathedral), 169
"Nuns of Our Lady" (Religieuses de Notre-Dame), 32

Ochino, Bernardino, 313
"Oeconomicus" (Xenophon), 71
Œuvres complètes (Montaigne), 251
Officina (Ravisius Textor), 144
Old World, 194
Order of Saint Michael, 66, 118, 135, 140, 266
Ordre du Temple, 8
Orléans, 271, 274
Orléans, University of, 70–1
Orléans, Charles d', 117
Osorius, Hieronymus, 18–9
Ossat, Arnauld d', 81, 303
Outlines of Pyrrhonism (Sextus Empiricus), 175
Ovid, 41, 67, 143

Paçagon (Pazagon, Patagon) family, 21–3
Paçagon, Mayer, 21–3
Paçagon, Moses, 21–2
Padua, 33, 209–10
Palais de l'Ombrière, 49–50, 59
Pallas, 256
Papessus, 39

Parc, Le, 31

Paris, 3, 5, 10, 13, 36, 43, 47, 113–4, 139, 145, 151, 206, 208–9, 224, 230, 236, 249–50, 269–73, 275–6, 280–2, 286–8, 305, 308

Parlement of Aix; *see* Parlements

Parlement of Bordeaux: M.'s ancestors and relatives in, 8–9, 20, 22–3, 25, 31, 33, 35, 49–50, 85; M. in, 38, 46, 48–64, 77, 109, 114–5, 118, 139, 142; resistance to Cour des Aides of Périgueux, 47–8; role and history, 49; grudging reception to newcomers from Périgueux, 50–2; M.'s protest, 51–2; troubles over religion, 52–5; M. "names the whole Court," 54–5; M.'s suggestions for remarks to Charles IX, 55; a sample report of M.'s, 56; M. in Chambre des Enquêtes, 57; seeks to rise to higher chamber, refused, retires, 57–8; M. a good magistrate, 58; learned some of his skepticism there, 62; met La Boétie there, 63, 69; La Boétie's role there, 70; M.'s mission there later from Montpensier, 140; composed mainly of Catholic loyalists, 226; a faction there opposes M.'s re-election as mayor, 230; M. protests children of councillors being exempted from taxes, 231; few members remain in Bordeaux during plague, 240; helps keep city loyal under Henry IV, 284; other references, 6, 83, 93, 95, 227, 237–8

Parlement of Grenoble, 49

Parlement of Paris, 49, 53, 57, 70

Parlement of Toulouse, 43, 49

Parlements (of Aix, Dijon, Rennes, Rouen), 49

Pascal, 126, 128, 162, 181, 314–8

Pasquier, Estienne, 44, 58, 282–4, 304–6, 310–2

Pater, Walter, 317

Pasternoster; *see* Lord's Prayer

Pau, 236–7, 270

Paul, Saint, 165, 167

Paulus, Aemilius, 143

Pavia, 210

Payen, Dr. J.-F., 318

Peletier, Jacques, 133

Penitents, 214

Pensées (Pascal), 314

Périgord, 5, 7, 77, 89, 140, 208

Perigordian(s), 48

Perigordian (dialect), 40

Périgueux, 45–8, 50, 56, 210

Péronne Manifesto, 237

Peugue (stream), 10

Phaedo (Plato), 264

Philip I, king of Castile (Don Philip), 145

Philip II, king of Spain, 272–3

Philopoemen, 119

Piacenza, 210

Pibrac, Guy du Faur de, 44

Picardy, 275, 277

Pilate, Pontius, 319

Pisa, 202, 210

Pisani, Jean de Vivonne, marquis de, 134

Pithou, Pierre, 229

Pittacus, 101

Pius XII, Pope, 32

Plantier des Juifs (Bordeaux), 19

Plato, 40, 168, 194, 258–9, 264, 316, 322

Platonism, 144

Plautus, 41, 120, 143

Pléiade, 11, 71, 118

Pliny (the Elder), 152, 164, 183, 191

Plombières, 202, 210, 219

Plutarch: La Boétie's translations of, 71, 93, 98–9, 114; his story of the well-shaped shoe, 98–9; Amyot's translation of, 109, 170; M.'s admiring knowledge of, 143–4, 152, 157, 164, 200; his popularity in M.'s day, 144; helps M. become himself again, 157; M.'s borrowings in "Apology," 164, 170, 174; predecessor of M. by his *Moralia*, 184; La Croix du Maine compares M. with him, 249; M. and Marie de Gournay read his "Love Stories," 282; his cultural relativism, 321

Poissy, Colloquy of, 37

Poitou, 47, 267–9

Polish, 319

Pompey, 119

Pope, Alexander, 162

Port-Royal, 314, 317

Port-Royal (Sainte-Beuve), 163, 317

Porta Judaica (Bordeaux), 19

Porte-Dijeaux (Bordeaux), 19

Portugal, 18, 20

Portuguese, 12, 18–21

Posidonius, 158, 165

Posthumous Works (La Boétie), 140

Poyanne, Bertrand de Baylens de, 134

Poynet, Antoine, 48, 51–2

Pratolino, 211–2

Présidial, 50, 56

Prévost de Sansac, Antoine, archbishop of Bordeaux, 52, 54, 56, 134, 230

Prince (Machiavelli), 287

Protestant(s), 30, 34–5, 37, 52–3, 55, 57, 71–3, 137, 140, 170–2, 178–9, 213, 225, 233, 246–7, 270–1, 274–5, 294, 301, 320

Protestantism, 23, 30–1, 52, 66, 85, 110, 178–9, 216, 225–6, 275, 313

Proumenoir de Monsieur de Montaigne (Gournay), 282–4

Proust, 320

Provence, 23, 117

Prunis, Canon, 208

Puy, Arnaud du, 23

Puy, Giraulde du, 22–3

Puy, Honorette du, 22–3

Pyrenees, 4

Pyrrho, 155, 165–6, 168, 175, 177–8, 180, 183, 307

Pyrrhonism, 174–7, 179–80
Pyrrhonist(s), 176–7, 196

Quartilla, 67
Querlon, Meusnier de, 208

Rabelais, 4, 36, 44, 198, 209
Raemond, Florimond de: succeeds M. in Parlement of Bordeaux, 58, 114; a militant Catholic, 58; quotes M. on his relations with his wife, 90, 93; on M.'s conversation, 127–8; identifies many unnamed characters in the *Essays*, 134–5; draws on M.'s skeptical arguments, 162, 312; visits M. in M.'s last years, 303; laments M.'s loss, 305–6
Ram, Dominique, 20
Ram, Thomas de, 20, 230
Rat, Maurice, 89
Ravisius Textor, 144
Reform, 35, 44, 66
Reformation, 234
Reformist(s), 52, 225, 235, 313
Religieuses de Notre-Dame, 32
Renaissance, 11, 117
René, king of Sicily, 57
Representative Men (Emerson), 317
Researches on France (Pasquier), 283
Revolution, 307, 309, 315
Rhine, 4
Rhodiginus, Coelius, 144
Richelieu, 309
Richer, Jean, 145
Rignac, 56
Rio, Antonio del, 22–3
Rio, Martin del, 22–3
Ritter, Raymond, 270
Roffignac, Christophe de, 50, 52–4
Rohan, René II, vicomte de, 235
Roman(s), 4, 39, 99
Rome: M.'s love of, 3, 204–5, 207; M. notes treatment of Jews there, watches a circumcision, 17–8; M.'s trip there, 33, 202, 204–6, 210, 214–5, 217–9, 223–4; Mattecoulon's duel there, 34; *Essays* examined there by papal censors, 170, 217–8; M. dismisses secretary there, 208; Pope helps him become a citizen, 216, 222; M. finds Roman upper classes gracious, 219; other references, 44, 209
Rome, University of, 217
Ronsard, 71, 117, 278
Rotrou, Jean de, 241
Rouen, 4, 57, 128, 194, 248, 280–2
Rousseau, Jean-Jacques, 162, 198, 310, 316
Rousselle, La, 4, 7
"Rules of Marriage" (Plutarch), 71, 98–9, 114
Russian, 319

Sacy, Monsieur de, 314
Saint-André (cathedral), 5, 9, 17, 26, 306

Saint-Angel, Jean, 48, 56
Saint Bartholomew's Day Massacre, 140, 151, 216, 225
Saint-Bernard (chapel), 307
Saint-Bernard, Dom Marc-Antoine de, 86–9
Saint-Brice, 247, 267
Sainte-Beuve, 162–3, 207, 241, 310, 314, 317–8
Sainte-Foy-la-Grande, 37, 234–7, 240
Saint-Emilion, 37
Saint-James (priory), 229
Saint-Jean d'Angely, 274
Saint-Martin, Arnaud de (brother of M.), 26, 29, 32–3, 89–91, 113–4, 131, 150
Saint-Martin, Jean de, 307
Saint-Michel (church and parish, Bordeaux), 5, 7
Saint-Michel, Thomas de, 8–9
Saint-Michel de Montaigne, 9, 14, 37, 306
Saintonge, 237, 304
Saint Peter's (Rome), 214
Saint-Quentin, 9
Saint-Sauveur, Claude de, 269, 272
Saint-Seurin (church), 5, 9, 19
Salligny, baron de, 34
Sallust, 143
San Chirico, 211
Sand, George, 316–7
Santiago de Compostela, 7, 231
Saragossa, 21
Sarlat, 70, 205
Sarlat, Rue de (Bordeaux), 10
Satire Ménippée, 229
Sauvage, Denis, 143
Scaliger, Julius Caesar, 12, 71, 312
Scandinavia, 318
Schaffhausen, 210–1
Schomberg, Gaspard de, 284
Scipio Africanus the Elder, 14, 119, 204, 286
Scipio Africanus the Younger, 119, 257
Sclavonia, 214
Scripture (Gospel, Holy Writ), 66, 103, 107, 134, 148, 160, 258. *See also* Bible
Sebond, Raymond: hard reading for Pierre de Montaigne, 9, 163; M.'s mediocre opinion of, 11; M.'s translation of, 14, 57, 103–13, 224; Pierre Bunel gives his book to M.'s father, 35, 44, 163; M.'s changes in his Prologue, 107–8; some of his ideas congenial to M., 108, 160, 182; how M. came to translate him, 109–10, 163; expansion and improvements M. made in text, 110–2. M.'s "Apology for Raymond Sebond," 162–80: a counterattack against one group of Sebond's critics, 163–4, 167–8, 178, 183, in which M. soon abandons Sebond, 164, 170–2; probably composed mostly without him in mind, 170–2, 174–5; anti-Protestant, 178–9; made into an "Apology" at request of Margaret of Valois, who had read Sebond's book, prob-

ably in M.'s translation, 171–2, 174–5, 224, 266
Ségur, Jacques de, baron de Pardaillan, 134
Seine, 204
Sénancour, Etienne de, 317
Seneca, 84, 86, 128, 144, 153, 157, 159, 170, 188, 200, 283, 310–1
Sensible Man Reasoning . . . (Gamaches), 87
Sententiae (Stobaeus), 144
Sévigné, Madame de, 315
Sextus Empiricus, 62, 175
Shaftesbury, Anthony Ashley Cooper, third earl of, 316
Shakespeare, 194, 312, 316
Sheffield, John, 162
Siena, 202, 210–1, 224
Silhon, Jean de, 162
Sinigaglia, 210
Sleidan (Sleidanus), Johann, 143
Society of Jesus, 32, 215
Socrates: tested by his wife's malignity, 101; a hero to M., 144, 166, 177, 200, 248, 251, 257, 263; a hero to M.'s time, 144; beauty of his death, 152, 197, 299; knew the benignity of nature, 160; "wisest man that ever was," 166; his quest for truth, 166; saw self-knowledge as the key, 182, 184; virtue easy for him, 196–7, 222; can teach us our natural resources for living, 248, 255, 263, 301; perfection of his simple humanity, 251, 263, 301; a model of versatility, 257; corrected his natural disposition, 262; M. not unlike him, 263; his ecstasies and daemon, 297; finds death indifferent, 299; a believer in absolutes, 322; other references, 76, 79, 169, 264
Soissons, 209
Solon, 152
Sophocles, 45
Sorbonne, 36
Sources and Evolution of Montaigne's Essays (Villey), 147
Spain, 4, 6, 18, 20, 32, 275
Spaniard, Spanish, 4–5, 20, 103, 171, 273–4
Spanish (language), 9, 12–3, 106
Sparta, 119
Spartanism, 11
Spurina, 298
Staël, Madame de, 317
Stafford, Sir Edward, 271–2, 274–6
Stendhal, 317
Sterne, 317
Stevenson, R. L., 317
Stobaeus, 144
Stoic(s), 152, 166, 168–9, 196, 263
Stoicality, 310
Stoicism, 144, 157, 175, 193
Street of the Jews' Well (Bordeaux), 19
Strowski, Fortunat, 147, 308, 318
Suffolk, duke of, 145

Swiss, 6, 219, 222
Switzerland, 202, 210, 218

Tacitus, 252
Talbot, John, earl of Shrewsbury, 5, 49
Talpin, Jean, 41
Taprobanians, 56
Tausin, Monsieur de, 223
Tempest, The (Shakespeare), 194
Terence, 41, 120, 143
Textor, Ravisius; see Ravisius Textor
Thackeray, 317
Thales, 249
Thann, 212
"That Brute Beasts Make Use of Reason" (Plutarch), 164
Theologia naturalis; see Natural Theology (Sebond)
Theophrastus, 176
Thibaudeau (Prefect of the Gironde), 307
Thibaudet, Albert, 315, 319–20
Thomas, Simon, 43–4
Thorigny, Odet de Matignon, comte de, 271–5
Thou, Jacques-Auguste de: pronounces M. "a most worthy magistrate," 58; stops at M. in 1589, finds M. absent, is well entertained by his wife, 86, 284; reports M.'s account at Blois of his mediation between Navarre and Guise, 140–1, 283; urged by M., who would keep him company, to accept ambassadorship to Venice, 206; friendship with M., 229; tribute to M., 306
Three Truths, The (Charron), 313
Throckmorton, Francis, 275
Tiber, 204
Tivoli, 211–2
Toledo, Father, 215
Toulouse, 4, 9, 22–4, 35, 43–5, 103, 184
Toulouse, University of (Faculty of Law), 43–5
Tournelle (Parlement of Bordeaux), 49, 57–8, 61, 114
Tours, 272, 285, 287, 304
Trans, Germain-Gaston de Foix, marquis de, 52, 54–5, 118, 135, 140, 224, 304
Travel Journal (Montaigne): general, 201–22; references to the Jews, 17–8; shows how much M. misses La Boétie, 81; M.'s frequent and violent attacks of the kidney stone, 191, 221; M.'s love of travel, 207–8; history of the *Journal*, 208, 211; M.'s attempt to live life of those he visits, 218–9; written partly in Italian, 219; terse and meager on road back to France, 224; first good edition is in Italian, 318; other reference, 223
Trent, 210
Trinquet, Roger, 267–8
Triumvirate, 154

Truth of the Christian Religion (Mornay), 313
Tullius Marcellinus, 152
Turenne, Henri de La Tour d'Auvergne, vicomte de, 235–6, 247, 272, 274
Turkish, 319
Turnèbe (Turnebus), Odet de, 282
Turnebus (Turnèbe), Adrianus, 12, 44, 106, 109
Tyndareus, 86

Ubiquitism, 213
Ulysses, 164
Urbino, 210
Utopians, 56

Vaillac, Louis Ricard Gourdon de Genouilhac, baron de, 238–9
Valerius Maximus, 144
Valois, Margaret of, queen of Navarre: hates to be seen chewing, 134; M.'s warning to her in "Apology," 168; asked M. to defend Sebond in his "Apology," 171–2, 174–5; helps select M. as mayor of Bordeaux, 224, 266; sketch, 225; furious at Biron for firing on Nérac while she there, 227; godmother to Gursons' daughter at Cadillac in 1582, 228; expelled from court (1583), taken back reluctantly by Henry of Navarre, 232, 234, 236–7; at odds with Navarre over Ferrand incident, 237
Valzargues, René de, 134
Varro, 165
Vassy Massacre, 37, 226
Vatican Library, 219
Venetian, 121
Venice, 44, 139, 202, 205–6, 210–1, 237, 303
Ventadour, Gilbert, duc de, 135
Venus, 68, 76, 264, 291
Verneuil, François de, 56
Verneuil, Guillaume de, 56
Verneuil, Martial de, 56

Verona, 18, 210, 214
Verteuil, abbé de, 94
Veuillot, Louis, 317
Vicenza, 210
Villa, La, 81, 202, 206, 210–1, 213, 219–21, 224
Villa d'Este, 211–2
Villanueva; see Lopez de Villanueva
Villanueva (Calatayúd), 21
Villebois (forest), 271, 274
Villegagnon, 194
Villeneuve; see Louppes de Villeneuve
Villeneuve, Bertrand de, 22–3
Villeneuve, Jean de (President), 22–3, 25, 50, 140, 230
Villeroy, Nicolas IV de Neufville, seigneur de, 281
Villey, Pierre, 147, 171, 174–5, 250, 318
Villon, 117
Vinet, Elie, 12, 232
Viola Animae (Dorland), 110
Virgil, 41, 45, 143
Virgin Mary, 34
Viterbo, 210–1
Voltaire, 314–6
Voluntary Servitude, Discourse on (La Boétie), 71–3, 113, 130, 179, 205
Vulcan, 264

Walsingham, Sir Francis, 271–2, 275
Webster, John, 312
"Whether Land or Water Animals Are Cleverer" (Plutarch), 164
Wisdom, Of (Charron), 313–4
Woolf, Virginia, 319
World War I, 318

Xenophon, 71

Ymbert, Esther, 270

Zeitlin, Jacob, 171, 175, 308
Zweig, Stefan, 319
Zwinglians, 213

Rouen

SEPT. 5, 1580
Beaumont-sur-Oise

La Fè

OISE R.

SEINE R.

Meaux

MAR

Paris

Epernay

Chartres

L O I R E   R.

Orléans

Blois

Tours

Montrésor

F R A N C E

BAY

Niort

La Rochelle

St.-Jean d'Angély

OF

Cordouan Tower

SAINTONGE

Cognac

Angoulême

Limoges

Sauviat

Pontaumur

BISCAY

GIRONDE R.

FOREST OF
VILLEBOIS

Clermont-Ferrand

MEDOC

Thiviers

Thiers

L'Hôpital Rochefort

LY

Montaigne

Périgueux

Bordeaux

Sarlat

Cadillac

DORDOGNE R.

RHÔNE R.

Nérac

Agen

Mont-de-Marsan

GARONNE R.

Moissac

Hagetmau

Montauban

BEARN

Navarrenx

Toulouse

Pau

S P A I N

MEDITERRANEA

GIRONDE R.

DRONNE R.

Périgueux

ISLE R.

Coutras

GARONNE R.

Libourne

Castillon

Montaigne

Le Fleix

Bergérac

DORDOGNE R.

Bordeaux

Feuillas

Ste.-Foy-la-Grande

palacios